AF904691

Social Media Algorithms

Social Media Algorithms

Edited by

Adele Kuzmiakova

ARCLER
PRESS

www.arclerpress.com

Social Media Algorithms

Adele Kuzmiakova

Arcler Press
4164 Lakeshore Road
Burlington, ON L7L 1A4
Canada
www.arclerpress.com
Email: orders@arclereducation.com

© 2025 Arcler Press

ISBN: 978-1-77956-420-7 (Hardcover)

This book contains information obtained from highly regarded resources. Reprinted material sources are indicated and copyright remains with the original owners. Copyright for images and other graphics remains with the original owners as indicated. A Wide variety of references are listed. Reasonable efforts have been made to publish reliable data. Authors or Editors or Publishers are not responsible for the accuracy of the information in the published chapters or consequences of their use. The publisher assumes no responsibility for any damage or grievance to the persons or property arising out of the use of any materials, instructions, methods or thoughts in the book. The authors or editors and the publisher have attempted to trace the copyright holders of all material reproduced in this publication and apologize to copyright holders if permission has not been obtained. If any copyright holder has not been acknowledged, please write to us so we may rectify.

Notice: Registered trademark of products or corporate names are used only for explanation and identification without intent of infringement.

Arcler Press publishes wide variety of books and eBooks. For more information about Arcler Press and its products, visit our website at www.arclerpress.com

ABOUT THE EDITOR

Adele Kuzmiakova is a machine learning engineer working at the intersection of machine learning, computer vision, and natural language processing. Adele attended Cornell University in New York, United States for her undergraduate studies. She studied engineering with a focus on applied math. Some of the deep learning problems Adele worked on include predicting air quality from public webcams, developing a real-time human movement tracking, using 3D computer vision to create 3D avatars from selfies in order to bring online clothes shopping closer to reality, and creating visual stories and photobooks from photos on mobile devices. She is also passionate about exchanging ideas and inspiring other people and acted as a workshop organizer at Women in Data Science conference in Geneva, Switzerland in 2022 and 2023.

TABLE OF CONTENTS

List of Figures .... *xi*

List of Tables .... *xiii*

Preface .... *xv*

Chapter 1 Introduction to Social media Algorithms 1

Introduction 2

1.1. Algorithms, Social Media, and Big Data 3

1.2. Social Media Algorithm 13

1.3. The Impact of Algorithms on User Experience 24

1.4. Navigating Social Media Algorithms for Businesses 26

1.5. Tips to Win Over Social Media Platform Algorithm 28

1.6. The Pros and Cons of Social Media Algorithms 30

References 40

Chapter 2 Instagram Algorithm 45

Introduction 46

2.1. Instagram 46

2.2. History of Instagram 49

2.3. Instagram Features and Tools 53

2.4. Instagram Algorithm 63

2.5. How to Get on the Instagram Explore Page? 68

2.6. Instagram Reels Algorithm 76

References 106

Chapter 3 TikTok Algorithm 107

Introduction 108

3.1. Overview of TikTok Algorithm 108

3.2. How to Make a Blue Search Comment on TikTok? 118

3.3. How to Get Unshadowbanned on TikTok? 119
3.4. Social Media and User-Generated Content (UGC) 122
References 134

Chapter 4 Facebook Algorithm 137
Introduction 138
4.1. The Facebook Algorithm: How It Works and How to Make It Work for You? 138
4.2. Working with Facebook's Algorithm 144
4.3. Facebook Algorithms and User Polarization 147
4.4. Prioritizing Original News on Facebook 152
4.5. Navigating the Algorithm: Troubleshooting Why Facebook Ad Is Not Delivering 163
References 174

Chapter 5 YouTube Algorithm 177
Introduction 178
5.1. A Brief History of the YouTube Algorithm 178
5.2. How to Make a YouTube Channel? 180
5.3. Quality Content Is King 189
5.4. How Marketing Works on YouTube? 192
5.5. Monetization 197
5.6. YouTube Channel Goals You Can Control 202
5.7. Best Techniques to Use YouTube to Promote Your Business 204
5.8. Collaborations 209
5.9. Using Social Media to Promote Your Channel 212
5.10. Use Your Channel to Promote Your Merchandise 214
References 215

Chapter 6 LinkedIn Algorithm 217
Introduction 218
6.1. Basics of LinkedIn 218
6.2. LinkedIn as a Social Media 227
6.3. The Role of the LinkedIn Social Media in Building the Personal Image 237
6.4. The System of LinkedIn Algorithm 244
References 251

Chapter 7 Twitter Algorithm 253
Introduction 254
7.1. Overview of Twitter (X) Algorithm 255
7.2. How Does the Twitter Algorithm Work? 257
References 277

Chapter 8 Pinterest Algorithm 279
Introduction 280
8.1. What Is the Pinterest Algorithm? 280
8.2. How Does the Pinterest Algorithm Work? 284
8.3. Pinterest Algorithm Changes – A Timeline of Important Updates 297
8.4. How to Beat the Pinterest Algorithm 298
References 307

Chapter 9 Threads Algorithm 309
Introduction 310
9.1. Define Thread 310
9.2. Working Threads Algorithm 312
9.3. Tips for Working with the Threads Algorithm 314
9.4. Understanding the Threads Algorithm and User Control 318
9.5. Things the Threads Algorithm 320
9.6. Create a Threads Account 328
References 339

Index 341

LIST OF FIGURES

Figure 1.1. Posts by SEO.

Figure 1.2. Sponsored post.

Figure 1.3. Social media and content marketing on LinkedIn.

Figure 1.4. Social media content which is posted.

Figure 1.5. Post recency.

Figure 1.6. Social media stories.

Figure 1.7. Social media algorithm explore example.

Figure 2.1. Part of the Instagram app.

Figure 2.2. Instagram explore algorithm.

Figure 2.3. Instagram explore feed.

Figure 2.4. Instagram explore algorithm.

Figure 2.5. Instagram explore ads.

Figure 2.6. Instagram explore refresh.

Figure 2.7. Instagram explore not interested.

Figure 3.1. The typology of user-generated content.

Figure 4.1. This flowchart illustrates the insertion of constraints into the previously unfiltered feedback loop.

Figure 4.2. Citations in news articles. The top snippet cites an article by another publisher. The cited article cites another article from the same publisher.

Figure 4.3. News feed ranking at Facebook.

Figure 4.4. Reasons for non-delivery of your Facebook ads.

Figure 6.1. The reasons for activation on LinkedIn according to age groups.

Figure 6.2. Recommendations on LinkedIn sorted by professions in Serbia.

Figure 6.3. AI classification pipeline for LinkedIn algorithms.

Figure 7.1. Twitter is the most popular microblogging service.

Figure 7.2. Marketing and advertising with Twitter.

Figure 7.3. The Twitter (X) algorithm.

Figure 7.4. Social media platform.

Figure 7.5. The key parts of this system, roughly in the order they'd be called during a single timeline request, starting with retrieving candidates from candidate sources.

Figure 7.6. Embedding spaces.

Figure 7.7. The Twitter algorithm to maximize engagement.

Figure 7.8. Respond quickly to replies.

Figure 8.1. The smart feed worker in action.

Figure 8.2. Steps of Pinterest algorithm work.

LIST OF TABLES

Table 6.1. Differences in the purpose for using LinkedIn between age groups

Table 6.2. Differences in the purpose for using LinkedIn between the participants with different professions

PREFACE

In today's digital era, where social media is a dominant force shaping communication, culture, and even commerce, it is crucial to delve into the intricate mechanisms that govern the content we encounter daily. Social media algorithms, the sophisticated and often enigmatic systems operating behind the scenes, dictate what appears on our feeds, when it appears, and why. These algorithms have evolved into powerful entities, profoundly influencing our online experiences, interactions, and perceptions.

This textbook aims to unravel the complexities of social media algorithms, providing a comprehensive exploration of their foundations, functionalities, and far-reaching effects.

For businesses and content creators, navigating social media algorithms is both an art and a science. Understanding how to optimize content to align with algorithmic preferences can be the difference between success and obscurity. This textbook will delve into practical strategies for leveraging algorithms to maximize reach and engagement, offering insights into algorithm-friendly content creation, timing, and audience targeting.

This book on social media algorithms is structured into nine chapters, each focusing on the algorithmic frameworks of major social media platforms, offering a deep dive into their unique characteristics and impacts.

Chapter 1 introduces the foundational concepts of social media, providing an overview of how algorithms have become central to user experience and content distribution. It sets the stage for understanding the specific algorithms discussed in subsequent chapters. Chapter 2 focuses on the Instagram algorithm, exploring how it curates content, influences user engagement, and prioritizes posts based on factors like interaction history and content type. Chapter 3 examines the TikTok algorithm, known for its highly personalized content recommendations and its role in driving viral trends through its For You Page (FYP).

Chapter 4 covers the Facebook algorithm, detailing how it uses machine learning to tailor news feeds, prioritize posts from friends and family, and manage the visibility of sponsored content. Chapter 5 analyzes the YouTube algorithm, emphasizing its reliance on watch time, engagement metrics, and user behavior to recommend videos and drive content discovery. Chapter 6 covers the LinkedIn algorithm, which focuses on professional networking, highlighting how it surfaces relevant content, job opportunities, and industry updates based on user profiles and connections.

Chapter 7 discusses the Twitter algorithm, particularly its shift from a chronological feed to a relevance-based timeline, and how it prioritizes tweets, retweets, and trending topics. Chapter 8 looks at the Pinterest algorithm, explaining how it uses user interests and interactions to suggest pins and curate personalized boards. Chapter 9 explores the Threads algorithm, providing insights into its role in thread ranking, content visibility, and the promotion of high-quality discussions.

Offering readers a thorough understanding of how these invisible forces shape our online lives, a marketer, or simply a curious user, this exploration will equip you with the knowledge to navigate and critically engage with the digital landscape of today and tomorrow.

CHAPTER 1

INTRODUCTION TO SOCIAL MEDIA ALGORITHMS

Contents

Introduction 2

1.1. Algorithms, Social Media, and Big Data 3

1.2. Social Media Algorithm 13

1.3. The Impact of Algorithms on User Experience 24

1.4. Navigating Social Media Algorithms for Businesses 26

1.5. Tips to Win Over Social Media Platform Algorithm 28

1.6. The Pros and Cons of Social Media Algorithms 30

References 40

INTRODUCTION

Social media are technological platforms that are incorporated into people's daily lives in ever-more-pervasive ways. These spaces of interaction are where everything comes together: our closest friendships, news, interest groups, and interpersonal communication. Due to the convergence of mass and interpersonal communication, social network site stocks are highly valued since these platforms serve as both media and phone companies' platforms. Social media, once restricted to the Cultural Industry, is now able to operate more efficiently within a capitalist system as a result of its increasing personal and exponential growth in integration into people's daily lives.

The shift from the TV broadcasting-based Culture Industry that dominated the second half of the 20th century to the new Internet-based mediation structure encourages significant adjustments to the classic Monopoly Capitalism functions of propaganda, advertising, and programming (Bolaño, 2015). These are essential for the system's colonization of the lifeworld (Habermas, 1981).

Advertising's goal is to guarantee the economic subsystem's colonization of the real world by acting as a mediator between the market and consumers. Propaganda mediates conflicts between the citizenry and the state, allowing administrative subsystems to colonize the real world. According to Bolaño, a program's third function is to represent decisions made in the real world over mediating structure by providing content in a flow that can draw in an audience that will eventually become a commodity. However, in a public broadcasting system, the third role can be fulfilled through public services, accountability, and so forth.

The important thing to remember is that interaction is how this primary function appears in the context of social media and the Internet. The much more complicated issue of how the propaganda function is carried out in the current capitalist mediation structure is not something we will get into here. At the moment, Internet monitoring is the primary means by which the State colonizes the real world. Apart from the dissemination of content rooted in the real world, the interaction feature permits monitoring of social media platforms that generate user profiles as well as government agencies.

In contrast to broadcasting, which involves a select (powerful) segment of the media staff logically organizing content via radio or TV programming (Williams, 2003), social media automates this process by organizing content according to the user's preferences and taking into account their interactions with other users, businesses, and other organizations. The audience is a commodity sold by traditional mass media (Smythe, 1977). Audience prices are determined by the demographic group profile of the current television-watching audience and vary based on the schedule, when advertising runs, and other factors. According to Bolaño (2015), profiles are established through qualitative and primarily quantitative surveys that utilize samples drawn from the entire population of people who watch or listen to radio at any given time.

Because a large portion of respondents to these surveys are disinterested in the products being advertised, the system as a whole is rendered nonfunctional, leading to inefficiencies and higher expenses. This issue is greatly mitigated by social media, where market-consumer mediation operates with previously unheard-of efficiency. Algorithms are a new component that is essential for the completion of all its mediation functions in social media environments.

As stated on page Gillespie (2014, p. 167), "[Algorithms] are encoded procedures that, based on predetermined calculations, transform input data into a desired output." According to Wilson (2016), algorithms are everywhere and play a major role in the operation of services like Netflix recommendations, Google searches, Twitter trends, and Facebook newsfeeds. Even friend interactions on social media are arranged based on algorithms-generated patterns. Algorithms allow for the tracking of user navigation on the Internet, producing data that is used to create highly customized advertisements. Social media monitors users' interactions with other profiles, whether they belong to businesses, individuals, or content creators, in order to disseminate propaganda, advertising, and content in a tailored manner.

1.1. ALGORITHMS, SOCIAL MEDIA, AND BIG DATA

One of the main forces behind the 1970s capitalist system restructuring that led to the end of the Fordist accumulation regime and the beginning of the flexible accumulation regime was the development of information and communication technologies (ICTs) (Harvey, 1989). ICTs have given outdated technologies a powerful disruptive edge, speeding up the trend of creative destruction within the capitalist system. Furthermore, by automating and codifying a variety of tasks in software, ICTs have strengthened what Marx refers to as the labor subsumption by capital (Bolaño, 2002). Since the last 10 years, the cultural industry has been affected by ICTs. This has included a drop in the circulation of newspapers and magazines as well as, more recently, an audience's adoption of second screens, which has resulted in a decrease in viewer attention. In other words, the cultural industries' commodity audience has undergone a severe devaluation process.

This procedure is associated with the pursuit of profitability in the online market, which was a primary factor in the collapse of the NASDAQ stock market bubble. Based on the anticipation of Internet popularization in the 2000s, there was a promise of high profitability, which prompted the indiscriminate opening of technology companies and the speculation that followed. But the great majority of companies were not profitable enough to offset the large sums of money that speculative capital had invested in that industry. The truth is that by the end of the previous millennium, Internet search and content sites still hadn't figured out how to turn a profit from the digital world other than through financial speculation. Numerous initiatives were created, including the subscription service and the advertisements that appeared on users' screens when they visited particular websites. The majority of Internet users, however, were unwilling to pay for content and found pop-up advertisements to be disruptive because they appear on computer screens involuntarily rather than through controlled and expected television advertisements that are aired during regular programming.

Authors like McChesney (2013) and Van Dijck (2013) claim that tracking users online using cookies—files that browsers download when they visit specific websites—and gathering user path data is the way to break free from the aforementioned impasse. It was possible to track down users' profiles using that data and present them with customized advertisements. By fusing real-time data collection with user tracking, social media has refined this logic to provide users with a customized experience for both content and advertising. Though they are still major content producers of news, videos, series, and movies, big media companies can view this transformation as a defeat because they are no longer the main targets of the advertising industry. Social media companies, whose algorithms mediate people's interactions with mass-media companies and other people, hold the power to distribute the flow of content and advertisements.

These businesses position themselves as impartial go-betweens for users, content creators, and advertisers by relying on the fictitious mathematical objectivity of algorithms. Pasquale (2015) observes that algorithms "are constantly making controversial, value-laden decisions, despite their claims of objectivity and neutrality." Although the owners of these devices assert that algorithms only display the world, the devices nonetheless create images of it. Pasquale points out that although people know very little about the giants like Google and Facebook, their algorithms do. Pasquale claims that algorithms are like "black boxes."

According to Cormen and associates (2009), an algorithm is a precisely defined computational process that accepts a value or set of values as input and outputs another value or set of values. As a result, an algorithm is a set of instructions for computing that converts input into output. Algorithms are the computational codes that underlie the software that we use. Algorithms contain instructions on how software should respond (output) to commands from users (input). Computational algorithms, then, are the outcome of numerous advances in computer science and mathematics that are employed by business to create new goods and increase profits.

Social media interactions between people are mediated by computers and software, and algorithms control human-software interaction. The ads and content that are suggested for this user would be the output of social media algorithms that use data gathered from the tracking of user interactions with the profiles of businesses and other users as the input. That output is the outcome of statistical computations performed on massive amounts of data that were gathered with the aid of computers with powerful processing units. The use of algorithms has become ubiquitous in daily life. They influence the financial markets, Google search results, Netflix movie recommendations, social media platforms, and more, making Lawrence Lessig's(2006) well-known adage that "the code is the law" an uncomfortable reality.

Additionally, computational codes are increasingly permeating our social media interactions. Van Dijck (2013) argues that social media can be viewed as a network that fosters interactions as a social value, facilitating human connection. However, these platforms are also automated systems that create and modify interactions to determine users' preferences and needs. "Social media sites like Facebook track users by encoding connections between users, objects, and ideas" (idem). The author claims that social media companies frequently emphasize how well they facilitate human interaction in their institutional propaganda, while downplaying the extent to which these interactions are automated. According to the source, the use of algorithms to automate interactions enables a "detailed and intimate knowledge of the desires and tastes of people," which is employed by platforms to create tools that define and direct particular needs.

Although algorithms were created to solve problems, they are data-driven and inert (Gillespie, 2014). In order to provide personalized content and advertising, algorithms require vast amounts of data, which are gathered by tracking user interactions. Thanks to computers with powerful processing capabilities, social media algorithms can compile this data in real time. The term "Big Data" refers to the enormous quantities of data, which can only be processed with the help of such powerful computers. Shutt and O'Neill (2013) argue that there is a misconception that Big Data encompasses all data, where N = All, meaning the sample would include every member of the specified population. However, those not captured by Big Data would be ignored by this reasoning, making it impossible for a sample to truly represent the entire population in statistical terms.

On the other end of the spectrum, the writers are equally mistaken in believing that N = 1. According to statistics, this would imply that it would be feasible to deduce from a single person the traits of a certain population. But in the Big Data era, N = 1 takes on new significance since it is now feasible to store vast amounts of data about a single person and create a sample that encompasses all of their events and behaviors, allowing conclusions to be drawn about them. It's known as "user-level modeling" by data scientists, and it involves building data models that can forecast the preferences and behavior of a particular service's user (Idem). "A model is an attempt, whether it be mathematical, biological, or architectural, to understand or represent the nature of reality." Consequently, it is challenging to uphold the objectivity claims for social media given that models are created through a specific lens.

In their extremely negative analysis of the Cultural Industry, Adorno and Horkheimer (1949) state that "for everyone something is foreseen; so that no one escapes." The two German philosophers actually believed that the distinctions among the different kinds of content generated by the Cultural Industry were just a way to statically classify and measure consumers for the sake of industry planning. According to Habermas (1981), the Cultural Industry would thus encourage the colonization of everyday life by the lifeworld. It was the continuation of the system's instrumental rationality, to which the employee would be exposed both during work and during leisure time. The viewpoint of Adorno and Horkheimer is widely regarded as a biased one regarding the Cultural Industry, which totally strips people of their agency and presents an incredibly inflated picture of the ability of mass culture companies to predict audience preferences.

With a margin of error far smaller than that seen in the traditional Cultural Industry, social media algorithms truly predict something for every individual user. This is not a force of expression or metaphor, but rather the ability to correctly predict and distribute content or advertisements to the appropriate user. This surveillance and control over people's daily interactions also represents a hitherto unseen colonization of the lifeworld by the rationality of economic and administrative subsystems. Naturally, it would be incorrect for us to deny the existence of utopian energies. Social movements utilize social media as a tool to spread and mobilize support for their demands. Similar movements oppose the encroachment of instrumental rationality in digital networks. Contradictions in capitalism are inherently flawed. However, it is difficult to ignore the Frankfurter statement when we consider the advertisements and personalized content users receive based on the information gathered by social media.

From a different angle, we can also draw the conclusion that algorithms ensure that the entire Culture Industry operates in a way that is far more covert and focused on the market than Foucault's (1975) analogously organized "disciplinary society," where the individual's submission is connected to the partition of space into enclosed areas and the subsequent scheduling of working hours. Algorithms and the Internet economy appear to support Deleuze's (1992) theory of a shift from that analogous disciplinary society to a digitally structured "control society," where spaces converge without boundaries and a never-ending clock prevents people from completing their tasks.

1.1.1. Algorithms, Mass Communication, and Social Media

We can define the algorithmic task in terms of the microeconomic and microsocial aspects of the various culture industries as follows:

Algorithms arrange the cultural content available online, replacing the antiquated TV schedule with an automated device that translates viewer habits and preferences into demands from advertisers. Producers and consumers appear to be independent entities that discover the web to be the ideal tool for maintaining their reciprocal independence within a strictly commercial framework. The operation's ideological nature is apparent (Bolaño, 2016), leading to a more fetishist interpretation that confounds both roles within the oversimplified concept of "prosumer." It is true that programmers lost influence in all cases, giving preference to advertisers, but this was accomplished through a process that creates an alluring illusion of equality.

In doing so, algorithms automatically focus public attention and create various audience commodities that online players sell to advertisers in a highly effective manner. The inability of this social logic to maintain focus in a fully dialogical communication system is its flaw. In actuality, and herein lies the paradox solution, what is sold is not merely an audience, as in the case of broadcasting, but also an apparent direct channel, free from the intervention of other human interests, between consumers and advertisers. This appearance is a result of the system's automatic nature, which upholds the false notion of technological neutrality.

An interactive communication that was not possible in the Culture Industry organization of the XX Century is made possible by algorithms. As previously stated, interaction serves the same purpose in building an audience as programs or public services. However, in order to be beneficial to the state and capital, its revolutionary and critical potentials must be neutralized. In the last case, Habermas (1961) claimed that the classic bourgeois public sphere encountered the same issue during the shift from competitive to monopolist capitalism. He believed that the Culture Industry held the key to solving this issue. Reactivity then takes the place of interactivity (Williams, 2003). These days, a very similar procedure occurs.

Individual capitals compete to make micro decisions that determine the entire social logic. In Internet-based markets, algorithms are the primary advantage of individual capitals vying for dominance or protecting barriers against new competitors. Producing algorithms and keeping them under wraps gives monopolistic advantages. In the end, this is the main goal of any capital and the foundation of every specific business in the digital economy. Thus, information democratization is still far off. As with the tendencies of capital accumulation, Marx and Engels argued that concentration and centralization are the main trends in the Internet economy, where the typical market structure is still an oligopoly.

Conversely, Van Dijck and Poell (2013) highlight that mass media and social media are not at all neutral when it comes to influencing modern-day social interactions. The authors list four social media traits—programmability, popularity, connectivity, and datafication—that are becoming more and more common in day-to-day living. These four traits are intriguing because they help distinguish the socioeconomic shift from an era where mass media dominated society as social mediators to a current historical moment where social media companies start to impose their logic on people's interactions with administrative and economic subsystems. The boundaries between computer-mediated communication and mass communication are being rapidly eroded by ICTs.

This stream of content, news, and advertisements serves both an economic and cultural purpose. For instance, a newscast's news flow prioritizes some facts over others and skews viewers' perceptions of what is being reported. Economic interests also organize the programming flow. Schedules are set with the intention of reaching a specific type of audience who would be available to watch the broadcast program. The schedule of a broadcast program determines its chances of success, as Jost (2010) notes, since it might not reach the target audience or pique their interest less than the competitor's broadcast content. As a result, one of a broadcaster's strategic roles is to create a programming flow that, while taking into consideration the content offerings of other channels, delivers the right television genre to the target audience at the appropriate time. In addition to these two, the advertiser stipulates that a target must be created in order "to build a stable public, with more or less the same characteristics from week to week."

Programmability in social media is derived from user interaction tracking rather than prearranged program flow throughout the day. Because social media algorithms are proprietary and considered trade secrets, social media arranges the content flows that are accessible to individuals based on metrics and parameters that are not available for user accountability. It offers a fresh approach to audience sales in addition to automating the exchange of content and interactions. Individuals receive propaganda and advertising that is customized based on their past interactions, so the right advertisement is shown to the right person.

Popularity would be the second social media characteristic. Social media platforms have legitimized popularity, a power that the mass media still holds. Actors, politicians, and musicians are becoming more and more public figures, or they are gaining symbolic capital from social media exposure. Agents who are adept at using their prominence and visibility in new media to their advantage can attract followers for their ideas and work without having to go through the mass media's filters. Connectivity can be considered the third characteristic of social media. In terms of connectivity, Van Dijck and Poells (2013) refers to the socio-technical capacity to link content and ads to user activities. The term is derived from technical hardware language. Instead of using the terms connectivity or interactivity, we prefer to use computer-mediated interaction (Primo, 2007).

Datafication, or the capacity of networked platforms to turn many previously unquantifiable aspects of the world into data, would be the fourth feature. Not only is it possible to quantify the demographic or profile information that consumers provide in online surveys, but it is also possible to automatically extract metadata from smartphones—such as location data—based on user interactions and actions. (Idem).

Here, we favor the concept of quantification, which embodies a long-standing trend that started in the XII Century, according to Crosby (1997). It symbolizes both the general division between manual and intellectual labor in ancient Greece as well as the internal process of abstraction that has been a hallmark of capitalist development since its inception (Sohn-Rethel, 1995). Recent manifestations of this long-term tendency include the rise of informatics, the logical division between hardware and software, and the subsumption of intellectual labor (Bolaño, 2012), which define the current capitalist reorganization…

1.1.2. Interactivity, Social Media, and Surveillance

Marxist theorists like Brecht in the 1930s and Enzensberger (1970) in the 1970s had already suggested that the media might enable people to be both producers and receivers, thereby affecting a type of popular, communitarian, contra-hegemonic communication, free from the control of capital and the state. In order to combat the forces of disconnection through the organization of the disconnected, Brecht (1964) believed that radio needed to be a tool of both communication and diffusion. Bolaño (2015), paraphrasing Williams, referred to this movement as the "listener rebellion."

When Williams (2003) examined television as a cultural form and the opportunities it provided for truly democratic communication in the 1960s, he distinguished between reactive and interactive media.

On the other hand, the electronic industry has always been concerned about the search for more interactive media. However, as noted by Van Dijk and Des Vos (2001) and Primo (2007), the need for technological advancements that boost interactivity has always been driven by the desire for profit and has been centered on human-machine interaction, following predetermined parameters set by programmers of technological systems. Devices designed to entice users included television remote controls, computer operating systems with user-friendly interfaces, and other technological advancements. These were "selling arguments" for electronic product advertising (Sfez, 1992). According to this bias, the "new communicative possibilities" of emerging technologies are qualities that warrant the purchase and use of new goods.

According to Van Dijk and De Vos (2001), interactivity is defined from a transmissionist perspective and is consistent with the emitter-message-receiver model in many definitions within the communication sciences. Rafaeli (1988) defined interactivity as "an expression of the extent that in a given series of communication, any third (or later) transmission (or message) is related to the degree to which previous exchanges referrer to even earlier transmissions." This definition is among the first and most well-known in the field of communication. Still, according to Williams (2003), an interactive system should provide the user with the opportunity to create and react in unexpected ways. However, "the range of choices, both in detail and scope, is pre-set" (Williams, 2003) in reactive systems. Williams' definition of interactive television states that it must permit "viewer rebellion." Primo (2007) states that Williams, however, would view a large portion of the technological resources currently found on television sets as reactive.

The fact that the term "interactivity" has multiple definitions stems from its multi-discursive nature (Jensen, 1988) – (i) "The concept of interaction of sociology; (ii) the interaction concepts of communication studies; and finally (iii) the concept of interaction of computer sciences" (Idem) are the three domains of knowledge that Jensen maps out and examines the various applications of interactivity.

The relationship between two or more individuals who, in a particular circumstance, mutually adjust their behaviors and actions to the other is the model for the concept of interaction in sociology. This social process includes social systems and particular, sharply defined situations; interactive patterns are more akin to physical interaction. Furthermore, the idea incorporates "symbolic interaction." Put another way, partners who are in the same social context engage in a reciprocal exchange and negotiation about meaning. A circumstance that media studies and communication would refer to as communication. As a result, while unidirectional communication can occur in sociological studies, interaction cannot occur in isolation from communication.

Regarding the concept of interaction, there is no agreement or precise definition in the fields of communication and media studies. Interaction can refer to how audiences construct meanings in response to specific content, how people communicate with one another, or something more closely associated with sociology in communications research within audience study groups. As mentioned earlier, another model for the idea of interaction in communication studies is the transmissionist model, which focuses solely on technology.

The relationship between humans and machines, also known as human-computer interaction (HCI) or human-machine interaction, is the foundation of the computer science interaction model. Jensen claims that batch processing—in which a significant amount of data is gathered prior to computer processing—is where the model got its start. Users could use dialog boxes, choice menus, and partial results to influence the process. By using "dialog traffic" or a "interactive mode," users were able to influence how the program operated. Computer-mediated communication, or communication between two people mediated by a machine, is not covered by the computer science model of interaction. Jensen states that while interaction (man-machine) can occur without communication, computer-mediated communication cannot occur without interaction (human-computer).

For the development of our argument, the interaction concept of "control" in computer science (Jensen, 1998) is crucial. In order to reach a consensus definition of the terms interaction and interactivity, Jensen presents the Workshop Seillac example. According to Guedji (1980), "Interaction is a style of control and interactive systems exhibit that style." Furthermore, according to Jensen (1998), "the concepts of "interaction" and "interactivity" in computer and media studies appear to be synonymous, even though sociology doesn't normally use the derivative "interactivity." In the context of the emergence of "new media," synonymous usage has also proliferated within the media studies community. Accordingly, "a certain feature of new media that distinguishes it from traditional media is often characterized by the concept of 'interactivity' or the combination of 'interactive media'" (Idem).

With the exception of mediated communication, Jensen believes it would be more beneficial to uphold the interaction concept in light of its robust sociological definition. The use of media and computer-mediated communication is referred to as interactive communication. Jensen defines interactivity as "a measure of a media's potential ability to let the user exert influence on the content and/or form of mediated communication" in this manner. Even with the addition of the potential for social media users to function as prosumers (Toffler, 1981), Jensen's concept of interactivity (Jensen, 2008) ignores the sociological aspects of the interaction concept, making it unproductive for understanding the role of social media in the modern era. We think that in social media, interaction—in the strong sociological sense—and interactivity—in the man-machine sense—are closely related.

According to Van Dijck (2013), social media platforms standardize human interaction through their codified architecture, which allows for the personalized insertion of propaganda, advertising, and content into users' lives while also keeping an eye on them. Because of the data created by user interactions on social media platforms, interaction on those platforms thus turns into a means of control and surveillance. This interaction coding plays a key role in what Foster and McChesney (2014) refer to as "surveillance capitalism," which is the emergence of the Warfare State—a political-economic structure in which the US government invests heavily in military hardware in order to bolster its own economy and maintain military hegemony on a worldwide scale. Daniel Guerin (1973) coined the term "Military-Industrial Complex" to describe the convergence of interests between US military forces and industry corporations.

Foster and McChesney (2014) claim that three methods of absorbing surplus value—massive military spending, sales efforts that entail significant investments in advertising, and financialization—have strengthened the digital communications revolution since the 1970s. This revolution is linked to technological advancements like computers, digital technology, and the Internet. Each required new methods of control and surveillance, as was mentioned. As a result, surveillance became ubiquitous and was linked to three different domains: (1) corporate-based marketing and the media system; (2) militarism/imperialism/security; and (3) the finance industry (Foster; McChesney, 2014).

Social media and algorithms meet the new requirements for monitoring and control, which improves the efficiency of sales efforts, the spread of advertising, and the financialization of the economy. The state and market are now better able to keep an eye on people thanks to new technologies. Algorithms are the tools that the market and the state use to jointly exercise control and surveillance. Big digital companies, however, consider those algorithms to be trade secrets. There is a significant power and information asymmetry because, although big technology companies have access to a vast amount of data about social media users, the general public is largely unaware of the uses made of this data. "Dataveillance" produces a mutually beneficial exchange of personal information about people's lives (Pasquale, 2015).

They resemble dark boxes. Users of social media are completely unaware of how that data is used and who has access to it, and they have no idea what criteria are used to rank and categorize them. By stifling advertising and propaganda into the content stream, social media mediatizes the interests of the market and the state in a way that is far more obvious than that of mass media. In addition to creating what Gillespie (2014) refers to as "calculated audiences," algorithms also infiltrate our daily lives (Wilson, 2016), act as gatekeepers in social reality, and establish the agendas of particular groups (Just; Latzer, 2017). Moreover, they serve as the technological foundation for monopolistic businesses like Facebook and Google.

1.2. SOCIAL MEDIA ALGORITHM

An algorithm is a set of guidelines intended to carry out operations, solve particular tasks, or reach conclusions. Algorithms in computer programming control the computer's operations, including sorting components, finding data, and identifying objects.

Algorithms are the data, signals, and rules that control how social media platforms work. These algorithms decide which content is ranked, filtered, chosen, and suggested to users. Algorithms have an impact on our decisions and the content we view on social media.

1.2.1. Why Are Social Media Algorithms Important?

Every social media network has a diverse user base with a range of interests. In the absence of a filtering system, users are forced to sift through an overwhelming amount of posts.

Here's where algorithms are useful. Social media companies use smart algorithms to act as intelligent advisors, carefully selecting and matching content to users based on shared interests.

Understanding the ins and outs of algorithms and why they are important is essential for any social media marketing strategy:

1.2.1.1. Filter Out the Content Noise

A new Facebook post or TikTok video that is uploaded to the internet joins millions of other content creations. Algorithms connect users with their preferences by sorting and acting as librarians. This helps users find what they like more quickly and avoids overburdening them with content. Users can find interesting posts, interact with people who share their interests, and explore their interests thanks to algorithms.

1.2.1.2. Show Users More of What They're Interested In

Social media sites extend user engagement through complex algorithms. Based on user information such as actions, behaviors, and interests, these algorithms regulate the visibility, order, and recommendations of content. For example, you will see more posts about gadgets if you interact with them. A better user experience is produced by this personalization, which also increases user engagement.

1.2.1.3. Personalize User Experience

Users now have more influence over how they interact with content. Algorithms use information to tailor content suggestions. You can curate your content by choosing "Not interested," hiding posts, or filtering comments on social media sites like Instagram.

1.2.1.4. Maximize Organic Reach

Gaining an understanding of social media algorithms will improve your online presence. As more people discover your content, the algorithm improves its ability to match up users with related interests. In order to maximize the distribution potential of their content, marketers and creators can optimize it for algorithms. The algorithm spreads the word about a post to more people when it receives a lot of engagement.

1.2.2. Working of Social Media Algorithms

Comprehending the functioning of social media algorithms is akin to disentangling the complex strands that dictate the virtual fabric of user experiences. These algorithms choose the content for our feeds, acting as invisible guides. Let's examine how social teams can benefit from social media algorithms and how they work.

1.2.2.1. Algorithms Search for Relevant and Valuable Content

Systems for curating content that are algorithmically driven, like the Instagram Feed and Facebook News Feed, keep track of user actions, interests, and behavior to suggest relevant content. For example, you'll probably see more basketball content if you interact with it.

By adjusting and picking up on user interactions, these algorithms seek to improve the content recommendations and make sure the content is still relevant.

1.2.2.2. Signals and Important Factors Social Algorithms Consider

Algorithms collect user signals to match them with relevant content. Key signals include:

1. **User Engagement:** Likes, shares, and comments indicate that users find the content interesting and relevant.
2. **Relevance:** Keywords and hashtags give content context and improve its visibility.
3. **Timing and Frequency:** Posting consistently and at the right time when your audience is active can boost visibility.
4. **Recency:** Newer posts are prioritized over older ones.
5. **User Interactions:** Accounts followed, interactions, and click-through rates on links signals relevance and content quality.
6. **Profile Authority:** Follower count, consistency, and engagement impact organic reach.
7. **Location:** Algorithms take into account the location and demographics of users when curating content. Content may be promoted to users in similar locations.
8. **Content Type:** Different content types, like videos, images, and text, are treated based on user interaction. Many platforms favor videos because they're more engaging.
9. **Virality:** Content gaining popularity and shares signals relevance to the algorithm.
10. **Watch Time:** This is the duration users spends watching videos (IG Reel, YouTube Shorts).

1.2.3. Social Media Algorithm Example

There's a good chance that if you use any social media platforms, you've encountered the active algorithm. These are a few instances that you may have overlooked (Figure 1.1).

1. Twitter shows content based on the keywords users follow. For example, I follow the "SEO" keyword, and X (formerly known as Twitter) recommends posts with the keyword on my Explore page.

Figure 1.1. *Posts by SEO.*

Source: https://media.sproutsocial.com/uploads/2023/10/social-media-algorithm-x-tag.png.

2. LinkedIn's algorithm shows content that my first-degree connections are engaging with. In this post, for example, over 313 of my first-degree connections follow this account, so LinkedIn prioritizes the sponsored post on my Feed (Figure 1.2).

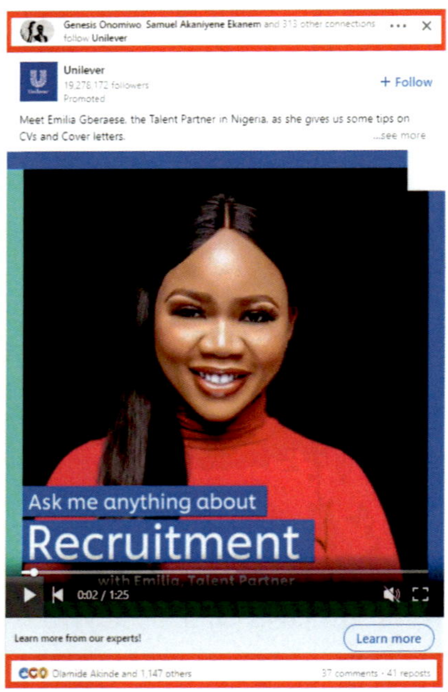

Figure 1.2. *Sponsored post.*
Source: https://media.sproutsocial.com/uploads/2023/10/social-media-algorithm-linkedin-reco.png.

3. LinkedIn suggests content for users with similar keywords. I love reading about social media and content marketing on LinkedIn, so it's no surprise they push this content type my way (Figure 1.3).

Figure 1.3. *Social media and content marketing on LinkedIn.*

Source: https://media.sproutsocial.com/uploads/2023/10/social-media-algorithm-linkedin-suggested.png.

4. Twitter suggests accounts to follow based on the content they post and what you've liked (Figure 1.4).

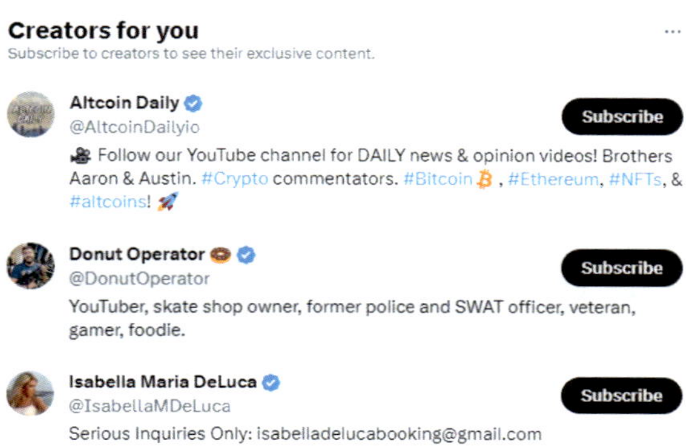

Figure 1.4. *Social media content which is posted.*

Source: https://media.sproutsocial.com/uploads/2023/10/social-media-algorithm-twitter-suggested-creators.png.

1.2.4. Social Media Algorithms by Platform

Each social media network has a different algorithm for selecting and displaying content. These platforms detect user preferences by searching for particular ranking signals. Let's examine a few social media sites and the rank signals unique to each that should be noted.

1.2.4.1. Twitter Algorithm

Instead of organizing content chronologically, the Twitter algorithm uses artificial intelligence (AI) to select content based on user preferences, interests, and past interactions. Twitter claims that its algorithm scans 500 million tweets every day to show you only the most relevant ones on your timeline.

In 2023, the updated Twitter algorithm considers:

- **Location and Language:** Twitter shows you content based on your location, especially in their "Trends for You" section.
- **User Interactions:** Content is recommended based on your activity, including who you follow and interact with.
- **Engagement Level:** Tweet popularity is determined by user engagement metrics such as likes, Retweets and replies.
- **Relevancy:** The relevance of a Tweet is based on the keywords used, the user's interests and previous interactions.
- **Recency:** Recent Tweets hold importance, especially in the "Trending Topics" and "What's Happening" sections.
- **Profile Reputation Score:** Active profiles engaging with others gain higher visibility; Twitter also uses TweetCred, a PageRank algorithm, to rate a profile's credibility based on its followers, past activities, safety status and device usage.
- **Similar Accounts:** Profiles are categorized based on the niche or topic discussed.

1.2.4.2. Facebook Algorithm

As the social media giant with over 2 billion active users, Facebook is unmatched in its size. To manage the content on this colossal platform, Facebook utilizes numerous algorithms to identify the content that users might find engaging. The updated algorithm considers:

- **Timing:** Facebook's algorithm prioritizes timing as a key signal for ranking content in user's feeds.

- **Demographics:** The user's location, language, and gender can help predict their content preferences.
- **Account Credibility:** The algorithm ranks accounts with credibility, a strong following, and engaging content.
- **Content Type:** Facebook's algorithm prioritizes the type of posts users engage with most. So, users who watch more videos will get more video content.
- **Relevance:** Posts with similar keywords or hashtags are recommended to users with shared interests.
- **Engagement Levels:** High engagement, including comments, shares, and likes, indicates quality content and since Facebook is all about creating meaningful posts, it ranks it higher.
- **Facebook Connections:** Content from the accounts you follow is prioritized over those you don't follow.

By combining these signals, Facebook's algorithm determines a post's relevancy score, which indicates the likelihood that a user will interact with it.

1.2.4.3. Instagram Algorithm

One of the most varied social media networks is Instagram. Instagram is separated into five sections, according to CEO Adam Mosseri: Feed, Stories, Explore, Reels, and Search. Algorithms, classifiers, and processes are used in each section to customize content recommendations according to user behavior.

1.2.4.3.1. Instagram Feed

A combination of content from accounts you follow, related profiles you might find interesting, and customized advertisements make up your Instagram feed. In the feed, posts are ranked based on several signals (Figure 1.5):

- **Post Recency:** Recent posts from accounts take priority, appearing before older ones.
- **People You Follow:** Posts from those you follow appear organically on your feed. For creators, this means having more followers increases your visibility.
- **User Activity:** Posts you've liked, shared, saved or commented on convey your content preferences.
- **Content Type:** Users who prefer photos will see more photos. The same goes for videos and carousels.

- **Post Information:** Posts with many likes, shares, comments, and saves signal relevance to users with similar interests or locations.
- **Interaction History:** Your interactions with an account's posts and frequency influence the appearance of their content in your feed.

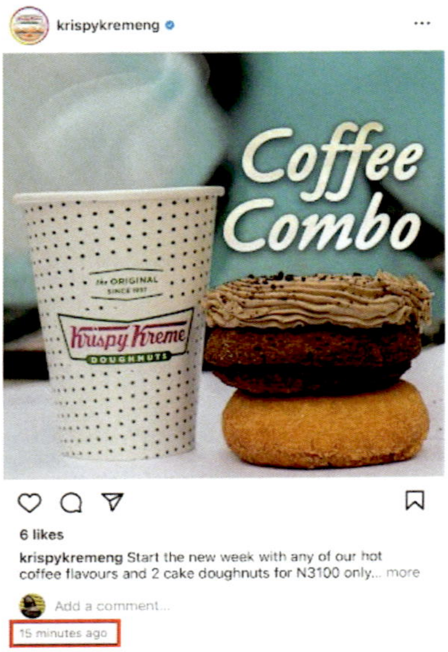

Figure 1.5. *Post recency.*

Source: https://media.sproutsocial.com/uploads/2023/10/social-media-algorithm-insta-krispy.jpg.

-

1.2.4.3.2. Instagram Stories

Users can upload images or videos to Stories, an in-app feature that expires in a day. This is how it appears (Figure 1.6):

Figure 1.6. *Social media stories.*

Source: https://media.sproutsocial.com/uploads/2023/10/social-media-algorith-insta-stories-example.png.

The ranking factors for stories are quite similar to those of the IG Feed. Stories use engagement signals such as:

- **Viewing History:** Frequently viewing an account's stories would result in its prioritization.
- **Engagement History:** Liking or responding to stories is an engagement metric that impacts story rankings.
- **Closeness:** The algorithm considers your relationship with the story's creator, including mutual follows, shared locations, and DM interactions.

1.2.4.3.3. Instagram Explore

Explore simplifies the discovery of new posts without needing active search. Here's what it looks like on Instagram (Figure 1.7):

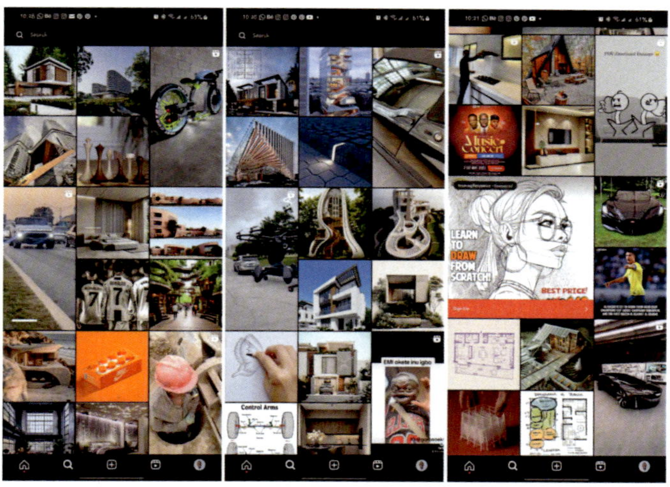

Figure 1.7. *Social media algorithm explore example.*

Source: https://media.sproutsocial.com/uploads/2023/10/social-media-algorith-ig-explore-example-1024x751.png.

The grid comprises content recommendations from accounts you don't follow but Instagram believes you might enjoy. Signals Instagram considers include:

- **User's Past Interaction:** Content is ranked based on previous engagements with posts.
- **Post Popularity:** The number of likes, comments, shares, and saves influences visibility.
- **User's Explore Activity:** History of a user's interaction on the

Explore page, including liked posts and similar content.

- **Account Information:** The frequency of interaction with the account in the past few weeks.

1.2.4.3.4. Instagram Reels

Reels are designed for users to explore new content from accounts they don't follow, similar to Explore. Key signals for Reels content include:

- **User's Activity:** Recent interactions with Reels, such as likes, saves, shares, comments, and engagement.
- **Interaction History:** Your interaction history with accounts, even if you don't follow them.
- **Relevance:** The content's relevance is determined by popularity signals like likes, saves, and comments.
- **Account Information:** An account's popularity, including follower count and engagement level, informs content recommendation.

1.2.4.4. TikTok Algorithm

TikTok's algorithm is a recommendation system designed to curate the For You Feed for each user considering the following signals:

- **User Interactions:** Your likes, views, shares, comments, searches, and interactions with accounts shape your feed. Accounts you follow or suggested for you
- **Location:** Recent and popular content in your region impacts your feed.
- **Video Details:** TikTok uses video quality, captions, sounds or hashtags to recommend content.
- **Device and Account Settings:** This includes the language, device type and country.
- **Watch Time:** The number of replays and completed videos influences your feed.

1.2.4.5. YouTube Algorithm

YouTube's algorithm considers many signals to rank videos on its homepage, including:

- **Video Performance:** YouTube video performance is measured in terms of engagement metrics such as likes, shares, and comments.
- **Click-Through Rate:** YouTube's algorithm assesses the likelihood

of user interaction with a video to recommend it to other users.

- **Watch Time and Retention:** Videos with longer watch time indicate quality content that retains viewer attention.
- **Recency:** Newer videos are promoted to subscribers who interact with the channel.
- **User Watch History and Actions:** Video watch time and post-interaction actions, like liking and commenting, signal relevance to the algorithm.
- **Search History:** What has the user searched for? Is it a recurring search?
- **Demographics and Location:** Videos uploaded by creators in a particular location are pushed to local viewers before broader promotion.

1.2.4.6. LinkedIn Algorithm

LinkedIn's algorithm uses several ranking signals that contribute to the success of a post on the platform. Here are some to watch out for:

- **Quality Over Quantity:** LinkedIn's algorithm filters posts into three categories: spam, low-quality, and high-quality.
- **Relevance:** The algorithm assesses post relevance based on keywords, hashtags, and comments.
- **Engagement Probability:** LinkedIn uses machine learning models to predict post engagement, especially within the first hour.
- **Personal Connections:** LinkedIn's algorithm prioritizes posts from your first-degree connections and those you engage with.
- **Consistency:** The algorithm rewards pages that post regularly with increased visibility.
- **Credibility:** Author expertise, insightful content and meaningful comments enhance post ranking.
- **Recency:** Recent posts hold significance for LinkedIn's algorithm.
- **Content Type:** The algorithm loves short-form videos and well-structured long-form content.

1.2.4.7. Pinterest Algorithm

The Pinterest algorithm ranks content using key ranking signals such as:

- **Topic Relevance:** Keywords, hashtags, and user interactions determine content relevance to users.

- **Pin Quality:** Your pin's level of engagement, such as likes, saves, and comments defines pin quality.
- **Domain Quality:** Website safety and visitor engagement impact Pinterest rankings. If visitors feel safe on your website, Pinterest ranks your content highly.
- **Account Quality:** Pinterest assesses your account credibility and posting consistency as a ranking signal. If you're considering Pinterest marketing, then ensure your account is on the good side.
- **Recency:** The algorithm considers how recently a pin was published and how recently it was updated.

1.2.4.8. Reddit Algorithm

Reddit's algorithm is designed to rank content based on what's Hot and Best, guided by key signals like:

- The number of upvotes, downvotes, and total votes it gets. Reddit uses votes as a signal to determine post relevance.
- Recent posts gain more traction and visibility. If you're marketing on Reddit, ensure you consistently post valuable content.
- The types of comments it gets. For example, a comment with nine up-votes and two down-votes will rank higher than a comment with one-up votes and no-down votes.

1.2.4.9. Tumblr Algorithm

If you use Tumblr for marketing, here are some signals to watch out for:

- **User Interaction:** Tumblr considers likes, reblogs, comments, and follows to expand content reach to a broader audience.
- **Post Content:** The algorithm uses tags, text, images, and multimedia to understand the post context and make recommendations.
- **Post Timing:** Newer posts receive higher visibility and are prioritized over older ones.
- **User Preference:** Past user interactions, content engagement and followed blogs influence content recommendations.

1.3. THE IMPACT OF ALGORITHMS ON USER EXPERIENCE

Without a doubt, social media algorithms have completely changed how we use platforms. Although they aim to improve user experiences by tailoring content and making it more relevant, they also bring up issues with content visibility and the possibility of echo chambers. Let us examine two crucial facets that are impacted by algorithms: content visibility and personalization.

1.3.1. Personalisation and Its Effects

The purpose of algorithms is to show us content that they think will appeal to us the most, thereby personalizing our feeds. By providing content that is suited to each user's preferences, personalization could improve user experiences.

Let's say, for instance, that you regularly interact with posts regarding travel. The algorithm might then give you access to more travel-related content in the future, like inspirational traveler stories, travel advice, and stunning scenery.

It is imperative to acknowledge, nevertheless, that personalization may restrict exposure to a range of viewpoints. By customizing our feeds to fit our interests, algorithms run the risk of unintentionally propagating preexisting biases and beliefs and creating information bubbles.

For example, if you are politically inclined and only interact with content that supports your beliefs, the algorithm might prioritize presenting you with more of the same, which could shield you from opposing ideas and help create echo chambers.

Algorithms, however, can also introduce users to fresh and interesting content that they might not have otherwise found.

It is possible for algorithms to recommend content from creators you may not be familiar with but are likely to enjoy by analyzing your behavior, including the posts you like, share, and comment on. This may result in coincidental discoveries that broaden your views and expose you to new ideas.

1.3.2. The Influence of Algorithms on Content Visibility

The content that is displayed and, in turn, the visibility and reach of user posts are largely determined by algorithms. Algorithms are designed to highlight interesting content for users, but they can also pose problems for companies and content producers who want to reach a wider audience. Businesses must comprehend how algorithms work if they hope to improve the visibility of their content in the fiercely competitive social media space.

Through an understanding of the factors that algorithms consider most important, like engagement rates, relevancy, and recentness, companies can better position their content to show up more frequently in users' feeds.

This could entail creating captivating headlines, attention-grabbing images, and promoting audience participation through shares, likes, and comments.

To make sure that their work is seen by as many people as possible, content creators also need to manage the influence of algorithms. In order to gain new followers, they might have to strike a balance between producing content that speaks to their current audience and trying out novel concepts.

Creators are able to fine-tune their strategies and adjust to the constantly changing algorithms by analyzing the performance of their posts and comprehending the patterns that surface.

Algorithms can also introduce users to niche content and lesser-known creators that they might not have otherwise come across. Algorithms that analyze user behavior and interests can suggest content that matches users' tastes even if it hasn't yet become widely known.

For aspiring authors, musicians, artists, and other creators, this can be a blessing because algorithms can assist them in connecting with a readership that recognizes and values their special gifts. In conclusion, algorithms have definitely changed how people use social media platforms, but there are drawbacks to their effects. On the one hand, by customizing content to each user's preferences, personalization can improve user experiences. However, it can also reduce exposure to different viewpoints and aid in the development of echo chambers.

Similar to this, algorithms can help companies and content producers become more visible, but they also pose difficulties due to their dynamic nature. To get the most out of social media, users, and content creators need to be aware of the nuances of algorithms.

1.4. NAVIGATING SOCIAL MEDIA ALGORITHMS FOR BUSINESSES

Companies that want to succeed online need to understand how to use social media algorithms wisely. Here, we'll look at ways to boost exposure and interaction, comprehend algorithm modifications and updates, and adjust to the constantly changing social media scene.

1.4.1. Strategies for Better Visibility on Social Media

In order to distinguish themselves from the noise generated by algorithms, companies ought to concentrate on creating captivating content that appeals to their intended audience. To increase visibility on social media platforms, one must cultivate real relationships, promote user interaction, and make use of influencers and sponsored promotions.

1.4.2. Understanding Algorithm Changes and Updates

Social media companies are always improving user experiences by tweaking their algorithms. It is critical to keep up with algorithmic trends, updates, and user preference shifts. Businesses can capitalize on new opportunities and retain visibility by modifying their strategies in response to these shifts.

1.4.3. AI's Role in Social Media Algorithms

The truth is that social media would not have taken off in the first place without AI. The creation and curation of algorithms that learn about users and make thoughtful decisions based on the data gathered has been greatly aided by artificial intelligence (AI).

Here are some ways AI plays a role in social media algorithms:

1. **Flagging of Misinformation and Fake News:** Social media companies employ AI to weed out harmful, disrespectful, and offensive content as well as identify fake news. For example, Twitter employs human moderation teams, AI-driven algorithms, machine learning models, and user reporting to detect and flag false content. To verify the veracity of the information shared, the algorithm examines the content of tweets and account histories.
2. **Moderate Content for User Safety:** It's reasonable to say that trolls, who participate in offensive behavior like posting hateful comments and, in more extreme cases, harassing others, can make social media unpleasant.

   Content moderation tools are used by platforms to flag questionable posts and comments in order to preserve high-quality discussions. Reddit, for example, employs machine learning models to identify questionable comments, which are then examined in more detail by human moderators. Similar to this, Facebook employs an AI tool to identify fraud and abuse in posts, photos, and videos, with human reviewers filling in as necessary.
3. **Personalize Content Delivery:** In order to personalize content recommendations, AI-driven algorithms segment users based on explicit (likes and follows) and implicit (video-watching time) details. Users can hide offensive words from their feeds and direct messages, follow hashtags, and choose their favorite keywords.

   Content recommendations are informed by user data, which includes feedback, actions, and behavior. Related posts with similar keywords are suggested.

4. **Provide Real-Time Analytics:** Data can be gathered, processed, and analyzed by AI algorithms instantly upon generation. Generative AI is used by social media giants like Facebook, which records billions of users every day, to make quick predictions, comprehend user relationships, and instantly handle security threats. In order to provide users with personalized recommendations, Facebook's AI algorithm starts tracking users' in-app behavior as soon as they log in. This includes tracking user engagement, content performance, and trending topics.

1.5. TIPS TO WIN OVER SOCIAL MEDIA PLATFORM ALGORITHM

The next stage is to become proficient at utilizing the algorithm with your content strategies now that we have a basic understanding of how social media algorithms operate. The precise method to follow is as follows:

1.5.1. Focus on the Quality

Social media algorithms greatly depend on signals like the quality and relevancy of the content. Because the algorithms are designed to present content that users are likely to find interesting, these signals are essential. Content quality is the most important ranking factor across all platforms. Hence, providing the content your audience wants is essential to passing the quality test. Depending on what your audience wants to see, it can be instructive, inspirational, or entertaining.

If you are a well-known fashion influencer on Instagram, for example, your followers would anticipate receiving style advice and fashion inspiration from your posts. If you have a do-it-yourself YouTube channel, your subscribers would anticipate you to provide step-by-step instructions and simple workarounds for any manual task. Making sure your audience sees content that is relevant to them is crucial. Additionally, since audience expectations and engagement are key factors in determining content quality across all social media platforms, make sure the content you create meets and exceeds these expectations.

1.5.2. Attract Likes, Comments, Shares, and Saves

One significant ranking factor for social media algorithms is audience engagement. Naturally, the secret to getting more likes, shares, and comments on your content is to produce content that promotes social media interaction. So how do you get that? Asking for it is an easy way to boost engagement that works well.

1.5.3. Know the Best Time to Post Content

The social media algorithm that determines how content appears in the feeds of your followers is heavily influenced by the time you post content. Here, recency is the primary factor that affects how your social media posts are displayed.

Posts that are recent are typically prioritized over ones that are days or weeks old, giving them a higher ranking on the feeds. The best times to post on social media must be taken into account if you want to improve the chances that people will see and interact with your content. But keep in mind that posting during optimal times does not ensure interaction.

The quality of the content you produce will ultimately determine whether or not your posts receive attention, even though publishing at the right times can help. Every social media platform has a best time of day for content posting.

1.5.4. Follow Trends to Gain Traction

Trending topics are given priority on social media platforms because they increase user engagement. Because of this, the algorithms try to show users more of this kind of content so they will continue to scroll through their feeds. It's not necessary to follow every trend, but it can be beneficial to look into trends that fit with the messaging of your brand. To achieve this, think about using resources like Google Trends to find out what's popular on the internet generally and social listening apps to find out what's going on in your industry. Additionally, keep an eye out for ways to incorporate popular sounds and effects into Instagram Reels and TikToks, which are short-form videos. By doing this, you can interact with your audience and increase the visibility of your content.

1.5.5. Experiment to Know What Works Best

Providing value to your audience on social media is the only way to beat the algorithm and increase your visibility. Therefore, the secret to understanding what motivates greater engagement in content is to experiment with it, whether you are a marketer or a business owner. Start by observing what information your audience is interested in before you start experimenting. Additionally, keep an eye on what your nearby rivals are promoting on social media. After you've done that, experiment with different interactive content formats to see which ones increase user engagement, such as pictures, surveys, videos, and stories. Examine the results of each and every content experiment you conduct. To improve assessment, closely monitor performance metrics like clicks, reach, and engagement to determine which of your content experiments are most well-liked by your target audience. As soon as you identify your best-performing content, you can start producing more of it to appear higher in feeds.

1.5.6. Share More Video Content

It's true that static posts do not reach as many people as video content. Numerous websites, including TikTok, Instagram, and so on, prefer moving images over still ones. Their social media feed algorithms are set up to prioritize showing users' feeds with more video content. Short films are also frequently promoted on social media platforms because it can be difficult to share regular video content. They take about 3 to 15 seconds to make and require very little time. Since video content engages users more thoroughly, it is encouraged. It achieves the platform's objective of keeping users on the feed for extended periods of time. For this reason, the user feed of most algorithms is programmed to display more motion or video content. Creating content of this kind can increase your reach on social media.

1.5.7. Find Out Your Publishing Frequency

In the context of experimentation, publication interval and frequency are also relevant. While some brands never deviate from a predetermined posting interval, others do so periodically. Their approach to social media marketing is based on what is effective for them.

Every social media platform should require a different posting strategy and approach. The posting tactics used on Instagram are not appropriate for other platforms, such as YouTube. In a similar vein, sharing several videos every day on TikTok or Instagram does not ensure viewership.

The recommended posting frequency for major social channels are:

- **Instagram:** 3–7 times per week.
- **Facebook:** 1–2 times a day.
- **Twitter:** 1–5 Tweets a day.
- **LinkedIn:** 1–5 times a day.

Therefore, it takes trial and error and brainstorming to determine what posting schedule works best for you. You should be able to track the effectiveness of your content with an absolutely accurate analytics tool in order to comprehend that.

1.6. THE PROS AND CONS OF SOCIAL MEDIA ALGORITHMS

The platform design process incorporates social media algorithms for a variety of use cases, including data sorting and content ranking at a scale and speed that is not feasible for humans. Notably, by limiting content that is unlawful, harmful, or inappropriate, algorithmic content moderation serves as the foundation for social media security. Digital platforms' efficacy and safety are guaranteed by algorithms.

Even though social media algorithms are highly capable technologically, there are many obstacles in the way of keeping billions of people safe online in the midst of a wealth of content. There is a bipartisan concern in Congress regarding the potential impact of algorithms on the offline consequences of social media use. Policymakers need to be aware of the trade-offs and consequences of this quickly developing technology if they plan to regulate how digital platforms use algorithms. This explainer contrasts the many advantages of social media algorithms with their drawbacks and offers a quick high-level summary of them.

1.6.1. Impacts to Children's Online Safety

1.6.1.1. Benefits of Algorithms

In particular, algorithmic recommendation systems can assist marginalized youth—such as LGBTQ+ youth and youth who identify as racial minorities—in locating important resources that foster self-discovery and connections with like-minded peers. As a result, powerful social networks are formed that are crucial to a child's upbringing. Algorithms for content moderation protect kids' online privacy by identifying and eliminating harmful content, including that which is associated with self-harm. In addition to preventing the spread of content that may encourage substance abuse, sexual harassment, or other harmful behavior, this can help create a safe online environment for children.

1.6.1.2. Limitations of Algorithms

Social media businesses create algorithms that show users personalized content and keep them interested for long stretches of time. Algorithm addiction has been related to poor sleep quality, which in turn has been connected to mental health issues in young people (e.g., depression, anxiety).

Users are encouraged to stay on the platform longer by algorithmic recommendations, and research indicates that the more time spent online, the more likely it is that they will encounter inappropriate content for their age, unattainable beauty standards, or cyberbullying. For instance, an algorithmically suggested picture may intensify negative emotions or social comparison for a child who has low self-esteem. Children and adolescents who are overexposed to harmful content face significant risks to their mental health, especially if they belong to vulnerable groups.

Finally, even with the best of intentions, algorithmic recommendations that use personal data may track and take advantage of children's online activity by showing them targeted advertisements. Many teenagers claim to feel powerless over the personal data that social media companies gather about them.

1.6.2. Impacts to Online Speech

1.6.2.1. Benefits of Moderation Algorithms

Many social media platforms aim to protect their businesses from liability and reputational harm, just like the majority of businesses do. The risk of harmful content on digital platforms has been successfully decreased by implementing proactive community guidelines, hiring trust and safety teams, and using algorithmic content moderation. Social media companies could be prevented from using algorithms to filter speech, which could have far-reaching effects like an increase in graphic and dangerous content.

Platforms must keep funding the creation of cutting-edge content moderation technologies in light of the proliferation of hate speech, misleading information, and violent threats on the internet.

1.6.2.2. Limitations of Moderation Algorithms

Although social media companies employ algorithms to filter out harmful content from their platforms, there are increasing worries that this gives them too much editorial power. Should artificial intelligence (AI) be the final arbiter of truth, or possess the highest level of expertise in this regard?

Shadow banning and algorithmic downranking are used to promote some types of content while suppressing others. False positives, or content that is mistakenly categorized as harmful by screening algorithms, can be removed, for example, blocking too much content). Unfair censorship can cause information gaps and have a negative effect on content creators. Many fear that as algorithms are used more frequently, marginalized communities may inadvertently be silenced, despite social media's main goals of promoting free speech and communication.

1.6.3. Improving Political Literacy

1.6.3.1. Benefits of Recommendation Algorithms

Social media is the main source of political news for many Americans. In light of social media's role in social activism and civic engagement, algorithmic recommendations facilitate user connections with people who share similar values. This can foster the development of cooperative networks, promote group action, and raise public awareness of social issues among political participants.

In the digital sphere, algorithmic recommendations can also promote the unrestricted flow of ideas and information, which is essential to a healthy democracy. Social media provides users with access to reliable, factual information sources. For instance, certain platforms employ algorithms to amplify posts from election offices and append precise voting data to posts about elections.

1.6.3.2. Limitations of Recommendation Algorithms

Regretfully, we are more likely to pay attention to bad news according to human psychology. Content that is more controversial and attention-grabbing has a tendency to go viral and rank higher in users' feeds due to algorithmic amplification, which is the result of designing algorithms based on human behavior. This phenomenon may unintentionally lead more users to news that is extremely politicized on the left or right.

In addition, algorithms prioritize displaying political news according to the political beliefs of each user in an effort to customize their experience. This feedback loop has the potential to isolate users from other points of view and place them in echo chambers or filter bubbles. This division of ideas has the potential to produce confirmation bias and unintentionally polarize public opinion.

In conclusion, the surge of artificial intelligence (AI) producing content may result in an increase of election-related misinformation, such as deepfakes representing election officers. Subsequently, these platforms' algorithms repetitively disseminate this content. The overwhelming distribution of AI-created images, videos, and audio on social media makes it challenging to distinguish truth from falsehood, potentially damaging the public's trust in democracy.

1.6.4. Transparency and Explainability Around Algorithmic Decision-Making

1.6.4.1. Benefits

Research, accountability, and public trust in platforms could all be raised by providing clear information sharing, audits, impact assessments, disclosure requirements, or transparency reports regarding automated content moderation systems.

The application of AI algorithms is frequently seen as a threat to transparency, indicating that information about this sophisticated technology is still not widely available. This is known as the "black box problem," which is the inability to comprehend how algorithms arrive at their conclusions. Users often express confusion, for instance, about why certain social media posts are sent to them or why their content was removed. The content that billions of people view, use, purchase, and consider on the internet is determined by algorithms; however, it is often difficult or prohibitively expensive to obtain information about these internal workings.

1.6.4.2. Limitations

Researchers must have access to comprehensive data from the AI systems that social media companies use in order to advance transparency. Algorithms are private, well-maintained mathematical formulas. It is important to think about how to carry out efficient algorithm audits without jeopardizing the integrity of platforms' trade secrets and intellectual property rights. Giving away all the details of algorithms could incite bad actors to take advantage of AI systems for their own ends, like running international disinformation campaigns. Given how competitive these technologies are on a global scale, it is especially critical that America continue to be a leader in AI innovation.

1.6.5. Mitigating AI System Bias

1.6.5.1. Benefits of AI Innovation

The computer scientists who created algorithms must carefully plan and regularly assess them to ensure that they function as accurately and efficiently as possible. Algorithms are constantly being tested by social media software engineers to optimize platform design and deliver optimal user experience. In order to take accuracy, discrimination, and other ethical issues into account, AI algorithms are trained and retrained.

Content shared by people of various backgrounds, genders, sexual orientations, and ethnicities should be equally visible according to algorithms. Social media algorithms, for instance, can be trained to identify and remove offensive or harmful stereotype-promoting content from online advertisements.

1.6.5.2. Limitations of AI Innovation

Humans create and train algorithms, and all people are flawed by unconscious prejudice. This implies that social media algorithms might be biased by design, which could make societal issues worse or disproportionately harm marginalized groups. Automation bias against specific groups based on their race, gender, sexual orientation, political affiliation, or ethnicity can result from algorithms that are trained on incomplete, skewed, or unrepresented data. Algorithms, for instance, may suggest or magnify content that is divisive and perpetuates racial stereotypes, thus sustaining historical injustices. On the other hand, content that defies cultural norms may be disproportionately screened and suppressed by algorithms, which could support biased opinions and limit opportunities for marginalized groups.

1.6.6. Collecting User Data on Social Media

1.6.6.1. Benefits of Algorithms

Through the use of data to generate customized recommendations, algorithms improve user experiences on the internet. Algorithms use user behavior analysis to deliver curated content that aligns with their interests, thereby creating a personalized online experience.

Algorithms can also prevent data breaches and cyberattacks by keeping an eye out for unusual or undetected activity. They are able to promptly identify and prevent security breaches, protecting people's personal data, including account information.

1.6.6.2. Limitations of Algorithms

Since algorithms depend heavily on data to function properly, there are several privacy concerns. The type of information that is being gathered and deduced about certain users worries them. Social media algorithms, for instance, might suggest content depending on a user's search history, location, or demographics. The Privacy Paradox is the term used to describe the wide range of factors that influence people's comfort level in disclosing information and level of concern about their privacy online. Another issue is the way algorithms handle data storage and transfer, particularly in light of the possibility that social media companies will do so without users' knowledge or consent. Concerns regarding users' ability to opt-out of such practices and the sale of their information have been raised by the potential aggravation of these issues caused by the monetization of personal data through targeted advertising.

1.6.7. Language Complexities in Content Moderation

1.6.7.1. Benefits of NLP Algorithms

Computer programs can understand human language as it is typed or recorded thanks to Large Language Models and Natural Language Processing (NLP) algorithms. Real-time sentiment analysis and speech translation are made possible by these algorithms, and they are crucial for the detection of harmful speech. Digital platforms can scan millions of online conversations for hate speech, harassment, profanity, and other inappropriate language by utilizing natural language processing (NLP).

NLP algorithms continue to learn about new linguistic fads, like slang, slurs, and unclear euphemisms, as the volume of online content rises, improving its capacity for content moderation.

1.6.7.2. Limitations of NLP Algorithms

Currently, over 7,000 languages are spoken in the globe. The natural complexity of language can have a detrimental effect on NLP's performance. For many languages other than English, algorithmic detection is faulty, as evidenced by recent research. Due to the bias of most AI models being trained mostly on English-language content, a sizable portion of online content is susceptible to uneven moderation. This flaw raises the possibility of either excessive or insufficient global speech moderation. For instance, false information in languages other than English is more likely to proliferate on social media without being noticed.

1.6.8. Social Media Algorithms and Section 230 Immunity

1.6.8.1. Benefits of Section 230 Immunity

Due to its ability to exempt social media companies from liability for user-generated content, Section 230 of the Communications Decency Act is arguably one of the most significant pieces of legislation pertaining to tech policy.

The question of whether decisions made by algorithms should be shielded from liability under Section 230 has been the subject of debate recently. In the past, courts have generally construed the application of algorithms as a conventional editorial function that, while falling outside the purview of Section 230, passively arranges content. Lawsuits may arise if digital platforms were made to answer for the decisions made by their algorithms. Startups and smaller platforms that lack advanced content moderation systems or cannot afford liability charges may be disproportionately harmed by this liability.

1.6.8.2. Limitations of Section 230 Immunity

There are currently no legally binding safety and efficacy requirements for algorithms. Some contend that the protections provided by Section 230 for platform design actions need to be reconsidered and revised. Should the digital platform face consequences for intentionally hosting or making money from content that contravenes its terms of service, for instance, if an algorithm flags harmful content but it is not taken down?

Given that the machine learning algorithm, as the name implies, "generates" new content, there is also growing concern about whether Section 230 protects the emerging application of generative AI on social media. These applications come with potentially serious legal risks as generative AI develops, and the debate over Section 230 policy is evolving quickly. Congress and the courts have not yet responded to the Section 230 versus generative AI question.

1.6.9. Role of Human Moderators in Content Moderation

1.6.9.1. Benefits of Increased Use of Algorithms

When social media first started out, content moderation was handled by small teams of staff members who made snap judgments about what to remove. AI is necessary because of the sheer amount of content available on today's digital platforms. When platforms use automated content analysis systems, a significant amount of inappropriate content can be removed by the tools' algorithms before it is seen by a human moderator for additional consideration. This protects workers from ongoing exposure to obscene conspiracy theories, violent disturbing images, and other stimulants that pose serious risks to their mental health. Because of algorithms' sophisticated capabilities, content moderation can be done more quickly and extensively while relying less on human moderators.

1.6.9.2. Limitations of Increased Use of Algorithms

As content moderation moves toward automation, it's critical to remember that AI algorithms are fallible and can draw the wrong conclusions. Because algorithms may struggle to understand the meaning or context of social media posts, a human-in-the-loop method is still required to guarantee that content removal is accurate. When algorithms identify content that may be harmful, human moderators ought to be able to review or override the machine's judgment.

The active role of human oversight is crucial in guaranteeing the responsible use of AI systems. Regrettably, numerous trust and safety teams saw their size reduced by recent tech sector layoffs; this could mean businesses are cutting back on the resources they allocate to finding harmful content.

1.6.10. Detecting Extremist Networks

1.6.10.1. Benefits of Moderation Algorithms

Digital platforms that have algorithmic detection systems installed are better able to anticipate illicit activity and take action before offline attacks take place.

In 2017, Facebook, Twitter, Google, Microsoft, and other major tech companies established the Global Internet Forum to Counter Terrorism, which invests in the development and dissemination of cutting-edge technological tools used to identify terrorist propaganda. One example of how machine learning algorithms can predict people's trajectories toward violent extremism is by analyzing their online behavior.

1.6.10.2. Limitations of Recommendation Algorithms

Algorithms' role in radicalization and recruitment of extremist networks is questioned by concerned critics. Algorithms have the potential to link vulnerable actors—young adults in particular—with others who share their interests and may search for, consume, and distribute harmful content online.

Gonzalez was heard by the Supreme Court in 2022. Google: the plaintiffs in this case claimed that YouTube's algorithmic recommendations helped and encouraged ISIS during an international terrorist attack. This was not the first instance of social media platforms being investigated for possible links to offline violence. For instance, prior to mass shootings, a large number of domestic terrorists are especially active on social media.

Although many mainstream platforms create sophisticated AI tools to reduce offline violence, it can be difficult to effectively moderate content because violent extremism is a contentious concept. Simply put, a lot of threat actors are shifting their tactics to smaller platforms without content moderation.

1.6.11. Detecting Child Sexual Abuse Material

1.6.11.1. Benefits of Moderation Algorithms

U.S. According to federal law, digital businesses must notify the National Center for Missing and Exploited Children (NCMEC), which then notifies law enforcement, of any known child sexual abuse material (CSAM). Thousands of photos showing child abuse are flagged by popular social media sites every day utilizing algorithmic detection techniques.

The Tech Coalition is an alliance of multinational corporations, ranging in size from small startups to the biggest in the world, that collaborate to proactively advance AI technology in order to combat online child sexual exploitation. Members of the Tech Coalition, for instance, have access to sophisticated image classification and hash-matching technologies. Using algorithms, this technology finds and compares social media posts to the NCMEC's database of images that have been linked to child abuse.

1.6.11.2. Limitations of Moderation Algorithms

Algorithms on social media that support pedophile networks face far more serious accusations and repercussions than those that suggest a cheap shirt, which could lead to a poor purchase. Recommendation algorithms facilitate the connection of a large network of social media accounts that spread CSAM, according to startling investigations. One can only guess the severity of the issue on smaller platforms or direct messaging apps if CSAM spreads on public feeds via large tech companies.

In an effort to evade detection on the internet, offenders are always refining their techniques, forcing platforms to catch up and update their algorithms. For instance, the growth of AI-generated CSAM, in which machine learning algorithms use real children's photos as source material, worries researchers at the Stanford Internet Observatory.

REFERENCES

1. Adorno, T., & Horkheimer, M. (1949). *Dialética do esclarecimento* [Dialektik der Aufklärung]. Rio de Janeiro: Zahar, 2006.
2. Alonzo, R., Hussain, J., Stranges, S., & Anderson, K. K. (2021). Interplay between social media use, sleep quality, and mental health in youth: A systematic review. *Sleep Medicine Reviews, 56.* Available at: https://www.sciencedirect.com/science/article/abs/pii/S108707922030157X?via%3Dihub.
3. Barrett, P., Hendrix, J., & Sim, G. (2021). How tech platforms fuel U.S. political polarization and what government can do about it. *Brookings*. September 27, 2021. Available at: https://www.brookings.edu/articles/how-tech-platforms-fuel-u-s-political-polarization-and-what-government-can-do-about-it/.
4. Bolaño, C. (2012). Intellectual work, communication, and capitalism: The reconfiguration of the subjective factor in the current productive reorganization. In C. Bolaño, G. Mastrini, & F. Sierra (Eds.), *Political economy, communication, and knowledge: A Latin American perspective* (pp. 1-12). New York: Hampton Press.
5. Brecht, B. (1964). The radio as an apparatus of communication. In J. Willett (Ed.), *Brecht on Theatre: The development of an aesthetic* (pp. 51-53). London: Eyre Methuen.
6. Campbell, K. (2023). Why do people click on bad news? Negativity bias. *Reputation X.* July 29, 2023. Available at: https://blog.reputationx.com/what-makes-us-drawn-to-negative-online-content.
7. Cormen, T. H., Leiserson, C. E., Rivest, R. L., & Stein, C. (2009). *Introduction to algorithms* (3rd ed.). Cambridge: The MIT Press.
8. Costa, R. D. (2004). Sociedade de controle. *São Paulo em Perspectiva, 18*(1), 161-167.
9. Crosby, A. W. (1997). *A mensuração da realidade: A quantificação e a sociedade ocidental, 1250-1600*. São Paulo: UNESP.
10. Deleuze, G. (1992). Postscript on the societies of control. *October, 59*, 3-7.
11. Doty, D. (2019). A reality check on advertising relevancy and personalization. *Forbes*. August 13, 2019. Available at: https://www.forbes.com/sites/daviddoty/2019/08/13/a-reality-check-on-advertising-relevancy-and-personalization/?sh=68c5eb297690.
12. Enzensberger, H. M. (1970). *Elementos para uma teoria dos meios de comunicação* [Baukasten zu einer Theorie der Medien]. São Paulo: Conrad, 2003.

13. Field, H., & Vanian, J. (2023). Tech layoffs ravage the teams that fight online misinformation and hate speech. *CNBC*. May 6, 2023. Available at: https://www.cnbc.com/2023/05/26/tech-companies-are-laying-off-their-ethics-and-safety-teams-.html.
14. Foster, J. B., & McChesney, R. W. (2014). Surveillance capitalism: Monopoly-finance capital, the military-industrial complex, and the digital age. *Monthly Review, 66*(3), 1-31.
15. Foucault, M. (1975). *Vigiar e punir* [Surveiller et punir]. Petrópolis: Vozes, 1987.
16. Gillespie, T. (2014). The relevance of algorithms. In T. Gillespie, P. J. Boczkowski, & K. A. Foot (Eds.), *Media technologies: Essays on communication, materiality, and society* (pp. 167–193). Cambridge, MA: The MIT Press.
17. Gleit, N. (2020). Launching the largest voting information effort in US history. *Meta*. June 16, 2020. Available at: https://about.fb.com/news/2020/06/voting-information-center/.
18. Guedj, R. A. (1980). Report on the Seillac II workshop on the methodology of interaction. *Computers in Industry, 1*(3), 189-192.
19. Guerin, D. (1973). *Fascism and big business*. New York: Pathfinder Press.
20. Habermas, J. (1961). *Mudança estrutural da esfera pública* [Strukturwandel der Öffentlichkeit]. Rio de Janeiro: Tempo Brasileiro, 2003.
21. Harvey, D. (1989). *A condição pós-moderna* [The condition of postmodernity]. São Paulo: Loyola, 2012.
22. Horwitz, J., & Blunt, K. (2023). Instagram connects vast pedophile network. *The Wall Street Journal*. June 7, 2023. Available at: https://www.wsj.com/articles/instagram-vast-pedophile-network-4ab7189?mod=hp_lead_pos7.
23. Jensen, J. F. (1998). Interactivity: Tracing a new concept in media and communication studies. *Nordicom Review, 19*(1), 185-204.
24. Jost, F. (2010). *Compreender a televisão*. Porto Alegre: Sulina.
25. Just, N., & Latzer, M. (2017). Governance by algorithms: Reality construction by algorithmic selection on the internet. *Media, Culture & Society, 39*(2), 1-21.
26. Lau, T., & Akkaraju, U. (2019). When algorithms decide whose voices will be heard. *Harvard Business Review*. November 12, 2019. Available at: https://hbr.org/2019/11/when-algorithms-decide-whose-voice-will-be-heard.

27. Lessig, L. (2006). *Code. Version 2.0*. Cambridge: Basic Books.

28. Mattelart, A. (2008). *La globalisation de la surveillance: Aux origines de l'ordre sécuritaire*. Paris: Éditions La Découverte.

29. McCarthy, N. (2020). Facebook removes record number of hate speech posts [Infographic]. *Forbes*. May 13, 2020. Available at: https://www.forbes.com/sites/niallmccarthy/2020/05/13/facebook-removes-record-number-of-hate-speech-posts-infographic/?sh=78fe4a130356.

30. McChesney, R. W. (2013). *Digital disconnect: How capitalism is turning the internet against democracy*. New York: The New Press.

31. McCluskey, M. (2022). How addictive social media algorithms could finally face a reckoning in 2022. *TIME*. January 4, 2022. Available at: https://time.com/6127981/addictive-algorithms-2022-facebook-instagram/.

32. Milan, S. (2015). When algorithms shape collective action: Social media and the dynamics of cloud protesting. *Social Media + Society, 1*(2). Available at: https://journals.sagepub.com/doi/full/10.1177/2056305115622481.

33. Moerel, L. (2018). Algorithms can reduce discrimination, but only with proper data. *IAPP*. November 16, 2018. Available at: https://iapp.org/news/a/algorithms-can-reduce-discrimination-but-only-with-proper-data/.

34. Mohan, M. (2023). The rising costs of social media APIs: The Twitter-Reddit scenario. *Codedamn*. June 11, 2023. Available at: https://codedamn.com/news/api/cost-of-apis-twitter-reddit.

35. Nicholas, G., & Bhatia, A. (2023). The dire defect of 'multilingual' AI content moderation. *Wired*. May 23, 2023. Available at: https://www.wired.com/story/content-moderation-language-artificial-intelligence/.

36. Norberg, P. A., Horne, D. R., & Horne, D. A. (2007). The privacy paradox: Personal information disclosure intentions versus behaviors. *Journal of Consumer Affairs, 41*(1), 100-126. https://doi.org/10.1111/j.1745-6606.2006.00070.x.

37. Pasquale, F. (2015). *The black box society: The secret algorithms that control money and information*. Cambridge: Harvard University Press.

38. Peterson, J., Densley, J., Spaulding, J., & Higgins, S. (2023). How mass public shooters use social media: Exploring themes and future directions. *Social Media + Society*. Available at: https://journals.sagepub.com/doi/10.1177/20563051231155101.

39. Phillips, T., & Martin, J. (2023). Will generative AI create a break in the impenetrable wall that is Section 230? *Pillsbury Law*. June 16, 2023. Available at: https://www.pillsburylaw.com/en/news-and-insights/generative-ai-section-230.html.

40. Powers, S. M., & Jablonski, M. (2015). *The real cyber war: The political economy of internet freedom*. Chicago: University of Illinois Press.

41. Primo, A. (2007). *Interação mediada por computador: Comunicação, cibercultura, cognição*. Porto Alegre: Sulina.

42. Rafaeli, S. (1988). Interactivity: From new media to communication. In R. P. Hawkins, S. Pingree, & J. Wieman (Eds.), *Advancing communication science: Merging mass and interpersonal processes* (pp. 110-134). Newbury Park, CA: Sage.

43. Research Rooted in Machine Learning Challenges Conventional Thinking About the Pathways to Violent Extremism. *National Institute of Justice*. July 24, 2023. Available at: https://nij.ojp.gov/topics/articles/researchrooted-machine-learning-challenges-conventional-thinkingabout-pathways.

44. Riehm, K., Feder, K., Tormohlen, K., Crum, R., Young, A., Green, K., Pacek, L., La Flair, L., & Mojtabai, R. (2019). Associations between time spent using social media and internalizing and externalizing problems among US youth. *JAMA Psychiatry, 76*(12), 1266-1273. Available at: https://www.ncbi.nlm.nih.gov/pmc/articles/PMC6739732/#yoi190054r28.

45. Santos, F. P., Lelkes, Y., & Levin, S. A. (2021). Link recommendation algorithms and dynamics of polarization in online social networks. *Proceedings of the National Academy of Sciences*, 118(50). Available at: https://www.pnas.org/doi/full/10.1073/pnas.2102141118.

46. Sfez, L. (1992). *Crítica da comunicação* [Critique de la communication]. São Paulo: Loyola, 1994.

47. Shutt, R., & O'Neil, C. (2013). *Doing data science: Straight talk from the frontline*. Sebastopol: O'Reilly Media Inc.

48. Smythe, D. (1977). Communications: Blindspot of Western Marxism. *Canadian Journal of Political and Social Theory/Revue Canadienne de Théorie Politique et Sociale, 1*(3), 1-27.

49. Social Media Algorithms: Content Recommendation, Moderation, and Congressional Considerations. *Congressional Research Service*. July 27, 2023. Available at: https://crsreports.congress.gov/product/pdf/IF/IF12462.

50. Social Media and News Fact Sheet. *Pew Research Center*. September 20, 2022. Available at: https://www.pewresearch.org/journalism/fact-sheet/social-media-and-news-fact-sheet/.

51. Sohn-Rethel, A. (1995). *Trabalho spiritual e corporal: Para a epistemologia da história ocidental*. João Pessoa: UFPB/CCSA. (Original work published 1989).

52. Suzor, N. P., West, S. M., Quodling, A., & York, J. (2019). What do we mean when we talk about transparency? Toward meaningful transparency in commercial content moderation. *International Journal of Communication, 13*(18). Available at: https://ijoc.org/index.php/ijoc/article/view/9736.

53. Thiel, D., Stroebel, M., & Portnoff, R. (2023). Generative ML and CSAM: Implications and mitigations. *Stanford Digital Repository*. June 23, 2023. Available at: https://purl.stanford.edu/jv206yg3793.

54. Toffler, A. (1981). *The third wave*. New York: William Morrow.

55. Valencia, S. (2021). Misinformation online is bad in English, but it's far worse in Spanish. *The Washington Post*. October 28, 2021. Available at: https://www.washingtonpost.com/outlook/2021/10/28/misinformation-spanish-facebook-social-media/.

56. Van Dijck, J. (2013). *The culture of connectivity: A critical history of social media*. Oxford: Oxford University Press.

57. Van Dijck, J., & Poell, T. (2013). Understanding social media logic. *Media and Communication, 1*(1), 1-14.

58. Van Dijk, J. A., & De Vos, L. (2001). Searching for the holy grail: Images of interactive television. *New Media & Society, 3*(4), 443-465.

59. Vogels, E., & Gelles-Watnick, R. (2023). Teens and social media: Key findings from Pew Research Center surveys. *Pew Research Center*. April 24, 2023. Available at: https://www.pewresearch.org/short-reads/2023/04/24/teens-and-social-media-key-findings-from-pew-research-center-surveys/.

60. Williams, R. (2003). *Television: Technology and cultural form*. London: Routledge.

61. Wilson, M. (2016). Algorithms (and the) everyday. *Information, Communication & Society, 20*(1), 137-150.

CHAPTER 2

INSTAGRAM ALGORITHM

Contents

Introduction 46

2.1. Instagram 46

2.2. History of Instagram 49

2.3. Instagram Features and Tools 53

2.4. Instagram Algorithm 63

2.5. How to Get on the Instagram Explore Page? 68

2.6. Instagram Reels Algorithm 76

References 106

INTRODUCTION

Instagram is a social media platform owned by Meta Platforms where users can share photos and videos. With the help of hashtag organization, geographic tagging, and filter editing, users can upload media files that are geotagged. A post's audience can be set to either public or preapproved followers. Users can follow other users to add their content to a personal feed, view trending content, like photos, and browse other users' content by tags and locations. It's an image-focused social media platform that runs on Meta and is accessible on Windows 10, iOS, Android, and the web. Users can snap pictures, use the tools and built-in filters to edit them, and then post the edited images to Facebook and other social media sites. Around 32 languages are supported by it, including Hindi, English, French, Korean, and Japanese. Instagram first set itself apart by limiting content framing to a square (1:1) aspect ratio of 640 pixels, which matched the iPhone's display width at the time. This limitation was loosened in 2015 when the pixel count was increased to 1080. In addition, it added messaging capabilities, the capacity to combine several photos or videos into a single post, and a Stories feature that let users share content to a chronological feed that was visible to other users for a full day, much like Snapchat, its primary rival. By January 2019, 500 million people were using Stories every day. Instagram quickly gained popularity after being introduced for iOS in October 2010 by Kevin Systrom and Mike Krieger. In just two months, 1 million users had registered, 10 million in a year, and 1 billion by June 2018. April of 2012 saw Facebook Inc. purchased the service for roughly $1 billion in stock and cash. Instagram first launched for Android in April 2012, then for Windows 10 in October 2016, a feature-limited desktop interface in November 2012, a Fire OS app in June 2014, and an Instagram app for Android in October 2016. More than 40 billion images had been uploaded as of October 2015. Instagram is frequently praised for its popularity and impact, but it has also drawn criticism for its detrimental effects on young people's mental health, changes to its policies and interface, claims of censorship, and improper and illegal content posted by users. The rules that determine how content is ranked on Instagram are called the algorithm. All throughout the app (users' feeds, the Explore Page, the Reels feed, hashtag pages, etc.), it determines what content appears and in what order. This chapter will explain the fundamentals of the Instagram algorithm and provide helpful hints to help you make the most out of it.

2.1. INSTAGRAM

Instagram is a mobile location-based social network app that allows users to share images and videos. With the help of this service, users can share their images and videos on other social media sites and apply digital filters to them. Kevin Systrom and Mike Krieger founded the service in San Francisco, California, and on October 6, 2010, it was formally released exclusively for the iPhone. The application was originally known as Burbn, and its goal was to incorporate a number of features from well-known social media platforms, such as Foursquare. After Krieger joined the team, the two programmers made the decision to concentrate only on sharing photos.

Instagram is a hybrid of "telegram" and "instant camera." Systrom and Krieger desired a digital version of the nostalgic photos made popular by Kodak Instamatic and Polaroid. In contrast to the 4:3 aspect ratio that mobile device cameras employ, the photos that are uploaded to the mobile application are reshaped into squares. Apart from this unique feature, users can modify images using various manipulation tools. Instagram provides 20 filters that alter the picture's lighting and tone.

Instagram users have the ability to share photos, connect their account to other social networking sites, "like" and comment on images, and follow other users' feeds. Instagram users can add geolocated data to their content with an embedded feature that is based on location. Because it increases searchability, adding geographic identification metadata to Instagram content gives it a social and economic value. Following Twitter's lead, the service introduced hashtags as a new feature in January 2011. In order to find photos and other users on the platform, Instagram encourages users to use precise and pertinent tags. In addition, hashtags facilitated the development of numerous interest-based communities and the widespread distribution of photos. In 2012, web profiles were introduced, enabling users to utilize their account similarly to a social network website. Instagram is now a location-based social network app rather than just a location-based social photo-sharing app. Instagram launched a new feature for sharing 15-second videos in June 2013. Instagram released Hyperlapse in August 2014. With this new app, users can make time-lapse videos.

December 2010 saw 1 million users access the platform. There were 5 million Instagram users as of June 2011, and by September of the same year, that figure had doubled. As of August 2011, 150 million photos had been uploaded to the service, according to the company. In April 2012, Facebook revealed that it had acquired the service and that over 30 million accounts had been created on Instagram. The platform's statistics from the summer of 2014 showed 200 million active users (of whom 65% were from outside the US), 20 billion photos shared, 1.6 billion "likes" daily, and an average of 60 million photos uploaded every day. Additionally, the data reveals that women make up 68% of Instagram's user base and that 50% of accounts are owned by iPhone users and 50% by Android users. On December 17, 2012, Instagram revised its terms of service and gave itself permission to sell user photos for profit without asking permission or paying for them. A statement retraction of the contentious terms was sent out by Instagram in response to millions of users, including the National Geographic Society. Users migrated to other photo-sharing services, such as Pheed and Flickr, after the announcement. As a result, Instagram updated its terms of service to address the ownership and authorship of photos.

The members' cooperation and contribution of content is essential to Instagram's survival. Numerous studies contend that individual user motivations for cocreation can be linked to the structure of the network. Users that are structurally embedded tend to share more and have a high number of connections to other members of the network. A person's commitment, growth, and reputation are factors that influence their decision to share photos.

Consumer collective intelligence and the notion that the consumer is an active participant, resource, and cocreator of value form the foundation of the economics of photo sharing. Instagram uses user-generated content to encourage group collaboration. Sharing photos allows users to participate in the creation of value through thematic communities and network ties. Cocreation is a social process that is based on collaboration and interaction between people.

In addition to encouraging users to share photos, businesses use Instagram to build a visual brand for their goods and services, drive traffic to their websites, foster competitions, index content through hashtags, and create engaging campaigns. Instagram is used by the MTV television network to show behind-the-scenes photos from its shows. Nike posts images of people working out with their gear on Instagram. Starbucks uses hashtags to publish pictures that fans have tagged on their profile.

Using images and videos, politicians utilize Instagram to connect with voters on a more personal level. President Barack Obama has 4 million followers and 294,000 likes on a "thank you" photo he posted on election night. Numerous celebrities provide their fans with pictures and videos from both their personal and professional lives. Instagram is used by the media to spread visual content and foster stronger relationships with their audiences. Instagram is also used by photographers, anonymous users, and community organizations to share images, interact with friends, and advance causes. Two startups, Gramforacause and Gramming for Good, use Instagram to link up photographers with nonprofit organizations and use photography to promote social and environmental causes.

Instagram users' feeds already display advertisements in certain countries. The platform will gradually introduce sponsored publications along with advertising.

2.2. HISTORY OF INSTAGRAM

Burbn, a mobile check-in app developed by Kevin Systrom and Mike Krieger, was the inspiration behind Instagram's early development in San Francisco. When working on Burbn, Systrom closed a seed funding round with Baseline Ventures and Andreessen Horowitz on March 5, 2010, for $500,000 (equivalent to $682,200 in 2023) (Lagorio, Christine (2011)). They refocused their app on photo-sharing, which had grown to be a popular feature among its users, after realizing it was too similar to Foursquare. Instagram is a hybrid of the terms "instant camera" and "telegram," which they renamed.

2.2.1. 2010–2011: Beginnings and Major Funding

Shayne Sweeney joined the company in November as an engineer, Josh Riedel joined in October as the community manager, and Jessica Zollman joined in August 2011 as the community evangelist.

When Mike Krieger first uploaded a picture of South Beach Harbor at Pier 38 on July 16, 2010, it was at 5:26 p.m. The Instagram iOS app was formally launched through the App Store on October 6, 2010. Instagram raised $7 million (or $9,357,057 in 2023) in Series A funding from a range of investors, including Benchmark Capital, Jack Dorsey, Chris Sacca (through Capital fund), and Adam D'Angelo, according to a February 2011 report. Instagram was valued at about $20 million in the deal. In April of 2012, venture capitalists valued Instagram at $500 million (roughly $656,100,000 in 2023) contributed $50 million, or $65,610,000 in 2023. Joshua Kushner's investment firm, Thrive Capital, doubled in size following Instagram's sale to Facebook because he was the second-largest investor in the company's Series B fundraising round.

2.2.2. 2012–2014: Additional Platforms and Acquisition by Facebook

An Android version of Instagram's app was released on April 3, 2012, and in less than a day, it had been downloaded over a million times. Since then, the Android app has received two major updates: the first in April 2017, which added an offline mode that enables users to view and interact with content without an Internet connection, and the second in March 2014, which reduced the app's file size in half and improved performance. In addition to announcing that the aforementioned functionality was live at the time of the announcement, Instagram also revealed that they were investigating an iOS version and that they intended to make more features available offline. It was reported at the time that 80% of Instagram's 600 million users were based outside of the US. Facebook, Inc. (now Meta Platforms) acquired Instagram on April 9, 2012, for

$1 billion (or $1,312,000,000 in 2023) in cash and stock, with the intention of maintaining the company's independence. August 14, 2012, saw the deal approved by Britain's Office of Fair Trading, and August 22, 2012, saw the US Federal Trade Commission close its investigation and approve the deal. The Instagram and Facebook deal officially closed on September 6, 2012, with a purchase price of $300 million in cash and 23 million shares of stock.

According to CNN, the agreement was finalized shortly before Facebook's planned initial public offering. The acquisition price was contrasted with Yahoo!'s 2005 payment of $35 million for Flickr. According to Mark Zuckerberg, Facebook is dedicated to creating and expanding Instagram on its own. As reported by Wired, Systrom received $400 million from the deal.

Instagram introduced website profiles in November 2012, enabling users to view user feeds through a web browser with restricted features. Additionally, users could access a variety of badges and web widget buttons that connected to user profiles.

Named location tagging has been provided by the app using Foursquare API technology since its launch. Instagram began testing and transitioning to Facebook Places in March 2014.

2.2.3. 2015–2017: Redesign and Windows App

The user interface of the desktop website underwent a redesign in June 2015, adopting a more minimalist and flat design with increased screen real estate for individual photos, akin to the design of Instagram's mobile website. In addition, one row of images has three rather than five photos in order to conform to the mobile layout. The slideshow banner that was previously displayed at the top of profile pages, displaying seven picture tiles of the user's uploaded photos in a random order and alternating at different times, has been removed. Furthermore, the previously angular profile images were changed to circular ones.

Instagram finally released a Windows 10 Mobile app in April 2016, responding to years of public and Microsoft pressure to do so. Before, on November 21, 2013, a beta version of Instagram was made available on the platform for Windows Phone 8. With the release of the new app, support for album posts, direct messages, and videos (both creating and viewing live streams) was added. In a similar vein, an app for Windows 10 tablets and PCs was made available in October 2016. Instagram added a more simplified version of the Explore tab and allowed users to upload photos to its mobile website in May.

Instagram changed its look on May 11, 2016, introducing a black-and-white flat design theme for the user interface of the app and a less skeuomorphic, more abstract, contemporary, and colorful icon. When The Verge obtained a screenshot from a tipster in April, rumors of a redesign initially surfaced. However, an Instagram representative at the time only stated that the idea was still in the works.

Comment liking was introduced by Instagram on December 6, 2016. The user who left a comment does not, however, get notifications about comment likes in their notification inbox, in contrast to post likes. It is an option for uploaders to disable comments on their posts.

Since May 4, 2017, the mobile website has permitted picture uploads. Video uploading and image filters weren't available back then.

The Windows 10 Mobile app was retired on April 30, 2019, but the mobile website is still accessible as a progressive web application (PWA) with restricted features. The app will be updated to a PWA in 2020 and is still accessible on Windows 10 PCs and tablets.

2.2.4. 2018–2019: IGTV, Removal of the Like Counter, Management Changes

Instagram launched the feature that allows users to download a copy of their user data in April 2018 in order to abide by GDPR regulations pertaining to data portability.

On June 20, 2018, IGTV was released as a stand-alone video app. March 2022 saw the closure of the application and its removal from app stores due to low usage and a switch to short-form video content.

In a statement released on September 24, 2018, Krieger and Systrom declared their intention to leave Instagram. The announcement that Adam Mosseri will take over as Instagram's new CEO was made on October 1, 2018.

It was revealed at Facebook F8 that Instagram will test removing the like counts for user-posted content from being publicly displayed, starting in Canada. Only the original poster of the content would be able to see the like counts. According to Mosseri, the goal of this was to encourage users to spend more time interacting with the people they care about and less time worrying about how many likes they're receiving on Instagram. It's been suggested that having fewer likes than others may make users feel less confident about themselves. Initiated in May 2019, the pilot program was expanded to six additional markets in July. In November 2019, the pilot was made available everywhere. Instagram also declared in July 2019 that it would be introducing new tools to lessen harassment and offensive remarks on the platform. Instagram also started a trial run of removing the Following tab, which let users see a feed of the likes and comments made by people they followed, in August 2019. The feature was underutilized, according to head of product Vishal Shah, and some users were taken aback when they discovered their activity was being surfaced in this way. The change was officially announced in October.

Instagram set a cap on the quantity of posts that could be viewed in page scrolling mode if users were not logged in, effective October 2019. All users could access public profiles up until this point, even if they weren't logged in. Following the modification, the user must log in to continue viewing content after seeing a number of posts.

Instagram released Threads, a stand-alone app, in the same month. The app allowed users to communicate through video chats and messaging, similar to Snapchat. It included Instagram's photo editing tool built into the app, along with integration with the Close Friends feature, enabling users to send texts, images, and other media privately. However, due to low usage compared to other social media apps, and the fact that most of Threads' features were already available on Instagram, the app was discontinued in December 2021. Instagram's user base did not embrace Threads, as less than 220,000 people downloaded the app worldwide since its release—less than 0.1% of Instagram's monthly active user base—indicating that adoption efforts were unsuccessful.

2.2.5. 2020–Present: New Features

Co-Watching is a new feature that Instagram introduced in March 2020. Through video calls, users can now share posts with one another thanks to the new feature. Because of the COVID-19 pandemic-related social distancing, Instagram claims that they accelerated the launch of Co-Watching to meet the demand for virtually connecting with friends and family.

Instagram made a change to focus more on videos in August 2020 and added a feature called Reels. TikTok, a website that allows users to share videos, was the target market. August 2020 saw the addition of suggested posts on Instagram. Instagram shows users posts that are relevant to their interests from accounts they do not follow after they have scrolled through the previous 48 hours' worth of posts.

Instagram started testing a new feature called Vertical Stories in February 2021; some sources claim that TikTok served as inspiration. In the same month, they started experimenting with removing the option to share feed posts to stories.

Instagram introduced a new feature allowing four users to go live simultaneously in March 2021. Additionally, Instagram stated that as part of new child safety measures, adults would not be permitted to message teenagers who do not follow them

In May 2021, Instagram began enabling users in select regions to add pronouns to their profile pages.

On October 4, 2021, the largest outage to hit Meta services since 2008 occurred, bringing down Facebook, WhatsApp, and Instagram. Security experts determined that DNS might have been involved in the issue

Zuckerberg announced plans to introduce non-fungible tokens (NFTs) to the platform on March 17, 2022.

In September 2022, the company was fined $402 million by Ireland's Data Protection Commission for violating privacy laws that were recently enacted by the European Union due to its handling of minors' privacy data.

In December 2022, Instagram unveiled Notes following a mid-2022 trial period. With the help of this feature, users can share updates with specific individuals as brief text posts of up to 60 characters, and those individuals can respond by messaging them on Instagram.

Instagram added a new feature that lets users browse and share GIFs in comments in February 2023. Zuckerberg declared in the same month that Meta would begin offering blue verified badges for sale on Facebook and Instagram.

Meta debuted Threads on July 5, 2023. It's an Instagram-connected social network platform that lets users create public, short-form blog posts with text, images, and videos. You can also interact with other users and reblog their posts. Threads wants to rival Twitter.

Instagram started testing the removal of recent posts from different hashtags in April 2022. A year later, the system-wide and permanent modification was implemented, meaning that hashtags are now limited to displaying a curated collection of content from prominent users. In addition to Instagram's repeated claims that hashtags don't increase post views, these changes are purportedly an effort to stop the spread of false information.

Instagram declared in April 2024 that they would begin testing new tools in a few weeks to combat sextortion, which is an online form of blackmail involving the sending of private images.

Turkey blocked Instagram on August 2, 2024, following the removal of posts from users expressing sympathy for Hamas leader Ismail Haniyeh.

2.3. INSTAGRAM FEATURES AND TOOLS

Users have the ability to geotag images with a location, upload pictures and short videos, and follow the feeds of other users. If a user chooses to make their account private, they will need to accept requests from new followers. In order to share uploaded photos to other social networking sites, users can link their Instagram accounts to those platforms. An updated icon, instant tilt-shift, high-resolution photos, one-click rotation, optional borders, and new and live filters were all included in the app's September 2011 update. Originally, photos could only have a square, 1:1 aspect ratio; however, as of August 2015, the app can also handle portrait and widescreen aspect ratios. A map of a user's geotagged photos was previously viewable by users. Due to minimal use, the feature was discontinued in September 2016.

Posts can be stored into a private section of the app as of December 2016. Users can now arrange saved posts into named collections thanks to an update that was made in April 2017. In a private storage area, users have the option to archive their posts, making them invisible to other users and the general public. In addition to limiting the emergent behavior of deleting photos, which deprives the service of content, the move was perceived as a means of stopping users from removing images that are boring or don't receive the desired amount of likes. In order to facilitate user interaction with replies, Instagram announced in August that it would begin threading comments.

Since February 2017, posts have allowed to contain up to 10 images or videos, which display as a swipeable carousel. In August, an update was made to the feature that allowed portrait and landscape photos instead of just square ones.

Instagram introduced focus mode, a version of its portrait mode that softly blurs a photo or video's background while maintaining focus on the subject when it is selected, in April 2018. Instagram started to allow users with visual impairments to add descriptions to their photos using Alt text in November. Either manually by the uploader or automatically using Facebook's current object recognition technology, they are created.

Instagram introduced Instagram Live Rooms, a new feature that allows four users to go live simultaneously, on March 1, 2021.

Instagram revealed in May 2021 that creators would now be able to add closed captions to their videos on Instagram Reels and Stories, making their content more accessible.

2.3.1. Hashtags

Hashtags were added to Instagram in January 2011 in order to facilitate user discovery of each other's photos. In order to make photos stand out and draw in other like-minded Instagram users, Instagram encourages users to tag their photos with precise and pertinent terms instead of using generic terms like "photo."

Using hashtags, users on Instagram have started trends. The platform's most popular trends frequently emphasize a particular day of the week for posting the content. Popular trends include: #SelfieSunday, where users share a selfie on Sundays; #MotivationMonday, where users share inspirational photos on Mondays; #TransformationTuesday, where users share photos showing how the past and present have changed; #WomanCrushWednesday, where users share photos of women they find attractive or romantically interesting, along with its #ManCrushMonday counterpart focused on men; and #ThrowbackThursday, where users share a photo from the past, highlighting a special moment.

Instagram users can now follow hashtags to see relevant highlights of the topic in their feeds. This feature was introduced in December 2017. In an effort to stop false information from spreading during the 2020 US elections, the capability to search Recent hashtags was momentarily disabled. This was tested on a smaller group of users once more in 2022, and the capability to search recent hashtags was completely eliminated in April 2023. Only a carefully chosen collection of well-liked posts with a specific hashtag can now be seen by users. It has been observed that using hashtags is the only free way for a user to reach beyond their current followers. Instagram stated that this is to prevent abuse and that hashtags do not help users gain views.

2.3.2. Explore

Instagram unveiled the Explore tab in June 2012; it is a section of the app where users can view search results, popular photos, and photos taken nearby. Updated in June 2015, the tab now includes curated content, trending tags and places, and location search functionality. Instagram launched a Videos You Might Like channel in April 2016, an Events channel in August that featured videos from live events like concerts and sports events, and Instagram Stories in October. Following Instagram Live's debut, the tab was later extended once more in November 2016 to feature an algorithmically curated page featuring the top Instagram Live videos that were airing at the time. In May 2017, Instagram made another update to the Explore tab, this time to highlight public Stories content from surrounding locations.

2.3.3. Photographic Filters

Photographic filters are available on Instagram for users to apply to their photos. The Lux filter, which darkens highlights, lightens shadows, and boosts contrast, was added to Instagram in February 2012. Five new filters were added to the Instagram filter family in December 2014: Slumber, Crema, Ludwig, Aden, and Perpetua.

2.3.4. Video

In June 2013, Instagram—which had previously only allowed photo sharing—added the ability to share 15-second videos. In the tech press, some saw the addition as Facebook's attempt to take on Vine, the then-popular video-sharing app. Widescreen video support was added by Instagram in August 2015. Instagram extended the duration of its 15-second videos to one minute in March 2016. In February 2017, albums were introduced, enabling the sharing of videos lasting up to 10 minutes within a single post.

2.3.4.1. IGTV

In June 2018, Instagram released IGTV, a vertical video app. The Instagram website and app also offer basic functionality. Uploads to IGTV are limited to 10 minutes in duration and 650 MB in file size. However, verified and well-known users are permitted to upload videos up to one hour in length and 5.4 GB in file size. In contrast to video hosts where users must first locate a video, the app starts playing videos automatically as soon as it is launched, according to CEO Kevin Systrom. The app was discontinued in March 2022.

2.3.4.2. Reels

According to reports in November 2019, Instagram started testing a new video feature called Reels in Brazil before moving on to France and Germany. With a focus on enabling users to record quick videos set to pre-existing sound clips from other posts, it functions similarly to the Chinese video-sharing platform TikTok. This feature allowed users to create videos for up to 15 (later 30) seconds. Reels also works with Instagram's pre-existing editing tools and filters.

Instagram launched Reels in India in July 2020 in response to TikTok's ban there. Reels formally debuted in 50 countries the following month, including the US, Canada, and the UK. A reels button was added to Instagram's home page. Full-screen Reels ads were introduced by Instagram on June 17, 2021. The 30-second advertisements resemble standard reels. They can be identified from ordinary content by the sponsored tag located beneath the account name. As of 2022, user engagement lagged significantly behind TikTok even after Reels was TikTokified and the parent company Meta spent millions courting content creators.

2.3.5. Instagram Direct

Instagram introduced Instagram Direct in December 2013, a feature that allows users to communicate via private messaging (sometimes referred to as DMs or DMs; in other places, the messages might be called just directs or directs). Instead of the previous public-only requirement, users who follow one another can now send private messages with photos and videos. Users must accept in order to view private messages they receive from users they do not follow. These messages are identified as pending. A photo can be sent by users to up to 15 recipients. In September 2015, the feature underwent a significant update that included conversation threading and allowed users to share profiles, hashtag pages, and locations through private messages straight from the news feed. Users can now respond to private messages by clicking on a heart icon, using text, or using emoji. With Direct's built-in camera, users can snap a picture and send it to the other person without ever ending a conversation. A November 2016 update allowed users to make their private messages vanish after the recipient viewed them, and to receive a notification if the recipient screenshotted the message.

Instagram redesigned Direct in April 2017 to group all private messages together—permanent and transient—into identical message threads. Instagram introduced the ability to send links to websites in messages in May, along with the ability to send photos in their original landscape or portrait orientation without cropping.

Using WebSocket technology, Direct was made available on the Instagram website in April 2020, enabling users to send direct messages from a web version.

Facebook began integrating Instagram Direct into Facebook Messenger in August 2020. Following the update, which is being rolled out to a subset of users, the Facebook Messenger icon replaces the Instagram Direct icon.

A feature that stops adults from messaging users under the age of 18 who do not follow them was added in March 2021 as part of a set of new child safety policies.

In August 2023, Instagram made new changes to safeguard user privacy and stop spam and harassment. From accounts they do not follow, users can only receive one direct message at a time, and in order to send another, they must first approve the message request. The user can adjust this setting to accept an infinite number of messages from accounts they do not follow.

2.3.6. Instagram Stories

Instagram Stories is a feature that lets users take photos, apply layers and effects, and then post the images to their Instagram story. It was introduced in August of 2016. After 24 hours, images added to a user's story become invalid. The feature's resemblance to Snapchat was noticed by the media. CEO

Kevin Systrom told Recode that Day One: Instagram was a combination of Hipstamatic, Twitter [and] some stuff from Facebook like the Like' button. This was in response to criticism that it copied features from Snapchat. Every feature that someone has in their app has origins that can be found somewhere in the history of technology. Recode reported that Systrom compared the common features of the two social apps to the auto industry, even though he acknowledged the criticism as valid. Several automakers can coexist, sufficiently different from one another to cater to distinct consumer audiences. Systrom continued, "We decided that one of the really annoying things about the format is that it just keeps going and you couldn't pause it to look at something, you couldn't rewind." This was after adopting [Stories]. We executed that and completed all of that. Additionally, he revealed to the publication that Snapchat didn't start off with filters. They started using filters because Instagram offered them and many other people were attempting to use them as well.

Instagram Stories now has the ability to broadcast live videos, which vanish instantly after they end. This feature was added by Instagram in November.

Instagram introduced skippable advertisements in January 2017, allowing 15-second video and 5-second picture ads to run in between stories.

Augmented reality stickers were added to Instagram Stories in April 2017, mimicking some of Snapchat's features.

Instagram added support for face filters to its augmented reality sticker feature in May 2017, enabling users to overlay particular visual elements on their faces.

Later in May, TechCrunch published a story about the testing of Instagram Stories' Location Stories feature, which aggregates public Stories content from a specific location and shows it on an establishment's, landmarks, or other location's Instagram page. A few days later, Instagram revealed Story Search, allowing users to look up hashtags or locations and have the app show them relevant public Stories posts that contain the term.

Instagram updated its live-video features in June 2017 to enable users to either remove or add their live broadcast to their story for 24 hours after it was posted (Constine, Josh (2017)). Instagram began letting users reply to Stories content in July. Users could then send back photos and videos that included Instagram effects like stickers, filters, and hashtags.

In late August 2017, Instagram released Stories on its desktop and mobile websites. On December 5, 2017, Instagram debuted Story Highlights, also known as Permanent Stories. These are similar to Instagram Stories, except they never expire. They can be accessed from the desktop website as well and appear as circles beneath the biography and profile picture.

As of June 2018, 400 million users were actively sharing stories on Instagram every day, and 1 billion users were active on a monthly basis.

2.3.7. Verified Badges on Instagram

In December 2014, Instagram unveiled the verification feature, also referred to as the blue verified badge. With the help of this feature, users can validate the legitimacy of their accounts. In August 2018, Instagram started enabling users to request account verification. This was a big change from the previous setup, in which Instagram would usually start the verification process for accounts it thought were well-known or of public interest. With the release of this feature, users who qualified could apply for verification through the Instagram app directly. The Instagram blue verified badge is a symbol that appears next to the name of an account to indicate that it is legitimate, authentic, and affiliated with a prominent public figure, celebrity, brand, or other entity. It makes it easier for users to spot authentic accounts among the many profiles on the platform. On search results, profile pages, and comment sections, the badge can be seen as a blue checkmark next to the username of the account. Typically, Instagram sets certain requirements to be met in order to obtain the blue verified badge. These requirements include being notable, authentic, unique, complete, and abiding by the platform's terms of service and community guidelines. Instagram does not always verify accounts that fit its requirements; it verifies accounts at its own discretion. Although users can request verification through Instagram's settings, the Instagram team ultimately decides whether to approve requests. In 2021, Meta (previously Facebook) introduced paid verification on Instagram. This made it possible for qualified Instagram users to pay a fee to have their accounts verified, as opposed to depending only on fulfilling the platform's standard verification requirements.

2.3.8. Advertising

In April 2013, Emily White started working at Instagram as the Director of Business Operations. She stated that the company should be prepared to start selling advertising by September 2014 in an interview with The Wall Street Journal from September 2013. This was her way of bringing in business from a well-known entity that hadn't yet turned a profit for its parent company. In December 2013, White quit Instagram to work at Snapchat. According to a spokesperson, James Quarles joined Instagram in August 2014 as the company's global head of business and brand development. He was given responsibility for managing advertising, sales, and the creation of new monetization products.

American users' Instagram feeds will soon feature both image and video ads, the social media platform announced in October 2013. The first image ads will go live on November 1, 2013. On October 30, 2014, almost a year later, there were video ads. Instagram revealed plans to launch advertisements in the UK, Canada, and Australia in June 2014; the ads would begin to appear that fall.

Instagram revealed plans to introduce carousel ads in March 2015, giving sponsors the opportunity to showcase several photos with the option to include links to more material. In October 2015, the company introduced carousel image ads, and in March 2016, it introduced video carousel ads.

Instagram reported having 200,000 advertisers on the platform in February 2016. By September 2016, there were 500,000 of them, and by March 2017, there were 1 million.

Instagram introduced new features for business accounts in May 2016, such as business profiles, analytics, and the capacity to advertise on posts. Businesses needed to link a corresponding Facebook page in order to access the tools. Business accounts could view top posts, reach, impressions, engagement, and demographic data on the new Instagram Insights analytics page. Initially launched in the US, Australia, and New Zealand, Insights later extended to the rest of the globe in 2016.

Instagram business accounts now have the option to add product links that take users to a page where they can make a purchase or add them to a shopping list. This feature was added in November 2018. Instagram introduced the Checkout feature in April 2019, enabling retailers to sell goods straight from the Instagram app.

Instagram revealed in a blog post from March 2020 that they are making significant changes to their moderation policies to curb the spread of false information, hoaxes, and fake news about COVID-19 on the platform. They also stated that they would be removing COVID-19 accounts from account recommendations and that they were working to remove some COVID-19-related content from Explore that wasn't posted by a reliable health organization. Additionally, content in the feed and Stories that has been flagged as false by independent fact-checkers will begin to be de-ranked.

Instagram introduced a native affiliate marketing tool in June 2021, which allows creators to get paid commissions on sales. Commission-enabled posts are distinguished as affiliate posts by having the user-side label Eligible for Commission. MAC, Kopari, and Sephora were among the launch partners.

2.3.9. Stand-Alone Apps

Instagram has created and launched three independent apps with distinct features. Bolt is a messaging app that was released in July 2014 that allows users to quickly send images to friends by clicking on their profile photo. Once an image is seen, it disappears from the app. August saw the release of Hyperlapse, an iOS-only app that makes quick time-lapse films and tracking shots through the use of sophisticated algorithm processing. Although Microsoft released a Hyperlapse app for Windows and Android in May 2015, Instagram has not yet released an official Hyperlapse app for any of these operating systems. Boomerang is a video app that was released in October 2015 that loops short, one-second videos that are created by combining photos.

2.3.10. Third-Party Services

Due to Instagram's widespread popularity, numerous third-party services have been developed to work with the platform. These services include those for producing content for Instagram users to share on the platform, generating content from Instagram photos (including print-out versions), analytics, and alternative clients for platforms that Instagram does not officially support or has limited support for (like iPads).

In order to preserve community control, give developers a clear roadmap, and create a more sustainable environment centered around genuine experiences on the platform, including those geared toward content creation, publishers, and advertisers, Instagram announced in November 2015 that it would terminate feed API access to its platform as of June 1, 2016. Third-party clients are also not allowed to use the text strings "insta" or "gram" in their names. According to reports, these modifications were made mainly for security purposes (to stop automated click farms from abusing the service and account hijacking), as well as to deter third-party clients from replicating the full Instagram experience because of the service's increased monetization. In 2018, Instagram started to impose additional limitations on its API following the Cambridge Analytica scandal.

You can browse public Instagram profiles indefinitely without creating an account by using third-party services, and you can browse other people's Stories anonymously. Because users are aware that their Stories will vanish in 24 hours if they don't add them as highlighted, Stories are more genuine than standard photos posted as posts (though users can check who saw their Story for 48 hours after it was published). They are therefore extremely useful for market research.

2.3.11. Fact-Checking

With the help of outside fact-checking organizations, false information can be recognized, examined, and flagged as such on Facebook. This announcement was made on December 16, 2019, by Facebook. When content is rated as partially or completely false, it is removed from the hashtag pages and explore page. In addition, it is marked as such. Using image matching technology to locate additional instances of misinformation was introduced with the Facebook fact-checking program. Duplicate content on Facebook or Instagram will also be marked as false if it has been classified as false or partially false.

2.3.12. Algorithm and Design Changes

Instagram started rolling out a change in April 2016 that replaced the strictly chronological order of photos displayed in a user's timeline with an algorithmic one. Although Instagram claimed that the algorithm was created to show users more of the images posted by users they liked, a large number of users had negative things to say about the app, with many pleading with their followers to enable post notifications so they would always be aware of updates. In response to customers who were upset about the change, the company sent out a tweet, which they reiterated in 2020, but they remained firm and did not offer a way to reverse it. But in a December 2021 Senate hearing on child safety matters, Adam Mosseri revealed that the company is working on a version of the feed that would display user posts chronologically. Subsequently, he clarified that the company would launch two feed modes: the traditional chronological feed and one that would allow users to select their favorite users, whose posts would appear chronologically at the top with other posts mixed in below.

In order to stop posts from showing up in search results and the app's Explore section, Instagram has been using the ability to reduce the prominence of accounts (shadowbanning) that it believes may be generating spam and non-genuine engagement (including the excessive use of unnecessary hashtags). Instagram stated in a since-deleted Facebook post, "When creating content, we advise concentrating on your business objective or goal rather than hashtags." Since then, Instagram has come under fire for allegedly expanding the practice to include post censorship in ambiguous and inconsistent situations, especially when it comes to sexually suggestive content.

Instagram's December 2018 update incited fury among its user base. They discovered an attempt to change the feed's flow from the conventional vertical scroll to a horizontal scroll by swiping left, mimicking and capitalizing on the success of their Instagram Stories. A number of retractions were made, characterizing it as a bug or as a test release that had been inadvertently made available to too many people.

Instagram moved the activity feed to the top of the page in November 2020 by replacing it with a new Shop tab. The company claims that the Reels tab makes it easier for you to find short, entertaining videos from creators all over the world and people just like you, and that the Shop tab improves your ability to connect with brands and creators and discover products you love. The new post button was also moved to the top and replaced with a Reels tab. Users, however, have not taken well to the change. They have taken their complaints to Reddit and Twitter, and The New York Times has specifically criticized Reels, stating that it is difficult to use and confusing in addition to failing miserably as a TikTok clone.

In 2020, Instagram launched a feature called "suggested posts" that enriches a user's feed with posts from accounts Instagram believes the user would find interesting. The Verge, which claimed that suggested posts would keep users glued to their feeds, give Instagram more space for advertisements, and ultimately harm users' mental health, stirred controversy around the feature. However, Instagram executive Julian Gutman refuted the claims, saying the feature was not meant to keep users glued to their screens (Carman, Ashley, 2020). More controversy surrounded suggested posts after Fast Company said it would be hard to disable the feature (Grothaus, Michael (2020)).

Instagram announced a test modification to the suggested posts feature on June 23, 2021. In the Instagram feed, the company has decided to prioritize suggested posts over those from users they follow. The change was made in response to positive feedback.

2.4. INSTAGRAM ALGORITHM

Content on Instagram is ranked using a set of rules called the Instagram algorithm. It determines what content appears on every Instagram user's feed, the Explore Page, the Reels feed, Stories, and so forth, as well as in what order. Instagram disclosed last year that distinct algorithms power every aspect of the platform. These are each of the recognized ranking signals.

2.4.1. How Does the Instagram Algorithm Work?

To put it simply, the Instagram algorithm looks at user behavior and interests as well as content (such as Stories, reels, and feed posts) to deliver relevant content to the appropriate audience. Making each user's experience on Instagram as enjoyable as possible is the primary goal of the Instagram algorithm. Because it sounds less robotic, Instagram CEO Adam Mosseri calls the algorithm "ranking" and emphasizes the significance of giving some posts more weight than others.

"I understand that many of you are dubious about ranking," Mosseri stated in a 2022 Instagram reel, "but it truly does help us ensure that Instagram is more valuable to each and every user of the platform." Additionally, according to Mosseri, "Instagram doesn't have a single algorithm that controls what people see and don't see on the app" (Figure 2.1).

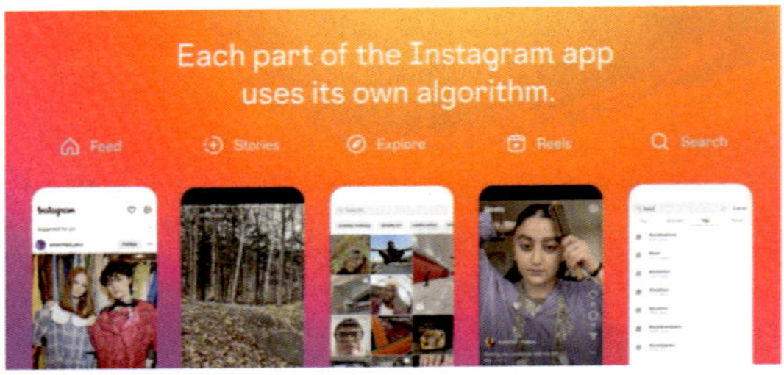

Figure 2.1. *Part of the Instagram app.*

Source: https://blog.hootsuite.com/instagram-algorithm/.

Rather, he claims that they employ a range of classifiers, algorithms, and procedures designed especially for every section of the app, including Feed, Stories, Explore, Reels, Search, and more.

2.4.2. Instagram Feed Algorithm

- **Your Activity:** We've talked a lot about this above – it's the content you like, share, save, or comment on.
- **Post Info:** Post popularity is first here, including not just how many people interact with the content but how quickly they do so. Other factors like date, time, and location come into play here, too.
- **Poster Info:** This signal aims to determine how interested you might be in the account that posted a particular piece of content, using signals like how often people have recently interacted with their account.
- **Your History with the Poster:** You're more likely to see content from people you follow, message with, or otherwise engage with. For brands, this means it's critical to encourage and respond to follower engagement.

2.4.3. Instagram Stories Algorithm

Recall that posts from accounts you do not follow are not included in Stories—aside from advertisements. Thus, Instagram Stories' algorithmic social media context revolves around prioritizing the content shared by accounts you follow.

For brands, that means you won't get new eyeballs here, but you still need to understand the algorithm to extend your organic reach.

- **Viewing History:** If you always watch an account's Stories, it will move to the front of your Stories list. If you tend to skip that account's Stories, it will move to the back of the line.

- **Engagement History:** Watching is good, but engaging is better.
- **Closeness:** This is similar to your history with the poster for the Feed algorithm, except in this case the algorithm is specifically evaluating how likely you are to be friends or family. This is a tough one for brands, so focus on the first two.

2.4.4. Instagram Explore Algorithm

According to Instagram, the Explore algorithm is made especially to present you with the kinds of content that you are most likely to "do something with." The three most crucial actions in this case are sharing, saving, and liking. Essentially, your Explore Page is a single screen that expresses your personality (Figure 2.2).

Figure 2.2. *Instagram explore algorithm.*

Source: https://blog.hootsuite.com/social-media-algorithm/.

The ranking signals are:

- **Post Info:** The level and speed of interaction with a post. This is more important for Explore than for any other Instagram surface.
- **Your Activity in Explore:** Similar to the equivalent ranking signal for Feed, except that this one more heavily weighs content type.
- **Your History with the Poster:** This is not as relevant to Explore, but if a post is ranking well on the other factors, this can give it an added boost.
- **Poster Info:** Same as for the Feed algorithm, here specifically looking for content from a wide range of accounts.

2.4.5. Instagram Reels Algorithm

Brands, pay attention. Reels have "an emphasis on entertainment," according to Instagram. In this case, the goal is to display content that viewers are most likely to enjoy, reshare, and watch through to the end.

Interestingly, they also want to show you content that you are likely to visit on the audio page. They do this in order to determine whether or not you will be motivated to create a Reel that is similar to theirs.

Here are the ranking signals:

- **Your Activity:** You get how this one works by now…
- **Your History with the Poster:** Again, this is less relevant here than in Feed, but it can be an added bonus.
- **Reel Info:** Basic details like audio track and visual, as well as that ever-important level and speed of engagement.
- **Poster Info:** Here this includes number of followers and level of engagement.

2.4.6. Top Instagram Algorithm Ranking Factors Overall

If you wanted to break down the Instagram algorithm ranking factors overall, here's what that would look like. The three most important ranking factors of the Instagram algorithm are:

1. **Relationship between the Creator and the Viewer:** Do you follow each other? Do you message each other or leave comments? If you have repeatedly interacted with a specific user in the past, you are more likely to see the new content they post. (This is very important for businesses: Active community management, including responding to DMs and comments, can improve a brand's visibility on Instagram.)
2. **Interest:** Does a user typically interact with this type of content? When the Instagram algorithm recognizes that a user enjoys a specific content type or format, it shows them more of the same.
3. **Relevancy:** Instagram decides how "relevant" every piece of content is. This includes an analysis of where it fits with trending topics as well as the timeliness factor (recent posts are considered more relevant than older posts).

2.4.7. Top Instagram Algorithm Changes for 2024

It's critical to stay informed about algorithmic changes as Instagram develops further. The top adjustments to the Instagram algorithm for 2024 are listed here.

2.4.7.1. Some Content Will Be More Restricted for Teens

Instagram will automatically assign teenagers to the most restrictive content control setting as of 2024. This implies that teenagers might find it more difficult to find potentially delicate content or accounts in areas like Search and Explore. The purpose of this modification is to encourage a safer online experience for younger users.

Restricted content will include:

- Violent content;
- Content about self-harm or suicide;
- Content about eating disorders;
- Nudity or sexually explicit content;
- Content that includes restricted goods.

2.4.7.2. Instagram's New Algorithm Is Less Focused on Reels

Adam Mosseri stated on an IG Live that the Instagram algorithm is changing to give more weight to other types of content, such as Stories and regular posts, after a heavy emphasis on reels in previous years. Users who complained that there were too many reels in their feeds prompted this change.

2.4.7.3. Replayed Reels Now Count Toward Your View Count

Previously, a reel's view count was only calculated on initial viewings; going forward, each time a reel is viewed, it will be added to the total views. As a result, when creators produce and distribute more reels, their view counts might rise.

2.4.7.4. Users Can Now Pay for a Blue Checkmark

Meta launched Meta Verified in 2023, offering users the option to purchase a blue checkmark to appear on their accounts. Enhanced algorithmic visibility and extra features, such as real-time access to a person for common account problems, are advantages for verified accounts. This modification has caused debate, though, as some people believe that verification ought to be earned rather than purchased. Currently under testing, the feature can be found in the US, UK, Canada, India, and Brazil. The worldwide launch is anticipated shortly.

2.4.7.5. Reels with Word Marks Are Ranked Lower

Mosseri has now verified the long-held rumors in an Instagram story. Word-marked reels will be ranked lower, no matter how many word marks there are. This includes watermarks from video editing software and wordmarks like the TikTok logo. Mosseri did clarify that videos without a word mark that were made outside of the Instagram app are unaffected.

2.4.7.6. European Users Can Now See Chronological Feeds

Instagram has announced that users in Europe will now be able to view Stories and Reels only from people they follow, arranged chronologically from newest to oldest, in response to the EU's Digital Services Act (DSA). This modification also affects search results, which will no longer be tailored to a user's interests and past behavior.

2.4.8. How to "Beat" the Instagram Algorithm and Get Your Content Seen

There isn't a magic bullet for beating the Instagram algorithm, despite everyone's desire to know how to do so. All it takes to beat the Instagram algorithm is to know how it operates and to take advantage of that knowledge. You can improve the likelihood that more people will see your posts by producing interesting, high-quality content, adhering to a regular posting schedule, and actively participating in the community. Remember to stay on top of trends and make use of tools like Reels, tagging, and hashtags to increase your exposure and reach even more.

Businesses can gain important insights into what is effective for their brand on the platform by using a business or creator account and monitoring analytics. In the end, it all comes down to developing a solid online presence on Instagram and having real, genuine connections with your followers.

2.5. HOW TO GET ON THE INSTAGRAM EXPLORE PAGE?

The Instagram Explore page is still one of the last bastions of organic reach, even though ad dollars still dominate social media discovery. Instagram's refined algorithm, which powers the Explore feed, is getting really good at suggesting users to check out content. Potential increases in reach, impressions, and revenue are among the benefits of having a brand listed on the Explore tab. It's a chance to develop a community and expand your audience. Find out about the most recent algorithmic changes and how to properly land on the Explore page.

2.5.1. Instagram Explore Page

A selection of publicly accessible material, including images, videos, Reels, and Stories, customized for every Instagram user can be found on the Explore page. Similar to TikTok's FYP, each user on Instagram has a unique Explore page that is generated by the Instagram algorithm.

The company claims that the posts that appear are selected based on various factors, including the users you follow, the images and videos you enjoy, and your connections on Instagram.

The Explore page can be a terrific way to find new posts, accounts, hashtags, or products you might like because you don't have to follow everyone you see.

Also, the feed is constantly evolving. Machine learning is used by the Instagram Explore page's algorithm to refine and enhance its content recommendations.

2.5.2. How to Use the Instagram Explore Page?

To access the Instagram Explore page, simply tap the magnifying glass icon located at the app's bottom. The Explore feed's top search bar allows users to look up accounts, keywords, hashtags, and locations (Figure 2.3).

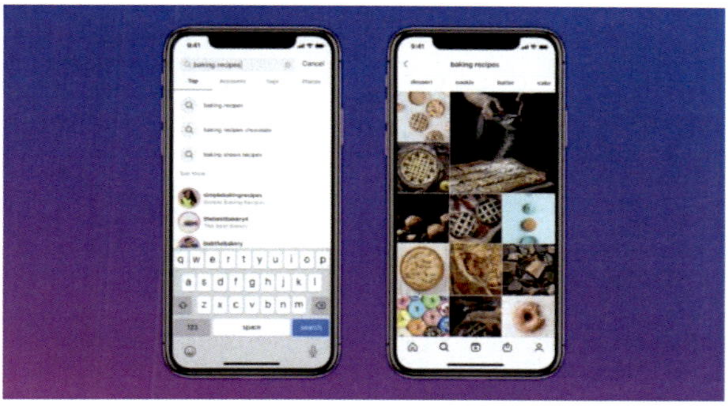

Figure 2.3. *Instagram explore feed.*

Source: https://blog.hootsuite.com/get-brand-instagrams-explore-page/.

The Explore page itself features a number of categories, including music, sports, travel, beauty, and food, in addition to a special Reels feed. The category options change to reflect your interests when you search for something.

A continuous scroll feed of related content appears when you click on a photo in the Explore feed. Thus, the Explore page can be thought of as a massive feed of portals to other feeds, each one more specific and narrowly focused than the last.

2.5.3. How Does the Instagram Explore Page Algorithm Work?

As previously stated, no two Instagram Explore pages are the same. This is so that users can customize what they see when they click on the Explore tab thanks to Instagram's Explore Feed Ranking System. The algorithm, also referred to as the Instagram algorithm, modifies what is displayed by applying machine learning to a variety of data sources and ranking signals.

Instagram engineers categorize the Explore page as an "unconnected system," in contrast to the home feed, which displays posts from accounts users follow.

Amogh Mahapatra, a machine learning researcher at the company, says in an Instagram blog post that the system selects posts "based on a user's activity across Instagram and are then ranked based on similar factors" (Figure 2.4).

Figure 2.4. *Instagram explore algorithm.*

Source: https://blog.hootsuite.com/get-brand-instagrams-explore-page/.

In other words, the selection of content on each Instagram user's Explore page is based on:

- The accounts you already follow;
- The content that people *you* follow like;
- The types of posts you engage with often;
- Posts with high engagement.

2.5.4. Why You Want to Appear on the Instagram Explore Page

By 2025, there will be 1.44 billion monthly active Instagram users, according to projections. There is a sizable audience for your content even if each Explore page is unique.

Benefits of appearing on the Explore page may include:

- **Increased Engagement:** When your content makes it to the Explore page, it's exposed to a wider audience than your followers. An engagement spike on that content usually follows.

- **More Followers:** If your post is compelling enough, some of your new audience will check out your profile and decide to follow you. (Make sure they're impressed by your amazing bio, highlight covers, etc.) Those new followers will also mean more engagement in the future.
- **More Conversions:** Make sure you have the right call-to-action ready for all those fresh eyeballs. You may even see a sales boost driven by product tags and Instagram shopping tools.

2.5.5. How to Get on the Instagram Explore Page: 10 Tips

Follow these tips to start showing up on people's Explore page in no time!

1. **Get to Know Your Target Market:** Your audience is already aware of you. So, go beyond "know your audience" to get to the Instagram Explore page. Learn about the target audiences you want to reach in Explore, as well as the content that these users are most interested in, by getting to know your Instagram demographics

   A good place to start is with the Explore feed on your business account. Examine posts, categories, and specialty feeds to identify strategies you could adopt.

   Some questions you might ask during this exercise include:

- What tone seems to resonate most with the audience?
- Is there a visual style that performs best?
- What type of content (Reels, carousels, static posts) earns the most engagement?
- What type of caption prompts the most responses?

2. **Share Engaging Content:** Increase your own Instagram engagement by learning more about the kinds of content that appeal to your target audience. Incorporate your brand's audience research into the social media content strategy.

   Since videos automatically play in the Explore tab and frequently take up more space in the feed, they have an advantage over static images in terms of engagement. However, engaging images can also be found in still images with product tags, carousel formats, or just beautiful imagery. Don't undervalue the impact of captivating captions, either.

   Adhere to each format's recommended practices. Offer something of value, such as excellent storytelling or loyalty rewards, share eye-catching images, and capture viewers' attention quickly.

Keep in mind that interaction extends beyond likes and remarks. Thus, strive to produce material that readers will want to save and/or share.

3. **Experiment with New Formats:** It's no secret, though, that Instagram wants Reels to be successful. Reels appear in both the Explore feed and a separate tab for a purpose. The entire home page of the Instagram app was redesigned to make room for the tab because it is so essential to the user experience.

   Gaining recognition in the Reels tab may also lead to recognition in the Explore tab. Please reconsider before sharing that TikTok again. Instagram's algorithm appears to deprioritize videos with the TikTok watermark.

   The takeaway from this is that Instagram rewards early adopters with greater reach when they encourage users to test out a new feature. Make sure you utilize that advantage.

   Experiment with various formats, such as carousels or Reels, to determine which verticals generate the greatest reach.

   Just remember that the platform is always changing which formats it prioritizes, so stay alert. (We advise bookmarking our Instagram updates feed to stay up to date.)

4. **Cultivate an Active Community:** Introducing users to Instagram communities is one of the main goals of the Explore page. As community-building is essential to Instagram's success, your marketing strategy should center around it.

   The likelihood that Instagram will suggest your brand to "lookalike audiences" on the Explore page increases with the activity of your brand community on the platform.

   Allow enough time for your audience to interact with your account. Engage in brand dialogues in the DMs, comment sections, and other popular brand venues. To ensure early engagement, encourage members of your community to enable post notifications.

5. **Post When Your Followers Are Online:** Instagram's algorithm gives timeliness priority (a.k.a. recency), so more of your followers will see your post if it is brand-new. Achieving a high level of engagement with your own followers is the prerequisite for being added to the Explore page.

- **Tip:** If your audience is online when you're not, an Instagram scheduler is your best bet.

6. **Use Relevant Tags:** Hashtags, account tags, and geotags are some more ways to increase your content's visibility within the Explore ecosystem.

   Recall that users can also search by hashtag and location on the Instagram Explore page. Someone can follow a particular hashtag if it piques their curiosity. To ensure that your content appears where people are looking for it, carefully consider the Instagram hashtags and geotags you use.

   Using account tags is an additional method of exposing your posts to new viewers. Be sure to tag relevant accounts in your posts, such as the CEO of the company, influencers, and brand partners, or the illustrator or photographer.

   Posts from your audience can be shared to foster community and increase visibility and interaction all at once.

7. **Pay Attention to Analytics:** Examine the things you're doing that your audience is responding to already. It's possible that they prefer your jokes over your motivational quotes or your carousels over your Reels.

   Get your audience to regularly tap hearts and leave comments, and their engagement will help you move up to the Explore page.

   To find out if your most popular posts have already appeared on the Explore page, check your analytics. To see the source of each impression you received, tap the blue View Insights button beneath your priceless post and swipe upward.

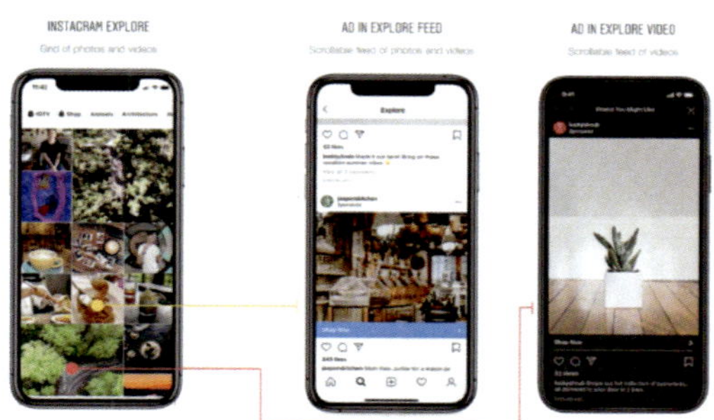

Figure 2.5. *Instagram explore ads.*

Source: https://blog.hootsuite.com/get-brand-instagrams-explore-page/.

8. **Consider Paid Placement in Explore:** Think about running an ad in the Explore feed if you're willing to support your organic efforts with some advertising funds.

You won't see these advertisements in the Explore feed grid right away. Rather, they place you in the next best spot, which is the scrollable photo and video feed that shows up when a user clicks on a grid post (Figure 2.5).

It's not the easy way out, lest you think so. Your Explore page ad needs to be just as interesting as the posts that surround it in order to have any effect. Sounds like a tall order, doesn't it?

9. **Skip the Shortcuts:** While buying followers or building Instagram pods might be profitable in the short term, these strategies typically don't pay off over time.

   Instagram's feed ranking is determined by machine learning, which is always learning from new data patterns. Instagram's @creators account explains, "so it can identify inauthentic activity and make adjustments." Instagram may suspend or even delete your account if they believe you are engaging in bot-related activities. Prioritize producing interesting content and developing a true brand community.

10. **Follow the Rules:** Though it should go without saying, if you violate Instagram's community or recommendation guidelines, the platform will not advertise your content to new audiences.

    Community guidelines are probably already familiar to you. They go over the fundamentals, like only sharing content that you are authorized to share, being mindful of the Instagram community, and abiding by the law.

    The recommendations on Instagram follow slightly more stringent rules. Even though a piece of content complies with community standards, it is still not always appropriate to recommend it to new audiences.

There are five categories of content that violate these recommendation guidelines:

- **Content that impedes Instagram's ability to foster a safe community:** Think anything that promotes self-harm, violence, or sexually suggestive content.
- **Sensitive or low-quality content about health or finance:** No miracle cures or "risk-free" investment opportunities.
- **Content that users have broadly indicated they dislike:** This one's a little vaguer, but it covers things like clickbait, engagement bait, and spammy giveaways.

- **Content that is associated with low-quality publishing:** Unoriginal content or news content that misrepresents its source.
- **False or misleading content:** Anything containing claims that have been debunked by expert organizations, vaccine misinformation, or false documents.

If your account has violated these rules, your content is far less likely to hit the Explore page.

2.5.6. How to Reset the Instagram Explore Page If You Don't Like What You're Seeing?

There are a few ways to reset your feed on Instagram if you don't like what you see on your Explore page. A simple workaround is to pull down and refresh the feed. Slide your thumb down the screen gently until the circle beneath the categories starts to spin (Figure 2.6).

Figure 2.6. *Instagram explore refresh.*

Source: https://blog.hootsuite.com/get-brand-instagrams-explore-page/.

For a more long-term fix, here's how to teach the algorithm what you don't want to see:

- Tap the post you don't like.
- Tap the three dots above the post.
- Select Not Interested.

The platform will avoid similar recommendations in the future (Figure 2.7).

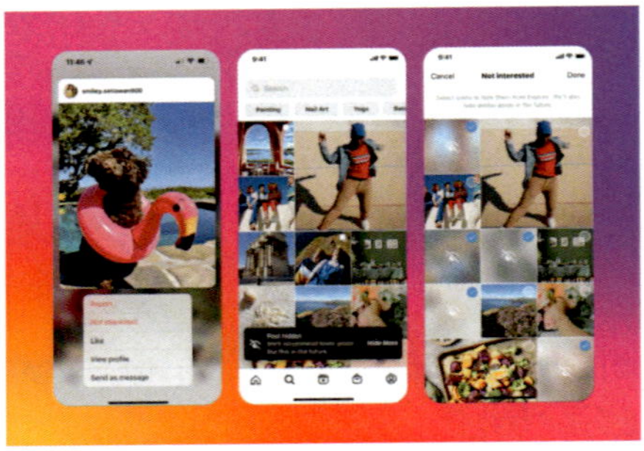

Figure 2.7. *Instagram explore not interested.*

Source: https://blog.hootsuite.com/get-brand-instagrams-explore-page/.

2.6. INSTAGRAM REELS ALGORITHM

In your quest to improve engagement for your business Instagram account, if you consider yourself a social media nerd (a term of endearment), you have undoubtedly already read our guide to the Instagram algorithm. However, it's crucial to be aware that Instagram Reels in particular have a unique algorithm that needs to be worked out if you want your content to stand out. Prepare yourself and step into the ring.

Naturally, Instagram introduced Instagram Reels—short-form videos—as a rival to TikTok in 2020. In just a few minutes, producers can create entertaining, captivating Instagram Reels by combining music clips, effects, and filters with basic editing tools. Unlike Instagram Stories, these creations remain visible for a full day. However, just like everything else on Instagram, the Instagram algorithm—the mysterious code that determines whether to show a video to the public or keep it hidden—will determine whether your video becomes virally popular, regardless of how great it is.

2.6.1. Instagram Reels

Videos that have been uploaded to Instagram are called Reels. Although a reel's maximum length is 15 minutes, the majority of excellent reels last between 7 and 15 seconds. Reels are typically rather short. Reels can consist of a single video, multiple clips combined into one, still images, or a mix of images and video. Both Instagram's built-in video editing features and third-party video editing apps can be used to create them.

The majority of Reels aren't just videos; they also use trending audio and text to make their points. There are a ton of serious, educational, and humorous Reels available as well as humorous ones. They're a great tool for building brand recognition for your company in a contemporary, approachable manner.

How to Make an Instagram Reel: Producing a brief but captivating video is a skill, and Instagram offers numerous avenues for achievement. You can use the Instagram app to edit and post a reel by following these steps.

- **Step 1: Open Up the Instagram Reels Editor:** This is the easy part—you can actually start an Instagram Reel three different ways. Here's a quick rundown of all three.

1. First, you can start a Reel from the Instagram news feed (otherwise known as the page that opens automatically when you enter the app) by hitting the plus button at the bottom.

2. Second, you can start a Reel from the Reel section, Reel simply. There's a camera icon in the top left. Hit that and you're ready to rock and roll.

3. Last, you can start an Instagram Reel from your profile. Just go to the plus button in the top right.

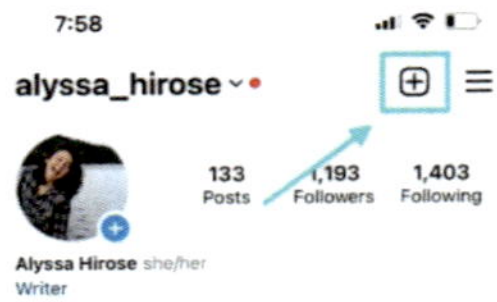

Note: The following two steps (2 and 3) can be done in any order. You can pick music first, then add your clips, or clips then music. You're the captain of your own life.

- **Step 2: Create Your Video or Select Clips from Your Camera Roll:** You can use the record button on your screen to shoot a Reel on the spot (but honestly, nobody does this—it's frankly a totally bonkers way to create content for Reels).

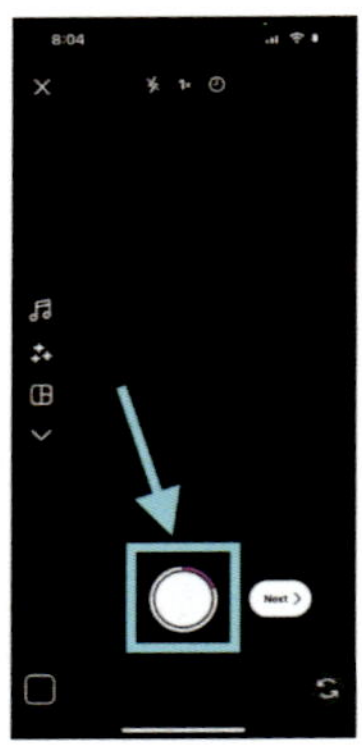

Instead, most social media managers will film video clips ahead of time. To access the clips in your camera roll, hit the square icon in the bottom left corner of your screen.

From there, you can choose videos from your photo and video library.

- **Step 3: Add Audio:** Guess what? There's also three ways to add music to your Instagram Reel.

1. You can select your audio at the same time you're selecting clips by hitting the music note icon on the left side of your screen.

2. Or, after you hit Next, you can open up the audio menu and access Instagram's music library by tapping the music note icon on the top of your screen.

3. Last one, you can also add audio from the clip editor itself (for a thorough rundown of the clip editor, check out step 5).

No matter how you get there, the audio selection menu for Instagram Reels looks the same.

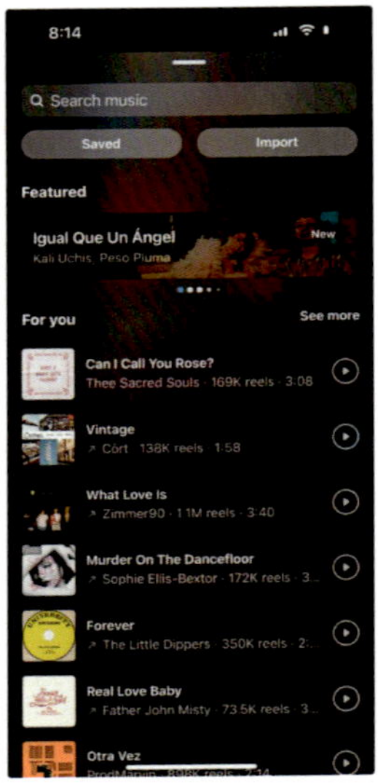

Search for the song you want or choose from trending songs (the ones that have a little upward arrow are trending).

- **Step 4: Add Text:** To make it a little easier on you, there aren't three ways to add text to an Instagram Reel. (There's two.)

1. First, you can add text when you're previewing your Reel by hitting the text icon at the top of your screen.

2. Or, once you're in the clip editor, you can add text by tapping Text on the bottom of your screen.

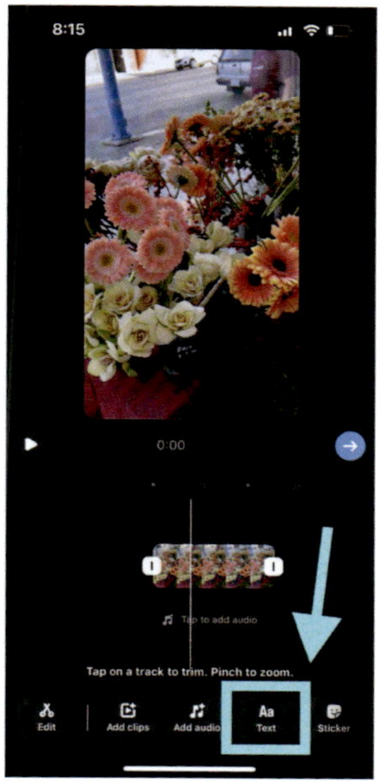

3. Once you type in your desired text, you can edit the size, font, color, and outline style.

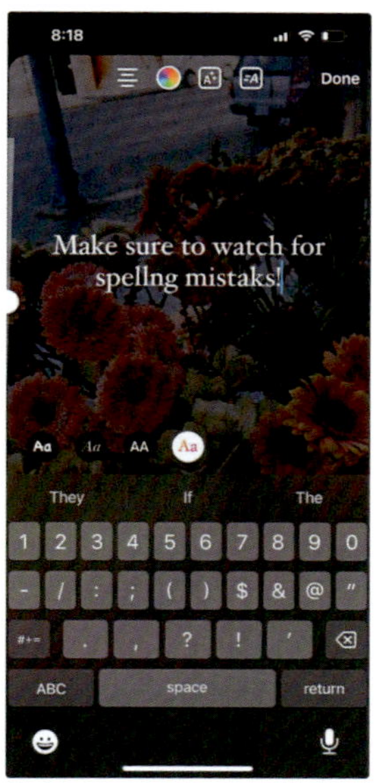

- **Step 5: Edit It Until You're Sick of It:** We joke. Mostly. Using Instagram's Reel editing tools, you can clip videos, change the order of videos, add transitions, split clips, change the playback speed, add stickers and more.

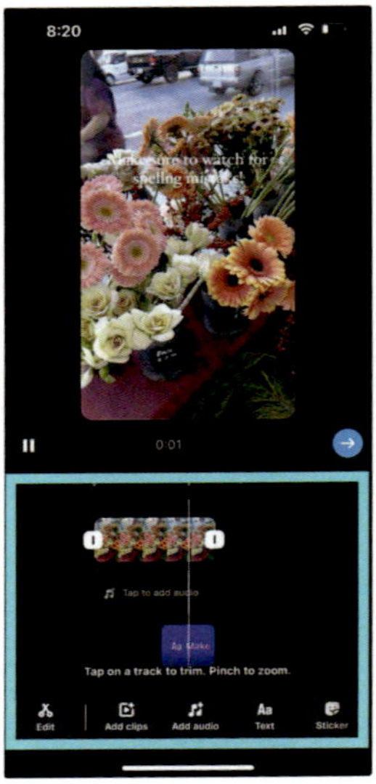

- This is the step that usually results in getting the chosen audio stuck in your head for the rest of the day. But hey, it's worth it.

Once you're totally happy with your Reel, hit the little blue arrow on the right side of your screen.

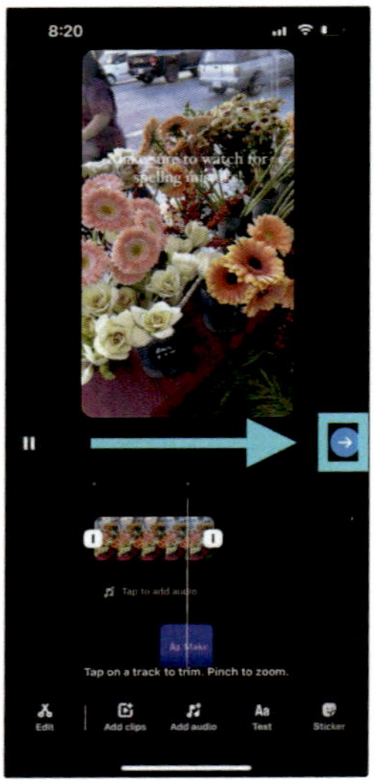

- **Step 6: Add a Cover Image:** Don't skip this step: a specific cover image will ensure that the Reel fits with your Instagram aesthetic. Tap Edit cover.

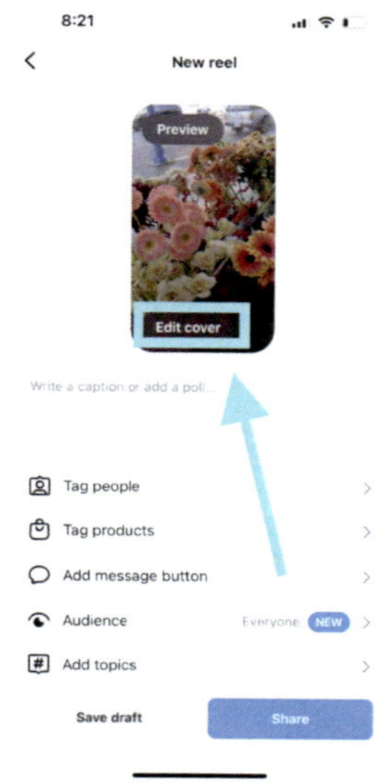

From there, you can choose a frame from your Reel to act as the cover image…

… or you can hit Add from camera roll to choose a different still image.

- **Step 7: Add a Caption:** You know the drill: write a great hook for this caption and include a call-to-action at the end. (If you're looking for over 250 awesome captions—plus more ideas—this is your sign).

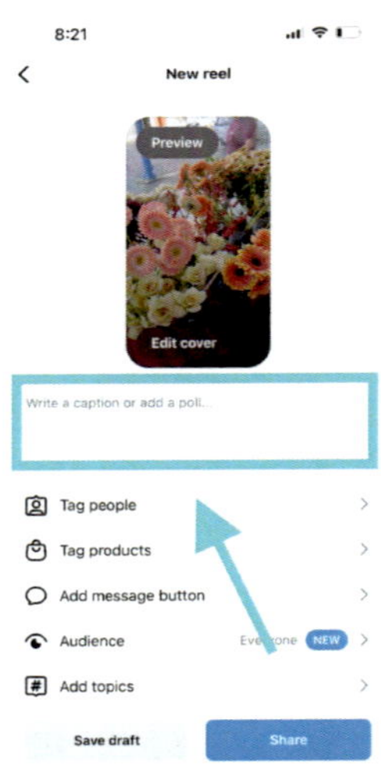

- **Step 8: Tag Other Users:** Hit Tag people and tag any relevant users, collaborators or creators.

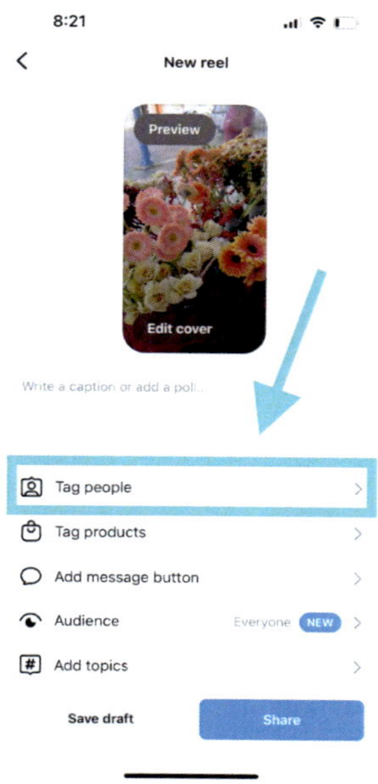

- **Step 9: Add Other Optional Details:** You can also change your audience, add products from your Instagram shop, add topics, add a location, set a fundraiser, add a reminder, and more before publishing your Reel. Although not required, adding more details to your post will make it easier for the algorithm to identify it.

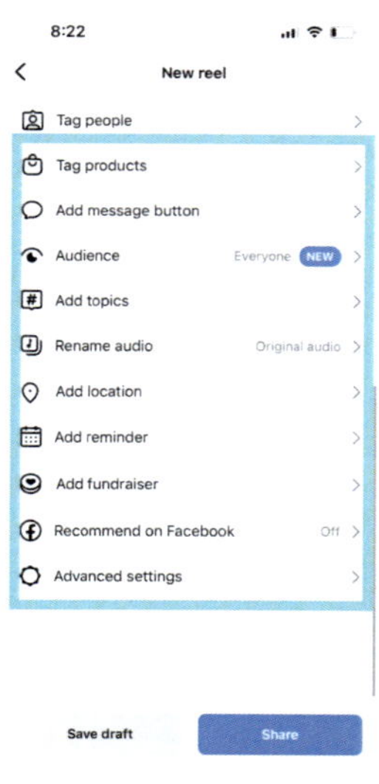

- **Step 10: Hit "Share":** You did it! Now's the time to hit Share.

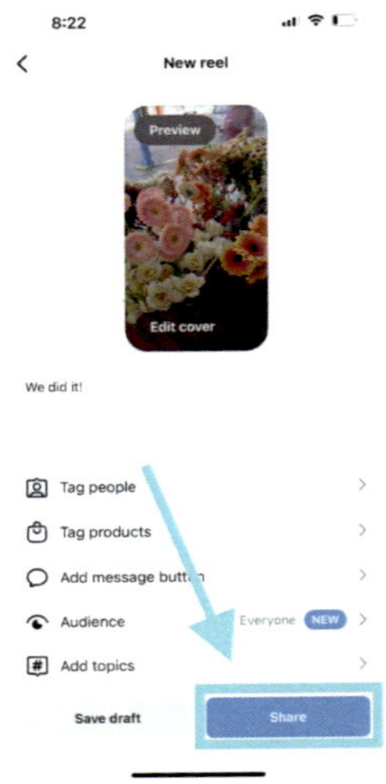

Or, you can schedule your Instagram Reel instead to reach the maximum number of users.

2.6.2. How Does the Instagram Reels Algorithm Work?

The Instagram Reels algorithm decides which Reels are shown to which Instagram user. You'll see Reels from accounts you follow in your main feed, but there are two other places Instagram Reels from other creators and brands can be discovered:

- **The Reels Tab:** This is basically Instagram's version of the TikTok For You page. Tap the Reels icon at the bottom of the Instagram app's home page for an endless, scrollable feed of Reels selected by the algorithm.

- **The Explore Tab:** Reels are also heavily featured in Explore, alongside Instagram Posts and Stories that the Instagram algorithm serves up.

There are multiple factors that go into determining when and where Reels appear.

2.6.2.1. Relationships

The Instagram algorithm observes how you engage with other users in addition to how you interact with content. If someone is obviously your best friend or superfan on Instagram, Instagram is more likely to share your most recent video with them as soon as it goes live. Examples of these behaviors include: do you both have followers and are searched for by name? Do you message or leave comments on each other's posts? However, if you have previously interacted with them in any way, Instagram also takes that into account. Larkers, raise your hands proudly! With Reels and Explore, you're likely to be shown videos from creators you haven't heard of.

2.6.2.2. Relevance of the Content

Instagram uses user affinity, which is a more sophisticated way of saying "likes." Instagram tracks the subjects or topics you engage with and attempts to present related content if you've previously liked or interacted with a Reel or post. The hashtags you use in your Instagram Reels, along with pixel, frame, and audio analysis, help the AI determine the subject matter of a video.

2.6.2.3. Timeliness

The algorithm gives fresh content precedence over archive Reels. The algorithm gods are human, too, and they want to see what's new. Continue to release those new drops!

2.6.2.4. Popularity

Instagram will recognize that you have something unique that users would find interesting if you have a dedicated following and upload content that regularly gets liked and shared. Although it may seem counterintuitive to have to be already well-known in order to gain popularity, Instagram's primary goal is to promote high-quality content, so if you already have a solid online reputation, the app will reward you.

2.6.3. Tips for Working with the Instagram Reels Algorithm

All of this is just a fancy way of saying that Instagram gives priority to Reels with fresh, entertaining, and timely content that it believes users will enjoy. In a recent carousel, Instagram's Creators account confirmed that maybe robots and humans aren't all that different after all. (The part that says "fun and relevant," not "embrace our robot brethren.")

2.6.3.1. Create Quality Content

Individuals anticipate humorous, engaging, and fascinating content when they click on the Reels tab.

That is therefore the goal of the algorithm. Reels currently has live people going through them to highlight the best ones, according to Instagram's @ creators account. We've got 10 ideas for Instagram reels to get you started, but making the "best" reel is a tall and highly subjective order. In summary, all you need to do to get started is try your hardest to make your audience laugh, teach them something new, or present a surprising twist or challenge.

2.6.3.2. Make Your Reels Visually Appealing

The algorithm rewards visually striking videos. If you want to get creative, try out all of Reels' bells and whistles. At the absolute least, shoot vertically and steer clear of low-res images and videos. Videos created using the app's filters and camera effects typically receive an algorithmic boost while maintaining viewer engagement.

2.6.3.3. Avoid Reposting TikToks

Even though Instagram Reels were once a TikTok trick, they don't want to be reminded of it. Reposting watermarked TikTok videos as Reels will get you banned. These are the facts, so we're not just speculating. "Content that is obviously recycled from other apps (i.e., contains watermarks or logos) detracts from the enjoyment of the Reels," the company writes in a post. Consequently, we are reducing the discoverability of this content in areas such as the Reels tab."

2.6.3.4. Use the Right Hashtags

Especially on Reels, hashtags are a fantastic way for creators to find new content, so be sure to include a minimum of a few in the description of each Reel. Use precise and informative hashtags for the greatest possible reach. This way, the algorithm will have an easier time sharing your photo or post with people who are interested in the same subject as it does if it can determine what it is about. (In addition, hashtags are free, not like Instagram ads!).

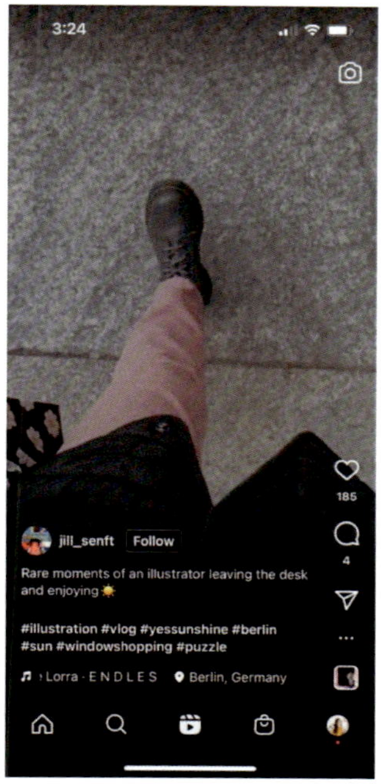

Instagram Reels allow for up to 30 hashtags, but according to Instagram best practices, using 3–5 thoughtfully selected hashtags will help you get the most out of them (our experiment, however, indicated the more hashtags you can use, the better). Use hashtags that accurately convey the topic of your post, do your homework, and investigate your niche communities.

2.6.3.5. Feature People in Your Reels

The social media team recently conducted an experiment to determine the engagement potential of Reels, and the results showed that Reels with human subjects perform remarkably well. Additionally, a video will be liked by the algorithm if users enjoy it. Though hyper-stylized product photos and illustrations can be entertaining, the Instagram audience is ultimately most entertained by faces.

2.6.3.6. Use Trending Music

Use a trending sound clip and the algorithm (or should we say… algor-rhythm) will reward you by spreading your Reel far and wide.

2.6.3.7. Create Content Outside of Reels, Too

The more Instagram content you share online—stories, posts, guides, and so forth—the greater the chance that someone will find you. Since the Instagram Reels algorithm is known to track your past interactions with other users, this is not surprising. The system will automatically show your most recent Reel to users who have been viewing your other Instagram posts.

2.6.3.8. Follow Instagram's Recommendation Guidelines

In its Recommendation Guidelines, Instagram explains how it chooses what and to whom to recommend. Think of this document as your social media code.

Instagram states that they "strive to avoid making recommendations that could be low-quality, objectionable, or sensitive, as well as recommendations that might be inappropriate for younger viewers."

For example, content that encourages self-harm, violence, or false information won't be recommended to someone. Play by Instagram's rules and maintain civility to maximize your reach.

2.6.3.9. Give the People What They Want

To better understand your audience and deliver content that resonates with them, use analytics. Reels analytics, which include performance metrics like reach, comments, and likes, are available to Business and Creator accounts on Instagram Insights.

There, you'll find detailed performance stats, including:

- Reach;
- Plays;
- Likes;
- Comments;
- Shares;
- Saves;
- Engagement rate.

Engagement reports for all your connected Instagram accounts now factor in Reels data.

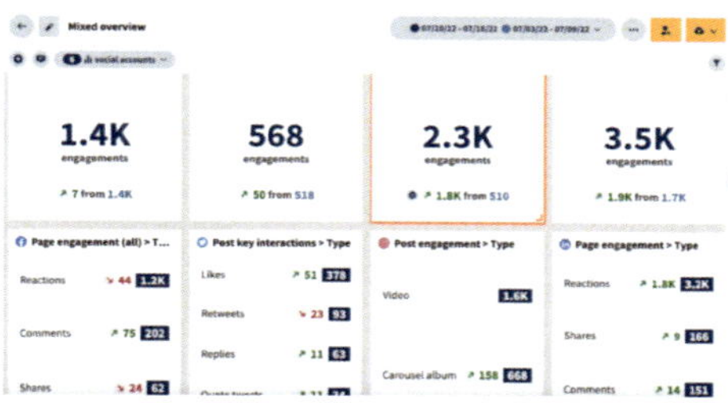

2.6.3.10. ...And When They Want It

It is imperative to post new content when the greatest number of your followers are online, as the Instagram Reels algorithm favors recent posts. Getting a spot on the Explore page requires achieving high engagement with your own followers, as we previously learned.

Here's how to schedule a Reel at the best possible time:

1. Record your video and edit it (adding sounds and effects) in the Instagram app.
2. Save the Reel to your device.
3. Tap the Create icon on the very top of the left-hand menu to open the Composer.
4. Select the Instagram Business account you want to publish your Reel to.
5. In the Content section, select Reels.

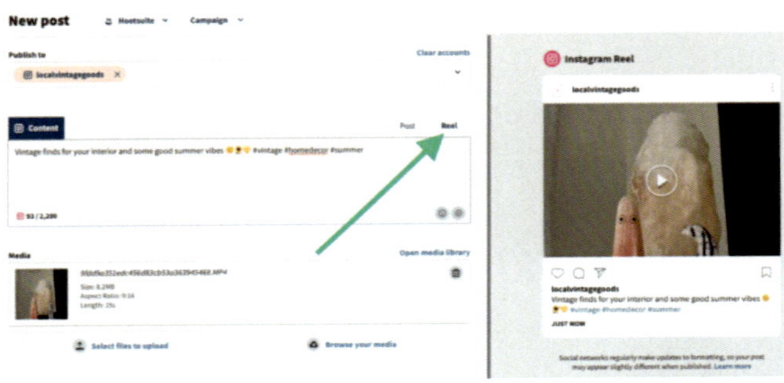

6. Upload the Reel you saved to your device. Videos must be between 5 seconds and 90 seconds long and have an aspect ratio of 9:16.
7. Add a caption. You can include emojis and hashtags, and tag other accounts in your caption.
8. Adjust additional settings. You can enable or disable comments, Stitches and Duets for each of your individual posts.
9. Preview your Reel and click Post now to publish it immediately, or…
10. …click Schedule for later to post your Reel at a different time. You can manually select a publication date or pick from three recommended custom best times to post for maximum engagement.

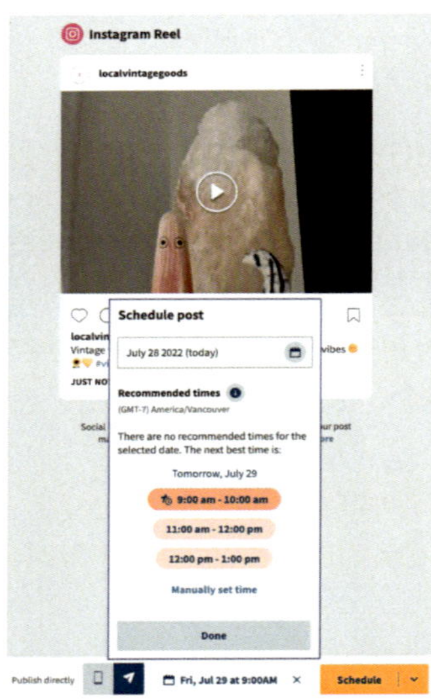

And that's it! Your Reel will show up in the Planner, alongside all of your other scheduled social media posts. From there, you can edit, delete or duplicate your Reel, or move it to drafts.

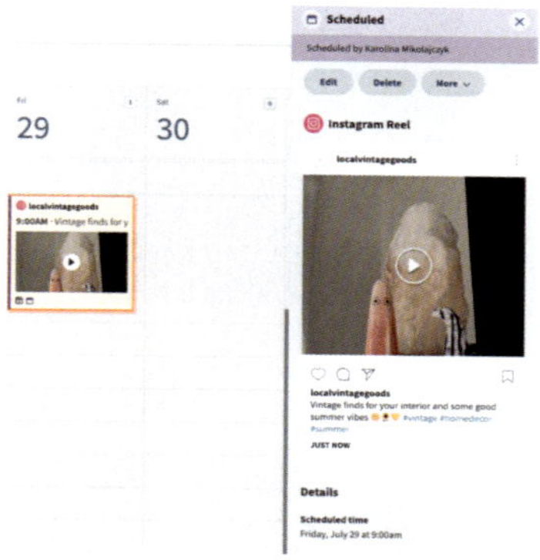

Once your Reel is published, it will appear in both your feed and the Reels tab on your account.

2.6.3.11. Cultivate an Active Community

Engaging your own brand community is the first step toward getting your Reels in front of valuable lookalike audiences on the Explore page. To be clear, this doesn't refer to shortcuts like purchasing followers or joining Instagram pods. Instead, it involves taking the time to engage authentically with others through comments and direct messages.

2.6.4. How to Download Instagram Reels?

To download a Reel on Instagram, take a look at the left-hand side of the screen: there, you'll see the "share" icon, which is shaped like a paper airplane.

Once you hit Share, a menu with lots of options pops up. **Download** is one of those options—to save the Reel to your camera roll, just tap that button.

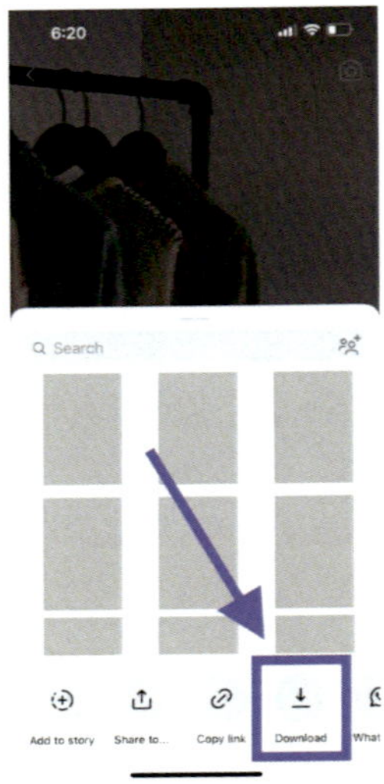

2.6.5. How Long Can Instagram Reels Be?

Reels created with Instagram's built-in Reel creator can have a duration of 15 to 90 seconds. However, all you need to do is use a third-party scheduling tool if you want to post Reels that are a little bit shorter—or much longer. Using Hootsuite, for instance, you can upload Reels to Instagram that are as short as three seconds or as long as 15 minutes.

It's best to use a different video editing app because, to be honest, Instagram's in-app video editor can be difficult to use (unless you have a small finger advantage). We've discovered that the ideal reel length for maximum engagement is between 7 and 15 seconds.

2.6.6. Instagram Reels Sizes

In a nutshell, Instagram Reels should have a 1080 x 1920 pixel resolution and a 9:16 aspect ratio. The unfortunate news is that Instagram Reels change in size based on the viewing orientation of the user. Only when the user is in Instagram's Reels section does the 9:16 ratio apply. The aspect ratio is 4:5 if the Reel appears in the Instagram newsfeed. This means that a portion of the video will be cropped out. When editing Reels, try to keep important content (like text) in the center of the screen to prevent this from happening.

2.6.7. How to Share a Reel on Instagram

Share because you care. There's lots of ways to pass on a great Reel, and all of them start with that little paper airplane icon in the bottom right of your screen.

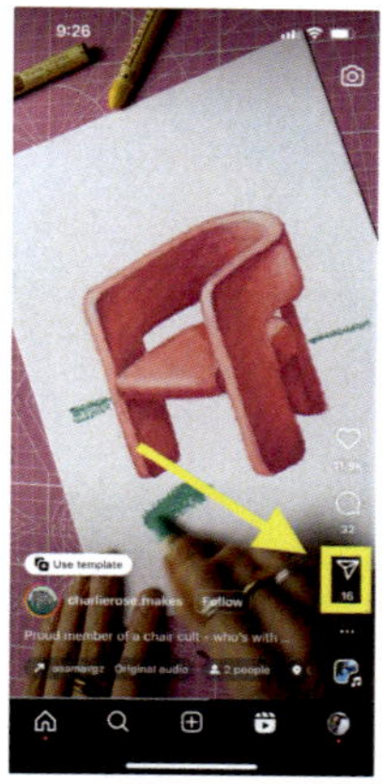

Once you tap that icon, you'll see suggestions to send the Reel as a direct message to people you commonly interact with on Instagram. You can also use the search bar to seek a specific user.

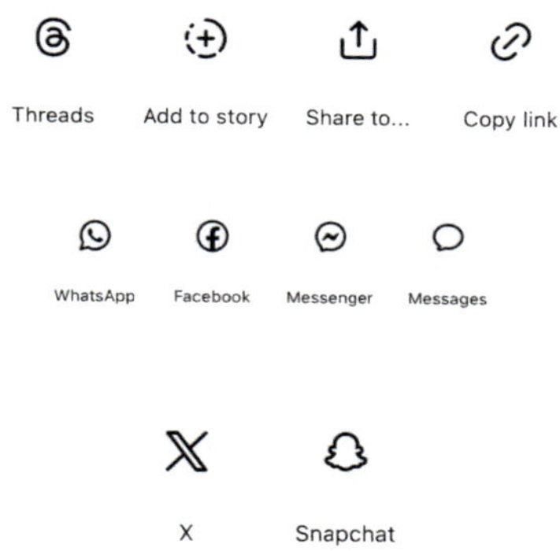

You can add the Reel to your story, post it to Threads, share it on Facebook, X (formerly Twitter), or Snapchat using the same menu. You can also choose to Copy the link and send it to anyone who has internet access. Your grandmother will be very happy to receive emails with links to all the Reels you enjoy.

2.6.8. Other Instagram Reels Tips

You know the basics, now it's time to get deep. Scroll on for advice that will make your Reels irresistible.

2.6.8.1. Adding Captions

Making your Reels' content caption-ready improves accessibility for all users.

You can use Reels' text editor to type your own captions, but it's much easier to use Instagram's caption generator instead. First, tap the sticker button located in the upper right corner of your Instagram Reel to enable automatic caption addition.

Then, select Captions.

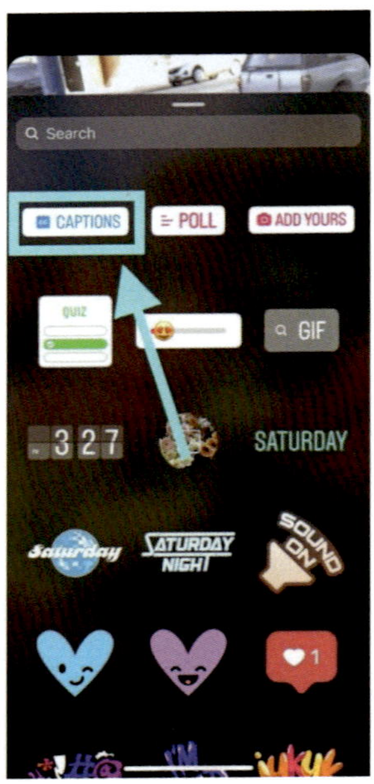

The captions will be automatically generated. Instagram is usually pretty good about interpreting audio…

...but if you need to adjust a word, just tap on it and use the keyboard to edit.

2.6.8.2. Boosting Reels

An adorable term for "turning a reel into an advertisement" is "boosting an Instagram reel." In essence, you can "boost" a reel by paying Instagram to display it to more users on a regular basis. You're spending money to make sure your Reel is seen, as opposed to relying solely on the Instagram algorithm.

Regretfully, no Instagram Reels with copyrighted music can be boosted. For any reel you want to promote, use royalty-free music or original audio.

Upload a reel to Instagram before trying to promote it there. Select the three dots located at the lower left corner of your screen.

Next, select Boost Reel.

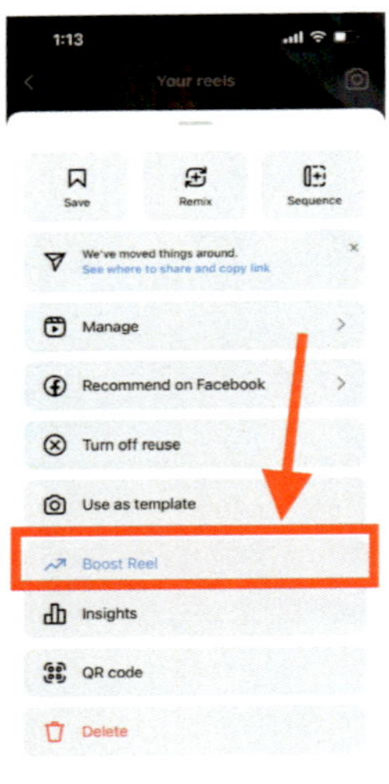

From there, you're able to choose the goal, audience, budget, and duration for your boosted Reel.

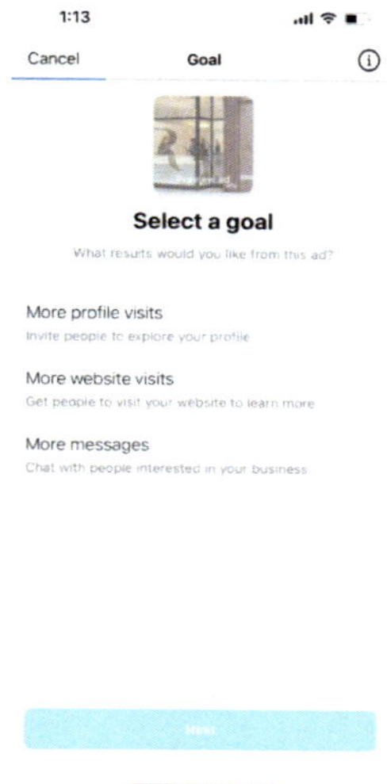

2.6.8.3. Scheduling Reels

As we mentioned above, scheduling Reels for the optimal post time is an excellent strategy for social media marketing (and it's also an excellent strategy for the sanity of a social media manager).

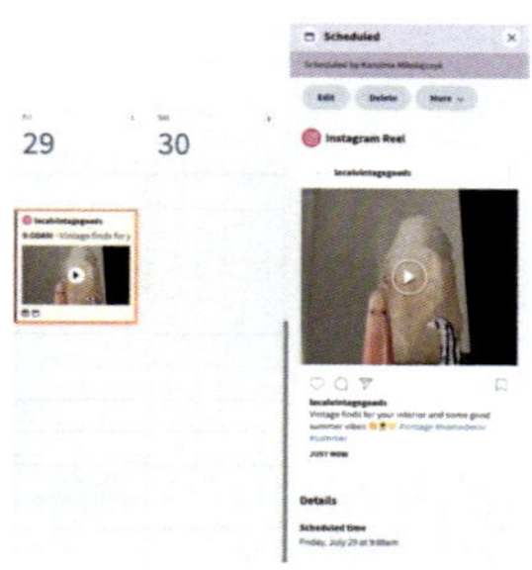

2.6.8.4. Using Great Hashtags

Hashtags can help you hack that pesky algorithm, and make it easier for you to reach your target audience.

2.6.8.5. Replying to a Comment with a Reel

Reacting to comments on Instagram with a Reel is one of the most entertaining ways to interact with your audience—on Instagram, engagement is everything. To use a Reel to respond to an Instagram comment, select the comment you wish to respond to first. In your Reel, this comment will show up as a sticker.

Hit Reply like you would to type a comment.

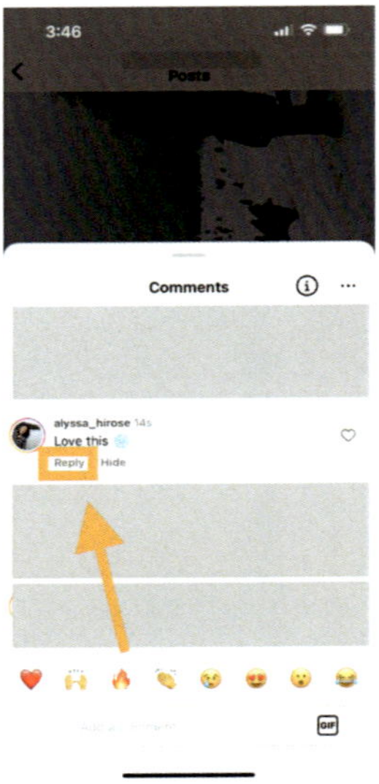

But instead of typing, tap the camera button.

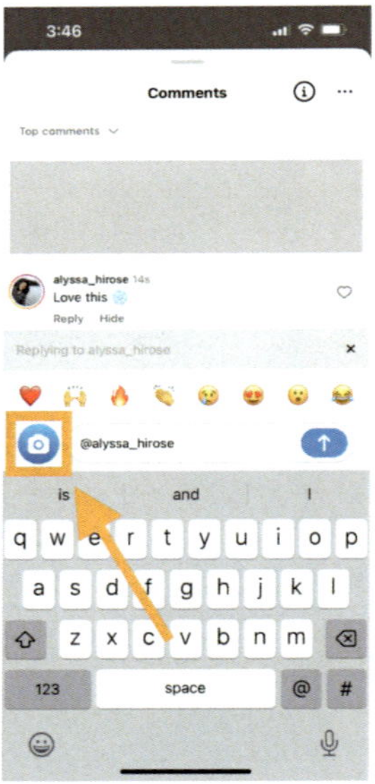

From there, Instagram will open the Reels editor and the sticker will automatically be part of the video.

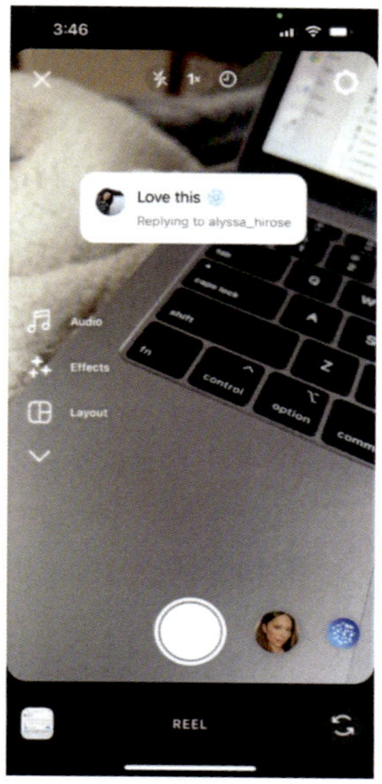

2.6.8.6. Splitting Clips on Reels

While entertaining viewers should be a reel's main objective, there are a lot of dull moments in real life. Here's how to split clips and remove anything unnecessary from your videos in order to edit out the least interesting parts.

In the Instagram Reels editor, tap Edit video.

Next, select Edit in the bottom left.

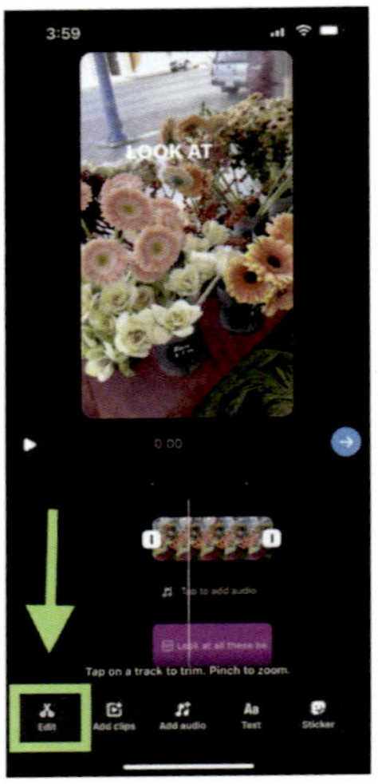

Locate the beginning of the section you want to omit or the point in the timeline where you'd like to split the clip. After positioning the playhead, which is a vertical line that indicates your current position in the video, to that location, choose Split.

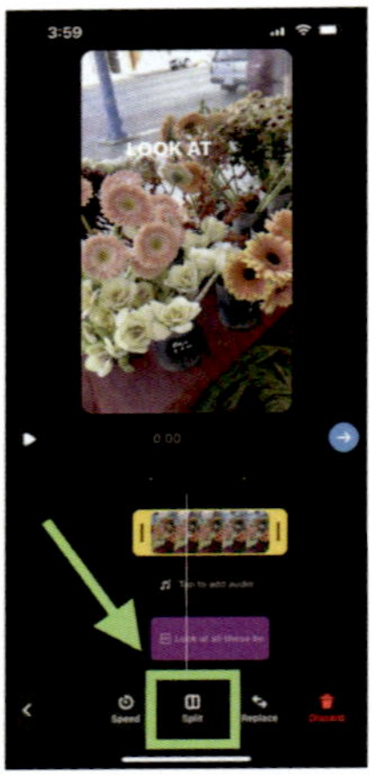

Next, advance the playhead to the next segment of the clip that you want to split (this would be the end of the segment you want to remove from the video, for example).

Now that your video has been divided into two parts, you have identified the portion you want to remove (we've circled it in blue in the image below). Click Delete to remove the clip.

2.6.8.7. Using Templates on Instagram Reels

Using a template rather than starting from scratch is one of the best ways to create Instagram Reels. Your chosen clips will be automatically edited by templates to a predetermined length that syncs with the audio. Here's a brief overview of one method, but there are other ways to find Reels templates on Instagram.

First, open up the Instagram Reels editor. Tap Templates at the bottom right.

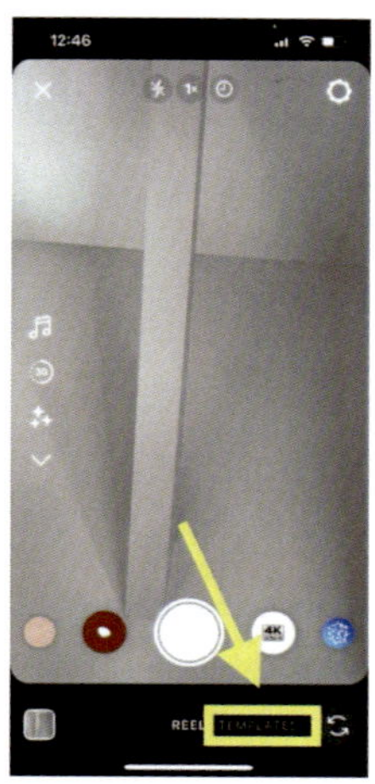

This will open up the Instagram Reels template library, where you can find templates that are trending and templates that Instagram think you'll like. Choose a template from this library.

From there, you can select the clips you'd like to use in the template by tapping Add media. Instagram will automatically trim the clips so they fit—and like magic, you're done.

- **Tip:** Instagram templates work best for aesthetic videos and general scenes/scenery—since IG does the clip-trimming for you, templates aren't as useful for clips that have a specific "good" part. For example, a long video of your dog catching a piece of popcorn might not work, as Instagram may cut out all the action.

2.6.8.8. Pay Attention to Reels Insights

Keep an eye on Instagram's insights to see how well your Reels are performing. With metrics like likes, shares, comments, and saves along with details about your audience and accounts reached, insights can offer insightful data and frank criticism that will help you refine your social media approach.

REFERENCES

1. Al-Bahrani, A. A., & Patel, D. (2014). Incorporating Twitter, Instagram, and Facebook in economics classrooms. *Journal of Economic Education, 66*(1). http://ssrn.com/abstract=2483255 (accessed on 9 October 2044).
2. Frier, S. (2020). *No filter: The inside story of Instagram*. Simon & Schuster. ISBN 978-1-9821-2680-3.
3. Hochman, N., & Manovich, L. (2013). Zooming into an Instagram city: Reading the local through social media. *First Monday, 18*(7).
4. Wasko, M. M., & Faraj, S. (2005). Why should I share? Examining social capital and knowledge contribution in electronic networks of practice. *MIS Quarterly, 29*(1).
5. Zwass, V. (2010). Co-creation: Toward a taxonomy and an integrated research perspective. *International Journal of Electronic Commerce, 15*(1).
6. Lagorio, C. (2011, June 27). Kevin Systrom and Mike Krieger, founders of Instagram. *Inc.* Retrieved October 4, 2011, from https://www.inc.com/ (accessed on 9 October 2044).
7. Bernstein, H. (2012, April 24). Photographers on Instagram. http://images.businessweek.com/slideshows/2012-04-23/photographers-oninstagram#slide7 (accessed on 9 October 2044).
8. Constine, J. (2017, June 20). Instagram Stories hits 250M daily users, adds Live video replays. *TechCrunch*. AOL. Retrieved June 20, 2017, from https://techcrunch.com/ (accessed on 9 October 2044).
9. Carman, A. (2020, August 19). Instagram rolls out suggested posts to keep you glued to your feed. *The Verge*. Retrieved May 5, 2021, from https://www.theverge.com/ (accessed on 9 October 2044).
10. Grothaus, M. (2020, August 20). How to disable 'Suggested Posts' on Instagram: You can't and here's why. *Fast Company*. Retrieved May 5, 2021, from https://www.fastcompany.com/ (accessed on 9 October 2044).
11. Carman, A. (2021, June 23). Instagram tests putting suggested posts ahead of your friends.' *The Verge*. Retrieved June 24, 2021, from https://www.theverge.com/ (accessed on 9 October 2044).

CHAPTER 3

TIKTOK ALGORITHM

Contents

Introduction 108

3.1. Overview of TikTok Algorithm 108

3.2. How to Make a Blue Search Comment on TikTok? 118

3.3. How to Get Unshadowbanned on TikTok? 119

3.4. Social Media and User-Generated Content (UGC) 122

References 134

INTRODUCTION

The content that appears on each user's For You page (FYP) is chosen by the sophisticated yet incredibly efficient TikTok algorithm. It uses machine learning to examine user interactions, preferences, and behavior in order to provide a tailored content experience. User interactions that indicate interest in particular types of content, likes, shares, comments, and watch time, are among the many factors taken into account by the algorithm. In order to align content with user interests, it also considers video metadata, such as hashtags, sounds, and captions. To further improve content recommendations, TikTok also keeps track of account and device settings, such as preferred language and location. As a user's preferences change, the content they see also changes because the algorithm is always learning and adapting. Because even inexperienced content creators can become highly visible if their work strikes a chord with a large audience, this dynamic personalization helps to keep users engaged while also fostering the viral nature of content on the platform. TikTok has experienced rapid growth and widespread popularity, largely due to its algorithm's ability to recognize and promote trending content and its emphasis on user engagement.

3.1. OVERVIEW OF TIKTOK ALGORITHM

A complex system called the TikTok algorithm customizes content for every user. It drives the Explore Page and the For You Page (FYP), influencing how users interact with the platform. Based on your previous interactions, the FYP recommends videos to you, and the Explore Page introduces you to new artists and trends. The algorithm depends on machine learning. The more likes, shares, and comments you make on TikTok, the more the algorithm learns about your preferences and improves its suggestions. Everything a user does on the app is analyzed, including the accounts they follow and the amount of time they spend on each video. This implies that as your tastes and emotional state evolve, so too may the kinds of videos you view. Your behavioral changes will be quickly detected by the TikTok algorithm, which will then suggest the most relevant content for you at that particular moment.

3.1.1. TikTok for You Page (FYP)

When users launch the app, the first screen they see is the TikTok for You Page (FYP). Based on each user's interests and past interactions, TikTok's algorithm curates a personalized feed full of videos it thinks will interest them. Users find new and popular videos on it, which makes it a great place for brands looking to get noticed. Businesses must have an appearance on the FYP in order to reach a more specialized and larger audience. Without the need for sponsored advertisements, it significantly increases reach and engagement. This exposure can result in a quick increase in followers, revenue opportunities, and brand awareness. Every user's FYP is unique due to its high degree of personalization. Brands want to appear on the front of prospective customers' minds, which means they need to produce content that appeals to their target market.

3.1.1.1. How Does for You Page (FYP) Work?

TikTok's algorithm powers the For You Page, sifting through a multitude of signals and interactions (more on these a little later) to find videos that users might find interesting. To view content that is relevant to their interests, TikTok users can choose to filter what shows up on their FYP.

In order to help the algorithm better understand users' preferences, TikTok even encourages users to share their feedback. Additionally, users have the option to restart their For You feed and sign up again, just like they did when they first downloaded the app.

A video is first shown by the algorithm to a narrow audience when it is first published. These users are selected according to their interests; they may not be followers of the creator. The video is then screened for a wider audience if the group's comments are favorable.

This cycle continues, enabling videos to go viral and show up on users' For You Pages. TikTok's adaptive algorithm ensures that trending and relevant content is always in front of the right audience.

3.1.2. Key Factors Influencing the TikTok Algorithm

Comprehending the elements that impact the TikTok algorithm is crucial to optimizing your visibility and interaction on the platform. You can increase the likelihood that your content will go viral and reach a wider audience by understanding the factors that influence the algorithm. Let's explore the factors that influence the TikTok algorithm to help you optimize your TikTok strategy.

3.1.2.1. User Interactions

1. **Engagement:** The TikTok algorithm is largely driven by engagement, which has a big impact on your videos' visibility and reach. The algorithm recognizes signals of high-quality content when users interact with a video by liking, sharing, commenting, or watching it through to the end. Videos that receive a lot of interaction have a higher chance of being featured on the For You Page (FYP), which opens up new viewers for them.

Videos with high completion rates are given priority by the algorithm because it shows that the viewers find the content interesting. The video's chances of getting broader exposure are further increased by shares and comments, which demonstrate active user interest and interaction. Because the algorithm rewards content creators who regularly create interesting videos, regular interaction with your content can also result in a growth in the number of followers. In practical terms, this means that the content you post on TikTok must provoke an emotional response. It's not enough to just land on a user's front end—you also need to engage them in some way with the video. Make sure your TikTok videos have a call to action, conduct a live Q&A session, and concentrate on producing material that is simple for other users to remix.

2. **Video Completion Rate:** Another significant metric in the TikTok algorithm that affects how content is promoted on the platform is the video completion rate. The algorithm receives feedback from users who watch a video through to the end, indicating that the material is interesting and should be shared with more people. This high completion rate suggests that viewers find the video engaging from beginning to end, increasing the likelihood that they will suggest it to other users on their For You pages. Videos with high completion rates are given priority on TikTok because they improve user experience by exposing users to engaging content.

3. **User Feedback:** To evaluate the caliber and applicability of content, the algorithm keeps a close eye on a variety of user interactions. The algorithm is informed that content is relevant and of high quality when users like, share, or comment on videos. Engagement is defined as positive feedback.

   Negative comments, however, also have an impact on the algorithm. Users indicate that a video is less engaging if they quickly swipe away, mark the video as Not Interested, or hide content from a specific creator. After that, the algorithm makes it less visible. In addition, TikTok tracks actions taken by users after watching a video, such as following the creator. Videos that have high engagement rates and positive feedback are more likely to gain traction and become viral. The user-selected content preference settings are also taken into account by the algorithm. TikToks that contain specific keywords will not appear in their personalized feeds if they have filtered those keywords.

3.1.2.2. Video Information

1. **Content Quality:** Because they grab viewers' attention and promote interaction, original, high-quality videos with crisp images, clear audio, and compelling storytelling are given preference by the TikTok algorithm. Engaging content that is well-produced does well on the platform, rewarding content creators who take the time to make visually appealing videos. Originality holds equal significance. Content that is original and creative stands out and is more likely to be liked and shared. In order to help original content reach a wider audience, the algorithm gives priority to innovative concepts and eye-catching styles. TikTok's algorithm may even exclude poor quality content from the For You Page since it doesn't perform well there. This covers content that has been copied and plagiarized as well as low-effort material that merely remixes current concepts and fashions without contributing anything new.
2. **Search Value/Trending Topics:** Trending topics and search value are two more crucial metrics for the TikTok algorithm. We look through every video to find out what kind of content it contains—hashtags, captions, even audio. Captions and hashtags with relevant keywords will aid the algorithm in deciphering the purpose of the video and the intended audience. Popular sounds are essential to the visibility of videos. You can improve your chances of showing up on users' "For You" pages by using well-liked audio clips. Videos that use popular sounds are often promoted by the TikTok algorithm, which aids in their increased popularity. But remember that uniqueness and high-quality content are still crucial. It's not enough to simply follow the latest trends; your TikToks should provide an original interpretation of them. One company that frequently uses social media trends to promote its products is Rare Beauty. They received 2.4 million views by promoting their new TikTok shop by participating in the POV trend. They made sure that their audience was informed of the new method to shop for Rare Beauty products in addition to producing a viral video.
3. **Performance Metrics:** Every video's performance metrics are gathered by the TikTok algorithm. The algorithm will interpret a video as valuable and engaging if it garners a high level of engagement during its initial showing to a small target audience. Likes, shares, and watch time are the three most significant performance metrics for the TikTok algorithm. Early success with a video increases the likelihood that it will be promoted further and seen by more people.

The algorithm keeps track of interactions, and as more people interact with the video, it becomes more popular and visible. Elevated levels of engagement imply that the content is meaningful to the audience, which is why the algorithm gives it top priority.

4. **Captions and Hashtags:** By classifying your content with popular and relevant hashtags, you can reach a larger audience. This increases the discoverability of your video and aids the algorithm in comprehending its context. The same is true for the captions, which ought to contain pertinent keywords that highlight the video's theme. In videos, text overlay is handled similarly to hashtags and captions.
5. **Content Diversity:** TikTok has stated that their goal is to expose their users to diverse content in order to avoid repetition on the FYPs and keep the users' feeds fresh, despite the fact that their algorithm is well-known for displaying users the kinds of content they have expressed interest in. As a matter of fact, according to a recent survey, 44% of TikTok users had opened the app expecting to find something specific, but instead had found something completely different.

Because of the layout of TikTok's feed, users frequently come across unexpected and entertaining content. TikTok's potential as a discovery engine, where creators share uncommon interests and helpful advice, is exemplified by hashtags like newfinds and tiktoktaughtme. TikTok creates a mix of familiar and novel content to pique users' interest, encourage viral trends, and broaden cultural awareness.

3.1.2.3. Device and Account Settings

1. **Language and Location:** The location of your account and your preferred language are taken into account by TikTok's algorithm. After that, it can deliver content based on your language preferences, making sure that users see videos that are easy to understand. Setting locations are just as crucial. TikTok makes region- and culturally-specific video recommendations based on geolocation data. This increases the likelihood that users will see content from producers in their own nation or area, which personalizes and engages the feed. It's critical for brands and creators to comprehend these factors. Developing content that is appropriate for the language and cultural quirks of their intended audience can greatly increase exposure and interaction. Material can resonate more deeply and have a higher chance of being promoted by the algorithm by utilizing local trends and cultural allusions.

2. **Device Type:** While device type information is not as important as some of the other metrics discussed earlier, the algorithm still considers it when determining which videos to recommend to FYPs. It takes into account the operating system and kind of device being used, such as a tablet or smartphone. By using this data, TikTok is able to maximize video performance and compatibility while guaranteeing a flawless viewing experience for its users. The processing power and screen resolution of various devices can vary, which has an impact on how videos are shown. TikTok can improve user satisfaction by customizing playback settings and video quality based on the type of device.
3. **User Preferences:** The TikTok algorithm is heavily influenced by user preferences and interactions, which shapes the content that shows up on each user's For You Page. Participating—liking, sharing, leaving comments, etc.) with particular kinds of videos instructs the algorithm to display more of that kind of information, resulting in a customized feed.

   However, users can help refine these recommendations by marking videos as Not Interested and filtering keywords to only show them content that they will find interesting. This dynamic system makes sure that the content displayed changes with the preferences of the user.

3.1.3. How to go Viral on TikTok?

A lot of people who create content want to know how to get a TikTok to go viral. However, as anyone who has inadvertently become viral on the platform can attest, success is not a given. Nevertheless, there are actions that you and other content producers can take to increase the likelihood of engagement and make sure that as many people as possible see your videos.

Here are a few things you should do to give your content the best chance to go viral:

3.1.3.1. Find Your Niche

Even though you may already know the kind of content you want to publish, it may not be what viewers are interested in seeing. If, for instance, your audience seems to be drawn to your college-related stories, despite your intense excitement for a scripted miniseries, consider turning those stories into scripted skits. The subject matter, duration, style, and timing of your videos all affect how viewers will interact with your material. Take your time experimenting with your content to discover your niche and gauge audience response in order to identify the best TikTok content ideas for you.

3.1.3.2. Post Consistently

Posting 1–4 times a day is recommended by TikTok while you figure out what kinds of content work best for you. Regular posting keeps readers interested and improves the likelihood that something will work well.

3.1.3.3. Use Trends to Your Advantage

It appears that content that aligns with current trends is prioritized by the algorithm. To join an already-thriving pool and improve your chances of showing up on other users' FYP TikTok feeds, use popular sounds or hashtags.

3.1.3.4. Use Accurate Keywords and Hashtags in Your Captions

A portion of the recommendation system is dependent on the content description. While a detailed synopsis is not necessary, the description should contain pertinent keywords to aid the algorithm in determining the appropriate placement for your video. However, if a trending hashtag has nothing to do with your post, don't include it just for the sake of including it.

3.1.3.5. Make Your Content Accessible

When editing your final video, don't forget to include your own captions or use the ones TikTok automatically generates. Users who have trouble hearing won't waste time attempting to interact with your content if they can't understand it.

3.1.3.6. Catch Viewers' Attention ASAP

Users are unlikely to stick with a video if they aren't immediately interested in it. To improve the likelihood that they will watch the entire video, grab their attention as soon as possible.

3.1.3.7. Interact With Your Audience

Make sure to get your name out there by leaving comments on other creators' videos and stitching or duetting content that speaks to you, as the algorithm appears to reward users who are very active. To foster community and boost engagement, reply to your viewers' comments.

3.1.3.8. Switch to a Pro Account

TikTok Pro provides information about your content that a standard account does not. Better understanding of content performance and viewer engagement is made possible as a result. You can monitor the effectiveness of your strategies and make required adjustments by keeping a long-term track of your numbers. By using these tactics, you might have a chance to get past the TikTok algorithm, figure out how to make a viral video, and become the internet celebrity of your desires.

3.1.4. TikTok Algorithm Updates and What the Future Holds

Algorithms are always changing to adapt to new developments in technology and user behavior. TikTok is no different, so let's examine the most recent adjustments it made as well as those that are still pending.

3.1.4.1. Recent TikTok Algorithm Updates

TikTok made major algorithmic changes in August 2023, especially for users in the European Union (EU). The goal of these modifications is to improve user control and privacy in response to the Digital Services Act (DSA). The customized content recommendation feature on TikTok is now optional for users in the EU. Alternatively, users have the option to select from a timeline of accounts they follow or well-liked local videos. This is a significant departure from TikTok's standard algorithm, which heavily customizes the For You Page (FYP) based on user behavior.

Instead of showing content based on algorithmic recommendations, users can now view content in the chronological feed option. By doing this, users have more control over what they see and TikTok's algorithm has less of an impact on their watching preferences. TikTok has also made more information about its algorithmic process available. The platform will now provide researchers with access to its data so they can examine it and gain insight into its methods for recommending content. TikTok has also expanded the options available to users for reporting objectionable content, resulting in a safer and more user-friendly platform. TikTok is also required by the DSA to prohibit targeted ads to users who are younger than 17. This action is intended to safeguard the mental health and privacy of younger users by preventing them from being exposed to offensive content or advertising tactics. TikTok revealed a second change to its content strategy later that year, encouraging creators to make longer videos. The platform's initial short-form video format was significantly altered by this shift, which aided in its quick ascent to popularity.

3.1.4.2. What's Next for the TikTok Algorithm?

TikTok is experimenting with a new feature that will let users post videos up to 60 minutes long, departing from the platform's focus on short-form content. There are currently no plans for a wider rollout; this trial feature is only available to a limited number of users. This action is perceived as a tactic to rival YouTube and entice users to spend more time on TikTok by providing a variety of content options. Extended video features have the potential to change the TikTok content scene by drawing content creators and viewers who want to watch more in-depth videos. Matt Navarra, a social media consultant, points out that platforms such as Netflix may be able to use this feature to directly promote longer content on TikTok. The platform's algorithm will keep adapting to user preferences as it develops, offering either short-form or long-form videos depending on specific interests.

The change comes as TikTok faces uncertain prospects in the U.S. due to a bill signed by President Biden that could ban the app if its parent company, ByteDance, doesn't divest its stake. TikTok and ByteDance have filed a lawsuit against the U.S., challenging the law's constitutionality.

Additionally, Reuters reported that TikTok is developing a separate recommendation algorithm for its 170 million U.S. users to operate independently from its Chinese counterpart, Douyin, in a bid to assuage U.S. lawmakers' fears over data privacy and security.

This would entail separating millions of lines of code and creating a separate code base for US consumers. TikTok has denied these claims, stating that the project would be impossible to complete within the given timeframe.

3.1.5. Factors That Don't Influence the TikTok Algorithm

Gaining an understanding of the TikTok algorithm is essential for making effective use of the platform; however, it's equally crucial to know what doesn't affect the algorithm. While many brands and creators may believe that certain factors influence their TikTok visibility and engagement, the algorithm's recommendations are not affected by these factors.

3.1.5.1. Follower Count

Although having a lot of followers may seem like a big deal on social media, TikTok's algorithm isn't directly impacted by it. The recommendation system on TikTok places more emphasis on how users engage with the content than how many followers a creator has. This implies that if an account has a small following and their videos effectively engage viewers, they can still become viral.

3.1.5.2. Account Age

Account age is not taken into account by TikTok's algorithm. No matter how long an account has been active, the recommendation system is made to highlight content that is engaging. This implies that the likelihood of new accounts becoming viral is equal to that of more established ones.

3.1.5.3. Previous Viral Videos

It's a common misconception that having viral videos on your profile will increase your chances of being promoted by the algorithm. However, this isn't the case. The TikTok algorithm evaluates every video on its own, giving more weight to the video's performance metrics right now than to the account's historical achievements.

3.1.6. What the TikTok Algorithm Doesn't Show?

To make sure you don't keep seeing the same videos or videos you've explicitly expressed disinterest in, TikTok filters some content from appearing on your For You page in an effort to continuously improve the user experience. That means the TikTok algorithm will not recommend the following types of videos:

- Content you've already watched;
- Spam content;
- Duplicate content;
- Content you've marked as "Not Interested;"
- Potentially harmful/upsetting content;
- Low-quality content;
- Content that promotes dangerous stunts or risky behavior;
- Graphic content;
- Content that violates community guidelines.

Upholding an upbeat and interesting atmosphere is very important to TikTok. This means that any content that encourages hate speech, disinformation, or discrimination of any kind is quickly taken down.

Videos that don't effectively engage users—like those with low completion rates or little interaction—are also given less priority on the platform.

3.2. HOW TO MAKE A BLUE SEARCH COMMENT ON TIKTOK?

It's likely that you've noticed a lot of blue comments under videos when recently scrolling through TikTok. If you want to join in on the blue comment action, you've come to the right place; we'll explain what these comments are all about and tell you how to make your comments go blue on your favorite creator's videos. These comments link to a search page, but how are people doing that?

3.2.1. Identify Important Keywords Used in a Video

TikTok highlights in blue words and phrases that are pertinent to the video. Thus, pay close attention to the creator's words and phrases throughout the entire video, as they may be related to the content. Next, search for any text that appears in the hashtags, caption, and video itself. It also helps to look at the terms and expressions that other commenters frequently use.

- For example, if you're watching someone do a red-carpet fashion review, relevant keywords might be the event name, the notable celebrities at the event, the fashion designers, the films or TV shows the celebrities are in, and "red-carpet" or "fashion review."
- Select well-known videos to make your comment more likely to appear blue. TikTok can better assess whether your keywords are relevant to the video by looking through more data from videos with a high number of views and comments.

3.2.2. Type the Keywords and Phrases into a Comment

All you need to do is copy and paste the pertinent words and phrases related to your video into a comment. You are welcome to leave a brief remark about the video or to include more in-depth analysis of the words or phrases that are pertinent.

- If the video has a suggested search at the top of the comments, copy that into your comment.

- Likewise, if other comments have blue text, use those words and phrases in your comment.
- For example, on a video about crocheting a sweater, you might comment "Crochet sweater tutorial" or "Your crochet sweater tutorials are so easy to follow, I've loved every one that I've made! I'm going to try this pattern ASAP."

3.2.3. Check Back on Your Comment after a Few Minutes

While you wait, check out some other videos on TikTok. Your comment won't turn blue right away. After that, return to the video and locate your feedback. The words in your comment will now be blue with a tiny magnifying glass next to them if TikTok determined that they were relevant to the video.

- TikTok directs you to the phrase's search results when you click on the blue text. You will see more videos about rollerskating when you click on your blue text, which is "rollerskating."

3.2.4. TikTok Chooses to Turn Comments Blue Based on Their Algorithm

There isn't a button or additional symbol available for you to use at this time to make your comments blue. Rather, TikTok uses an algorithm to make comments blue if words are frequently searched, used a lot, or have some relevance to the video.

- Although leaving pertinent keyword comments on well-liked videos increases the likelihood of getting blue comments, this isn't a foolproof strategy. Your comments may turn blue or not at different times.

3.2.5. Blue Comments Link to a Search for the Word or Phrase on TikTok

TikTok is currently testing an internal search feature that looks like these comments. The blue text in the comments leads to a word search related to the video's content. This is meant to increase the reach and views of content creators and assist users in discovering more content that interests them.

3.3. HOW TO GET UNSHADOWBANNED ON TIKTOK?

If your TikTok account isn't receiving any likes, views, or traffic to your videos, it could be because you posted something that violated the community guidelines and was shadowbanned. However, what is a shadowban and how can one be lifted?

3.3.1. What Is a Shadowban on TikTok?

Like every other social media platform, there are rules that you need to follow, and breaking those rules can get you banned. Similar to a ban, a shadowban is only in effect for a short period of time—roughly two weeks—and you are not informed that you are under one.

- It's also known as ghost banning or stealth banning.

  It's an automatic process done by TikTok's algorithm in order to protect other TikTok users from spam, copyright issues, and adult content. A shadowban will hurt your content in search results and keep it from appearing on the For You page or in hashtag results.

  TikTok doesn't tell you if you're shadowbanned, but there are a few indicators that you can look out for. In addition to your videos not showing up in hashtag search results or on the For You page, you'll also notice that, in comparison to your popularity, you're not gaining any new followers and that, on average, your videos are receiving very few views, comments, or likes.
- By having a friend (someone with a different TikTok account) search for your videos using the platform's search function, you can determine whether you've been shadowbanned. You may have been shadowbanned if your videos and account are not at the top of search results.

3.3.1.1. Getting Unshadowbanned

1. **Delete Your Most Recent Video:** After you uninstall and reinstall TikTok, you can repost the video if you are certain it does not violate any policies or guidelines.
- The most recent video you uploaded may have been the reason behind your initial shadowban once you become aware that you have been shadowbanned.
2. **Uninstall and Reinstall TikTok:** It may occasionally be necessary to update the app in order to remove your shadowban; in these cases, reinstalling it might be helpful.
3. **Switch to a Pro Account:** You can omit this step if you already have a Pro account. To track the effectiveness of your content, a Pro account provides insights and analytics. These tools make it simple to keep an eye on your audience reach and level of engagement.

- To do this, open TikTok, tap Profile > ☰ > Settings and privacy > Manage account > Switch to Pro account.
- You may have been shadowbanned if you observe an abrupt decline in your audience. Conversely, a steady decline in viewers may indicate that fewer people are watching.

4. **Delete Potentially Offensive Content:** Please remove any videos you uploaded that violate the community guidelines and rules. A shadowban cannot be removed until all of those videos are removed from your account.

- Your account could receive warnings about videos that violate community guidelines (in which case the offending videos won't be visible at all) or it could be permanently banned if you don't remove any that break TikTok's rules.
- Most videos that are considered "controversial" may be considered "offensive" to others.

5. **Post Original, Innovative Content That Follows Community Guidelines:** Post videos that don't include:

- hate speech
- copyrighted music (these can result in DMCA takedowns or content ID matches)
- inappropriate content (like drugs, fake news, and nudity)
- violence to anyone
- abuse of minors.
- Keeping up with trends will help you keep your content relevant. You can try to create more videos that are similar by using your Pro account to see which videos are hits and popular.

6. **Don't Spam Videos:** The TikTok algorithm has the ability to flag your activity as spammy and initiate a shadowban if you are active more frequently than usual. In order to prevent being marked as spam, try to upload no more than one video each day.

- Activity like you commenting or liking other videos might be seen as spammy, so you can take it slow on that end too.

7. **Update Your Profile and Description:** Verify that your bio does not contain any vulgar or offensive language, such as swear words. Use polite language at all times because the algorithm isn't smart enough to recognize irony and may misunderstand certain things.

8. **Check Your Profile Picture:** If your TikTok profile picture includes violent or sexual imagery, it can result in you getting shadowbanned.

- To change your TikTok profile picture, open TikTok, tap Profile > Edit Profile > Change photo.

3.4. SOCIAL MEDIA AND USER-GENERATED CONTENT (UGC)

Social media is used by brands to educate consumers about their goods or to foster a relationship between them and their customers (Ibrahim et al., 2020). "A group of Internet-based applications that build on the ideological and technological foundations of Web 2.0, and that allow the creation and exchange of user-generated content" is how Kaplan and Haenlein define social media. Social media brands are now inconsistent. A place designed for people to enjoy, connect, and share has been commercialized by the brands (Kaplan and Haenlein, 2010). Tiago and Verissimo (2014) claim that social media has enabled people to build international communities, freely exchange information, and find amusement in one another. The various social media channels assist customers in researching possible brands and their offerings. The writers also clarify that customers have the ability to impart information and experiences that shape their own opinions. From a branding standpoint, social media offers the ability to communicate with customers. These days, relationships are two-sided, with consumers and brands communicating with each other and potentially having conversations. Social media-savvy brands can now analyze customer feedback and gain deeper insights into their target audience (Tiago and Verissimo, 2014). Facebook and Instagram to determine which content significantly influences the behavior of users.

Content created by users on the platforms and content generated by brands (Djafarova and Bowes, 2021; Djafarova and Rushworth, 2017; Mayrhofer et al., 2019). TikTok is not like Instagram in two aspects. The first distinction is that content on TikTok is exclusively available as videos, most of which are based on songs or recordings. This sound clip can be a song snippet, dialogue from a TV show or movie, or user-generated sounds that have been shared. TikTok employs hashtags in a manner similar to Instagram's. But the use of sounds is the platform's main feature. Trends that originate from sound compositions and are frequently replicated by thousands of people have a significant impact on the TikTok app (Haenlein et al., 2020). Additionally, there are two primary formats in which the content is offered on TikTok compared to Instagram. Content that the TikTok artificial intelligence algorithm believes the user is likely to enjoy is displayed in the feed named "For You." The user can view content from other users they have followed on the app in the other feed called "Following." Although users can follow others on TikTok, compared to Instagram, it has been observed that these users are less likely to be social connections, like family and friends. As such, TikTok is more akin to YouTube, where users watch content provided by creators who are unknown to them offline, rather than Instagram and other social media platforms like Facebook (Haenlein et al., 2020).

One where customers own the power and use their own content to determine marketing outcomes. User-generated content has become a major online force since the advent of social media. According to O'hern and Kahle (2013), user-generated content refers to the unique contributions that users make. These are communicated with other users or businesses through a variety of media formats, including sound recordings, social media posts, videos, and reviews (O'hern and Kahle, 2013; Hanus, 2013). According to Mayrhofer et al., (2019) and Yu and Yuan (2019) media outlets have begun to emphasize the importance and value of brand related UGC, and often recommend that companies try to encourage their consumers to create content on their behalf. The reasoning is partially due to UGC being much cheaper to accomplish, but also stated to be more effective than traditional marketing (Dunn & Harness, 2018). It has been concluded that user-generated content blends in more seamlessly with other content on social media, therefore, is seen as effective (Mayrhofer et al., 2019). According to Ashley & Tuten (2014), consumers that are engaged with a brand often participate and share social content, such as consumer-generated stories. Consumers now share their opinions on products and brands with their personal network on social media platforms.

		User Contribution Objective	
		Product Promotion	Product Innovation
Direction of UGC Knowledge Flows	C2C Knowledge Row	Informing	Pioneering
	C2B Knowledge Row		Co-Creating

Figure 3.1. *The typology of user-generated content.*

Source: https://researchportal.hkr.se/ws/portalfiles/portal/44152590/Grupp16_Handley_Kobiela.pdf.

The "typology of UCG" (Figure 3.1) was developed to distinguish between the various types of user-generated content and to describe the potential advantages and/or difficulties associated with each kind. The term "user-generated content" is broad and used to characterize a variety of distinct phenomena. The purpose for which UGC is created is described by the term "objectives." Furthermore, the post's target group is defined by the knowledge flows (O'hern and Kahle, 2013).

In their 2013 study, O'hern and Kahle distinguished four categories of UGC, observing that these varied in two distinct ways (Figure 3.1). The creation of user-generated content (UGC) is driven by two primary objectives: firstly, to promote products and brands by showcasing their advantages and disadvantages; and secondly, to stimulate additional user-generated content. A desire for new products is the second factor that has been found to explain why UGC is produced. This goal is driven more by the desire to develop their own product or to enhance an already-existing one than by the desire to promote. The path of knowledge flows resulting from the UGC process is shown in the second dimension. In order to reach other users and offer suggestions, fresh perspectives, or product designs, user-generated social media content and product reviews are intended. Information flows from customer to customer (C2C). Instead of focusing on other users, some content is made by users specifically to share knowledge with a business. The dimension is described by the authors as customer-to-business (C2B) knowledge flows because of the particular kind of user-generated content. Informing, pioneering, co-communicating, and co-creating are the four categories of user-generated content (UGC) that were distinguished using these dimensions (O'hern and Kahle, 2013).

When a user posts something that compliments or criticizes a brand or product and targets other customers, that content is considered informative. According to a study by Jonas (2010), younger consumers regarded brand-generated content as less credible than informative user-generated content. Furthermore, product reviews are one type of media content that O'Hern and Kahle (2013) identified as brand-related user-generated content. Additionally, Cheng and Ho (2015) state that a review's perceived value is correlated with the author's experience and number of followers. Research has shown that a review's perceived credibility and trustworthiness have a positive impact. This can be achieved by building a larger following or demonstrating a well-established level of expertise in the subject matter (Cheng and Ho, 2015).

UGC influences consumer decision-making and is viewed as more credible when posted by common people rather than celebrities, claim Muda and Hamzah (2021). The statement's primary justification is that users who come across user-generated content (UGC) can relate to the content and creator because of the similarities in their own lives. The authors also mentioned that customers who have a sense of community with the UGC find it easier to make decisions about what to buy. When someone shares needs and opinions related to a product, for instance, a user searching for that product is more likely to view that person as credible and trustworthy. Investigating the account of the UGC poster also helps the viewers gain credibility. According to Muda and Hamzah (2021) the viewer's perception of credibility may be bolstered by learning more about the posting individual's preferences, personality, and values through perusing their profile. Muda and Hamzah (2021) also discovered that a favorable attitude toward the user-generated content viewed increases the likelihood of word-of-mouth spreading on social media. When the credibility and trustworthiness of the video are higher, viewers are more inclined to share it with others (Muda & Hamza, 2021). Moreover, Davcik and associates. According to (2022), users of social media engage with user-generated content by liking, commenting on, and forwarding posts to others.

3.4.1. TikTok Usage

TikTok has quickly risen to prominence as one of the most widely used social media sites globally, especially with younger users. Users of the app can make, share, and find short films—which are usually accompanied by music or sound bites—on the app. Users can easily create engaging content with it thanks to its variety of creative tools, which include editing features, effects, and filters. TikTok's highly personalized For You page is well-known for keeping users interested and promoting longer interaction times by curating a stream of videos based on individual preferences through an algorithm. In addition to providing entertainment, TikTok has evolved into a forum for activism, education, and marketing, with companies using the app to connect with new customers. The core elements of the TikTok experience are challenges, hashtags, and viral trends, which frequently result in high participation and quick content distribution. A sense of connection and engagement is fostered by the community-driven nature of the platform, where users can readily interact, collaborate, and respond to others' content. TikTok is becoming a major player in the social media scene as its influence on popular culture, consumer behavior, and digital communication increases with its continued evolution.

3.4.2. Perception of UGC

Individual differences were observed in the participants' perceptions of user-generated content. Every interviewee for the study stated that they sensed and appreciated the presence of user-generated content on the platform. The participants gave this explanation: they thought that TikTok creators were approachable and individual. According to O'hern and Kahle (2013), the UGC typology characterizes informative content as a user's presentation of a product, outlining its benefits and drawbacks, with the intention of educating and entertaining other consumers. In the interviews, most participants said that when it came to brand-related content, the informative kind of user-generated content (UGC) caught their interest. Mayrhofer and colleagues. UGC fits in more naturally on the platform, according to (2019). This was said because the respondents thought regular television or other online advertising was more abrupt than user-generated content (UGC) on TikTok. They claimed that people thought UGC and the other content were similar.

The respondents also made it clear that, in their opinion, TikTok's user-generated content was more credible than conventional advertising on other platforms. Consumers find informative user-generated content (UGC) more trustworthy than brand-controlled content (Jonas, 2010). The content on TikTok is created by regular people, which makes it more authentic, according to the respondents. The majority of respondents stated that in their opinion, a legitimate creator presents the product in all its glory and outlines both its advantages and disadvantages. Furthermore, a few participants expressed that, in order to preserve credibility, it is critical that the video remain unsponsored.

Numerous participants clarified that when the user posting the content was not associated with or sponsored by the brand, there was a greater sense of perceived credibility and trust toward the user-generated content. UGC created by common people is generally more trusted by users than content created by celebrities, according to Muda and Hamzah (2021). When asked how they determined if the content creator was sponsored or not, the majority of interviewees said they looked for a statement from the creator indicating that the video was sponsored. If not, it was assumed that the TikTok video was not sponsored. Furthermore, Muda and Hamzah (2021) asserted that individuals who perceive a degree of similarity between themselves and the creator are more likely to trust and believe in the content.

Regarding how they felt about videos that promoted products, the respondents had similar thoughts. During the interviews, the ability to identify common needs and relate to sponsored products, as well as the way the product is portrayed in the video, were the key points raised. Moreover, Muda and Hamzah (2021) asserted that users who are exposed to user-generated content (UGC) explore the user's profile in greater detail to learn about their preferences, values, and personality. The results of the interviews show that when using TikTok, this was not the respondents' experience. The interviewees clarified that, in cases where they are unfamiliar with the viewed individual, their interpretation of the video primarily relies on the features of the TikTok post.

The participants reported feeling a sense of similarity with the content creators they encountered because, for the most part, they are regular people.

A lot of people said that the common beliefs could alter their perception of a brand or product and create a need for it. The participants also mentioned that their interest in a product increases if they see a lot of people talking about or owning it. According to the majority of respondents, TikTok has affected their desire to buy goods. One example of this was that TikTok creators piqued the respondents' interest in a product and encouraged them to consider buying it. One respondent said they had initially disliked a product, but after seeing other creators on TikTok praising it, they began to consider whether or not to buy it again. Conversely, another participant reported that their inclination to buy a particular product diminished upon witnessing numerous TikTok creators criticizing it.

Purchase intentions are higher when user-generated content is present (Mayrhofer et al, 2019), and it is claimed to be impacted by the capacity for knowledge and opinion sharing, which has been said to foster trust between viewers and content producers (Majeed et al., 2021). This was reflected in all of the respondents' responses, the vast majority of which emphasized that content is viewed as more credible when it is supported by facts and is presented in an understandable manner in the video. Conversely, the respondents indicated that they would be less inclined to purchase the product if the maker disclosed a drawback.

3.4.3. Electronic Word-of-Mouth

Participants claimed to be able to relate to and exchange ideas with other TikTok users. According to several participants, they read the UGC post's comment section to see if other users shared their opinions. The relevance that other users' comments were thought to have when determining the credibility of the content that was being viewed was brought up by the participants.

This occurred both when the content creator presented a positive and negative view of a brand or product. According to Rosario et al. (2019) electronic word-of-mouth is a consumers' presentation of opinion of brand related experiences, which can be in the form of comments on social media. The respondents discussed eWOM during the interviews, stating that they look to the comments section for other users' opinions to verify the accuracy of the video content. It was mentioned multiple times that when more people shared their thoughts or experiences on the TikTok post related to the brand, the participants felt that their influence grew. All of the participants indicated that they used the comment section as a tool to determine whether or not other people shared their beliefs.

Numerous participants clarified that user-generated content could potentially impact their prior perceptions; however, opinions were found to rise when other users discussed a brand or product in the comment section. The quantity of likes and comments on a post may influence how people perceive it (Lee et al., 2020) and more is regarded as more convincing (Teng et al., 2014). In the course of the interviews, the respondents explained that the more they considered the opinions of others, the more persuasive the content was. According to the interviewees, one's ability to trust a user's opinions increased with the number of likes and comments on a particular post. Furthermore, it was mentioned that the content's credibility was affected by the commenters' relatability. The participants clarified that being able to relate to people and determine whether opinions are shared is essential to them.

Several respondents mentioned that the TikTok comment section helped users discover others who agreed with them and assisted them in gathering data to aid in decision-making or the creation of a brand image. Wang and associates. According to (2012), when there is a perceived sense of comfort and similarity in opinions and values, the shared opinions have an impact on the recipient. The participants' perceptions were found to be influenced by both positive and negative opinions. However, it was mentioned that the respondents found it important to clarify their own opinions based on the amount of user interaction (likes and comments) on the post.

3.4.4. Parasocial Relations

The participant illustrates how a parasocial relationship has affected their perception of a friendship between themselves and the TikTok creators they follow (Xiang et al., 2016). Several participants mentioned that they could have a bigger influence on other creators' decisions when they knew them better during their description of their relationships with them on TikTok. For example, the respondents thought that a review from someone they felt they had a relationship with would be sufficient to convince them to make the purchase.

The degree to which the respondents knew the creator was related to the perceived relations reported in the findings. According to the participants, getting along with someone who held similar beliefs and values made you feel more like you know them. Xiang and associates. (2016) claimed that in addition to influencers or celebrities, parasocial interactions can also occur between social media users. Numerous participants reported feeling a personal connection to the creators, recognizing their values, preferences, and personality. Furthermore, users' inclination to purchase is influenced by parasocial interactions (Xiang et al., 2016). According to the respondents, there was a greater desire to try a product or service that the content creator recommended if they could relate to the person or knew their preferences. Furthermore, as per Xiang et al. (2016) Social media users' parasocial relationships can be defined as those in which the observer perceives a genuine friendship or relationship. According to the majority of participants, they view TikTok creators as friends because they are familiar with their interests and occupations, as well as the media character. Many participants in the interviews said they were unable to name or characterize their relationships to other creators. Despite going on to describe their interactions, many of the interviewees said they had never been in a relationship. The parasocial interactions are as Yuan and Lou (2020) and Gleason et al. (2017) explained the short-term perception that the consumers get when viewing the content, in comparison to parasocial relationships which is the long-term perception. Similar to the statement made by MK, many of the participants stated that their TikTok feed changes continuously and therefore the media creators the participants encounter change as well.

Gleason and associates. (2017) have reported that individuals who engage in frequent social media interactions with one another may form a parasocial relationship that manifests either consciously or unconsciously. The results that have been presented indicate that the participants believe it is difficult for them to build a relationship with TikTok creators. These claims are primarily motivated by the fact that the respondents' TikTok feed is constantly shifting and that the creators who initially appear may eventually vanish. The participants mentioned that they might forget about a user's disappearance and find new content to engage with. Still, the respondents' responses also revealed the prevalence of long-term parasocial relationships. According to Sokolova and Kefi (2020), parasocial relations arise when the parties involved perceive a strong connection between their shared values or interests, which may impact their desire to make a purchase (Hwang & Zhang, 2018). Participants who talked about their relationships with content creators said that a user's desire to make a purchase could be swayed if the user's intentions, preferences, and personality were known. Those who were able to identify and explain their relationships with TikTok creators during the interview revealed that they follow users with whom they have a sense of connection. The participants also mention that the creator's communication is more trustworthy because of their expertise. Breves et al. and Ohanian (1990). (2021) claimed that the communicator's experience could have an impact on the message's credibility. Many participants also mentioned that if they have a personal connection to the creator, there is a higher chance that they will make a purchase. The respondents stated that the video could affect their choice to buy if the messenger had similar qualities to them, such as the same body type, hairstyle, or style. One respondent went on to say that although they generally don't feel a connection to creators on TikTok, they did find some videos relatable because the creator and the respondent share similarities.

The videos that the interviewed individuals found relatable influenced the respondents. Similarly, the majority of the participants stated that they feel a stronger persuasiveness to the poster when they can relate to the creator. According to Martensen et al. (2018), when social media figures post personal content, the viewers' possibility to relate increases and influences viewers' persuasion. As stated during the interviews, when the respondents could relate to the content and the creator, they stated that it influences their perception of content.

3.4.5. Brand Perception

Every participant has reported seeing posts on TikTok that are related to brands. Some participants asserted that there was evidence of brand-generated content. Numerous people observed that brands are utilizing the comment section on TikTok to actively communicate with customers. Furthermore, while none of the participants followed brand-owned TikTok accounts, many were aware of the content and kept up to date with it. On TikTok, however, the respondents said that the majority of the posts were made by other users when discussing their brand experiences.

This assertion is consistent with what Gensler et al. (2013) pointed out that because social media gives users a platform to readily connect with other users and share their brand experiences, users have become more active creators of brand stories. When inquired about whether they had previously seen brand-generated videos on TikTok, every participant said they had. On these kinds of videos, people's perspectives differed. While some participants found this content enjoyable, others didn't feel the same way.

Hudson and others. (2016) claimed that when customers follow a brand on social media, their desire to make a purchase may grow. According to the information provided, the respondent stated that the brand-generated content on their TikTok feed had a positive influence. Furthermore, most of the respondents had a favorable opinion of brands that don't prioritize promoting and selling their goods. Rather, it was valued when companies used the platform to interact with their customers. Furthermore, consumer-brand communication has the ability to increase the company's knowledge and trust (Hudson et al., 2016).

Many of the participants discussed their perceptions of brands and how they have experienced others' influence on them when using TikTok during the interviews. The empirical data demonstrates that the respondents' viewpoints were not in agreement. On the one hand, the participants said that something they had seen on TikTok had altered their overall opinion of the brand. Even though it was stated that everyone's perception of the product was influenced, some participants thought that other users' posts on TikTok lacked the ability to alter their perception of the brand. The significance of brand presence on the app—which is said to happen in the form of comments or videos—was also emphasized by the participants' responses.

3.4.5.1. Anthropomorphism

Many respondents who were questioned about user-generated content (UGC) and its impact on TikTok stated that when brand-owned accounts repost UGC, it improves the perception of the brand. It was said that when a business demonstrates that "regular" people enjoy its products, it builds participants' trust toward the brand. The new digital era has changed the way that brands market themselves, and on Tik Tok some brands seem to have created a brand persona or "spokesperson" that participates in conversations on the app, with the personality of a human being (Ashley & Tuten, 2014; Fournier, 1998). When brands acknowledged their consumers on TikTok, the participants explained a positive change in their view of the company. The communication between brands and consumers were explained by the respondents as reposting original posts or communicating through the comments.

When a brand was clearly present on the platform, the participants said they saw it as personal. The responders liked it when companies built a rapport with their customers by humorously interacting with users on TikTok. Customers who adopt an anthropomorphic viewpoint about a brand do not perceive its actions as authentic. Perception of the brand's actions arises from interpreting them or applying intuition to them (Delgado-Ballester et al., 2019). The anthropomorphic viewpoint was recognized in many participants' responses, despite it not being expressed explicitly. The majority of respondents stated that they associated human characteristics with brands that were active on TikTok, which changed their opinion of the brand. According to the participants, consumer communications from brands are "cool" and "fun." Furthermore, some participants expressed that when there is clear communication, they feel more connected to a brand. As previously mentioned, a relationship is formed between customers and brands when customers begin to associate a brand with human traits and personalities (Fournier, 1998). Another respondent clarified that they now view brands using TikTok as "more modern," even though they were previously thought to be "old" and "not cool."

3.4.5.2. Utilitarian Benefits

Many of the respondents preferred videos where the creator clearly demonstrated the features and fundamental operations of the product, according to information gleaned from the interviews (Yu and Yuan, 2019). Participants reported feeling a shift in their perception of the product after hearing the creator go through the features and useful benefits of it. Educating respondents through UGC also helped them acquire knowledge, which increased their interest in purchasing products after they saw and understood the information.

Participants reported feeling more credible and trusting of the content when the utilitarian and hedonic benefits were demonstrated in a video. Numerous participants clarified how a product's clear representation aids in their decision-making. The hedonic and practical functions are linked to the happy attributes, like colors, which explains the utilitarian benefits. Additionally, it was mentioned that social media content may offer utilitarian and hedonic benefits that favorably affect consumers' decisions (PerezVega et al., 2018).

In a TikTok video, the participants demonstrated a positive affection sparked by the attributes explained. Many people have said that the desire to purchase increases when the product's creator displays it and explains its features. However, the respondents indicated that if the user explains the drawbacks, it would probably result in no purchase when asked if the attributes could negatively affect their decisions.

As stated by Perez-Vega et al. (2018) Social media could be used to convey the practical advantages. The participants share what they know about the utilitarian product benefits that are present in the TikTok content. Furthermore, consumers' perceptions of the benefits can impact their initial intentions regarding the product (Perez-Vega, 2018). A significant number of participants expressed that they found the videos that discussed the benefits to be informative and useful, and that it had assisted them in determining whether the purchase was necessary.

3.4.5.3. Brand Loyalty

The empirical data demonstrated that brand-related user-generated content (UGC) on TikTok has impacted participants' brand perceptions in both positive and negative ways, as the content they encounter reflects both positive and negative brand experiences that users have had with the app. Some participants said they felt a shift in brand loyalty for a product rather than other users on TikTok influencing their loyalty to the brand.

This demonstrates that customers have the power to both positively and negatively influence their opinions of a brand and their loyalty to its products (Ashley and Tuten, 2014). When asked if TikTok users had altered their perceptions of a product, the majority of participants said that the platform had forced them to try it, which had made them feel devoted to the brand. Repurchasing a brand's goods over time demonstrates a customer's favorable opinion of the brand and its offerings (Srinivasan et al., 2002). Conversely, another participant expressed that they don't think TikTok has affected their brand loyalty. Numerous participants expressed agreement that their TikTok experience did not alter their brand loyalty. It was mentioned that when a user expresses negative opinions about a brand, they usually look into the issue further to come to their own judgment. This opinion was not, however, shared with regard to product loyalty. Brand loyalty is said to be related to marketing communication (Sasmita & Suki, 2015). The participants clarified that they have repurchased products because UGC, as a communication tool, has made them aware of them.

REFERENCES

1. Abbas, L., Fahmy, S. S., Ayad, S., Ibrahim, M., & Ali, A. H. (2022). TikTok intifada: Analyzing social media activism among youth. *Online Media and Global Communication*, *1*(2), 287–314.
2. Ashley, C., & Tuten, T. (2014). Creative strategies in social media marketing: An exploratory study of branded social content and consumer engagement. *Psychology & Marketing*, *32*(1), 15–27.
3. Bae, S., & Lee, T. (2010, November 17). Gender differences in consumers' perception of online. *Springer Science+Business Media*, *11*, 201–214.
4. Bell, E., Bryman, A., & Harley, B. (2019). *Business research methods*. Oxford: Oxford University Press.
5. Benjamin, R. (2019). Race after technology: Abolitionist tools for the new Jim code. *Social Forces*.
6. Breves, P., Amrehn, J. H., Liebers, N., & Schramm, H. (2021). Blind trust? The importance and interplay of parasocial relationships and advertising disclosures in explaining influencers' persuasive effects on their followers. *International Journal of Advertising*, *40*(7), 1209–1229.
7. Charisi, V., Imai, T., Rinta, T., Nakhayenze, J. M., & Gomez, R. (2021, June). Exploring the concept of fairness in everyday, imaginary, and robot scenarios: A cross-cultural study with children in Japan and Uganda. In *Interaction Design and Children* (pp. 532–536).
8. Currás-Pérez, R., Ruiz-Mafé, C., & Sanz-Blas, S. (2011). What motivates consumers to teleshopping? The impact of TV personality and audience interaction. *Marketing Intelligence & Planning*, *29*(5), 534–555.
9. Davcik, N., Langaro, D., Jevons, C., & Nascimento, R. (2022). Non-sponsored brand-related user-generated content: Effects and mechanisms of consumer engagement. *Journal of Product & Brand Management*, *31*(1), 163–174.
10. Delgado-Ballester, E., Palazón, M., & Peláez, J. (2019). Anthropomorphized vs objectified brands: Which brand version is more loved? *European Journal of Management and Business Economics*, *29*(2), 150–165.
11. DeVos, A., Dhabalia, A., Shen, H., Holstein, K., & Eslami, M. (2022, April). Toward user-driven algorithm auditing: Investigating users' strategies for uncovering harmful algorithmic behavior. In *Proceedings of the 2022 CHI Conference on Human Factors in Computing Systems* (pp. 1–19).
12. Djafarova, E., & Bowes, T. (2021). Instagram made me buy it: Generation Z impulse purchases in the fashion industry. *Journal of Retailing and Consumer Services*, *59*(1).

13. Djafarova, E., & Rushworth, C. (2017). Exploring the credibility of online celebrities' Instagram profiles in influencing the purchase decisions of young female users. *Computers in Human Behavior*, *68*(1), 1–7.
14. Duffett, R. G. (2015, January 22). Facebook advertising's influence on intention-to-purchase and purchase amongst Millennials. *Internet Research*, *25*(4), 498–526.
15. Dunn, K., & Harness, D. (2018). Communicating corporate social responsibility in a social world: The effects of company-generated and user-generated social media content on CSR attributions and scepticism. *Journal of Marketing Management*, *34*(17–18), 1503–1529.
16. Garcia, K. (2020, October 21). Here's how TikTok is changing the way businesses advertise. URL (accessed on 4th October 2024).
17. Geng, R., & Chen, J. (2021). The influencing mechanism of interaction quality of UGC on consumers' purchase intention – An empirical analysis. *Frontiers in Psychology*, *12*.
18. Gensler, S., Völckner, F., Liu-Thompkins, Y., & Wiertz, C. (2013). Managing brands in the social media environment. *Journal of Interactive Marketing*, *27*(4), 242–256.
19. Haenlein, M., Anadol, E., Farnsworth, T., Hugo, H., Hunichen, J., & Welte, D. (2020). Navigating the new era of influencer marketing: How to be successful on Instagram, TikTok, & Co. *California Management Review*, *63*(1), 5–25.
20. Hanus, M. D. (2019). Distinguishing user experience when customizing in a user-generated content advertising campaign and subsequent effects on product attitudes, reactance, and source credibility. *Journal of Interactive Advertising*, *19*(1), 74–85.
21. Herrman, J. (2019, March 10). How TikTok is rewriting the world. Retrieved from *The New York Times*: https://www.nytimes.com. URL (accessed on 4th October 2024).
22. Horton, D., & Wohl, R. R. (1956). Mass communication and para-social interaction: Observations on intimacy at a distance. *Psychiatry*, *19*(3), 215–229.
23. Hudson, S., Huang, L., Roth, M. S., & Madden, T. J. (2016, March). The influence of social media interactions on consumer–brand relationships: A three-country study of brand perceptions and marketing behaviors. *International Journal of Marketing in Research*, *33*(1), 27–41.
24. Hwang, K., & Zhang, Q. (2018). Influence of parasocial relationship between digital celebrities and their followers on followers' purchase

and electronic word-of-mouth intentions, and persuasion knowledge. *Computers in Human Behavior*, *87*, 155–173.

25. Ibrahim, B., Aljarah, A., & Ababneh, B. (2020). Do social media marketing activities enhance consumer perception of brands? A meta-analytic examination. *Journal of Promotion Management*, *26*(4), 544–568.
26. Ismail, A. R. (2017). The influence of perceived social media marketing activities on brand loyalty: The mediation effect of brand and value consciousness. *Asia Pacific Journal of Marketing and Logistics*, *29*(1), 129–144.
27. Jain, N., Olmo, A., Sengupta, S., Manikonda, L., & Kambhampati, S. (2022). Imperfect ImaGANation: Implications of GANs exacerbating biases on facial data augmentation and Snapchat face lenses. *Artificial Intelligence*, *304*, 103652.
28. Literat, I., & Kligler-Vilenchik, N. (2023). TikTok as a key platform for youth political expression: Reflecting on the opportunities and stakes involved. *Social Media+ Society*, *9*(1), 20563051231157595.
29. Metaxa, D., Park, J. S., Robertson, R. E., Karahalios, K., Wilson, C., Hancock, J., & Sandvig, C. (2021). Auditing algorithms: Understanding algorithmic systems from the outside in. *Foundations and Trends® in Human–Computer Interaction*, *14*(4), 272–344.
30. Shen, H., DeVos, A., Eslami, M., & Holstein, K. (2021). Everyday algorithm auditing: Understanding the power of everyday users in surfacing harmful algorithmic behaviors. *Proceedings of the ACM on Human-Computer Interaction*, *5*(CSCW2), 1–29.
31. Zulli, D., & Zulli, D. J. (2022). Extending the internet meme: Conceptualizing technological mimesis and imitation publics on the TikTok platform. *New Media & Society*, *24*(8), 1872–1890.

CHAPTER 4

FACEBOOK ALGORITHM

Contents

Introduction 138

4.1. The Facebook Algorithm: How It Works and How to Make It Work for You? 138

4.2. Working with Facebook's Algorithm 144

4.3. Facebook Algorithms and User Polarization 147

4.4. Prioritizing Original News on Facebook 152

4.5. Navigating the Algorithm: Troubleshooting Why Facebook Ad Is Not Delivering 163

References 174

INTRODUCTION

In spite of what you might have heard, Facebook continues to rule the social media world. After 20 years, Facebook has rapidly expanded to 3 billion users. This unexpected rise is partially attributable to a change in Facebook's algorithm, which makes use of an advanced tool that uses artificial intelligence (AI) to give users a highly customized experience.

Make sure Facebook remains a part of your current social media strategy. It's not hopeless if it's not producing the desired outcomes. There is no secret code or riddle to work out when it comes to the Facebook algorithm. It is always changing and adapting to new trends. Social media teams must continuously refine, test, and fortify their approaches in order to maintain audience interest and remain relevant.

Facebook's algorithm, which consists primarily of a set of rules and machine learning tools, is heavily influenced by AI. These guidelines determine who views your content based on metrics for authenticity, consistency, style, and engagement. It is a machine that performs its assigned tasks as per its programming.

Making the user experience unique is the main goal of the Facebook algorithm update. Making sure that no two feeds are the same and offering total personalization and customized content is the aim.

The engine that is enabling Facebook to achieve its goal of a personalized platform is artificial intelligence (AI). These algorithms are ideal for identifying user patterns, reaching out to existing audiences, finding new audiences, and recommending related content. This is an essential advantage for any brand trying to reach out to a particular demographic among the billions of users that are online.

Brands have a better chance of achieving organic reach on social media platforms when AI and algorithms are integrated. Organic growth is less expensive and frequently produces long-term outcomes for building a devoted following. Prior to the Facebook algorithm change, brands needed to put in a lot of work to identify their target market and maintain their top spot in the feed. Now, the Facebook algorithm will (in a sense) assist your content in finding your audience if publishers can optimize and personalize their content.

4.1. THE FACEBOOK ALGORITHM: HOW IT WORKS AND HOW TO MAKE IT WORK FOR YOU?

Although not the only factor influencing reach, Facebook's algorithm is undoubtedly one of the more powerful ones. It will be considerably more difficult for you to get your posts seen by the people who are most important to your business if you are not keeping up with changes to the Facebook algorithm. Facebook made significant algorithmic changes in 2019 that gave users more control over what appeared in their news feeds. Users can now see the reason behind the appearance of a particular post on their feed. Thankfully, brands have a lot of options for ensuring user engagement with their posts—even in the absence of sponsored advertisements.

4.1.1. How the Facebook Algorithm Works?

Like search engine algorithms, Facebook's algorithm ranks every post that could appear in a user's news feed according to the likelihood that the user will find the content interesting.

Facebook prioritizes posts from friends over brands, emphasizing "meaningful interactions."

Facebook's algorithm uses four main factors or signals:

- A listing ("inventory") of the posts available to show;·Signals from each post that tell Facebook what it is;
- Predictions on how users will react to each post in the inventory;
- A final score based on all of the ranking signals.

Facebook uses user behavior data and considers the behavior of all users on the platform when determining its ranking factors. Facebook focuses on three main categories:

- Who users typically interact with;
- The type of content: videos, images, links, etc.;
- The post's popularity.

Facebook began conducting direct user surveys in May 2019 in an effort to learn more about the content users are interested in seeing. Facebook asked users questions such as these:

- Who are your close friends?
- What posts do you find valuable?
- How important is this Facebook Group to you?
- How interested are you in seeing content from this Page you follow?

Facebook modified its algorithm to improve user experience with the news feed in response to those comments. One way to do this was to display additional content from the Groups and Pages that users have been following or interacting with the most. The news feed would then start to display other content lower.

4.1.2. How to Use the Facebook Algorithm Effectively?

Facebook's algorithm changes may seem to be intended to make it more difficult for posts from your brand to be seen without displaying advertisements. And perhaps that contributes to it. After all, Facebook depends on ads for its revenue, so it makes sense that the company would encourage brands to follow suit.

However, Facebook's higher ups are also aware that displaying content to users that they don't actually want to see is a surefire way to drive them off the network. That implies that since Facebook's audience would be smaller, brands would be less inclined to pay for ads. Let's just assume that there is a combination of factors at play here: Facebook wants users to be satisfied with the content they see in their news feeds, but it also encourages brands to provide more engaging content if they want to reach users without having to turn every post into an ad. (Tandoc, E. C., Jr., & Maitra, J., 2018)

Facebook's algorithm favors the development of more genuine or meaningful interactions, so in order to encourage genuine interactions, your brand must produce better content.

Here are 11 ways you can make the Facebook algorithm work for you:

1. **Post Content at the Right Time:** Posts with higher levels of engagement are given priority by the Facebook algorithm, so it's critical to know when your audience is online and at their busiest so you can publish during those periods. Check out the ideal times to post on Facebook to get you started. That will serve as a jumping off point for you as you examine your Facebook analytics to learn more about your target audience and adjust the timing of your posts.
2. **Post Often and Regularly:** Brands with a regular posting schedule tend to receive higher levels of engagement. Facebook's algorithm favors recent content, so make it a point to regularly post excellent content. To ensure you have content ready to go, we highly advise making a Facebook content calendar.
3. **Focus on Video Content:** The popularity of video content has grown over the last few years. Don't wait any longer if you haven't started using video marketing. According to a survey by Wyzowl:

- 96% of people have watched an explainer video to learn more about a product or service.
- 84% of people say that they've been convinced to buy a product or service by watching a brand's video.
- 74% of people say they've been convinced to buy or download a piece of software or app by watching a video.

Additionally, Facebook changed its algorithm to display more original, excellent videos in users' news feeds starting in May 2019. When making video content for Facebook, keep these three ranking factors in mind:

- **Intent and Loyalty:** Create videos that will bring users back again and again.
- **Length and Duration:** Your video needs to be engaging enough to get viewers to watch at least one minute, but you can likely skip creating videos longer than three minutes.
- **Originality:** Like all social media platforms, Facebook prefers original content that isn't repurposed from other platforms

Don't be afraid to use Facebook Live as well. Notifying your followers when you go live is a great way to boost engagement.

4. **Drive Discussion Instead of Fishing for Engagement:** You know those posts that your younger cousins used to share all the time: "like if you remember this" or "comment a number and I'll do this?" Well, Facebook is now penalizing brands using those same tactics to get comments, tags, and likes. While that doesn't mean you should never use posts like that (they can be an engaging way to poll your followers), Facebook wants to encourage creators to drive discussions instead of simply asking followers to "like" something.

   Use questions to start a discussion and promote debate. There are ways to promote discussion on subjects linked to your brand, even though you don't want to post content that is overtly controversial. If you offer email marketing services, for instance, you may want to find out what your followers think about cold emailing.

5. **Say "No" to Clickbait and Low-Quality Content:** Facebook not only forbids engagement-baiting posts but also takes a strong stance against clickbait. Links and thumbnails used in clickbait are created specifically to grab attention and encourage clicks. Clickbait is typically sensationalized, deceptive, or both.

   Aside from clickbait, there are a few other types of content that Facebook frowns upon:

- Misinformation and fake news;
- Content that's offensive but doesn't meet the threshold for prohibited content;
- Links to sites that don't add value or that contain stolen or scraped content;

- Misleading health information;
- Faked videos that have been flagged by third-party fact-checkers.

6. **Encourage Employees and Partners to Share and Engage:** You have an automatic method to take advantage of the Facebook algorithm if you employ staff members or work with Facebook influencers. To make your content stand out on other users' news feeds, ask your staff members and business partners to share and interact with it.

   Facebook gives preference to posts from users you know, so you're more likely to see updates from friends and family than from companies you follow. Your content will reach a wider audience if you encourage your partners and staff to share your posts with their networks. Furthermore, content from friends and family is 16 times more likely to be read than that from your brand. See these fantastic Facebook post-boosting suggestions for some fantastic methods to expand the audience for your content.

7. **Focus on Images and Tags Instead of External Links:** It's no secret that Facebook prefers to retain users on its network rather than direct them to other websites. Facebook prioritizes content that is native to the platform and de-emphasizes posts that contain external links. This is not to say that posts containing external links will never be viewed; rather, it means that you should have a variety of content, with a focus on native Facebook content that engages users and keeps them on the network.

   Facebook loves visual content in addition to using native content. And so do those who follow you. As a matter of fact, BuzzSumo discovered that Facebook posts featuring images receive 3x as much engagement as those without. Make sure every post has a visual (GIF, picture, video, infographic, etc.).

8. **Create Facebook-Specific Content:** Initiate the process of crafting distinctive and captivating captions for your posts—even if you are recycling previously shared content on Facebook. Don't just impart the same information. To keep it from getting monotonous, vary it up a little. This isn't limited to the captions on your posts; you can also use an image editing tool to create visually appealing posts or a video editing tool to turn posts into videos.

9. **Leverage Facebook Groups:** One of the greatest ways to guarantee that your followers are seeing your content at the top of their news feeds on a regular basis is to join Facebook groups. By starting a

new group for your brand on Facebook, you can take advantage of the group's power. This group is a place to promote conversation, offer advice on products, amusement, help with user issues, and other useful content for your followers.

10. **Focus on the Right (Narrow) Audience:** Facebook offers great tools for audience targeting that let you control exactly who sees your content. Narrowing your audience may seem counterintuitive, but the result will be a rise in engagement. As a result of higher engagement, the Facebook algorithm will reward your content and make it appear higher in users' news feeds.

11. **Run Facebook Ads:** While your organic (free) content will play a significant role in building and maintaining relationships with your audience, Facebook advertising is the most effective and efficient way to increase brand awareness on the network. You can precisely target the people you need to reach in order to expand your audience with Facebook's audience targeting. You'll then be in a better position to determine the kind of content that appeals to the audience you wish to target.

Facebook advertising is already used by 93% of online marketers because of its excellent return on investment. You can maximize your advertising efforts by combining Facebook advertising with the 10 tips we've already discussed. The best way to reach as many members of your target audience as you can while still promoting your organic content to build the relationships you're starting is to combine paid and organic efforts.

4.1.3. How Does Facebook Recommend Content?

Brands and content producers have a great chance to reach new audiences through Facebook's recommendation system without having to resort to paid advertising.

Since this recommendation system is unique, no two users will see the same set of recommendations, which is consistent with Facebook's goal of offering personalized, insightful, and relevant recommendations.

Complying with Facebook's guidelines is essential if you want to increase the chances that your content will be recommended. Facebook's Community Standards, a comprehensive set of guidelines detailed in their Transparency Center, must be adhered to by all content.

Content pertaining to violence, crime, suicide or self-harm, child exploitation or nudity, bullying or harassment, spam, inauthentic behavior, and misinformation are a few examples of content that violates these standards and will be deleted. But meeting these requirements by themselves does not ensure that a recommendation is eligible. The Recommendations Guidelines on Facebook are meant to be more stringent than the Community Standards. Therefore, not all content that is allowed on the platform is appropriate for suggestions.

If you want to be recommended to Facebook users, avoid these five types of content:

- Content compromising safety, like discussions of self-harm, suicide, eating disorders, sexually explicit material, or promotion of regulated products;
- Sensitive or low-quality content, such as 'miracle' health supplements or questionable financial schemes;
- Disliked content by users, like clickbait or engagement bait;
- Low-quality publishing, such as news content lacking transparent authorship; and
- False or misleading content, including fake news or claims debunked by independent fact-checkers, like vaccine misinformation.

4.2. WORKING WITH FACEBOOK'S ALGORITHM

Here are some tips to help you optimize your content, engagement, and overall Facebook strategy:

1. **Understand What Your Audience Wants to See:** Facebook indicates it prioritizes content that is "meaningful, relevant, and informative." So what does that mean, exactly?

- **Meaningful:** Content that, based on previous usage patterns, the user will want to watch videos on and discuss with friends and family. This also takes into account overall engagement.
- **Relevant:** Content is ranked according to your most active users, the kind of content you typically enjoy, and the number of user interactions it has received.
- **Informative:** Content someone will find "new, interesting, and informative," which will vary by user.

  You must comprehend the distinct interests and behaviors of your target audience in order to determine what will be interesting, pertinent, and educational to them. You can find these qualities with the aid of audience research.

2. **Create Accurate and Authentic Content:** Facebook says, "People on Facebook value accurate, authentic content." They also specify that the types of posts people "consider genuine" will rank higher in the algorithm. Meanwhile, they work to reduce the ranking for posts people find "misleading, sensational, and spammy."

   Here are a few tips to let the algorithm know that your content is genuine and factual:

- **Write Clear Headlines:** Make sure the headline accurately sums up what readers can expect from your post. You can definitely use creativity in the captions of your posts, but avoid using deceptive or clickbait titles.
- **Be Truthful:** Simply said, speak the truth. Avoid sensationalizing, embellishing, or flat-out lying.

On the flip side, here are some things to avoid:

- Content that impedes community safety, like violence, self-harm, or use of regulated products.
- Content with low-quality health or financial claims, like miracle cures or get-rich-quick schemes.
- Unoriginal content or unattributed news content
- False claims and misinformation
- Facebook algorithm words to avoid, such as racist, homophobic, or violent language

3. **Don't Try to Manipulate the Algorithm:** But wait, isn't this post all about how to manipulate the algorithm? No, this post is about understanding how the algorithm works so you can learn what Facebook considers valuable for its users.

   It is your responsibility to determine how those general guidelines relate to your target audience. Next, produce content that appeals to them and gives the algorithm signals for a higher ranking.

   It is strictly forbidden to try to trick the algorithm in order to get more exposure for your content than it deserves. This could entail using other black-hat techniques (also known as "inauthentic sharing") to increase reach, such as purchasing interactions or comments.

   Attempting to game the algorithm with clickbait, engagement bait, or misleading landing pages will not help you; Facebook works hard to restrict their distribution. Moreover, purchasing likes can narrow your distribution.

Additionally, users now have more authority to report, block, and hide content that they deem unnecessary thanks to new feed preference controls. Your audience is likely to catch you scamming even if Facebook's moderators miss it.

4. **Engage with Your Audience:** Facebook's algorithm gives priority to posts from Pages with which a user has meaningful history interactions. Increasing your reply game is therefore essential.

Don't let someone lose the chance to comment on your post if they take the time to do so. Responding to their comments increases the likelihood that they will leave more comments on your posts in the future. Naturally, this gives the algorithm more of those delicious engagement signals. If you ignore them, they'll probably stop talking as well.

5. **Get Your Audience to Engage with Each Other:** Recall that the algorithm favors content that users want to discuss and share with their friends. Well, getting users to share and discuss your content with their friends is a fairly simple way to send that signal.

   Facebook claims that its algorithm uses "action-bumping logic" to show a post to a user again if it sparks a lot of discussion among their friends.

   Check out our tips for increasing Facebook engagement to encourage sharing and discussion among your audience.

6. **Post at the Right Time:** Facebook's algorithms make your content visible to users who weren't online when it was originally posted. However, as this post has made clear, one important indicator of a post's potential value is its level of engagement. And if you post when a larger portion of your audience is online, you have a higher chance of receiving that engagement—particularly crucial early engagement.

   To put it simply, scheduling your post for optimal visibility increases the likelihood that it will be seen by readers—even those who aren't online at the moment!

   Because of how crucial this subject is, we've written an entire post on when it's best to post on Facebook.

7. **Don't Forget the Basic Status Post:** It can be tempting to look for intricate Facebook algorithm tricks in an attempt to increase your engagement rates. Don't overlook the modest status update, though. (A post devoid of an image, video, or link).

   According to research, status updates typically receive one of the highest percentages of engagement (0.11%). The percentage of photo posts is only slightly higher, at 0.12%. The percentages for videos and link posts are substantially lower, at 0.08 and 0.04, respectively.

While we're not advocating that you fill your Facebook page with nothing but status updates, they can be a useful tool for conveying straightforward information and achieving high engagement rates.

8. **Expand Your Reach via Your Best Advocates:** The Facebook algorithm may give your staff greater authority and credibility than your brand page. This is a result of their increased authority and credibility among their own friends and supporters.

   Another fantastic group of supporters that can help you increase your reach and establish the legitimacy of your brand is affiliate marketing. Assist them in expanding your targeted audience on Facebook by providing them with resources and training so they can use their own algorithm signals to do so.

9. **Collaborate with Influencers:** Influencers have the same power to increase your reach as do your employees. Collaborating with influencers who possess a substantial and active fan base notifies the Facebook algorithm that your material is reliable and pertinent.

   Make sure an influencer is a good fit for your brand and has a loyal following before working with them. By doing this, you can make sure that their brand-related posts are sincere and meaningful to their followers, as opposed to forced or unauthentic—which would send the wrong message to the algorithm.

10. **Monitor Analytics and Insights:** Keeping track of and evaluating your own performance is the best way to comprehend the Facebook algorithm. It is possible to spot trends and patterns in engagement for your particular page by keeping an eye on analytics and insights.

    Afterwards, you can make the necessary adjustments and optimizations to your content strategy based on this data to better tailor it to your audience's preferences.

4.3. FACEBOOK ALGORITHMS AND USER POLARIZATION

In social media applications like Facebook, algorithms control the vast majority of what a user sees on their main content page. Through networking and personalization, Facebook has leveraged artificial intelligence to help create a sense of community and user engagement on its platform. With the help of these AI, advertisers are better able to target specific demographics through social media marketing. It has been demonstrated that the same algorithms that correctly suggest products can also push users toward more extreme viewpoints, creating real-world conflicts and consequences.

4.3.1. Facebook and Algorithms

Three main objectives make up Facebook's business model: increasing network size, improving user engagement on an individual basis, and implementing targeted advertising. The platform uses algorithms, which are synonymous with artificial intelligence, to accomplish these objectives. The News Feed's content selection, friend and group recommendations, and the ads that eventually seem to read your mind are all powered by these algorithms. The majority of user interactions with the application translate into user responses, which the algorithm assesses prior to the subsequent content display iteration. This sets these algorithms apart from being straightforward formulas; instead, these programs adapt based on user behavior, adjusting their approach to optimize engagement, increase networking, or target the right brain with an advertisement.

4.3.1.1. Social Networking Marketing

Facebook's primary source of income is advertising, which enables all users to continuously use the app for free. This new media distribution platform, like television and newspapers before it, produced a novel and efficient way for businesses and goods to reach large audiences. However, in contrast to more traditional media, the application's social theme gives advertisers access to friend networks and user data. Social networking marketing is the term used to describe this increased level of interaction that is currently driving the advertising industry. By using a user's network and information-sharing capabilities, this strategy can reach a larger and more relevant audience, such as Facebook Friends and Groups. In addition to instant communication, this created a sizable market for media advertisements, which helped to support the expansion of online platforms.

The ability of social networking marketing platforms to gather data from user behavior is arguably its biggest benefit. Along with Friends, groups, interests, and other information, this data also includes particular user interactions with media content. On a larger scale, this enables the platform to target related users with relevant ads more successfully. Advertisers will invest more in an application's ads if the application has a higher success rate in customer feedback. This ability to match the advertisement with the consumer is a crucial point of competition among social media companies.

News Feed and recommendation algorithms use this same data to determine what content or suggestion to show the user next. The algorithms anticipate which content will elicit the greatest positive user response, as elaborated in one of the reviewed articles, and they relentlessly pursue this objective at every turn. But the trouble starts when these algorithms can't control human inclinations, which show up as an increased interest in sources and content that support and validate the user's preexisting opinions.

4.3.2. Bias Propagation

Recommender algorithms have been demonstrated to reduce the variety of content displayed as they identify the primary topics and attributes of a user, as they gain more and more knowledge about the user. The degree of this effect varies depending on the platform, but Facebook users in particular are drawn to more partisan sources, according to a study conducted at UVA's McIntire School that examined the effects of these "echo chambers" on a variety of social media platforms. Even though this might not seem like much on a personal level, these polarized and affirmative bubbles have culminated in extreme global effects that are real, such as the election of Trump in 2016, the genocide against Muslim Rohingya citizens in Myanmar, and the rise of conspiracy theories and their related communities.

The influence that these echo chambers have over fact-checking systems that are designed to try and thwart false information. Users' experiences with echo chamber effects from iterative algorithmic interactions were more important to take into account than a simple fact-check flag, regardless of their political stance or orientation.

The best external research that can be done is a black-boxed approach because these algorithms are the trade secret of these applications. The articles in this review of the literature focus on the user interface input to this black-box artificial intelligence in order to examine and lessen the potentially divisive impact that over time pure algorithmic control may have. The first piece, written by Lorian Leong, delves into how newcomers in Myanmar interacted with the Facebook algorithm and comprehended it. L. Elisa Celis et. Al, suggest a simple boundary approach to counteract the unbridled divisive inclinations of an iterative algorithm approach.

4.3.3. Facebook Users in Myanmar

According to Lorian Leong, a study was carried out in Myanmar in the early part of 2016. It involved speaking with several Myanmarese citizens one-on-one and having them navigate the application and News Feed on their own.

Following the overthrow of the long-standing military regime in 2011, a large number of Burmese citizens began to have access to the internet and its resources. Facebook and smartphones served as the primary access points for everyone to view their friends' activities and news. Facebook received very little criticism because of its remarkable difference from the costly, constrictive internet of the past. These researchers had the chance to watch how users interacted with a new algorithm presence in their daily lives as networks and usage expanded swiftly. (Leong, 2020).

Leong focuses on the concept of "domestication" of algorithm technology through Facebook, or how this phenomenon is woven into the fabric of daily life. The algorithm dictates what users see and suggests, and the way users respond and contribute data also shapes the trajectory of this algorithmic presence. The audience can utilize a framework that revolves around the dual meaning of technology in various cultures and societies when utilizing this social media technology. The Facebook application's "double articulation" acknowledges it as both a physical tool for communication and information access and a metaphor for Myanmar's openness and freedom of the press.

This is significant because, although Friends and Groups are at the core of Facebook's application, Myanmarese internet users' symbolic access to information alters the way Facebook is primarily used in that nation. One of the initial conclusions of this exploratory study with informants from Myanmar was that, even though they did not actually know the individuals, they frequently added new accounts and connections especially for the purpose of sharing information. This was occasionally added on top of social motives as well, since having more Friends makes an account seem more social, knowledgeable, and connected to other people. Despite Facebook's intentions of fostering personal connections, the interpretive flexibility of its Myanmarese users causes the platform to be used much more heavily toward the information domain.

We relate these exchanges to interacting with the News Feed algorithm: most users are aware that by adding connections, the algorithm will display data on their feed because of what they have done. Leong highlights a notable discrepancy between the algorithm's perspective and reality, namely the lack of differentiation between "type" of connection—that is, whether the connection is with an anonymous informant or a real-life friend. Only the iterative actions in the algorithm-maintained user feedback loop determine which connections are prioritized. The algorithm will learn from more interactions with news connections that these connections are more valuable to the user and will therefore show up more frequently.

Although this illustrates the influence that users and culture can have on the adoption and domestication of algorithm technology, it also shows how vulnerable users and culture are to the algorithm's power. Following a sharp increase in anti-Islamic propaganda on Facebook, over 700,000 Rohingya Muslims in Myanmar were forcibly forced to flee their country in a mass exodus that began not long after this study was completed. After realizing the potential of Facebook's platform and the social media dissemination of information, military and government officials began disseminating hate speech among Myanmarese citizens who now have unfettered access to information. The world was alerted to the dangers of this new, unregulated social platform by tension and violence, which resulted in the mass exodus.

4.3.4. Controlling Algorithmic Polarization

To manage the output of a news feed, "regulatory mechanisms" are required. The "constrained algorithm" approach is one suggested method for handling this, and this demo shows it on a website with percentage limits and a news search bar. This concept restrains the actions of otherwise "greedy" algorithms, which aim to maximize the rate of short-term reward at each step (Figure 4.1).

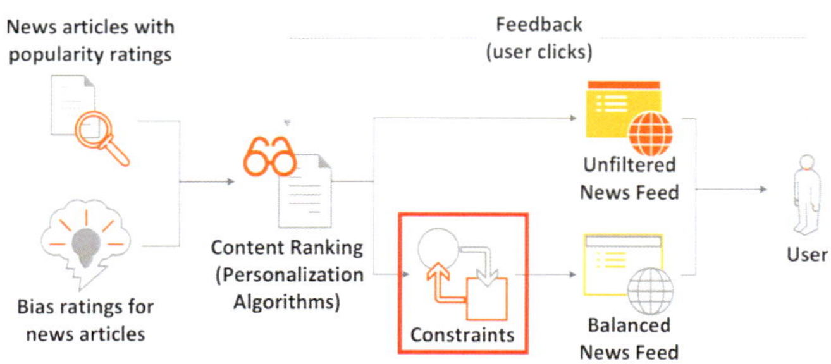

Figure 4.1. *This flowchart illustrates the insertion of constraints into the previously unfiltered feedback loop.*

Source: White, Z. (2021). Facebook algorithms and user polarization. Charlottesville, VA, USA.

The additional step added to each iteration of a News Feed display is depicted in this graphic. The user-accessible percentage graph displays the "constraints" applied to the search results at the top, with options for conservative and liberal balancing limits. These indicate the proportion of each point of view that is included in the feed and are fulfilled by each News Feed display in the "balanced" output.

In this demo, each click by the user takes them to an external news story, but also records as a "reward" for that instance of content. The algorithm updates its information on the user: specifically, the predicted success rate of a certain topic or viewpoint. Therefore, in the next iteration, the greedy algorithm displays more content aligned with the viewpoint of that article. This occurs for both the unconstrained and balanced feeds on this sample website because personalization is not explicitly prohibited by the constraints. The majority of articles that are displayed still reflect the user's political views, but the percentage limits provide enough of a different perspective to potentially break up the "echo chambers" that are otherwise encouraged online. The constrained algorithm takes these limitations into account at each stage, and any inclusion that causes the News Feed's quantified polarization to rise above a certain point is removed until the constraints are met. The algorithms behave similarly in most other respects.

4.4. PRIORITIZING ORIGINAL NEWS ON FACEBOOK

Every day, a significant amount of news is published online, and many people now get their news mostly from this source. The quality of news has an impact on people's preferred platforms and methods of consuming news. Numerical expression of news quality can lead to major platform and user improvements. We consider a number of factors when evaluating news quality, and originality stands in contrast to repetitions, slightly altered text, and coverage that makes reference to original news. Although creating original news is time-consuming and expert-only, it is what starts the normal news cycle and propels the news industry as a whole. People all across the world are informed by original news, which ranges from breaking news, eyewitness accounts, and vital updates during emergencies to in-depth investigative reports that unearth fresh information. It is in everyone's long-term interest to prioritize original news on the internet.

Here, we first examine the online news landscape, utilizing the Facebook platform as an illustration. We tabulate the range of news originality, from entirely unoriginal to highly original news, to facilitate a quantitative approach. Despite a sizable inventory that must be properly indexed and processed in order to identify the original news, our static analysis indicates that highly original news are uncommon. We also investigate the dynamics of the Facebook news life-cycle and discover that, usually, news posts receive the most exposure in the first few hours, with a lengthy tail following. This suggests that the computation of an originality score, which is used to enhance News Feed ranking, needs to happen quickly.

Aiming for fast response times and high search quality at scale, we develop a near real-time system and create a synthesized signal for news originality. Following pairwise-labeled data (same subject or different subjects), specialized BERT embeddings are used to cluster news articles covering the same news event together. We ultimately choose a two-stage clustering algorithm that is both highly scalable to large datasets and effective after testing a number of clustering algorithms against pairwise data that has been human-labeled. Every hour, our system makes incremental updates to better capture the dynamics of the news. We found that behavioral cues, like citations of earlier posts, can also be utilized to assess news originality instead of content alone. Given the strong incentives to manipulate the distribution of online news, integrity considerations are especially crucial. We remove news items created within suspicious activity patterns in order to de-bias our algorithms. First, we compare our originality signal's performance offline to ratings made by qualified journalists. An A/B test is used for online evaluation, and the effect on news article ranking is also tracked. The News Feed ranking system incorporates the signal.

Our contributions include:

- We analyze the dynamics of the news life-cycle and the landscape of news originality before putting forth a quantitative method for understanding the news ecosystem. The amount of work required to produce news content is how we classify the originality of the news.
- We design a near real-time system and propose a methodology to process individual news articles on a large scale. It generates an artificial score to determine the originality of news by utilizing the three-step clustering method and the PageRank algorithm. In particular, PageRank normalization within clusters is new. This technique is transferable to other news delivery systems.
- We develop quantitative and qualitative methods to enable live-data analysis of news quality scores and perceived news quality. These techniques can measure entire news ecosystems as well as focus on specific news articles and their distribution. Both news publishers and consumers—who increasingly rely on online news—benefit from such analyses.

4.4.1. Background

This section begins with an introduction to the news citation graph and a review of the PageRank principles. Next, we present our ranking at Facebook using our originality signal. However, our contributions are not Facebook-specific; other social media platforms employ conceptually similar ranking systems.

4.4.1.1. The News Citation Graph

Google created the PageRank algorithm in the beginning to rank websites and pages to enhance search results. In mathematics, the process of ranking vertices in a graph is based on a random walk algorithm. A website that receives a lot of links from heavily trafficked websites is considered to be heavier. Every Web page propagates its page weight to the pages it links to. When it comes to the news industry, Del Corso et al. presented a corresponding graph-based ranking algorithm that prioritizes credible news sources and noteworthy news events, with each vertex representing a news source (Gianna M Del Corso, et al., 2005)

Ye and Skiena developed MediaRank, an automated ranking system for news sources. They demonstrated that PageRank values are positively correlated with reporting quality as determined by peer reputation and other metrics by applying the PageRank algorithms to news reporting citations. Zhang and associates developed a set of signals to assess the reliability of news gathered from knowledgeable annotators. Their indicators were divided into two groups. The first group consists of content indicators, such as studies, organizations, and so forth, that are identified by the articles themselves. According to Cresci et al., context indicators in the other group necessitate examination of outside sources, such as author reputation and/or peer recognition based on the PageRank algorithm.

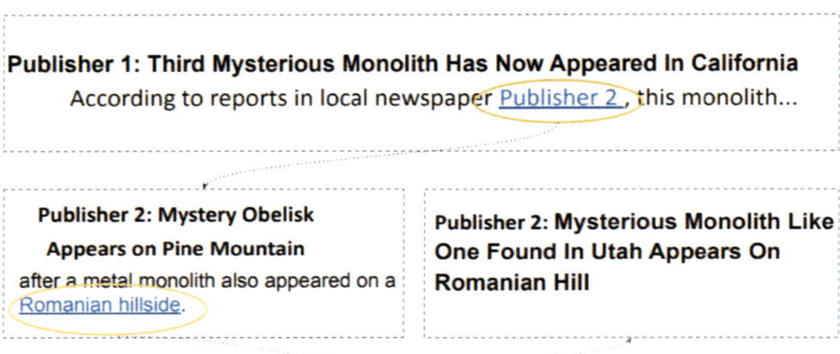

Figure 4.2. *Citations in news articles. The top snippet cites an article by another publisher. The cited article cites another article from the same publisher.*

Source: https://arxiv.org/pdf/2102.08465.

Similar to citations in academic papers, it is common to cite credible peers in the news industry, and such citations are important indicators of news source quality. Therefore, we introduce the news citation graph at news article level, instead of the domain level, to estimate the credibility of individual news articles. The idea is that when a news article f is disproportionately cited by its peers, this indicates higher journalistic credibility. Whereas academic papers itemize their references and use reference numbers in citations, news articles follow a different style. We only consider citations in the form of links in a news article to other news articles. (Stefano Cresci, Roberto Di Pietro, ET AL., 2015) (Figure 4.2).

Citations from news articles are shown in Figure 4.2. The news article by Publisher 1 is the source of the example at the top. This article references a number of sources, one of which is displayed: a news story from a different publisher that references a different piece from the same publisher. A publisher will get cited in a lot of other articles and publications if they break the story about a significant news event.

We take snapshots of the news ecosystem and index all our notation by time t. In particular, V is the set of all news articles at time t, and $v \in$ V denotes an individual article. We cluster such articles by news event or news story, denoting individual clusters C $\subset$ V. When a news article v cites another article u, we represent this by a directed edge ev, $\in$ E, where E is the set of edges in the citation graph. We also say that ev, is$v$'s outbound edge and u's inbound edge. Using these directed edges, we can compute the PageRank values of individual vertices by iteratively applying the following formula on every vertex in the graph in a topological order:

$$n_v = \frac{1-d}{|\mathcal{N}|} + d \sum_{u \in \mathcal{B}_v} \frac{n_u}{|\mathcal{B}_v|}, \qquad (1)$$

where; nv is the PageRank of article v (initialized to 1) at time t; Bv denotes the set of adjacent vertices (neighbors) of vertex v; |Bv| is the number of neighbors of v; and d is a (constant) damping factor, usually set to 0.85. The latter parameter dampens the propagation of weights through multiple edges.

The News Article Representation It's critical to consider the degree of similarity between two articles when determining an article's originality. Cosine similarity is frequently used to accomplish these checks on vector embeddings. Previous work uses the BERT (Bidirectional Encoder Representations from Transformers) network architecture to generate the necessary embeddings, and has achieved state-of-the-art results in numerous natural language processing tasks across various applications. BERT handles previously unseen words by breaking them down into known subword fragments. It can also be updated on a regular basis to handle emerging keywords such as "COVID." Original BERT models were DNNs pre-trained on the BooksCorpus and the English Wikipedia. However, BERT networks can be specialized to a given use case by adding one dense layer and training it on adequate labeled data. Along these lines, Reimers and Gurevych proposed a SentenceBERT architecture that uses the Siamese network structure in the context of semantic similarity estimation.

4.4.1.2. News Feed Ranking

Scholars and business alike have studied news ranking in great detail. This topic is covered in a number of publications from the information retrieval community. A news source ranking system called NuzzleRank was introduced by Nuzzle in 2018. It combines a number of signals, such as publisher authority data, into a single score.

Facebook's News Feed displays events from users' social graphs in addition to news content. Ranking goals take into consideration communities (friends, family, etc.), News Feed integrity (e.g., to prevent unlawful activities and discourage clickbait), and long-term user satisfaction. A user's News Feed, which contains the most recent updates from their friends, groups they have joined, and pages they have followed, appears when they log into Facebook. The four stages of News Feed ranking are roughly inventory, signals, prediction, and relevance scores. Many signals are extracted from a piece of content once it is posted, including the publication time and engagement numbers. The probabilities of potential individual user actions for each piece of content in the inventory, should they see it, are estimated using those signals. In terms of notation, P(like) denotes the likelihood that a user will like the content, and P(comment) represents the likelihood that a user will comment on the update. In the final step, we aggregate these forecasts and calculate a ranking relevance score for every content item. This system uses our news originality signal, which is summed up in Figure 4.3. Facebook's News Feed ranking takes into account a variety of signals, and our originality signal only slightly alters the user experience.

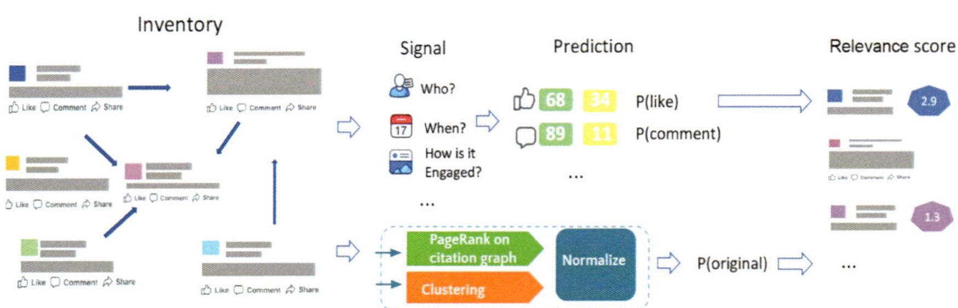

Figure 4.3. *News feed ranking at Facebook.*

Source: https://arxiv.org/pdf/2102.08465.

4.4.2. Problem Analysis

Here, we assess the state of news originality and provide inspiration for our work. Next, we look into the evolution of news articles on social media sites. Using the originality signal in News Feed ranking requires an understanding of the news life-cycle.

4.4.2.1. The Landscape of News Originality

Our quantitative approach to news originality uses content buckets:

- Completely unoriginal, scraped or spun content with no editorial effort;
- Highly unoriginal, with very low editorial effort;
- Somewhat unoriginal, may be editorially produced but heavily cite other content without original reporting or analysis;
- Potentially original but lacking peer recognition;
- Recognized as original by peers: breaking news, eyewitness reports, exclusive scoop, investigative reporting, and so forth.

Content that has been scraped is taken verbatim from other sources without any editing. Spun content is taken from a website or post and uploaded by people or computers with very little changes. Rearranging paragraphs, changing words, and paraphrasing are common techniques. One can quickly create a lot of content without scraping by automating the spinning of already-existing content. Spun and scraped material has the potential to overshadow original work and diminish its value, so it should be removed or distributed less widely than original work.

Simple text edits result in incredibly unoriginal articles. The majority of news stories, in our opinion, actually fit into the third category of being a little unoriginal. These articles don't take much work to write, but they might contain helpful information.

Content that does not fit into previous buckets and may be unique, but for a variety of reasons does not receive peer recognition during the news cycle is included in this bucket labeled as potentially original. This is often the case with opinion pieces that get little traction. Citation signals, therefore, are unable to differentiate between articles that are not original and this bucket.

A great deal of work goes into fact-checking the material for the highly original news pieces, which also feature lucid storytelling, excellent writing, and striking images. Well-considered and unique news articles are frequently highly referenced by colleagues in the field and enhance the standing of individual content producers. Owing to the time and knowledge needed, original news articles are hard to come by. Distribution of original content should be prioritized in order to expand its audience and ultimately benefit readers and the news industry.

It is generally challenging to evaluate the originality of each article on its own since doing so would necessitate a thorough content analysis combined with knowledge of current affairs. Making the distinction between rumors and fake news and accurate reporting would be especially difficult. Consequently, we extract further insights from the online news dynamics and the news citation graph. Specialized systems based on text hashing, fingerprinting, and text similarity metrics handle the unique cases of scraped and spun content. As a result, our work does not handle such content, which in reality does not show up in users' News Feed inventories.

4.4.2.2. The Dynamics of Online News

Online news can be readily indexed and preserved, although social media platforms typically prioritize recently released content. News reporters work hard to break a new story because of this. In order to reconsider this widely held belief and ascertain how to incorporate it into our work, we monitor the trends in user engagement metrics and analyze a sizable amount of news articles that are shared on Facebook. We also examine the effects of adding important information a few days after the original publication, and we visualize the life-cycle of typical online news stories. It turns out that the same pattern holds true for news about politics, entertainment, and both local and global news.

Johnson and Johnson's Ebola vaccine received approval on November 11, 2019. According to our inventory, 34 related articles were published on 17 websites on that particular day, and user engagement metrics peaked. The publisher that first broke the story, which attracted the most traffic, specializes in life science and medicine. The World Health Organization formally approved the vaccine two days later, on November 13. This news was reported by numerous mainstream publishers, and we saw an increase in inventory. But after seven days, traffic was essentially flat and virtually nonexistent, suggesting that this did not lead to another engagement peak.

According to our data analysis, ranking interventions are only beneficial at the beginning stages of a news story's existence. This has an immediate effect on News Feed ranking architecture and implementation, creating difficulties for ranking deployment as well as signal computation. As a result, we only pay attention to news items that were released in the previous seven days. Our intervention with respect to originality ranking does not significantly impact users' News Feed experience because we do not modify the current post inventory. Nonetheless, reporters and publishers who create intelligent and unique content ought to benefit from the overall effect.

4.4.3. Estimating News Originality

It makes sense that both the method and the caliber of news content are considered aspects of news originality. But computationally capturing these ideas seems difficult, particularly when the process of creating content is still opaque. Expert writers and raters frequently find that a single passage is insufficient to assess originality and require more context. Relevant background information includes the extent to which current events have received coverage, as well as the opinions of colleagues within the news ecosystem regarding a particular news item. A fundamental tenet of our work is that while appropriate context may offer sufficient signals to estimate originality, direct content analysis is neither sufficient nor necessary.

We create a news citation graph for the complete news inventory at a specific time in order to capture the context of individual news articles. The PageRank algorithm is used to assess each article's peer recognition on this graph. A news article may be cited by multiple publications or it may be a local news article that receives numerous citations from a major publisher; PageRank effectively handles both scenarios. Here, we highlight the application of global PageRank values that aren't limited to specific news stories. This is so because high-quality articles frequently reference unrelated background information and could be referenced under upcoming news stories.

We try to capture news ecosystem dynamics and emulate how professional raters or journalists estimate news originality level. To this end, PageRank values cannot be compared across topics and news events with very different amounts of news coverage. For a given news event or news story, we consider the entire news coverage as a cluster. Our insight is that articles with the highest global PageRank values within each news-event cluster are most likely to be original. Hence, we estimate news originality by normalizing global PageRank scores nv within each cluster Cv:

$$s_v = \left(\frac{n_v^p}{\sum_{u \in C_v} n_u^p}\right)^{\frac{1}{p}}, \; p > 0 \tag{2}$$

where; Cv is the cluster of article v; and the p constant defaults to $p = 1.0$. Increasing p would favor articles with higher nv values.

Notably, we are unable to assess an article's originality before colleagues have cited it. Delays are introduced, and a near-real-time system is needed to provide originality scores early in the news cycle.

When using originality scores sv in News Feed ranking, we first convert them into P(original) $\in (0, 1]$ as follows:

$$\text{P(original)} = \frac{\max(s_v, \theta) - \theta}{1 - \theta}. \tag{3}$$

here; $\theta \in (0, 1]$ is the promotion threshold, that is, only contents with $s\,t\,i > \theta$

can be promoted. Then, we add P(original) to the relevance score as a second-order term:

$$\text{Relevance} = \alpha_1 \cdot P(\text{comment}) + \alpha_2 \cdot P(\text{share}) + \alpha_3 \cdot P(\text{like}) + \cdots + \alpha_n \cdot P(\text{click}) \cdot P(\text{original}). \tag{4}$$

In this case, the weights αi maximize long-term user satisfaction, and P(comment), P(share), P(like), and P(click) represent the probabilities of the corresponding events for the news article in question. It is evident that our originality signal is only one factor in News Feed ranking, which boosts content that has been acknowledged by peers. Certain content types are elevated by other signals.

4.4.4. Implementation and Scaling

According to our initial research, news stories that are frequently cited by other articles typically have a higher degree of originality. As a result, we start by creating a citation graph of every news item that was released during a seven-day period. We then use scalable clustering techniques to group news articles by story or event, normalize PageRank values within each cluster, and compute global PageRank values for individual articles.

4.4.4.1. PageRank with Integrity Considerations

Using the Facebook Crawler tool, we index every news article shared on the network. Using a Facebook social plugin or by copying and pasting the link, the Facebook Crawler tool crawls the HTML of an application or website that has been shared on Facebook. Other open-source crawlers accomplish the same thing. Anyone can access and analyze the well-maintained, publicly available Web crawl data repository known as Common Crawl.

Only news articles published within a seven-day moving window are included in the graph. Following HTML parsing, we go through the output to obtain every tag that defines a hyperlink to another website. Links within the tag that have distinct URLs can still lead to the same website. In order to give each news citation graph vertex a unique ID based on a canonical URL, we resolve all of its URLs to canonical URLs. We create an edge between the two news article vertices if the referenced Web page is also a recent news article. We determine the PageRank values for each news article using this news citation graph.

According to Du et al., the raw citation graph is susceptible to link farming. In other words, the graph can be altered to add numerous inbound edges to a target page by modifying the interconnected link structure of the pages. Before using the PageRank algorithm, we ignore a number of citation types in order to thwart such manipulations. One common example is self-linking edges in G^t that reference an article written by the same publisher, as seen in Figure 4.2. Some websites link to other websites that don't actually contain any content; instead, they automatically reroute users to phishing websites or back to the original article. The possibility of manipulation is reduced by these integrity filters. Typically, a filtered snapshot of the citation graph taken every hour has between 300 K and 500 K edges. The PageRank calculation does not include news articles that do not have any incoming or outgoing citations. Attempts to influence PageRank in Web searches have been effectively addressed despite their lengthy history.

With graphs that show cycles—which are produced when well-known Web pages are updated to link to pages that were published later—the original PageRank computations perform admirably. Since news posts on social networks are usually not edited, our news citation graph, in contrast to the Web link graph, primarily consists of links to older content. On acyclic graphs, PageRank computations become much simpler and only need one linear-time graph traversal. In actuality, though, our citation graph has enough cycles to call into question these ease of abstractions.

4.4.4.2. News Event Clustering

We now describe our method of clustering. Using the PageRank scores of other articles in the same cluster, we normalize the PageRank scores of individual news articles. It seems sense that a major national news event and a local breaking news story would have comparable levels of originality; however, original articles within larger clusters receive higher PageRank scores and more citations. Computational scalability is crucial in addition to cluster normalization; on a typical day, our inventory snapshot comprises 2 million–3 million articles, which we aim to process in a matter of minutes.

Noting that articles with identical titles may have different PageRank scores, we use the titles of the articles to estimate the topical similarity of the articles. To group duplicate article titles into mini-clusters, we first lowercase the titles, remove punctuation, and hash the titles. We compute a vector embedding based on the robust and flexible BERT DNN for every unique title. Apart from effectively managing synonyms and synonymous phrases, BERT facilitates transfer learning.

Vector-based clustering algorithms are supported by BERT-based vector embeddings that are optimized to capture title similarity using cosine similarity.

The ability to process millions of titles in a matter of minutes and quality concerns influence the choice of algorithms, which we need to guarantee regular updates to the news originality signal. K-Nearest-Neighbors (KNN)-based clustering algorithms are a good place to start, but determining *K* is difficult, and for any given *K*, these algorithms run the risk of yielding inconsistent results in our application. The set of unique article vectors is converted into an undirected KNN graph G. For each vector, we find its *K* = 5000 nearest neighbors based on cosine similarity (1 – cosine distance) and use cosine similarity for edge weights between adjacent vertices v_i^t and v_j^t. Lightweight edges are ignored, and subgraphs are defined by connected components of the resulting graph. Reasonable weight thresholds are found with a form of binary search guided by a subgraph size target.

4.4.4.3. Scalability

One of the main performance bottlenecks is the construction and processing of the KNN graph with *K* = 5000 nearest neighbors per vertex. On an average day, one server's RAM can accommodate all of the previous week's news articles, allowing for reasonably quick processing. For the following reasons, though, this architecture is not sufficiently scalable.

4.4.5. Evaluation and Deployment

We assess each of the news originality signal's functional components separately, as well as the signal as a whole with the assistance of expert raters, before embedding the signal into News Feed ranking and testing various scenarios to ensure that everything functions as it should. An industry-standard method is used to assess the production deployment: before it is made available to the majority of users, an A/B test is conducted using real data on a small number of users.

4.4.5.1. Evaluation of Embeddings and Clustering

We ask experienced raters to evaluate pairs of news articles as part of our rating flow. For every pair of articles, the raters designate a similarity level: distinct subjects with some shared contents, same subjects with different aspects, and same subjects. We gather 100 K pairs of randomly selected English news titles for training, with 40% going toward fine-tuning, 10% toward validation, and 50% toward testing. In addition, we gather an additional 10,000 pairs of news articles to assess the effectiveness of clustering. We select a certain number of closest neighbors based on text similarity and/or document embeddings in order to sample likely-positive examples. The neighbors further away who are close enough to make the labeling task nontrivial provide likely-negative samples.

4.4.5.2. Evaluation by Professional Raters

We sample the most viewed news articles classified as original and the most viewed article not classified as original from the most viewed news domains over a seven-day period in order to evaluate the accuracy of our citations score signal. Our team of expert raters has extensive experience in the news industry and employs a methodical approach to ensure impartial evaluation of every article on a three-point news originality scale. Around 90% of the time, our predicted labels match these results for the rating of 3.0. Stated differently, our signal achieves 90% precision in recognizing original news.

4.4.5.3. Production Deployment and Evaluation

The purpose of the originality signal is to increase the distribution of original news articles in the relevance score calculation. Recalculating it hourly from scratch ensures that it is available early in the news cycle. It just takes a few minutes to build the news citation graph and news clusters, but there are currently crawling and vector embedding bottlenecks in place. Although it takes time for original articles to be cited in practice, if the workflow were to be run more frequently, original articles might be found and promoted sooner. Such advancements are probably possible with additional infrastructure optimization. We carefully examined the available data and conferred with the publishing and academic communities before proposing changes to Facebook's News Feed ranking. Specifically, we conducted an A/B test on real data for a few weeks, with a small test group using the updated ranking rules and the control group using the previous production ranking rules. We calculated the increase in view counts at various thresholds in order to estimate the impact, and we discovered that our method performs well at various thresholds. No statistically significant declines in our proprietary metrics were seen either during the A/B test or following the full product launch. In June 2020, our signal was made available for English-language content in Facebook's News Feed ranking system for the majority of users, following further inspections and discussions. Publishers might attempt to tamper with our originality signal. In order to prevent misuse, PageRank can be safeguarded, while Facebook's integrity enforcement and monitoring specifically target coordinated inauthentic activities.

4.5. NAVIGATING THE ALGORITHM: TROUBLESHOOTING WHY FACEBOOK AD IS NOT DELIVERING

Facebook is a powerful platform that has revolutionized the way businesses engage with their target audience in the vast world of digital marketing. With its enormous user base and powerful targeting tools, Facebook gives marketers unmatched chances to connect with and win over new clients.

Nevertheless, success cannot be assured by merely producing and launching an advertisement. Advertisers frequently encounter difficulties when their ads don't produce the expected outcomes.

In order to comprehend the reasons behind this, we must delve deeply into the intricacies of Facebook's algorithm.

4.5.1. Unraveling Reasons for Non-Delivery of Your Facebook Ads

There are several reasons why your Facebook ads might not be delivering. We've delved deep into the most common reasons below (Figure 4.4):

Figure 4.4. *Reasons for non-delivery of your Facebook ads.*

Source: https://www.artworkflowhq.com/resources/navigating-facebook-algorithm.

1. **Ad Disapproval:** If Facebook's advertising policies or guidelines are broken, the ads may not be approved. Ad disapproval can be due to a number of factors:
   - **Violation of Community Standards:** Facebook reserves the right to reject ads that include objectionable, violent, or improper content that violates its community standards.
   - **Misleading or False Claims:** Ads that present false information or make up facts about goods, services, or deals might not be accepted.
   - **Restricted Content:** Ads endorsing specific delicate content, like gambling, alcohol, or adult products, might need more

scrutiny and could be rejected if they don't follow Facebook's guidelines.

- **Prohibited Content:** Ads that promote illegal goods or activities—such as weapons, drugs, or discriminatory content—will probably not be accepted.

2. **Ad Under Review:** Facebook's review process can occasionally take longer than anticipated, which keeps ads in the review stage. Reasons for ads being under review include:
   - **Increased Ad Volume:** During peak times or periods of high influx of ad volumes, the review process may take longer.
   - **Complex Ad Content:** Ads with complex features, such as advanced targeting options or specific industries, may require additional review for compliance and accuracy.
   - **Manual Review Triggered:** Certain factors, such as targeting sensitive topics or keywords, may trigger a manual review by Facebook's team.

3. **Low-Quality Ad:** Facebook's standards and guidelines for ad content may not be met by low-quality ads. Some factors contribute to the low quality of advertisements:
   - **Engagement Bait:** Ads that artificially increase interactions through deceptive methods or engagement baiting might be classified as low quality.
   - **Withheld Information:** Ads that omit important details or deceive viewers by obscuring their intent or nature could be rated as low quality.
   - **Sensationalist Language:** Ads that employ sensational or exaggerated language but don't offer much substance or pertinent information could be labeled as low quality.

4. **Excessive Text:** Facebook has restrictions on how much text is allowed on an advertisement image. A text-heavy ad may only be delivered to a limited audience. Excessive text in advertisements can be attributed to various factors.
   - **Overlay Limitations:** Facebook restricts the quantity of text that can be displayed on an advertisement image in order to preserve an eye-catching experience.
   - **Image-to-Text Ratio:** High text-to-image ratio advertisements may be viewed as less visually appealing, which could limit their reach.

5. **Spending Limit Reached:** The advertisements will stop running if the campaign's budget or spending cap is met. There are a few reasons why you might have spent too much:
   - **Budget Allocation:** The allocated budget for the campaign has been fully utilized or depleted.
   - **Campaign Duration:** The campaign has run for the specified timeframe, and the budget has been exhausted within that period.
6. **Ad Frequency and Ad Fatigue:** Ad fatigue may result from continuously playing the same advertisement for the same audience. Users' engagement may decrease as a result of desensitization or loss of interest in an advertisement after seeing it too frequently.

   Ad frequency is taken into consideration by Facebook's algorithm, which may restrict the distribution of ads to the same users if they are shown too frequently.
7. **Ad Auction Competitiveness:** Advertisers bid for ad placements through Facebook's auction-based ad delivery system.

   Your ads may receive few impressions or not be shown at all if your bid is not competitive enough with other advertisers vying for the same audience.

   Now that we've looked at the main reasons behind Facebook ads not delivering, let's look at how we can fix it.

4.5.2. Tips and Tricks to Navigate the Facebook Algorithm

Gaining an understanding of and proficiency with the Facebook algorithm will greatly improve your advertising endeavors. The following advice will assist you in navigating the Facebook algorithm:

1. **Understand Your Audience:** Comprehending your target audience is essential for successful Facebook advertising. A thorough understanding of your target market will enable you to produce content that appeals to them, increasing reach, improving ad performance, and fostering higher levels of engagement. Here's how you can do this:
   - **Conduct Audience Research:** Use Facebook Audience Insights, Google Analytics, and other tools to gather data about your target audience demographics, interests, and behaviors.
   - **Create Buyer Personas:** Develop detailed profiles of your ideal customers, including their age, gender, preferences, and

pain points. This will help you tailor your content to their specific needs and interests.

– **Monitor Audience Engagement:** Analyze the performance metrics of your Facebook posts and ads to gain insights into what content resonates the most with your audience. Adjust your strategy based on these findings.

2. **Create Compelling Content:** To draw in and hold the interest of your audience, you need to provide interesting and timely content. It increases organic reach, motivates people to interact with your posts, and raises the possibility that more people will see your ads.

   To conduct compelling content, here's what you can do:

   – **Conduct Content Research:** Stay updated on industry trends, popular topics, and what your competitors are doing. This will help you create content that is timely, relevant, and valuable to your audience.

   – **Use Captivating Visuals:** Include visually appealing and brand-consistent high-quality photos, videos, and graphics. More people are drawn to and engage with visual content more often.

   – **Craft Compelling Headlines and Ad Copy:** Create headlines and ad copy that are clear, succinct, and visually appealing while conveying the importance and pertinence of your content. Make use of persuading language and speak to the concerns of your audience.

3. **Use Visuals and Multimedia:** Users' attention can be drawn in by visually stimulating content while they browse through their Facebook feeds.

   You can improve the appeal and uniqueness of your content by adding images and multimedia components. Use the advice below to add interest to your visuals:

   – **Use High-Quality Images and Videos:** Make sure your images are well-designed, lucid, and visually appealing. Well-edited videos and high-resolution photos can improve the overall quality of your content.

   – **Experiment with Different Formats:** To add variety and hold the attention of your audience, experiment with different kinds of visual content, like infographics, GIFs, and live videos.

- **Add Captions and Subtitles:** If you use videos, consider adding captions or subtitles so that users who prefer silent or muted browsing can access your content. This has the potential to expand audience reach and boost engagement.

4. **Utilize Facebook Audience Insights:** You can find useful information and insights about your target audience with Facebook's Audience Insights. You can learn more about their demographics, interests, habits, and intent to buy by utilizing this tool.

   With the help of this data, you can improve your targeting tactics and produce more specialized and successful advertising campaigns. You can use audience insights in the following ways:

   - **Access Audience Insights:** Navigate to the Facebook Ads Manager, select "Audience Insights" from the "Plan" dropdown menu. Choose the appropriate audience segment to analyze.
   - **Analyze Demographics:** Review demographic information such as age, gender, location, and language to understand the composition of your audience and tailor your content accordingly.
   - **Explore Interests and Behaviors:** Identify the specific interests, hobbies, and behaviors that your audience engages with. Use this information to refine your targeting and create content that aligns with their preferences.
   - **Identify Purchase Intent:** Discover the types of products, brands, or industries your audience is interested in. This insight can help you tailor your messaging and promotions to align with their purchase intent.

5. **Experiment and Test Different Strategies:** Facebook's algorithm is always changing, so what functions now might not function in the future.

   You can find the most effective strategy for your audience, maximize your campaigns, and outperform the competition by trying and testing a variety of approaches. There are different ways to test your strategies:

   - **A/B Testing:** Make several versions of your ads with different targeting, ad copy, and/or images. Run these versions concurrently to evaluate their differences in performance and determine which components work best.
   - **Test Different Objectives:** Examine various campaign goals,

such as conversions, lead generation, and brand awareness. Evaluate how well each goal is performing, then adjust your plan of action in light of the findings.

- **Monitor Analytics:** Examine your campaigns' performance metrics on a regular basis, paying particular attention to reach, engagement, click-through rates, and conversions. Make data-driven decisions and improve your upcoming campaigns by utilizing these insights.

4.5.3. Understanding the Facebook Ad Algorithm

The intricate system of computations and guidelines that controls the distribution, visibility, and interaction of advertisements on the Facebook network is known as the "Facebook ad algorithm." In order to present users with the most pertinent and interesting content based on their interests, behaviors, and preferences, it employs a range of signals and data points for the purpose of evaluating and ranking ads.

Understanding Facebook's ad algorithm is essential to running a successful Facebook campaign. In this section, we will delve further into understanding the Facebook ad algorithm and examine important variables that affect the performance and delivery of ads.

1. **Ad Relevance:** A key component of the Facebook ad algorithm is ad relevance. It assesses how well the interests and preferences of your target audience are matched by your advertisement. The likelihood that an advertisement will be seen by the intended audience increases with its relevance.

   For example, your advertisement's relevance score will be higher if the creative and messaging are in line with the values of the users it is targeting, such as those who are environmentally conscious and promoting a new line of eco-friendly skincare products.

2. **Ad Engagement:** User actions like clicks, shares, likes, and comments are referred to as engagement. Additionally, the Facebook ad algorithm is influenced by the amount of engagement your ads receive.

   Ad delivery increases when users actively interact with your ads, as this tells Facebook that the content is worthwhile and relevant.

   Let's say you are promoting a new product through a Facebook ad campaign. Because of its precise targeting and interesting ad content, your advertisement has a high ad relevance score. Nevertheless, there aren't many likes, comments, or shares during the advertisement's initial phase of engagement.

The low engagement in this instance might be interpreted by the Facebook algorithm as an indication that the advertisement is not connecting with the intended audience.

Because of this, if the algorithm determines that the advertisement is not interesting or relevant enough, it may only show it to a smaller audience.

Conversely, suppose that over time, the advertisement begins to garner more attention. Positive feedback is shown by users starting to like, comment on, and share the advertisement.

In this case, the Facebook algorithm receives an increased level of engagement as a signal that the ad is worthwhile and pertinent to the intended audience.

Consequently, the Facebook algorithm might react by increasing the ad's delivery and reaching more people. A broader audience, comprising users with comparable interests and actions to those who interacted with the advertisement, might see the advertisement.

3. **Ad Performance:** Ads that perform well are more likely to be shown to a larger audience on Facebook, as the social media platform strives to deliver ads that yield positive results for advertisers.

   Assume you have Campaign A and Campaign B, two Facebook ad campaigns that are running concurrently and have comparable targeting and ad content. Nonetheless, the two campaigns' performances diverge significantly.

   The advertisements in Campaign A have a low cost per result, a good conversion rate, and a high click-through rate (CTR). Consumers are actively interacting with the advertisements, and the campaign is producing favorable results like sign-ups, purchases, and website visits.

   Conversely, Campaign B is not doing as well as it should. The advertisements have a high cost per result, a low conversion rate, and a low CTR. The campaign is not producing the expected results, and users are not interacting with the advertisements.

   In this case, more people will see Campaign A advertisements than Campaign B due to Facebook's algorithm. Now that we know how Facebook ad algorithms operate, let's examine the possible reasons why your Facebook ads might not be performing as expected.

4.5.4. Exploring the Different Types of Facebook Ads

Facebook provides a variety of ad formats to meet the needs of different audiences and advertising objectives. With the distinct features and capabilities of each ad type, advertisers can select the best format for their campaigns.

Let's delve into the various types of Facebook ads and explore their key characteristics.

1. **Photo Ads:** One of the most popular and basic ad formats on Facebook are photo ads. They are composed of a call-to-action button, ad copy, and a single image.

   Enhancing the appeal and distinctiveness of your content can be achieved by incorporating images and multimedia elements. Use the advice below to add interest to your visuals:

   – **Use high-quality images and videos:** Ensure that your visuals are well-designed, clear, and visually appealing. High-resolution photos and well-edited videos can enhance the overall quality of your content.

   – **Experiment with different formats:** To keep your audience engaged, try incorporating various types of visual content, such as infographics, GIFs, and live videos.

   – **Add captions and subtitles:** If you include videos, consider including captions or subtitles. This allows users who prefer silent or muted browsing to still access your content, potentially expanding your audience reach and increasing engagement.

   Product displays, event promotions, and showcasing brand imagery can all be accomplished with photo ads. Marketers have the ability to select visually striking images that pique viewers' interest and inspire action.

2. **Video Ads:** An interesting and dynamic method to interact with your audience is through video advertisements. Facebook provides a number of video ad formats, such as in-feed videos, stories ads, and in-stream videos, in response to the growing popularity of video content.

   Video advertisements are a great way to showcase product features, share client endorsements, and effectively communicate your brand message. They make it possible to tell stories and draw in viewers with gripping audio and visuals.

3. **Carousel Ads:** Advertisers can display several photos or videos in a single ad unit by using carousel ads. Customers can view various

offerings, product variations, or sequential storytelling by swiping through the carousel cards.

This type of advertisement works well for showcasing a variety of goods, providing step-by-step instructions, or narrating a brand story in sections. Carousel advertisements boost user engagement and conversions by offering an engaging and interactive visual experience.

4. **Slideshow Ads:** Slideshow advertisements are a less complex option for audiences with slower internet connections than video ads. They are made up of multiple photos or videos that have been combined to resemble a slideshow.

5. **Collection Ads:** These combine an engaging mobile shopping experience with the power of images or videos. Advertisers can display a main image or video in this ad format, with several product images underneath it.

   Users are redirected to a full-screen Instant Experience after tapping on the advertisement, where they can easily browse through a selection of products and make purchases. Collection advertisements work especially well for e-commerce companies trying to increase sales and product discovery.

6. **Instant Experience Ads:** These, formerly known as Canvas ads, offer mobile users an immersive full-screen experience. With the help of these advertisements, marketers can provide engaging, multimedia-rich experiences with images, videos, carousels, and more.

   Instant Experience advertisements aim to draw in viewers and offer a captivating medium for product placement, brand storytelling, and experience sharing.

7. **Lead Generation Ads:** The purpose of lead generation advertisements is to collect user data and produce leads. These advertisements include a lead form that users can fill out on Facebook, saving them the trouble of leaving the app.

   Lead generation advertisements are useful for companies looking to grow their consumer base or nurture leads for additional conversion because they make the process of gathering user data easier.

8. **Dynamic Ads:** Personalized and automatically generated, dynamic ads show goods or services according to the user's browsing habits or interactions with your app or website. The products or content

featured in these advertisements are dynamic and tailored to the specific needs of each user.

Retargeting campaigns can benefit greatly from dynamic ads because they increase conversion rates by reminding users of the exact products they have looked at or expressed interest in.

9. **Messenger Ads:** Advertisers can interact more interactively and conversationally with users by utilizing Facebook Messenger, a popular messaging app. These advertisements can show up in the conversation threads and inbox of the Messenger app, giving marketers the opportunity to start discussions, respond to user questions, and increase interaction.

   Businesses wishing to offer individualized customer care, encourage chatbot interactions, or enable direct communication with their audience may find messenger ads helpful.

10. **Sponsored Messages:** Businesses can send targeted, personalized messages to users who have interacted with their Messenger account in the past through sponsored messages, a particular kind of advertisement.

    Through these advertisements, which show up as direct messages in the user's Messenger inbox, companies can send out customized promotions, pertinent content, or follow-up messages. Through tailored dialogues, Sponsored Messages are a useful tool for re-engaging users and nurturing leads.

REFERENCES

1. Beam, M. A., Hutchens, M. J., & Hmielowski, J. D. (2018). Facebook news and (de)polarization: Reinforcing spirals in the 2016 US election. *Information, Communication & Society*, *21*(7), 940–958.
2. Celis, L. E., Kapoor, S., Salehi, F., Keswani, V., Vishnoi, N. K., & Weng, P. (2019). A dashboard for controlling polarization in personalization. *AI Communications*, *32*(1), 77–89. https://doi.org/10.3233/AIC-180606.
3. Cresci, S., Di Pietro, R., Petrocchi, M., Spognardi, A., & Tesconi, M. (2015). Fame for sale: Efficient detection of fake Twitter followers. *Decision Support Systems*, *80*, 56–71.
4. Del Corso, G. M., Gulli, A., & Romani, F. (2005). Ranking a stream of news. In *Proceedings of WWW*. ACM, Chiba, Japan, 97–106.
5. Geschke, D., Lorenz, J., & Holtz, P. (2018). The triple-filter bubble: Using agent-based modelling to test a meta-theoretical framework for the emergence of filter bubbles and echo chambers. *British Journal of Social Psychology*, *58*(1), 129–149.
6. John, N. A., & Dvir-Gvirsman, S. (2015). I don't like you any more: Facebook unfriending by Israelis during the Israel-Gaza conflict of 2014. *Journal of Communication*, *65*(6), 953–974.
7. Kitchens, B., Johnson, S. L., & Gray, P. (2020). Understanding echo chambers and filter bubbles: The impact of social media on diversification and partisan shifts in news consumption. *MIS Quarterly*, *44*(4), 1619–1649. https://doi.org/10.25300/MISQ/2020/1637.
8. Larsson, A. O. (2018). Diversifying likes: Relating reactions to commenting and sharing newspaper Facebook pages. *Journalism Practice*, *12*(3), 326–343.
9. Leong, L. (2020). Domesticating algorithms: An exploratory study of Facebook users in Myanmar. *Information Society*, *36*(2), 97–108. https://doi.org/10.1080/01972243.2019.1709930.
10. Liao, S.-H., Hsian, P.-Y., & Wu, G.-L. (2014). Mining user knowledge for investigating the Facebook business model: The case of Taiwan users. *Applied Artificial Intelligence*, *28*(7), 712–736. https://doi.org/10.1080/08839514.2014.927695.
11. McPherson, M., Smith-Lovin, L., & Cook, J. M. (2001). Birds of a feather: Homophily in social networks. *Annual Review of Sociology*, *27*(1), 415–444.
12. Schubert, E., Sander, J., Ester, M., Kriegel, H. P., & Xu, X. (2017). DBSCAN revisited, revisited: Why and how you should (still) use DBSCAN. *ACM Transactions on Database Systems (TODS)*, *42*(3), 1–21.

13. Seargeant, P., & Tagg, C. (2019). Social media and the future of open debate: A user-oriented approach to Facebook's filter bubble conundrum. *Discourse, Context & Media*, *27*, 41–48.
14. Tandoc, E. C., Jr., & Maitra, J. (2018). News organisations' use of native videos on Facebook: Tweaking the journalistic field one algorithmic change at a time. *New Media & Society*, *20*(5), 1679–1696.
15. Usher-Layser, N. (2016). Newsfeed: Facebook, filtering, and news consumption. *Phi Kappa Phi Forum*, *96*(3), 18–21.
16. Ye, J., & Skiena, S. (2019). MediaRank: Computational ranking of online news sources. In *Proceedings of KDD*. ACM, Anchorage, AK, USA, 2469–2477.
17. Zhang, A. X., et al. (2018). A structured response to misinformation: Defining and annotating credibility indicators in news articles. In *Proceedings of WWW*. ACM, Lyon, France, 603–612.

CHAPTER 5

YOUTUBE ALGORITHM

Contents

Introduction 178

5.1. A Brief History of the YouTube Algorithm 178

5.2. How to Make a YouTube Channel? 180

5.3. Quality Content Is King 189

5.4. How Marketing Works on YouTube? 192

5.5. Monetization 197

5.6. YouTube Channel Goals You Can Control 202

5.7. Best Techniques to Use YouTube to Promote Your Business 204

5.8. Collaborations 209

5.9. Using Social Media to Promote Your Channel 212

5.10. Use Your Channel to Promote Your Merchandise 214

References 215

INTRODUCTION

A mainstay of the global cultural landscape, YouTube is used by millions for information, entertainment, and everything in between. Parents use it to keep their kids entertained, and students use it to learn. However, discovery is something that is frequently a mystery. Although YouTube is essentially a massive search engine, most of its users are watching its recommendations and not much else. So how does the YouTube algorithm actually work? How do people get the content they do? Why does certain content go viral seemingly overnight? Something appears to be recommended more and more the more people watch it until it becomes viral.

The secret sauce of YouTube, akin to other social media platforms, is its algorithm, which guarantees that users receive the exact content they desire from the website. Social media companies use algorithms, which are collections of mathematical or scientific rules, to decide which content users want to see first and in what order. Like other algorithms, YouTube's goal is to present content that users are most likely to interact with based on their past interactions with similar content.

5.1. A BRIEF HISTORY OF THE YOUTUBE ALGORITHM

In order to address the question of what the YouTube algorithm is, let's take a brief look at how it has evolved over time. And the current state of it.

5.1.1. 2005–2011: Optimizing for Clicks and Views

As per the founder Jawed Karim's (a.k.a. the star of Me at the Zoo), YouTube was established in 2005 with the goal of crowdsourcing the video of Justin Timberlake and Janet Jackson's infamous Super Bowl performance. Thus, it makes sense that the videos with the highest views or clicks were initially recommended by YouTube's algorithm. Consequently, there were more deceptive titles and thumbnails (a.k.a. clickbait. The user experience was disastrous as viewers felt deceived, let down, or just plain irritated by the videos.

5.1.2. 2012: Optimizing for Watch Time

YouTube changed its recommendation algorithm in 2012 to encourage viewers to spend more time on each video. It also included the total amount of time spent on the platform. People watch videos for longer periods of time when they find them valuable and engaging. Or at least that's the theory. This change to compensate for viewing time was revolutionary. "[Watch time] had an immediate impact," claims Mark Bergan, author of Like, Comment, Subscribe: Inside YouTube's Chaotic Rise to World Domination. The majority of early YouTubers were creating TikTok videos, but as time went on, they produced gaming, beauty vlogging, alt-right podcasts, and other verticals that we now associate with the platform. "

Accounts that were big performers previously (like videos from eHow, or MysteryGuitarMan) dropped off almost immediately.

Some creators attempted to shorten their videos in an attempt to increase the likelihood that viewers would watch them through to the end after YouTube changed its algorithm. Some extended their videos to give viewers a longer viewing experience overall. YouTube stuck to its party line and said that if you create videos that people want to watch, the algorithm will reward you. It didn't comment on either of these strategies. Nevertheless, time spent is not always equal to quality time spent, as anyone who has ever spent any time online can attest. YouTube quickly adopted a new strategy.

5.1.3. 2015–2016: Optimizing for Satisfaction

YouTube started using user surveys in 2015 to track viewer satisfaction directly. Additionally, it gave precedence to metrics that measure direct response, such as Likes, Dislikes, and Shares (as well as the particularly cruel "not interested" button). Deep Neural Networks for YouTube Recommendations is a whitepaper that YouTube published in 2016 that details some of the inner workings of its artificial intelligence. Put succinctly, the algorithm had become far more individualized. Finding the video that each unique viewer wants to watch, as opposed to just the one that many others may have watched in the past, was the aim. Because of this, the chief product officer of YouTube stated in a panel in 2018 that 70% of YouTube viewers watch videos that the algorithm recommends.

5.1.4. 2016–Present: Dangerous Content, Demonetization, and Brand Safety

The scale and popularity of YouTube have led to a rise in the number of problems with content moderation over time. Furthermore, the topic of what the algorithm suggests has drawn the attention of journalists, the government, and creators alike in addition to advertisers. According to YouTube, it takes seriously its obligation to promote a wide variety of viewpoints while halting the spread of false information. For instance, early 2019 algorithm modifications resulted in a 70% decrease in the consumption of borderline content. (YouTube characterizes borderline content as deceptive or harmful material that almost doesn't break community guidelines. On the other hand, offensive material is taken down right away. Creators are impacted by this problem because they worry about inadvertently breaking the dynamic community guidelines, or receiving strikes, demonetization, or worse as a form of punishment. (Previous CEO Susan Wojcicki stated that enhancing community guidelines for creators' transparency was one of YouTube's top priorities in 2021).

Brands and advertisers are also impacted because they don't want their name and logo to be associated with white supremacists. Politicians in the United States are growing more worried about the social media algorithms' impact on society. Senate hearings have called on YouTube and other platforms to answer questions regarding their algorithms. Additionally, Democrats proposed the "Protecting Americans from Dangerous Algorithms Act" at the beginning of 2021. Researchers have discovered that the new YouTube algorithm has made progress in lowering the quantity of hazardous content it presents in recent years. However, despite alleged algorithmic changes, evidence of YouTube endorsing alt-right content was discovered during the most recent 2024 Finnish election. It appears that we are still in the dangerous YouTube content territory.

5.2. HOW TO MAKE A YOUTUBE CHANNEL?

It doesn't take long to start a YouTube channel, regardless of your motivation. You can alter the look of your channel, make any necessary video edits, and even organize your videos into various playlists once it has been created and approved. Here is a quick 3-step checklist you can use when creating a YouTube account for your brand or company.

5.2.1. Create a Google Account

If you didn't already have one, this is crucial. Your Google username will be your YouTube username by default. Thus, this username is what other people see when you upload videos. Once you're on YouTube, though, you can alter it at any time. Google accounts are linked to Gmail accounts, which grant users access to all Google services and products, including YouTube, Google Play, and Maps. However, you will need to enter your first and last name before being able to access YouTube through your Google account. This is the name that YouTube will use to recognize you. As a result, you have the option of selecting a different name or your true first and last name.

5.2.1.1. Choose Your Character

You are aware of how crucial the name of your YouTube channel is. Almost equal numbers of well-known YouTubers go by both their real names and their brand names. This now really depends on your level of privacy preference and the subject matter of the channel content. For instance, the majority of gaming channels typically use a brand or made-up name, but the majority of vlogging channels typically use their full name. Use your imagination. You should use the brand name if your channel is going to be focused on an idea, concept, or brand. You should give the process of naming your brand a lot of thought. Here are some suggestions that you can combine:

- Alliteration, for example, "Charisma on Command;"
- Wordplay/Rhyming, for example, "Pewdiepie;"
- Try a single word, for example, "Vsauce," "Smosh."

That being said, your channel name isn't overly important as long as the content is quality. For example, most cannot even pronounce the channel name "Kurzgesagt," however their videos consistently pull millions of views. Pick a name you like and are passionate about, and stick with it. Once you have filled these required fields, select "Create Channel."

5.2.2. Customize the Appearance of Your Channel

This is significant because your channel's initial impression matters a lot. Of course, your videos are of the highest caliber, but in actuality, it's best to cover all the bases. You can alter a few fundamental things, like your;

- Channel's icon;
- Channel's art;
- Channel's description.

When you want to make these changes, go to your channel, and click the edit button next to the items you want to change.

5.2.1.2. Channel Icon

This could be a cool self-portrait, a professional shot, or even one that was captured with an iPhone. Make sure this photo catches people's attention because its primary goal is to entice them to click on your channel. A method supported by science is to include your face in the icon (if suitable), choose a face associated with your YouTube channel (e.g., Vsauce's icon), or simply use a photo of you grinning. You may also get ideas for the logo from your channel name. If you're really stuck, you can even get a very good quality logo made for as little as $5 by visiting the website fiverr.com. Here, you can also hire a professional editor to add your logo to your photos. Individuals also choose to draw themselves, which can be quite effective, particularly if you're not the most photogenic (like me).

5.2.1.3. Channel Art

As previously mentioned, you can use Fiverr to get a nice banner made for as little as $5. You can also use a wallpaper of your choice or a free stock photo from Pexels.com. This is not a very significant section of your channel, but you could use it to promote a book you've written or include a link to your website.

5.2.1.4. Channel Description

This is a crucial section of your channel. Even though there won't be as many viewers of your channel description as there are subscribers, it's still a good idea to include links to your website and any other social media profiles you wish to share. A lot of YouTubers also provide a FAQ here for frequently asked questions. If necessary, it's imperative to include a business email address here. Never use your private email address. This can be extremely useful for increasing the revenue you make on YouTube. You can also add a featured channels section, add a trailer to your channel. A channel trailer is important, as it lets people know what they can expect on your YouTube channel. You can also change how the videos are laid out and also enable 'channel comments' under the discussion section. Any change you desire to make can be done by clicking the settings icon (it is next to your subscribe button), then, enable the "customize the layout of your channel" option.

5.2.3. Start Uploading Your Videos

Simply log in and click the "upload" button to access the upload page whenever you'd like. It is located in the upper right corner of the YouTube page. You have two options when it comes to uploading your videos.

- Drag videos to the upload page;
- Click the large upload area to browse for videos from your PC; or
- Click the 'import' option; it is next to the 'import videos' area by the right of the upload page. This option allows you to upload videos you have saved in Google photos.

A picture slideshow that you can upload to YouTube is an additional choice. On the upload page, it is accessible on the right-hand side. Expert advice: when uploading videos from your pc\., make sure you choose public, unlisted, private, or scheduled, depending on your preferences. Remember that once you make your videos public, anybody can view them. Only people with a direct link can view the video when it is unlisted. When they are private, only you have access to them and you must first log in. You can specify the time that your videos will be accessible to the public when you want to schedule them. Other considerations that you should have.

- The maximum size of the video you wish to upload should be 128 GB if your web browser is up to date. If not, you will be limited to uploading videos that are no larger than 20 GB. Before you render your video, your video editing software should give you a decent idea of its size; in most cases, you won't be going over 20 GB.
- Videos uploaded to YouTube cannot be longer than 15 minutes unless you verify your account. This limit is lifted as soon as your YouTube account has been verified. Depending on the kind of content you want to create, this is something to keep in mind.
- The YouTube video editor allows you to add captions, titles, photos, clips, and transitions to your videos. Later, more details on how to precisely edit your video.
- If you want to easily manage your videos, put them into custom playlists

5.2.3.1. Setting Up a YouTube Brand

Reaching a major milestone for your YouTube channel and brand is the ultimate source of satisfaction. The first 1,000 subscribers is a milestone worth celebrating. For those who have never used YouTube before, getting this many subscribers may seem unattainable, but it's actually quite simple. YouTube functions best when combined with other websites and social media platforms, and it can be a powerful tool for growing your following and business. Let's go over some fundamental guidelines for having fun and having success with YouTube.

1. **Be Consistent:** You need to consistently upload worthwhile content to YouTube if you want to be successful. This is really quite difficult. You may assume that every topic has already been covered just by browsing the website, but this is untrue because you can take a well-liked topic and give it a fresh perspective. For example, there are plenty of tech "unboxing" videos online. However, you could create a "re-boxing" channel where you talk about various tech parts as you put them in their boxes. This is just a suggestion; please use your imagination to come up with something different.
2. **Give Your Videos Smart Names:** Creating a catchy title for your YouTube videos is another difficult part of creating content for the platform. Perhaps you already have an idea, but it might be too detailed or intricate. If you follow the guideline to make it as simple as possible, YouTube will automatically complete the name. Although the title of your video need not match an already-existing

video, it must still make sense and be applicable. There is a wealth of additional information about naming your videos effectively on the internet, so check it out if you are struggling to think of catchy titles. Remember to conduct your research!

3. **Make the Design of Your Channel Appealing:** Many visitors are forming an initial opinion of your brand and concept based on how your channel is designed. This is how viewers can engage with you and discover the values of your channel. Create a captivating header to highlight your business or brand. If you lack experience with graphic design, fonts, or color selection, there are experts available online who will assist you for a fair price. You might also ask a friend who is tech-savvy for assistance in coming up with an interesting channel style.

4. **Try Out Different Shooting Locations:** Making films in various locations will instantly add interest to your channel. Changing up the background or occasionally filming at a nearby coffee shop can help keep your videos engaging for viewers, though this may be difficult if you are limited to one location. This will keep them wondering and enticed to come back to find out what you'll do next.

5. **Be Lighthearted:** Try to laugh at yourself and your channel occasionally; it's not enjoyable to watch someone who is always too serious. Admitting your mistakes to your audience makes you seem more relatable and human, which sets you apart from the majority of other talking head content videos on the internet. To make your viewers feel astonished when they visit your channel, try to keep it interesting, lively, and impromptu. Additionally, though, always stay true to who you are. Make sure your videos reflect your sense of humor, if you have one. Be yourself if you're sincere. Genuineness and relatability are what people will respond to and value most. Even though you might not win over everyone, the people who really matter will value you.

6. **Utilize the Custom Thumbnail Option:** With this easy tweak, you can boost your YouTube views and subscribers. Simply use a well-liked font on various images from the internet to draw attention, and then use Photoshop to make adjustments to the picture. To help viewers quickly understand what they are about to see, you can change the title of the picture thumbnail to something different than the title of the video.

7. **Make Use of Annotations:** Those little pop-ups that appear in the middle of videos? Using these can really help to increase the

effectiveness of your content. Include an annotation for every video to encourage viewers to subscribe to your channel. Granted, it does require a little more work, but you will want annotations in every video as soon as you see an increase in the number of subscriptions.

8. **Don't be Afraid to Ask:** This is an easy-to-miss but sometimes forgotten tip. As your videos come to an end, make sure you ask viewers to "like" and subscribe to your channel. You can't get what you don't ask for. This is an excellent opportunity to explain to viewers what they can anticipate from your channel. For example, if you provide advice on home improvement projects, you could encourage people to subscribe to receive additional advice on the topic.
9. **Be True to Yourself:** You can only be yourself on your channel and in your videos; no matter how hard you try, you can never be someone else. Being in front of the camera can be intimidating for some people at first because it makes them compare themselves to others who are more comfortable with it. Recognize that being fake won't help you move past this. Rather, let your actual self shine through, and you will attract individuals who share your values.
10. **Make a Quality Trailer for Your Channel:** Video creators on YouTube now have the option to customize their channel, including a trailer that summarizes the content of the channel. The majority of people only attend movies after watching the trailer and being aware of what to expect. A minute and a half is the maximum length for your trailer, which should include some scenes from the content on your channel and an incentive to subscribe. If you actually work at what you make, people will come back.
11. **The Third Most Popular Site Online:** Not only is YouTube the most popular social networking site for creating videos, it is also the third most visited website worldwide. However, not many people are utilizing social networking to its full potential. The majority of YouTube users don't even use the site to develop their own brands, increase their online presence, or generate revenue. Many users haven't uploaded even a single video to YouTube. If you've never heard of this concept before, it's time to give YouTube some serious thought. These are a few of the causes:
    - **Cross Promotion:** You can use YouTube for cross-promotion, which is driving traffic to your other websites or blogs. Make sure you let viewers know where they can find you on your blog when your videos conclude. Remember to also remind

them to subscribe. YouTube can be useful as a supplement to already-existing blogs or websites, but it's not that great on its own. You have to regularly cross-promote your channel in order for this to work.

- **A Full-Time Income can Happen:** Indeed, it is feasible; some people have made a living solely from YouTube, particularly with Google's AdSense program. But when you first start out, make sure you are focusing on several sources of revenue.
- **A Chance to Grow your Business:** Viewers are more likely to engage with your content if you have videos posted on YouTube. The more content you have, the longer people will watch it, and the longer they watch it, the more likely it is that they will find your blog or other websites and subscribe to your content. Recall that quantity is important, but quality is just as important!

12. **The Importance of Optimized Titles:** The only way to succeed on YouTube is to stand out from the crowd, and titling your videos with something original and quirky is a great way to do this. This will encourage curious people to visit your channel. Having original, humorous titles helps to strengthen your points of view. But, in terms of YouTube marketing, you must understand some SEO fundamentals if you want to obtain as many views as possible. These pointers will help with that:

    - **Title Keywords:** This still affects your content even though it used to be much more beneficial for SEO. Because Google bots cannot read text posts, they cannot view videos. However, if you include your keywords in the title of your video, Google bots will recognize the topic.
    - **Utilize AdWords on Google:** Use Google AdWords to discover the most popular search terms at the moment. Try to focus on videos with a high search volume and little competition.
    - **Have a Descriptive Title:** While quirky titles can be advantageous, you should also let your audience know what to expect from your content. Be original, but make sure the words in your title relate to and make sense for the content of your video. It might take some time to become proficient at this, but if you work at it, you will.
    - **Go for Shorter Titles for Your Videos:** Remember that

Google removes the first 10 characters from your video title and substitutes "YouTube" with it. To make the most of this, try to keep your title lengths to 50 characters or less.

- **Omit "Video" from the Video Name:** When naming your video, there's no reason to use the word "video." This simply wastes character space and has no bearing on your YouTube search engine rankings. Nevertheless, there may be a slight change in the usual search results if this is done.
- **Customize Your Channel:** Utilizing YouTube's customization options is essential if you want to establish credibility with viewers. Make it distinct and new.
- **Be Professional:** A professional appearance is important to win over viewers' trust and respect, even if you are probably filming your videos from your room. Try to apply the same branding components on YouTube if your blog already has a following so that people can identify you on various websites and media.
- **Make a Bio:** To fully customize your channel, be sure to take advantage of YouTube's channel bio feature. You should keep your bio brief and to the point. In video descriptions, include a link to your blog, store page, or website.
- **Placing Subscribe Buttons on Your Website:** As previously mentioned, you ought to include a link to your website or blog in your YouTube videos. However, don't forget to include subscribe buttons from your blog on your YouTube channel.
- **Keep Your Videos Less Than Five Minutes Long:** Though there is no lack of in-depth, comprehensive content on YouTube, the videos that garner the most subscribers are under five minutes in length. According to research done in 2014, the average length of a YouTube video is 4:04 minutes, so for those of you who are just starting out, this is a good length to aim for. This will assist you in gaining a devoted fan base.

Keep it brief, simple, educational, and entertaining at first. You can experiment with different lengths once you have a following on your channel to see how people respond. Even though it could be difficult, it's a worthwhile challenge that will raise your chances of success on YouTube. Having excellent, one-of-a-kind artwork for your channel will greatly aid in the establishment of your brand online. If you are not proficient in graphic design, YouTube offers a service for creating channel art. Make sure to use a background head image that was created specifically for you and incorporates design elements from another website or blog.

13. **Using the Best Tools with YouTube:** YouTube offers a plethora of helpful tools, such as tools for creating and promoting videos, among other things. Using these will assist you in organically increasing your subscriber base, and over time, organic views translate into more subscribers. You can use the following video marketing tools to achieve the desired outcomes.
    - **Bulk Suggest Tool:** The Internet Marketing Ninjas developed this free tool, which makes it simple to obtain pertinent keyword research information for your content. It will search Google's and YouTube's "auto complete" databases, adding terms to your entry based on frequently searched keywords. This helps you better understand the search objectives of your target audience and subscribers by enabling you to quickly compare Google search terms with YouTube terms.
    - **WordPress Keyword Plugin:** Additionally, you can look up potential keywords using Google autocomplete search terms by using a WordPress plugin. This is located under the post editing options on your dashboard. This plugin also has the advantage of providing you with ideas for topics for articles and videos based on what is trending.

14. **Do Research on Competitors:** You can improve your content marketing campaign by learning more about your rivals. Analyzing your competitors can help you discover what works and strategies to increase viewer interest and engagement in your channel, but it shouldn't interfere with your creative ideas. The YouTube Analysis feature on BirdSong Analytics is the best tool for this. You can pay for this tool as you use it. You can use this helpful tool to get a variety of helpful reports and stats, like the following, with just the channel name.
    - Your competitor's channel's best upload time (in terms of getting likes).
    - The ideal day to upload for getting likes, according to your competitor.
    - When you should upload to receive audience comments, according to the competition.

- The best day to upload videos in order to get comments, according to your competition's channel.
- The way the length of your videos can impact viewing figures.
- The way the length of the videos can impact viewer engagement.
- Commonly used terms in video captions, and more.

Additionally, you can download an Excel spreadsheet containing a list of all the videos uploaded by your rivals, along with information about their duration, upload date, description, title, and number of views, comments, and likes. Experiment with conditional formatting and filters in the spreadsheet to gain even more insight into rival strategies. When using these reports for your video creation, make sure you check out multiple channels.

5.2.3.2. How Can You Get People to Share Your Content?

Every time you upload a video to your channel, you are contributing to your content, which needs to be effectively promoted on all of your social media platforms. You can use a semiautomated channel to share your content across numerous social media platforms by utilizing the RSS feeds on your channel. This tool can assist you in that regard:

5.2.3.2.1. DrumUp

With just one click, you can use this useful tool to schedule posts to appear on your social media feed. You can add multiple Facebook pages, multiple Twitter accounts, and multiple LinkedIn profiles with this tool. You are able to much more effectively promote your video content everywhere. Additionally, it lets you:

- Schedule your videos fast using their one-click schedule button. This distributes them across your different social media platforms.
- Preview what your snippets will appear like on social media once they have been posted to the platforms.
- Authenticate your various accounts on social media.

  As you can see, you have access to a wide range of tools for enhancing your YouTube channel, statistics, and views.

5.3. QUALITY CONTENT IS KING

The secret to success on YouTube in the past was having a large number of subscribers. The recommendation system of the platform gave preference to channels with a larger number of subscribers, giving their content a higher ranking. But YouTube's approach and algorithm have changed over time, putting more emphasis on high-quality videos than on subscribers. Content is king these days.

The main objective of YouTube is to maintain users' engagement on the site for as long as possible. It has changed its emphasis from advertising channels with sizable subscriber bases to providing content that is relevant to viewers' interests in order to accomplish this. The enhanced visibility of smaller channels on users' feeds indicates that this change is a gateway rather than a barrier. For small channel owners, this is a new era of empowerment.

The recommendation system on YouTube has advanced, utilizing a variety of metrics to determine the interests of users. These metrics consist of past searches and viewing behavior, active subscriptions, satisfaction tests, and more. Small channels now have a higher chance of being suggested to new viewers as a result.

This implies one thing for small channel owners: relevance and consistency are crucial. Creators need to make videos that appeal to their target audience and clearly define the niche of their channel in order to get the algorithm's attention. For videos to be discovered, their titles, tags, and descriptions must be optimized. It's crucial to keep in mind that while more impressions may result in more views, this is not a given. In the end, viewers make the decision about what to watch. Think Media, for example, received over 7 million impressions between May 1 and May 28, but only 280k viewers clicked on their videos. This proves that impressions are not guaranteed viewpoints, but rather opportunities.

Small channels have a special opportunity as recommendations become more content-based. Creators can boost their chances of drawing in new viewers and expanding their subscriber base by selecting a niche and optimizing their content for discoverability. This is a promise of future development and success rather than merely a shift. Now is the ideal moment to dedicate yourself fully to growing your small channel and producing interesting, high-quality content that appeals to your viewership.

5.3.1. A New Era on YouTube

YouTube is changing, and with it come the tactics that content creators must use to be successful. In order to support both established and up-and-coming creators in expanding their channels, subscribers must be replaced with more pertinent metrics and tactics.

5.3.2. The Current State of YouTube

5.3.2.1. Subscribers: A Vanity Metric

A YouTube creator's success used to be greatly influenced by their subscriber base. They are now more of a vanity metric, though. Since the platform changed from being a social graph to an interest graph, the relevance of your video to viewers' interests now determines its reach more than your subscriber count. This is a change that makes it easier for new creators to be found.

5.3.2.2. Algorithm Evolution

Viewer behavior now takes precedence over social connections in YouTube's algorithm. This means that rather than being based on what your friends and followers are doing, your recommended videos are based on your likes, searches, and viewing history. By presenting content that is more closely aligned with the interests of the viewer, this change seeks to improve the viewing experience.

5.3.3. Four Proven Strategies for YouTube Growth

The four tried-and-true methods to boost your YouTube presence are discussed in subsections.

5.3.3.1. Learn from Video Outliers

Analyzing outliers—videos that perform noticeably better than others on comparable channels—is one of the best ways to find popular video topics. Outliers show that a particular type of content is in high demand. By looking at rival channels, you can manually find outliers; alternatively, you can use programs like VidIQ, which speed up the process and offer insights on high-performing videos.

5.3.3.2. Trend Surfing

Producing content centered around current affairs, well-known individuals, and popular subjects is known as trend surfing. The YouTube algorithm favors content that speaks to viewers' current interests and frequently highlights smaller creators alongside more well-known ones. Use Google News to search for trends related to your channel's topics and subscribe to industry newsletters and content providers.

5.3.3.3. Master Video Packaging

The topic, title, and thumbnail of your video together make up its packaging.

Sufficient packaging is essential to drawing in clicks. For the best video packaging, use:

- Choose compelling topics;
- Write titles that create curiosity and include relevant keywords;
- Design eye-catching thumbnails;
- Optimize your video descriptions and scripts.

VidIQ and similar tools facilitate this process by offering insights into keywords, title ideas, and thumbnail inspiration.

5.3.3.4. Develop a Core Theme and Clear Strategy

While following trends can quickly grow your channel, long-term success requires a clear strategy and the development of a core theme. This entails determining your niche, comprehending your target market, and regularly generating content that is in line with the general direction of your channel.

5.4. HOW MARKETING WORKS ON YOUTUBE?

The process of using YouTube videos and advertisements to promote your business is known as YouTube marketing. YouTube is growing faster than any other platform because it is an incredibly powerful medium. After Google, it is the second most popular website worldwide. Since its launch, it has amassed almost 2 billion monthly active users worldwide. Therefore, YouTube marketing is the solution if you want to diversify your traffic sources or even just get your brand in front of your target market.

5.4.1. Top Advantages of YouTube Marketing

When viewers enjoy videos as much as we do, you should think about incorporating them into your marketing plan. Naturally, when we refer to a video, we mean YouTube. Here are six reasons to think about YouTube marketing if you haven't already included it into your overall strategy.

5.4.1.1. Heavy Traffic

With over 5 billion videos watched daily, YouTube is experiencing exponential growth in traffic compared to all other platforms combined. Advertising your content on other people's videos is a great way to reach an audience even if you don't make many videos for your company. As long as you meet their needs, you can be sure to find potential customers on YouTube thanks to its high traffic volume. These are some statistics from YouTube that you should be aware of:

- YouTube gets 30 million visitors per day;
- 300 hours of video are uploaded to YouTube every minute;
- 68% of YouTube users say that videos help them in their purchasing decisions;
- The number of small and medium business advertising on YouTube has doubled over the last two years;
- YouTube is available in a total of 76 different languages (this covers about 95% of the Internet population);
- YouTube has its own local versions in more than 88 countries.

5.4.1.2. Higher Visibility on Google

It's possible that you've noticed that videos are showing up in Google search results more frequently than other types of content. By producing excellent content for your website and uploading videos to YouTube based on it, you can capitalize on this. By doing this, you will build backlinks to your website and increase the frequency with which Google search will locate your company. You are also enhancing your company's online authority by using YouTube marketing. Your page will rank higher on the Google search engine result page the more authoritative you are on the search engine. Here are some YouTube tips to help you improve the authority of your website:

- Get other websites to embed your videos on their websites;
- Associate your website with your YouTube channel;
- Share your videos on other social media platforms;
- Use different video styles to engage more with your consumers.

5.4.1.3. Build Your Email List on YouTube

Using YouTube to grow your email list is a major benefit of YouTube marketing. You can directly embed your sign-up form into YouTube videos using a variety of available programs. A video can be momentarily stopped to allow viewers to sign up for your list and enter their information. This strategy facilitates the process of growing your email list while offering your audience high-quality content. These are a few of the most popular methods for growing your YouTube email list:

- Use lead magnets;
- Add annotations;
- Add cards;
- Run YouTube ads.

5.4.1.4. Higher Conversion Rates

A video replaces a million words if a picture can convey a 1,000 words. Videos, more than any other type of content, have the ability to elicit strong emotions. They breathe life into your business by transforming your messages from boring text to something lively and captivating. In a special way, they also support the development of authority and trust among others. This type of interesting and captivating content can boost your conversion rate by 80%.

5.4.1.5. Multiple Video Types

The variety of videos you can make to promote your brand online is another important benefit of YouTube marketing. Explainer videos, sales videos, social media videos, presentation videos, and video ads are the most popular categories of videos on YouTube. Reproducing a single piece of content across numerous formats is easier now. These pointers may help you decide what kind of videos to make:

- Make engaging and funny videos;
- Answer common questions (think of the most common questions you can get from potential customers about your business, your products, and services);
- Show how your brand works in behind-the-scenes videos;
- Create testimonials from customers;
- Go live.

5.4.1.6. Massive Media Library

In addition to having a sizable user base, YouTube boasts an enormous media library. The reason for this is that 300 hours of videos are posted to YouTube each minute. You can find anything you need under the sun and even beyond it with that much information. With a search engine this strong, YouTube allows you to locate the precise content you're looking for on a platform this size. This is the second-biggest search engine on the internet, with over 3 billion searches per month—much more than Ask.com, AOL, Bing, and Yahoo put together. All you need to do is optimize your YouTube videos if you're concerned about your content getting lost in this enormous ocean of data.

Every business has an incredible opportunity to increase traffic and customer base thanks to YouTube. But it's also a highly competitive environment. This implies that you can't just start posting videos to your channel and hope for instant results. Many large companies enter the YouTube marketing space without a plan, as evidenced by their low number of subscribers and views.

In actuality, making excellent videos is not enough to succeed on YouTube. It involves understanding how to tailor those videos to the search terms that users of YouTube use.

5.4.2. YouTube Marketing Strategy

YouTube offers businesses a plethora of opportunities. Companies are able to effectively promote their products thanks to its large user base. Let's explore how to develop and execute a YouTube marketing plan for your company.

1. **Create a Channel on YouTube:** You can use your standard Google account to create a channel. But the only person able to log in will be you. Create a brand account if you require an account that multiple people can access at once. It enables you to launch multiple YouTube channels.
2. **Research Your Target Audience:** You should research the demographics of your YouTube channel before making any videos. To satisfy user needs, find out the location, age, and viewing preferences of your target audience. You will be able to produce beneficial content by taking into account the needs and desires of your target audience. Compile all the pertinent data regarding the most popular videos that people have watched. Examine the analytics on your YouTube business account, if you have one. It will help you gain deeper understanding of the preferences of your audience. Learn more about the preferences and interests of your subscribers by looking through the comments, posing queries, or setting up a poll.
3. **Conduct Competitive Analysis:** There is fierce rivalry on YouTube, a sizable platform with a large number of business accounts worldwide. You can identify the opportunities your channel has by researching your competitors in the market. Determine who your top three most profitable rivals are first. You can accomplish this by using keyword tools to find the brands that rank highest for terms associated with your sector. To find useful information and inspiration, pay attention to their metrics, titles, descriptions, and comments under videos. Second, you should use a SWOT analysis to ascertain the advantages and disadvantages of your rivals.
4. **Create Videos based on the YouTube Algorithm:** YouTube uses a unique ranking system. Making recognizable thumbnails (pictures of your videos) and using keywords, along with optimizing your titles and descriptions, will help you rank highly. It will assist you in getting more views and giving you precedence over other

channels and videos. When writing a title, make sure to use the right keywords. Locate these terms and phrases in YouTube Analytics, then incorporate them into your titles. Don't forget to begin with the keywords. Write a title with 60 characters or less, aside from that. In order to write a synopsis of your video, you should utilize the most important keywords from your description. Add calls to action (CTAs) in the form of cards, end screens, watermarks, or bumper ads to encourage users to take the desired action. Lastly, give them encouragement to subscribe, like, comment, and share.

5. **Start Uploading Content to Your Channel:** Make a plan so that your videos will upload on time. Viewers will be aware of the upcoming time of the new video in this way. Make sure you select the day and time when there are the most views and engagement. Once you've uploaded some videos, you can use the analytics to determine when it's best to upload new ones.
6. **Provide All the Necessary Information on Your Channel:** You must optimize your channel in order to make the search easier. You should think about taking a few actions to make it easier for users to find you. Start by finishing your profile. Don't forget to use channel art, upload your logo, and complete the channel description. Additionally, you can include any other channels or resources that you think your subscribers would find useful. Secondly, ensure that links to your website and social media profiles are included in your channel. Thirdly, make a trailer for your YouTube channel to inform viewers about your product and introduce your business. Explain to users why they should subscribe to your channel and share your brand statement.
7. **Promote Your Videos:** If the titles of your videos contain relevant keywords, they may receive more attention. Think about setting up accounts on various social media platforms with engaging and high-quality videos. It will increase awareness and promote word-of-mouth advertising. There exist numerous efficacious methods for notifying your subscribers of newly uploaded content on your channel.
8. **Consider Influencer Marketing:** A sizable portion of opinion leaders' followers may be considering your product. Reaching out to influencers in your industry who are willing to promote your business and goods is always a smart move. Considering that 49% of consumers believe influencer recommendations, you can extend an invitation to collaborate.

9. **Measure Your Success:** You must monitor your progress after you post your first video. You'll be conscious of your successes and shortcomings in this way. This process will be made simpler by YouTube Analytics. Check it out to see how the subscriber count, audience demographics, traffic sources, and device reports have changed. The data you obtain will support the expansion of your channel. Gaining more insight into your audience will help you create content that better suits their needs.

Now that you understand how to create a YouTube strategy, it's time to look into the best tools for putting it into practice. One of the greatest channels for businesses using video marketing is YouTube. It presents marketers with a fantastic chance to engage with their audiences thanks to its billions of users and extremely high engagement rates.

5.5. MONETIZATION

The dynamic process of YouTube monetization enables content creators to make money off of the videos they upload to the website. Because of this financial incentive, YouTube has become a profitable platform for both pros and amateurs, providing a means of making money while sharing interesting content. Understanding the definition, prerequisites, and eligibility requirements for the YouTube Partner Program (YPP) is essential before starting this monetization journey.

5.5.1. Definition

The ability of content creators to profit from the videos they post on YouTube is referred to as "monetization." Ads that appear prior to, during, or following the video playback are the main source of revenue for this platform. In order for creators to take part in YouTube's monetization program, they must meet certain requirements that the platform has established.

5.5.2. Eligibility Criteria for the YouTube Partner Program (YPP)

The YouTube Partner Program (YPP) provides access to both advanced features and, more significantly, opportunities for platform monetization. In order to qualify for YPP, creators need to fulfill the following requirements:

- **Follow YouTube's Monetization Policies:** YouTube rules and regulations must be followed by creators in order for their work to meet community standards and be appropriate for advertising.

- **Watch Hours:** In the last 12 months, creators must have accumulated at least 4,000 watch hours on their videos. This measure assesses a channel's total viewership and engagement.
- **Subscriber Count:** It is necessary to have 1,000 subscribers at minimum. This benchmark indicates a sizable and active viewership for the channel.
- **Linked AdSense Account:** The YouTube channel of creators must be connected to an AdSense account. By connecting to Google's AdSense advertising platform, content producers can monetize the ads that appear in their videos.
- **Geographical Location:** Qualification for the Young Photographers Program is based on the creator's place of residence. Their area needs to have access to the program.
- **No Community Guidelines Strikes:** Channels that have a track record of breaking rules and regulations in the community could be excluded from YPP. Ensure that your record of no content violations is spotless.
- **Two-Step Verification:** Enforcing two-step verification as an additional security measure for the Google account linked to the YouTube channel is a security prerequisite.

5.5.3. Key Requirements: Subscriber Count and Watch Hours

- **Subscriber Count (1000):** Reaching a minimum of 1,000 subscribers indicates that the channel has a committed following of people who are interested in the programming. Notifications about fresh uploads are sent to subscribers, which boosts viewership.
- **Watch Hours (4000):** Around 4000 hours of viewing over the course of the previous year is a sign that the material is interesting and draws in viewers. This measure is essential for assessing the channel's general appeal and popularity.

5.5.4. The Seven YouTube Monetization Rules

These seven monetization guidelines are a good place to start if you want to make money from your YouTube content.

5.5.4.1. Create an AdSense Account

Get this rule out of the way first, as it will be a major prerequisite. Google's internal advertising network, AdSense, is used to market and sell advertising space across a variety of platforms, including YouTube. Connect your YouTube account to that account.

5.5.4.2. Learn the YouTube Partner Program Requirements

The YouTube Partner Program, or YPP, is what you should do next. Access to resources like the merchandise shelf and channel memberships is granted by membership. The requirements listed below must be fulfilled before YouTube will even give you a membership in the YPP.

- Prove you're following YouTube's monetization policies;
- Users must have watched your content for at least 4,000 hours ver the past 12 months;
- You need at least 1,000 subscribers;
- You need a linked AdSense account;
- You must be located somewhere where the YPP is available;
- Your channel has no community guidelines strikes against it;
- You're following YouTube's monetization policies;
- You have an extra layer of security via a two-step verification on the Google account associated with your YouTube channel.

5.5.4.3. Enable YouTube Monetization

After your application has been accepted, launch YouTube Studio, choose "Enable Monetization," and adhere to the prompts.

There are many rules to follow, and your channel will be monitored to verify that you comply. These policies include:

- Google AdSense policies;
- Community Guidelines;
- Copyright;
- Monetization policies;
- YouTube's Terms of Service.

5.5.4.4. Stay Within Copyright Laws

Get a Music License for Your Background Tracks. Copyrights are very important. Think about using Lickd to enhance your videos with quality music.

5.5.4.5. Things to Avoid If You Want to Monetize YouTube Content Effectively

Avoid these pitfalls, or you will scare away potential advertisers:

- Controversy and misleading or false statements. We have freedom of speech, but it comes with responsibilities. For example, you may get dinged by deliberately creating controversy with misleading, inflammatory language.
- Excessive bad language. A few swears won't get you in hot water, but, as in the movie rating system, excessive obscenities get you flagged.
- Misleading thumbnail previews. If your video is about how to clean an assault rifle and the thumbnail image is a basket of fluffy kittens, your video could get flagged for misleading content.
- Unnecessarily shocking content. Although this isn't a deal-breaker, advertisers are wary about being associated with controversial content of questionable taste, especially if there appears to be no reason for it.

5.5.4.6. Other Tips to Make Money on YouTube

Finally, expand your horizons and consider these other monetization methods:

- **Merchandising:** People love tchotchkes (e.g., t-shirts, mugs, hoodies, keychains, ball caps)
- **Affiliate Link Clicks:** Join an affiliate program and get commissions from referrals.
- Sell your video rights: Other brands might be interested in licensing your videos for their monetization purposes!
- **Get Fan Patronage:** Use platforms like Patreon to offer your viewers extra features and special perks for their monetary support.

5.5.5. YouTube Channel Monetization Policies

Let's go over two important aspects of YouTube's channel monetization guidelines. We have already discussed a few of these ideas.

5.5.5.1. Applying to the YPP (YouTube Partner Program)

It takes YouTube about a month, maybe longer, to review your membership application and reach a decision. YouTube will check these criteria during the application process:

- Main theme;

- Most viewed videos;
- Newest videos;
- Biggest proportion of watch time;
- Video metadata (e.g., titles, thumbnails, descriptions).

5.5.5.2. Avoiding Copyright and Monetization Mistakes on YouTube

As previously mentioned, copyright infringement on YouTube is a serious violation. As a result, you should only post videos that you have either made yourself or have permission to use. Moreover, videos that are created by others, audio and music tracks, and other copyrighted works are all covered by copyright. Policy infractions may lead to:

- Account termination or suspension;
- Removing all advertisements from your videos;
- Getting suspended from the YPP.

5.5.6. The Top 10 Ways to Monetize on YouTube

1. **YouTube Ads:** This is the most straightforward, conventional, and widely used method of making money. You can choose where these advertisements appear by using one of the many YouTube ad formats. They can appear before or during a video.
2. **Affiliates:** An affiliate program is when you watch a video and the host gives you a link to go to a business's website and think about buying their products and services. Every transaction that is successful earns you a commission.
3. **YouTube Premium:** With YouTube Premium, users can download videos and view content without advertisements. Fortunately, subscription revenue payments are made to video creators similarly to ad revenue payments, so you continue to receive payment for your videos under this service. The frequency with which Premium members view your videos determines the amount.
4. **Channel Membership:** A monthly subscription is required for channel memberships in order to receive special offers such as product discounts, one-on-one live chats, and access to exclusive videos.
5. **Patronage:** Think about allowing patrons to support your channel in exchange for special gifts via a third-party platform like Patreon. Speaking of treats, here are some.

6. **Merchandise:** Here's another strategy that we've already covered. Dozens of merchant platforms are currently available and ready to assist you in selling your branded products to your fan base.
7. **Paid Sponsorships:** Using, showcasing, or discussing a brand's or company's product or service in your video in exchange for a sponsorship is the strategy here.
8. **Super Features (Super Chat, Super Stickers, and Super Thanks):** These three "super" features can be found in chat messages displayed during YouTube live streams.

- **Super Chat:** This feature puts your chat messages front and center over everyone else's.
- **Super Stickers:** Similar to Super Chat, this feature allows users to purchase and exchange visually striking stickers that can be pinned to the top of a chat stream.
- **Super Thanks:** Users can show their favorite creators some love with this feature. In addition to receiving a featured comment in the chat, users can purchase an animated GIF.

9. **YouTube Shorts Fund:** If they fit the requirements, creators of Shorts will have access to this $100 million fund.
10. **YouTube BrandConnect:** For content marketing campaigns, this service links brands with YouTube creators and is presently available in the US, UK, and Canada.

5.6. YOUTUBE CHANNEL GOALS YOU CAN CONTROL

Setting realistic goals is crucial if you're just starting out on YouTube and want to see your channel grow. The majority of people make the error of concentrating on unachievable objectives like the quantity of subscribers or views their videos get.

These objectives may inspire you, but you may not always be able to achieve them. It is preferable to concentrate on controllable internal goals instead. These are the behaviors and actions that will help you accomplish your outside objectives. The following are a few instances of internal YouTube channel goals:

- Posting videos regularly;
- Creating high-quality thumbnails and descriptions;
- Engaging with your audience through comments and social media;

- Collaborating with other creators;
- Building a website to drive traffic to your videos.

5.6.1. Why Internal Goals Are More Effective?

There are various reasons why internal goals are more successful. First of all, you have control over them. Instead of depending on outside variables like viewer engagement or sponsorship opportunities, you can take action to achieve them. Second, you are laying a solid foundation for your channel by concentrating on internal objectives. In the long run, this may make achieving external goals simpler. For instance, you might see an increase in your subscriber count and views if you set a goal to post a video every week and work toward achieving it. Creating and sharing top-notch content on a regular basis will help you grow a devoted following and improve your visibility on YouTube.

5.6.2. How to Set and Achieve Your Goals?

To set and achieve your goals for your YouTube channel, follow these tips:

1. **Set Specific, Achievable Goals:** Rather than setting a goal like "I want to make $2,000 per month from YouTube sponsorships," try setting a goal like "I will post a video every week" or "I will create a custom thumbnail for each video." These goals are specific and achievable, and will help you to take action towards achieving your external goals.
2. **Track Your Progress:** Keep track of your progress towards your goals by using tools like a calendar or a spreadsheet. This can help you to stay motivated and see how far you've come.
3. **Celebrate Your Achievements:** Don't forget to celebrate your achievements, no matter how small they may seem. This can help you to stay motivated and continue working towards your goals.

5.6.3. YouTube Subscriber Goals

Now, you may be asking yourself, should I set goals for YouTube subscribers? After all, a lot of people consider having a large number of subscribers on their channel to be a sign of success on YouTube. You ought not to have subscriber targets. You have no control over how many people subscribe to your channel. All you can do is make sure your channel is in the best possible position to attract new subscribers by regularly producing excellent content, among other things. Yes, the number of subscribers serves as a success indicator. That being said, there are many channels with 500 subscribers that receive more views than, say, those with 1,000 subscribers. The number of subscribers doesn't matter.

You should concentrate on the things you can control as a content creator. Take your upload frequency, for instance. How much work you put into making and sharing videos is entirely up to you. Concentrating on uncontrollable factors is a surefire way to fail.

5.6.4. SMART Goals for YouTube

It's likely that if you've ever set goals, you've heard of the term "SMART goals." Unbelievably, you can use this idea to set practical goals for yourself as a YouTube content creator. Specific, Measurable, Attainable, Relevant, and Time-based is what SMART stands for. It has worked well in the past to set goals that fall into each of these categories, and YouTube is no exception. SMART objectives for YouTube might be:

- Upload 12 videos per month for 6 months;
- Spend 1-hour editing videos for 3 months;
- Comment on 10 videos every day for 1 year.

You'll see that none of these examples have anything to do with reaching a target quantity of views or subscribers. Your objectives need to be tied to things that you can directly influence with your own work. You will fail and become disappointed if you attempt to control something that you cannot control. Make sure your YouTube channel goals adhere to the SMART goals framework when you set them. To help you stay focused and to hold yourself accountable, go over your goals each day.

You now understand how to set YouTuber goals in a way that will lead to success in addition to knowing what some excellent goals are. Setting goals is essential for all content creators, but you have to be careful not to set uncontrollable objectives based solely on effort. In conclusion, don't limit your attention to purely external objectives like views and subscriber count if you want to expand your YouTube channel. As an alternative, make controllable internal goals and strive toward them. This will raise your chances of success and assist you in building a solid foundation for your channel.

5.7. BEST TECHNIQUES TO USE YOUTUBE TO PROMOTE YOUR BUSINESS

Platforms for videos have grown in importance as internet marketing tools for businesses. Particularly, the YouTube community has grown to become one of the most powerful in the social media space; monthly unique visitors reach over a billion, and YouTube searches rank second only to Google. The potential advantages of YouTube are immediately clear when you look at the numbers. However, due to its intense competition, YouTube isn't the best channel for every kind of business. It surpasses Facebook to become the second most popular website in the world, and hundreds of hours of video content are uploaded on it every minute.

It's simple for your video marketing efforts to be overlooked with all of this competition, particularly if the caliber of your material is poor. Although videos are among the most interesting content formats available, producing content at the caliber that YouTube viewers demand can be costly and time-consuming. However, don't let that stop you from creating video content; YouTube can still be a fantastic platform for hosting your videos, even though it can be difficult to attract viewers at times. Following that, sharing those videos on your other social media accounts on Facebook, LinkedIn, and Twitter will be simple.

5.7.1. Benefits of YouTube Video Marketing

Developing a YouTube marketing strategy has shown to be an effective approach for businesses and sponsors to connect with viewers. Brands can use the platform to connect with a wide range of consumers and develop a devoted following. Millions of subscribers have allowed many well-known YouTube creators to build enormous audiences. These channels have grown to be major sources of news, entertainment, current affairs, educational material, and much more. They are incredibly powerful nowadays.

Nevertheless, if done correctly, YouTube video marketing can offer your small business a number of fantastic advantages. Among the advantages of YouTube video marketing are:

- **Reach New Audiences:** Utilize YouTube's algorithm for recommendations to reach new viewers. This could be the most effective approach to connect with consumers who might not otherwise engage with your brand. They can quickly share your content on social media if they find it engaging enough. As a matter of fact, sharing videos online has grown in popularity.
- **Improve SEO:** Use YouTube's automated transcript generator to increase website traffic and gain the chance to achieve significant SEO benefits. YouTube provides a number of fields where SEO terms and phrases can be entered. There are many options available to you to maximize the visibility of your video content and draw attention to your business, including transcripts, descriptions, and keywords for your videos.
- **Drive Traffic to Your Website:** By creating engaging video content, you can use YouTube marketing to grow your audience and direct

viewers to your business website. Viewers may visit your website to find more content, get more information about your brand, or make purchases after watching your video.

- **Effectively Showcase Your Products and Services:** You can use YouTube to showcase products from your online store, make product-related instructional videos, and respond to frequently asked questions. Putting your product through its paces could entice people to visit your website and complete a purchase.

5.7.2. How to Create a YouTube Channel for Your Business?

Establishing a small business account is a reasonably simple procedure. The actions you must do to create it are as follows:

- You'll need a Google account with a business focus because YouTube is owned by Google. Don't use your personal Gmail or Google account, please.).
- Visit YouTube and enter your account information while logged into your business Google account. After that, you'll be able to set up a channel for your tiny company.
- You will be prompted to enter the name of your channel, which is typically just your company name or brand.

After it's created, you can customize it with features like banner art, a brief bio, and a channel image, which is also referred to as a channel icon. Simply search for "Customize Channel." Here are a couple more pointers:

- An 800 x 800 pixel channel icon is what you should have. The best possible image will result from doing this. Verify again that the profile picture you have chosen appears clear at this lowered size.
- Select a picture for your banner that effectively conveys the advantages you have over your competitors and represents your business or line of products.
- You have the chance to tell your audience a little bit about your brand and what kinds of content they can expect to see in the "About" section of your YouTube channel. Consider a few keywords that best capture the essence of your company. Keywords are terms or expressions that people frequently search for online.)
- Lastly, you can appoint more administrators or "managers" to your YouTube channel. You should designate other individuals as managers if more than one person is in charge of producing and overseeing the YouTube content for your company. They will then be able to administer, watch, and post on the channel.

5.7.3. Popular Types of YouTube Content

You must provide interesting content if you want to make marketing videos for your YouTube channel that are effective. As you create your videos, keep the following ideas in mind:

- **Listicles:** Lists are a common content type that can be both informative and entertaining in any format. They clearly outline the time and effort your audience will need to invest in consuming the content, as well as the potential value that can be obtained. Shorter lists show the opposite; longer lists are more valuable but take more time to complete. Try both and see which works best for your audience.
- **How-Tos:** Video tutorials that provide step-by-step instructions on how to use a product or solve common problems can be very helpful. They will assist potential customers in learning more about your goods and services in addition to assisting current clients in finding the answers to their queries without the need to contact customer service.
- **Behind the Scenes:** Providing a behind-the-scenes glimpse at your employees or operations can humanize your brand and provide customers with a better understanding of your company. They'll meet the people who run your services, discover how things are made, get a sense of your work culture, and more. People will feel more like they're part of your company's history rather than just another customer if you can provide them with this kind of insight.
- **Product Videos:** Customers can see your products up close and personal through videos without ever having to visit your store or make a purchase. This gives them the chance to find out exactly what your products are capable of and determine if they are suitable for their requirements.
- **Testimonials:** No matter how good you are at selling and promoting your goods, people will frequently put more faith in the thoughts and opinions of other customers. Testimonial videos give you the chance to leverage previous achievements to market your business and close deals. To encourage your clients to record testimonials, you could even provide a discount in return for their participation.

5.7.4. YouTube Posting Strategies

While producing excellent content is crucial, it is not the only factor to consider. It is imperative for small businesses to exercise strategic posting of those assets.

The following advice will help you understand how to make sure that more people in your target audience see your content.

5.7.4.1. Create Content Goals

You're probably already familiar with creating content goals if you're already producing content for other platforms, such as Facebook and Instagram. Companies create content for various purposes. It's possible that your only priorities are increasing engagement and expanding your audience. Alternatively, perhaps the focus of your social media endeavors is on transforming current followers into fresh subscribers or clients. Whatever your motivation, you should have specific objectives in mind as they will enable you to assess the effectiveness of your YouTube marketing campaigns.

5.7.4.2. Develop a Content Schedule

Your level of success on any social media platform, including YouTube, is largely determined by the quantity of content you create. Your company gains credibility on the platform the more you post worthwhile content that your fans can interact with. It is crucial to establish a content schedule that establishes the frequency and timing of your posts. Your YouTube following will eventually grow accustomed to knowing when you will post new videos. Advice: Although many people check other social media sites several times a day, YouTube users are more active at night and on the weekends.

5.7.4.3. Optimize Your Videos for Search

YouTube is well-suited to enable businesses to improve content with keywords, video tags, and other search-related elements because it is a member of the Google family of platforms and services. Making the most of these will help increase the visibility of your videos in YouTube's search results.

5.7.4.4. Encourage, Monitor, and Respond to Comments

Encouraging viewers to leave comments on your videos is a smart practice. This will facilitate beneficial communication between your company and its intended markets.

Additionally, it will encourage dialogue among your followers. Make sure to reply promptly to audience interactions and comments on your videos so that viewers feel their opinions are being taken seriously. Months later, a straightforward answer can help keep the brand-customer relationship strong.

5.7.5. Tips for Creating Effective YouTube Marketing Content

Building a successful YouTube marketing plan will help you expand your fan base and boost revenue. So how can one effectively market on YouTube? Here are some pointers to help you get off to a great YouTube marketing start.

5.7.5.1. Write Exciting Video Titles

The best way to produce viral content on the platform might be through the titles of your videos. Compared to other strategies, using evocative titles increases views and expands your audience more quickly. Thus, be sure to write unique video titles that entice viewers to click on your content.

5.7.5.2. Customize YouTube Video Thumbnails

The thumbnails you use are just as important, if not more so, than your titles. As long as they adhere to your brand style guide, these should be as striking as possible. Keep in mind that your video thumbnail serves as the viewer's initial impression of your content, so create something eye-catching for them.

5.7.5.3. Leverage YouTube SEO

The title, description, and transcript that the website automatically creates are three ways that YouTube SEO is used. But you should also pay close attention to the meta tags you select when uploading. To include important SEO terms and phrases, use that entry field.

5.7.5.4. Create Playlists on YouTube

If your content appeals to viewers, they will want to binge watch it repeatedly. Watching playlists is the simplest way for them to accomplish that. To better organize your content and entice viewers to watch your videos for longer, make playlists on your YouTube channel.

You can improve your marketing strategy and expand your audience by making engaging videos and uploading them to YouTube. YouTube is the world's most popular platform for sharing videos and is the best place to find any kind of video content. You're now prepared to launch your business YouTube channel and start posting amazing, viral videos that gain subscribers and views!

5.8. COLLABORATIONS

In the distinctive and varied world of YouTube, the pursuit of growth sometimes seems like a personal adventure.

But cooperation is a secret weapon you have at your disposal that can open doors to new audiences, boost engagement, and take your channel to new heights. Working together with other YouTubers is a smart move that has a lot of advantages beyond just making entertaining videos. Let's examine how working together can accelerate your YouTube growth and the most effective methods for doing so.

5.8.1. The Power of Collaboration: Partnering with Other YouTubers to Boost Your Channel

It can be difficult to stand out and develop a sizable following on the ever-expanding YouTube platform. There is intense competition among the millions of creators fighting for the attention of viewers. Collaboration is one tactic, though, that has consistently shown to be a game-changer for a lot of YouTubers. The popularity, development, and success of your channel can all be greatly increased by collaborating with other YouTubers. In order to help you grow your channel, we'll examine the value of collaboration in this section and offer advice on how to work with other creators productively.

5.8.1.1. Exposing Your Content to a New Audience

The chance to present your content to an entirely new audience is one of the biggest benefits of working with other YouTubers. Partnering with someone whose content is complementary to, or matches yours in some way, increases the likelihood that their subscribers will be interested in what you have to offer as well. An increase in viewers, subscribers, and engagement on your channel may come from this cross-promotion.

5.8.1.2. Networking and Building Relationships

Working together is more than just getting views and subscribers; it's also about networking and creating deep connections with other members of the YouTube community. You get the opportunity to meet people who share your passion for content creation when you collaborate with other creators. These connections may open up additional doors for future cooperation and offer insightful counsel and assistance.

5.8.1.3. Enhanced Content and Creativity

Adding new perspectives and ideas to your content through collaboration with other YouTubers can be beneficial. Working together and conducting a brainstorming session can produce creative and captivating videos that you might not have thought of on your own. Your content will ultimately be of higher quality if your collaborators push you to try new things, try new formats, and try out different styles.

5.8.1.4. Sharing Expertise and Skills

Every YouTuber has certain abilities and strengths. Working together gives you the chance to benefit from and draw on the knowledge of others. Whether it's marketing, scripting, or video editing, you can learn useful skills that will advance both your channel and your own development.

5.8.1.5. Combining Audiences for Greater Impact

The most fruitful partnerships often involve YouTubers who have sizable, devoted followings. Working together with content creators who have a sizable fan base will greatly expand the audience and impact of your channel. This helps your channel and gives you the opportunity to reach a wider audience with your message or content.

5.8.2. Different Types of YouTube Collaborations

The world of YouTube collaborations is vast and diverse. Here are some popular types to explore.

- **Guest Appearances:** Appear on another creator's channel for an interview, challenge, or collaborative video within their format.
- **Joint Productions:** Collaborate on a video concept from scratch, combining your unique styles and expertise to create something entirely new.
- **Series Collaborations:** Develop a multi-part series with recurring themes, where each episode features both creators in a new context.
- **Reaction Videos:** React to each other's videos, offering insights, opinions, and sparking conversation among your combined audience.
- **Challenges and Experiments:** Engage in friendly challenges or collaborative experiments within your niche, adding a layer of fun and excitement to the collaboration

5.8.3. Tips for Effective Collaboration

Now that we've discussed the benefits of collaborating with other YouTubers, let's look at some practical tips for making your collaborations successful:

1. **Choose the Right Partners:** Select collaborators whose content

aligns with yours and whose audience would be interested in your videos.

2. **Plan and Communicate:** Discuss your ideas and goals for the collaboration in advance. Clear communication is key to a successful partnership.
3. **Be Flexible:** Be open to compromise and adapt to your collaborator's style and preferences. Flexibility is crucial for a harmonious collaboration.
4. **Promote Each Other:** Promote the collaboration on both of your channels and social media platforms to maximize its reach.
5. **Give Credit:** Always credit your collaborators and link to their channels in your video descriptions and social media posts.

One of the most effective ways to build your channel and increase your audience is to collaborate with other YouTubers. Gaining new viewers for your content, forming connections with other members of the YouTube community, developing your creativity, and exchanging knowledge and abilities are just a few advantages. You can fully realize the benefits of this strategy and take your channel to new heights by adhering to the guidelines for productive collaboration. Therefore, don't be afraid to connect with other YouTubers and begin discovering the fascinating realm of teamwork. Working together could be the key to your channel's success!

5.9. USING SOCIAL MEDIA TO PROMOTE YOUR CHANNEL

You should promote your videos on your own as well if you want to maximize the impact of your content, even though YouTube is a search engine and its algorithm will help draw viewers to it. It's time to make changes if you're receiving fewer views and subscribers than typical. One choice is to advertise your channel on other social media sites, such as Clubhouse, Twitch, Instagram, TikTok, and many more. Here are some strategies for using social media to advertise your YouTube channel and videos:

1. **Create a Strong YouTube Channel:** Make sure your YouTube channel is fully optimized before promoting it on social media. This entails having an eye-catching channel trailer, an engaging and unambiguous channel banner, and a well-written channel description that includes pertinent keywords.
2. **Create High-Quality Videos:** Your videos' quality has a big impact on drawing in and keeping viewers. Make sure your videos are well-

produced, interesting, and educational. High-quality videos boost your search engine rankings and raise the likelihood that you'll show up in the section with suggested videos.

3. **Conduct YouTube SEO:** Search engine optimization (SEO) is a critical aspect of YouTube growth.
4. **Optimize Keywords for Better YouTube Visibility:** To Improve Your YouTube Visibility, research keywords and incorporate them into the titles, descriptions, and tags of your videos. To find out more about search volume and keyword rankings, use tools like VidIQ or TubeBuddy.
5. **Promote Your YouTube Channel on Social Media:** Post links to your videos on Facebook, Instagram, LinkedIn, Twitter, and other social media sites. Utilize hashtags that are pertinent to your industry and interact with your followers. Expand your network by interacting with other creators in your niche and sharing your videos in groups and communities that are relevant to them.
6. **Use Paid Advertising:** Use paid advertising on websites like Facebook Ads and Google Ads to promote your videos. This enables you to target particular locations, interests, and demographics while also reaching a larger audience.
7. **Collaborate with Other YouTubers:** One of the best ways to expand your audience is to work together with other creators in your niche. Seek out channels that cater to the same demographic and work together on videos or cross-promote each other's channels.
8. **Engage with Your Audience:** Interact with your audience on social media and reply to comments left on your videos. By doing this, you can create a community around your channel and inspire users to tell their friends and family about your content.
9. **Analyze Your Data:** To monitor the effectiveness of your videos and channel, use YouTube analytics.
10. **Analyze Content Performance to Drive Channel Growth:** Determine the most successful content type and produce more of it. Make better decisions and expand your channel by using this data.

To sum up, social media promotion of your YouTube channel and videos is crucial to the platform's expansion. To develop a devoted following, concentrate on producing top-notch content, managing your YouTube account, and interacting with your viewers. To expand your audience, work with other creators in your niche, use social media and paid advertising, and evaluate your results to improve your approach.

5.10. USE YOUR CHANNEL TO PROMOTE YOUR MERCHANDISE

Developing and selling products is a great method to advertise your YouTube channel. Merchandising brings your channel visibility, delights your fans, and may even bring in a little extra money. It's a win-win scenario, and there are lots of methods to produce goods. These three strategies will help you promote your YouTube channel with merchandise.

1. **Make t-Shirts for Your Channel:** One of the best ways to promote yourself is to make t-shirts for your YouTube channel. Start by making a straightforward logo or design for your channel, which can incorporate the name and URL of the channel. Next, visit a store that sells custom t-shirts and order the design to be printed on as many t-shirts as you want. Asking friends and family to wear the shirts is a good place to start if your channel is just getting started. Wearing your shirts in public allows your channel to get a lot of exposure since it will be seen by many onlookers.
2. **Put Your Channel Logo on Stickers:** Using stickers bearing your channel's logo is another powerful way to market your products. Sticker printing is very inexpensive, and if you sell these stickers for a low price, you can even turn a profit. Stickers with the Channel logo can be attached to laptops, binders, cars, and bulletin boards. If you place your stickers in a variety of locations, people may come across your logo while working, studying, strolling through the streets, or even stuck in traffic.
3. **Print Your Logo on Various Accessories:** You really can print your channel logo on an endless amount of accessories. Pens, erasers, water bottles, and phone cases are just a few examples of these accessories. Consider getting your logo printed on a range of accessories, then distributing them for free at a media gathering like VidCon. Although it might require some investment, this will undoubtedly pay off. Numerous individuals will gladly accept your accessories and unintentionally promote your channel.

There is a plethora of ways that you can use merchandise to promote your channel. Merchandising is beneficial to you, your fans, and your YouTube channel.

REFERENCES

1. Bergen, M. (2019, April 2). YouTube executives ignored warnings, letting toxic videos run rampant. *Bloomberg*. Retrieved from https://www.bloomberg.com/news/features/2019-04-02/youtube-executives-ignored-warnings-letting-toxic-videos-run-rampant.
2. Covington, P., Adams, J., & Sargin, E. (2016). Deep neural networks for YouTube recommendations. *RecSys '16 Proceedings of the 10th ACM Conference on Recommender Systems*, 191–198. https://doi.org/10.1145/2959100.2959190.
3. Evans, R. (2018, October 11). From memes to Infowars: How 75 fascist activists were "red-pilled" [Blog post]. Retrieved from Bellingcat website: https://www.bellingcat.com/news/americas/2018/10/11/memes-infowars-75-fascist-activists-red-pilled/.
4. Goodrow, C. (2021). On YouTube's recommendation system. *YouTube Official Blog*. https://blog.youtube/inside-youtube/on-youtubes-recommendation-system/.
5. Hayden, M. E. (2019, August 4). White nationalists praise El Paso attack and mock the dead. *Southern Poverty Law Center*. Retrieved from https://www.splcenter.org/hatewatch/2019/08/04/white-nationalists-praise-el-paso-attack-and-mock-dead.
6. Hilbert, M., Thakur, A., Flores, P., Zhang, X., Bhan, J., Bernhard, P., & Ji, F. (2024). 8–10% of algorithmic recommendations are 'bad,' but… an exploratory risk-utility meta-analysis and its regulatory implications. *International Journal of Information Management*, *75*, 102743. https://doi.org/10.1016/j.ijinfomgt.2023.102743.
7. Kaiser, J., & Rauchfleisch, A. (2018, April 11). Unite the right? How YouTube's recommendation algorithm connects the U.S. far-right. Retrieved October 28, 2019, from Medium website: https://medium.com/@MediaManipulation/unite-the-right-how-youtubes-recommendation-algorithm-connects-the-u-s-far-right-9f1387ccfabd.
8. Langer, G. (2017, August 21). Trump approval is low but steady; On Charlottesville lower still. *ABC News/Washington Post*. Retrieved from https://www.langerresearch.com/wp-content/uploads/1190a1TrumpandCharlottesville.pdf.
9. Markmann, S., & Grimme, C. (2021). Is YouTube still a radicalizer? An exploratory study on autoplay and recommendation. *Disinformation in Open Online Media*, 50–65. https://doi.org/10.1007/978-3-030-87031-7_4.

10. Masadeh, S., & Hamilton, B. (2020). The aftermath of the adpocalypse: Systemic bias on YouTube. *CHI*. http://critical-media.org/cobi/docs/Masadeh_Bias%20on%20YouTube.pdf.
11. Mock, B. (2007, April 20). Neo-Nazi groups share hate via YouTube. *Southern Poverty Law Center*. Retrieved from https://www.splcenter.org/fighting-hate/intelligence-report/2007/neo-nazi-groups-share-hate-youtube.
12. Newton, C. (2019, December 16). The terror queue: These moderators help keep Google and YouTube free of violent extremism—and now some of them have PTSD. *The Verge*. Retrieved from https://www.theverge.com/2019/12/16/21021005/google-youtube-moderators-ptsd-accenture-violent-disturbing-content-interviews-video.
13. Nigatu, H., & Raji, I. (2024). "I searched for a religious song in Amharic and got sexual content instead": Investigating online harm in low-resourced languages on YouTube. *Proceedings of the 2024 ACM Conference on Fairness, Accountability, and Transparency*, 141–160. https://doi.org/10.1145/3630106.3658546.
14. O'Donovan, C., Warzel, C., McDonald, L., Clifton, B., & Woolf, M. (2019, January 24). We followed YouTube's recommendation algorithm down the rabbit hole. Retrieved October 28, 2019, from BuzzFeed News website: https://www.buzzfeednews.com/article/carolineodonovan/down-youtubes-recommendation-rabbithole.
15. Pariser, E. (2011). *The filter bubble: How the new personalized web is changing what we read and how we think*. Retrieved from https://books.google.com/books?id=wcalrOI1YbQC&lpg=PP1&pg=PP1#v=onepage&q&f=false.
16. Spinelli, L., & Crovella, M. (2020). How YouTube leads privacy-seeking users away from reliable information. *FairUMAP*, 244–251. https://doi.org/10.1145/3386392.3399566.
17. Suciu, P. (2021). YouTube remains the most dominant social media platform. *Forbes*. https://www.forbes.com/sites/petersuciu/2021/04/07/youtube-remains-the-most-dominant-social-media-platform/?sh=5a0f8c456322.
18. Thompson, N. (2018, March 15). Susan Wojcicki on YouTube's fight against misinformation. *Wired*. Retrieved from https://www.wired.com/story/susan-wojcicki-on-youtubes-fight-against-misinformation/.
19. Tufekci, Z. (2018, March 10). YouTube, the great radicalizer. *The New York Times, Opinion*. Retrieved from https://www.nytimes.com/2018/03/10/opinion/sunday/youtube-politics-radical.html.

CHAPTER 6

LINKEDIN ALGORITHM

Contents

Introduction 218
6.1. Basics of LinkedIn 218
6.2. LinkedIn as a Social Media 227
6.3. The Role of the LinkedIn Social Media in Building the Personal Image 237
6.4. The System of LinkedIn Algorithm 244
References 251

INTRODUCTION

LinkedIn is a mobile app and website social media platform that focuses on business and jobs. Eric Ly and Reid Hoffman introduced it on May 5, 2003. LinkedIn has been a fully owned subsidiary of Microsoft since December 2016. Employers can post jobs on the platform, which is mainly used for professional networking and career development. Jobseekers can post their resumes. Since 2015, the majority of the business's income has come from selling recruiters and salespeople access to member information. More than 1 billion people from more than 200 countries and territories are registered members of LinkedIn. Members of LinkedIn's online social network, which includes both employers and employees, can establish profiles and connect with one another to potentially represent professional relationships in the real world. Anybody can be invited by members to become a connection, whether they are already members or not. Organizing offline events, joining groups, writing articles, posting job openings, uploading pictures and videos, and more can all be done on LinkedIn.

6.1. BASICS OF LINKEDIN

LinkedIn is a social media platform created exclusively for professionals in the business world. The website's objective is to give registered users the ability to create and maintain professional networks of people they know and trust. Professionals can use LinkedIn to research companies, find jobs, and stay up to date on industry news and business connections. In order to give decision-makers, employers, employees, and educators data-driven insight into trends that support workforce supply and demand alignment globally, LinkedIn collects data from LinkedIn profiles. These patterns include the times of year that people typically search for their next career move, patterns of work migration in particular regions, skills shortages in particular industries, and the stickiest cities, that is, regions where workers are less likely to leave. With its headquarters located in Sunnyvale, California, LinkedIn is a business-focused social media platform and social networking website that was established in 2002. Microsoft, a behemoth in software and cloud computing, paid $26 billion to acquire the business in 2016.

LinkedIn places more emphasis on a user's professional connections than other social networks like Facebook and Myspace, which are frequently used for recreational purposes only. Users create profile pages that resemble resumes in structure, allowing them to list their education and employment history, highlight specific skills, and summarize their career. When a user accepts an invitation from another to join their network, connections are made between them. Through job searches, third-party connections made at specific companies, and user recommendations, LinkedIn enables users to advance their careers. Although membership is free, users can view the complete profiles of any LinkedIn user and see more profiles in their search results by purchasing the premium service. LinkedIn was founded in 2003 by venture capitalist Reid Hoffman, engineer Eric Ly, engineer Jean-Luc Vaillant, product designer Allen Blue, and marketing expert Konstantin Guericke. Growth started out slowly. LinkedIn launched services in 2005 that let businesses post job openings and look for potential candidates on the network. LinkedIn offers businesses professional services in addition to the option to advertise on the platform. In 2007, LinkedIn finally turned a profit. In that year, LinkedIn boasted over 15 million members; by 2011, the global membership count had surpassed 100 million. $353 million was raised during LinkedIn's initial public offering (IPO) in the same year. Microsoft purchased LinkedIn in 2016 for a reported $26 billion. By 2024, there will be over a billion users on LinkedIn, representing more than 200 nations. Microsoft reported $15 billion in worldwide revenue from its LinkedIn division in its fiscal year 2023. Of that amount, $7 billion came from hiring software targeted at corporate recruiters and $1.77 billion from sales of premium subscriptions.

6.1.1. Difference Between LinkedIn and Other Forms of Social Media

LinkedIn differs from other social media platforms such as Facebook, Instagram, and Twitter because it was created with business networking in mind. Members typically only connect with people they already know or who they were introduced to by someone in their network, making it a more exclusive network. Because of this, LinkedIn is a great place to develop business connections rather than personal ones. Having said that, LinkedIn does provide certain features, like discussion forums and groups that are shared by other social networks. LinkedIn is the only social media platform designed specifically with business users in mind, out of those geared toward enterprise use.

6.1.2. Who Created LinkedIn?

Reid Hoffman, a former executive vice president at PayPal responsible for business and corporate development, was a co-founder of LinkedIn. Since its May 2003 launch, the website has amassed over 850 million members, of which roughly 191 million are from the U.S. With more than 200 countries and territories hosting more than 58 million registered users. Reid Hoffman reports that recruiters make up almost 30% of LinkedIn users. LinkedIn was purchased by Microsoft in June 2016 for $26.2 billion. Some experts claim that the vast amounts of semistructured data that LinkedIn members freely share, including skill sets, industry information, job titles, and geographic locations. — made the acquisition of LinkedIn a great value, despite the fact that it was one of Microsoft's most costly acquisitions to date.

6.1.3. Why Use LinkedIn?

LinkedIn is used primarily by three groups of people: individuals, sales reps and recruiters:

1. For *individuals*, LinkedIn is a great way to manage your career, find a job, research companies, connect with business contacts and get news about your industry.
2. *Salespeople* often used LinkedIn to generate leads and build relationships with potential customers.
3. *Recruiters* use LinkedIn to find candidates for open positions, research companies and connect with potential employees.

6.1.4. Membership to LinkedIn Work

The skills, employment history, and education sections of a LinkedIn member's profile page are highlighted, along with news feeds from professional networks and a few customizable modules that let you highlight your qualifications, experience, and job history, as well as recommendations from peers and past employers. LinkedIn membership is free at the basic level. Connections are members of a network. LinkedIn promotes connections to already be in a relationship, in contrast to other free social networking sites.

6.1.5. LinkedIn Premium Subscription

LinkedIn Premium subscriptions offer a variety of features intended to help users succeed in their careers and be more productive in addition to the features accessible to basic members. Here are a few of these characteristics:

- You can send InMail messages to any member, regardless of your relationship with them. This is a useful feature for recruiters, who frequently use recruitment sessions to get in touch with candidates they do not personally know.
- Advanced search filters enable users to narrow their search results to find exactly the right person they are looking for.
- You can see who has viewed your profile and when by using profile views. When members are looking for new job opportunities and would like to know possible employers who might be looking through their profile, this is helpful.

- Sales navigator is a tool designed specifically for salespeople that provides access to leads, account details and contact information.

6.1.6. History

6.1.6.1. Founding from 2002 to 2011

Reid Hoffman and the initial PayPal and Socialnet.com team members—Allen Blue, Eric Ly, Jean-Luc Vaillant, Lee Hower, Konstantin Guericke, Stephen Beitzel, David Eves, Ian McNish, Yan Pujante, and Chris Saccheri—founded the business in December 2002. Sequoia Capital spearheaded the company's Series A investment towards the end of 2003. LinkedIn attained a million users in August 2004. LinkedIn turned a profit for the first time in March of 2006. Around 10 million people used LinkedIn in April of 2007. The mobile version of LinkedIn was released in February 2008. Sequoia Capital, Greylock Partners, and other venture capital firms paid $53 million for a 5% stake in the company in June 2008, valuing it at about $1 billion after the money was invested. As part of its Asia-Pacific team expansion, LinkedIn established offices in Sydney and Mumbai in November 2009. In 2010, LinkedIn announced the acquisition of Mspoke, opened an international headquarters in Dublin, Ireland, and increased its 1% premium subscription ratio. Tiger Global Management LLC also invested $20 million in the company at a valuation of roughly $2 billion. That October, Silicon Valley Insider ranked the business number ranking of 10 on its list of the 100 most valuable startups. In private markets, the company was valued at $1.575 billion by December. A significant portion of LinkedIn's first year in India, which began in 2009, was devoted to learning about Indian professionals and teaching members how to use LinkedIn to further their careers.

6.1.6.2. 2011 to Present

January 2011 saw LinkedIn submit a request for an IPO. On May 19, 2011, the company debuted with its first share trade at $45 (about $60,00 in 2023) per share, trading under the NYSE symbol LNKD. On their first day of trading on the New York Stock Exchange, LinkedIn shares increased by as much as 171%, closing at $94.25, more than 109% above the IPO price. The site's underlying infrastructure was updated shortly after the IPO to enable faster cycles between revisions and releases. LinkedIn surpassed Twitter, which made $139.5 million, in advertising revenue alone in 2011 with $154.66 million. LinkedIn's increased success in the social media space contributed to the company's record-breaking fourth-quarter 2011 earnings. By this time, LinkedIn employed roughly 2,100 people full-time, as opposed to 500 in

2010. With a 10-year lease in place to house up to 2,500 employees, LinkedIn announced in April 2014 that it had leased 222 Second Street, a 26-story building currently under construction in San Francisco's SoMa district. The intention was to house all 1,250 employees based in San Francisco in one building as of January 2016, integrating the research and development team with the sales and marketing staff. They made the decision to move in March 2016. LinkedIn's shares fell 43.6% in a single day in February 2016 after an earnings report, to $108.38 per share. That day, LinkedIn's market capitalization dropped by $10 billion.

Due to non-compliance with the 2015 national legislation requiring social media networks to store citizens' personal data on servers located in Russia, access to LinkedIn was blocked by Russian authorities in 2016. Microsoft declared in June 2016 that it would buy LinkedIn for $26.2 billion, or $196 per share. Up until Activision Blizzard was acquired by Microsoft in 2022, this was the company's largest acquisition. The purchase would be financed entirely by debt and done in cash. Microsoft would permit LinkedIn to maintain its unique identity, culture, and autonomy. Weiner would continue in his role as CEO, reporting to Microsoft CEO Satya Nadella. Analysts speculated that Microsoft saw a chance to better integrate the professional network system with its products by integrating LinkedIn with its Office product suite. The agreement came to an end on December 8, 2016. LinkedIn announced at the end of 2016 that it would be adding 200 new positions to its Dublin office, bringing the total number of employees to 1,200. Since 2017, 94% of B2B marketers have disseminated content via LinkedIn. The new LinkedIn desktop version was unveiled shortly after Microsoft acquired LinkedIn. The goal of the updated version was to improve user experience on desktop and mobile devices. A few adjustments were made in response to comments from users of the previously released mobile app. Functions that were not frequently used were eliminated. For instance, there is no longer support for the contact tagging and filtering features.

Some users expressed dissatisfaction with the new user interface (UI) after it was released, citing bugs, slowness, and missing features from the previous version. Both free and premium users, as well as users of the desktop and mobile versions of the website, encountered the problems. Year 2019 saw the global launch of LinkedIn's Open for Business feature, which makes it possible for independent contractors to be found on the network. The same year saw the launch of LinkedIn Events. After serving as CEO for 11 years, Jeff Weiner announced his resignation in June 2020 and was named executive chairman instead. Ryan Roslansky, who had served as senior vice president of products, assumed the role of CEO. LinkedIn revealed at the end of July 2020 that it had let go of 960 workers—roughly 6% of the entire workforce—from the global sales and talent acquisition departments. CEO Ryan Roslansky blamed the cuts on the COVID-19 pandemic's effects in an email to all staff members. CyberNews reported in April 2021 that 500 million LinkedIn accounts had been compromised online. But according to LinkedIn, after looking into an alleged set of LinkedIn data that was put up for sale, we found that it is actually an amalgam of information from several different websites and businesses.

PrivacySharks reported in June 2021 that a hacker forum was selling over 700 million LinkedIn records. Later, LinkedIn clarified that this is not a breach but rather the result of data scraping, which is against their terms of service. In October 2021, Microsoft terminated LinkedIn's operations in China. Compared to $10.3 billion in 2021, LinkedIn's revenue in 2022 was $138 billion. LinkedIn eliminated 716 positions from its 20,000 employees in May 2023. The decision was made to simplify the company's operations, as stated in a letter from CEO Ryan Roslansky. Roslansky went on to say that this choice would generate 250 new job opportunities. LinkedIn additionally declared the end of its local job apps for China. Axios revealed in June 2024 that LinkedIn was testing a new AI assistant for its premium members who had to pay for it.

6.1.7. Network on LinkedIn

It is highly recommended that you begin by establishing connections with individuals you already know. The website provides resources to help you connect with the connections of your connections on a degree-by-degree basis for mutual gain. Think about personalizing your LinkedIn connection request by including a warm message, mentioning where you met, or mentioning the company you both work for. There are five ways that LinkedIn can be an effective networking tool.

1. **Alumni Search:** You can use this tool to look up people who went to the same school(s) as you, whether they are connections or not. This can be a great tool to find graduate programs that fit your career path, companies or organizations you want to get involved with, and people you can start building relationships with!
2. **Advanced Search:** You can locate people in your network, people you are mutually connected to, people from groups you follow, or people outside of your network by using the advanced search function. We strongly advise you to use LinkedIn's "get introduced feature" to connect with people who are not your initial connections.
3. **'Get Introduced' Tool:** We advise you to start with people who are second degree connections rather than jumping right into a relationship with a complete stranger. You can ask to be introduced

to your second degree connection by sending a personalized message to your mutual connection first using this tool.

4. **Joining Company Pages:** You can see the most recent updates, details about their services, possibly exclusive job postings, and the possibility that you already have a connection to the company through one of your connections by liking the pages of businesses that interest you.

5. **Your Connections:** The best networks almost always start with people you already know, such as friends, family, professors, former employers, and classmates. Make use of the connections you have, both online and off, to learn new things, build contacts, and seize opportunities.

6.1.8. Ways to Use LinkedIn for Online Marketing

Similar to other social media platforms, LinkedIn requires brands to employ efficacious tactics to establish an online presence that stimulates interaction and propels sales. Here are some ideas for how brands can use LinkedIn to craft impressive social media campaigns.

1. **Tell Your Brand's Story on LinkedIn:** According to some, LinkedIn is the biggest professional network in the world. Audiences on the social media platform are therefore willing to interact with and learn from companies and executives. Furthermore, the website gives brands the opportunity to produce content that inspires and has an impact on users. Therefore, in order to engage followers and increase brand visibility, businesses can use it to discuss their vision, passion, and story. Coca-Cola, for instance, demonstrates its commitment to the causes it supports by sharing fervently about them. The business uses LinkedIn to share employee stories and to commemorate international occasions that empower others.

2. **Activate Employees and Employee Advocacy:** Working with in-house influencers to promote brand or product awareness, expand audience reach, and foster authenticity are all benefits of this kind of partnership. Given the multitude of employee connections LinkedIn offers, it can serve as a useful tool for encouraging staff members to take on the role of brand ambassadors and advocates. For example, companies might advise staff members to use company-generated content on their personal pages on LinkedIn, tag the company page in updates sent to colleagues, and use company hashtags in their own content. In order to build credibility and collaborations with

executives and other brands, brands may also showcase employee testimonials about their experiences working for the company. Kellogg's is one company that uses LinkedIn to engage in employee advocacy. The consumer goods company started using the hashtag #LifeAtK to share content about its employees' experiences working for the brand. By uploading their own content with the brand's hashtag, Kellogg's employees additionally used it to promote the brand and brand-related events.

3. **Create User-Generated Content:** Similar to other social media platforms, LinkedIn can be used by brands to create content created by users in an effort to increase engagement. Because the platform is a professional network, businesses might come up with interesting queries about their employees' aspirations and career goals. Brands may also inquire about the thoughts and recommendations of audiences on matters related to work and personal development. For example, Adidas asked its followers to share their New Year's resolutions at the start of 2020. Adidas also regularly uses LinkedIn questions about goal-setting, coaching, and personal growth to increase engagement.

4. **Put Innovation into Spotlight:** Using innovation is another method to create content that is incredibly engaging. Highlighting a technological or product innovation can help your business stand out from the competition and could lead to new business opportunities, expanded customer bases, and alliances. Additionally, emphasizing innovation can assist businesses in using LinkedIn to tell brand stories in a more imaginative and captivating manner. Johnson and Johnson distinguishes itself from competing brands with cutting-edge inventions. For example, the company frequently shares information on technological achievements and offers insights on the brand's scientific leaders on its LinkedIn Page. Additionally, Johnson & Johnson finds ways to deliver cutting-edge developments and present these discoveries, whether it be through new technology used for product development or innovation in health processes.

5. **Showcase Brand Products and Services:** Don't believe that promotions for goods and services are limited to the brand's Facebook or Instagram pages. You can recommend new goods and services on Linkedin. Businesses should, however, target professional audiences with relevant and enticing brand offerings in their advertisements. For instance, each time Nestlé releases a new product on the professional platform, the company showcases

technological innovation and a breakthrough in the creation of new products, ingredients, and packaging.

6. **Produce Video and Image Content Using LinkedIn:** An increase in video content is anticipated this year. It's true that in 2020, brand marketing strategies will still place a high value on video social media content. Employing image and video formats, businesses can create dynamic and captivating content on LinkedIn. Brands, for example, can create videos that highlight company achievements and awards, highlight employees and their activities, highlight company best practices, highlight socially conscious initiatives, and highlight prominent leader interviews. Also, businesses and staff members can produce content in real time by using LinkedIn's Live Video feature. The aforementioned campaigns have the greatest potential to attract and involve brand fans. Nike offers an excellent example of how to promote video content on LinkedIn. The company's official LinkedIn page has inspirational films and behind-the-scenes looks at product development. The few businesses that use motion graphic image content to pique audiences' attention are Nike among them.

7. **Highlight Brand's Social Good Campaigns:** Campaigns for cause marketing can boost sales, give your company a more authentic image, and increase audience engagement. Additionally, social good campaigns can help you win over millennial consumers' hearts. As a matter of fact, 91% of millennials have a preference for socially conscious brands. Given that millennials make up 87 million of LinkedIn's user base, the platform can be a useful tool for connecting with this specific demographic. Brands can use the platform to showcase employees' posts about company-organized cause marketing campaigns or to highlight causes that the company supports. For instance, Mattel actively collaborates to support and assist communities and organizations. The brand's official LinkedIn page highlights the causes it is committed to. Moreover, Mattel gains extra interaction from staff members sharing content linked to cause marketing on their personal accounts.

8. **Partner with LinkedIn Influencers and Brand Ambassadors:** Working with influencers is another way to use the platform for your brand's influencer marketing campaigns. Prominent corporate executives and brand evangelists are regarded as reliable information sources. As a result, their followers value and respect their opinions. Influencers on LinkedIn already have a built-in following, so brands can use them to reach new audiences, acquire new followers, and

establish connections with prospective customers. Mercedes-Benz uses LinkedIn to work with influencer partners and brand ambassadors in addition to producing content under its own name. The brand benefits from increased follower engagement and a larger audience reach.

9. **Feature Company Behind-the-Scenes:** Behind-the-scenes content is one way to authentically and creatively tell the company's story and raise brand awareness. Brands might use LinkedIn, for instance, to highlight product development, employee daily activities, early looks at upcoming releases and promotions, and brand-related initiatives on the company's LinkedIn profile. These programs enable brands to create interesting and carefully chosen content. The employees of Walt Disney are the primary focus of the company's LinkedIn page. The brand uses behind-the-scenes posts to create extremely interesting content. For example, the business shows daily work activities and conducts employee interviews about their jobs. Walt Disney shares more real and relatable content as a result, increasing brand awareness.

6.2. LINKEDIN AS A SOCIAL MEDIA

One of the most significant professional networking sites in the world already is LinkedIn. Users can network with other users in the same industry or a different one by uploading their professional career. Nevertheless, users can publish and/or share articles on pertinent topics on the platform, which can also be used as a job exchange and information portal in addition to social networking. Particularly for B2B companies, a LinkedIn company profile ought to be a component of the contemporary marketing mix. LinkedIn gives the chance to actively connect with relevant target groups; as of April 2021, there were over 756 million users worldwide, with 198 million daily active users in Europe.

1. **Social Recruiting and Employer Branding:** LinkedIn is a useful tool for hiring new staff members. Companies can use a profile to showcase themselves as their own brand and post job openings and information for prospective candidates. These are available through LinkedIn's job search function or directly through the company profile. With just a few clicks on LinkedIn, users can apply for the jobs that are advertised and filter for different offers.
2. **Content Distribution of Website Content:** LinkedIn provides an extensive range of design choices for business postings. It is possible to carry out surveys, share images or videos, and publish blogs and

articles. Members are able to like or share posts from company pages that they follow. The members' contacts can then see these interactions in their feed. In this manner, company updates that are engaging and creative can gain a large following even though they have fewer followers.

3. **Sponsored Posts and Targeted Publishing:** On LinkedIn, you can use specific posts to target user groups above a certain size. You can filter this by area, age, industry, career level, and so forth. The main benefits of LinkedIn Sponsored Postings are their increased reach and the follow button within the post, which allows users to directly follow the company profile and never miss any updates.
4. **Highlighting Different Business Areas:** There is no requirement that the LinkedIn company presentation stick to a single business niche. Sub-company profiles that are independent but linked to the main profile can be made using what are known as focus pages. For instance, Eduvision features two main pages: Eduvision Opleiding en Training, which is the main page, and Eduvision Fort- und Weiterbildung DACH, which is the focus page and offers content in German for the German-speaking region. Additionally, businesses can expand the corporate culture section and separately describe different business areas on LinkedIn's paid career page.
5. **Employee Profiles as a Reach Catalyst:** When it comes to their professional history, employees of your company who are active on LinkedIn can link to your profile as an employer. In this manner, other users who click on the user profiles of your employees will also learn about your business. Furthermore, this enhances the company page's reputation because it positively affects the quantity of followers and the stated number of employees who are active on the network.
6. **Analysis for Post Optimization:** LinkedIn provides free statistics on followers, post updates, and visitors. Businesses can then use these to determine which kinds of postings receive less reach or which posts have been especially well received by the community.
7. **Internationalisation:** LinkedIn is a useful tool for businesses looking to advertise their goods and services both in the German-speaking market and in English-language publications. As was previously mentioned, LinkedIn has a strong international focus and is particularly well-liked outside of the DACH market.

6.2.1. LinkedIn Social Networking

LinkedIn is a social networking site with many benefits that was created especially for the business community. It makes it possible for professionals to network, exchange knowledge, and locate job openings. More than 830 million people use LinkedIn across more than 200 nations and territories. When it comes to social networking, LinkedIn offers a lot of advantages. Some of the most significant ones are listed below:

1. **Expand Your Network:** Making connections with people you know and those you'd like to get to know is made easier with LinkedIn. Your network will grow the more people you connect with. This can be useful for obtaining recommendations, discovering job openings, and remaining current with news in the field.
2. **Build Your Reputation:** You can improve your professional reputation by using LinkedIn wisely. By contributing to conversations, joining groups, and sharing insightful content, you demonstrate your expertise to clients and prospective employers.
3. **Find Job Opportunities:** LinkedIn is a widely used platform by recruiters to locate and establish connections with possible job seekers. You can make a profile on LinkedIn, look for jobs, and connect with recruiters if you're seeking for a new position.
4. **Learn About New Opportunities:** Discovering new prospects in your industry can be greatly facilitated by using LinkedIn. To keep up with the newest trends, you can read articles, watch videos, and go to virtual events.
5. **Promote Your Business:** LinkedIn is a useful tool for businesses to market their goods and services to prospective clients. You can connect with relevant professionals, exchange content, and establish a company profile.

Here are some tips for you if you're a beginner and using LinkedIn for social networking:

- Ensure that your profile is accurate, engaging, and comprehensive. This comprises your work history, skills, headline, and summary. Make use of keywords in your profile to make yourself visible to people looking for experts in your area.
- Post insightful content frequently. This could include blog entries, videos, articles, or even just your opinions on news from the industry. Take part in group discussions and make a pitch. This is a fantastic method to meet other professionals and find out about upcoming events.

- Participate in events. LinkedIn offers a range of online and offline events that you can go to in order to network with other business people. Make an effort to connect with the people you wish to. Never be reluctant to write a personalized note to someone you respect or who might prove to be a useful connection.

6.2.2. Social Networking Site for Business People and Professionals to Connect

Most people only focus on Facebook and Twitter when they discuss social media. Even though these are the most popular social media platforms, there are plenty more that are also successful. As one of the most significant social media platforms on the internet, LinkedIn has amassed about 100 million users. Over the past few years, it's likely that you have received an invitation to join LinkedIn from a friend or colleague. Did you accept? If not, you are losing out on a great chance to network. Do you even have a LinkedIn account? Because they are unaware of this platform's potential for business exposure and expansion, many local businesses choose to ignore it. When it comes to online business networking, LinkedIn is the most widely used social networking platform. It is a platform that enables professionals and businesspeople worldwide to connect with other professionals, irrespective of their industry.

It's a fantastic setting where people can meet many people who share their interests in business and the professional world. LinkedIn users have the ability to showcase their latest project updates and allow other users to see what they are working on. The connection's objectives include information sharing, product and service marketing, employment placement, establishing business-to-business connections, and much more. Although LinkedIn is essentially free to use, there are premium paid packages available with additional features. Similar to other social networks, LinkedIn operates. To participate, all you have to do is sign up and create a profile with all the personal details you wish to share about yourself, including your work history, education, accomplishments, and more. Then, to enhance visibility for your profile, you can quickly link your account to other websites, blogs, and social networking sites.

6.2.2.1. LinkedIn Statistics

Statistics aggregated by *Amodiovalerio verde* show the following numbers:

- LinkedIn has approximately 147 million members.
- The standard Linked in member is aged 25 to 54 years old.
- 66% of LinkedIn members are located in Europe and N. America.

- LinkedIn's members have grown by 45% worldwide compared to January 2011.
- Over 40% of members of LinkedIn are employees in companies that employ 10,000+ employees.

Quantcast has the following statistics:

- LinkedIn has more than doubled their monthly visits to 94.3 million in Sept 2011 from 45.8 million in 2010.
- Quantcast divides users on LinkedIn into three categories: addicts, regulars, and bystanders. Around 1% of members are addicts, and they will regularly use LinkedIn for interaction. Around 33% of users are regulars, meaning they will interact with the site more than once but fewer than 30 times in a month. The remaining 66% are passersby, who will only visit the location or communicate with media once every month.
- The age range of 18 to 34 accounts for about 26% of all LinkedIn members, whereas the age range of 35 to 50 accounts for 70% of all members. About 39% of LinkedIn members make more than $100,000 annually, and about 75% of members have college degrees.

6.2.2.2. What This Means for Your Business

Based on these figures, it's easy to conclude that LinkedIn is a significant component of social media that, when used correctly, can grow your company. LinkedIn is here to stay, so you can use this potent social media tool to confidently focus your efforts on growing your business. Just by signing into your LinkedIn account, you could be able to stay up to date on news and developments in your industry. Making connections with other companies in your sector can be quite beneficial. It offers fantastic business opportunities that would not have been possible without it. For example, you can network with other businesses in the fashion design industry if you own a fashion design company. By doing this, you will be able to connect with other businesses in that field, such as distributors and marketers, who can help you grow your company even more, and you will also have access to a wealth of information. One resource you can use to locate highly qualified candidates is LinkedIn. LinkedIn is a platform where a lot of job seekers and freelancers with skills that can expand your business are available.

The quality of your profile and the extent of your outreach to others are what drive LinkedIn's success. Put another way, LinkedIn is more focused on business relationships, whereas social media sites like Facebook and Twitter are more focused on social networking. With so many options at their disposal,

LinkedIn gives small business owners the ability to improve their companies. If you are serious about expanding your company, you should learn how to use this excellent marketing tool. It could be difficult for you to choose which social networks to use with so many available on the internet. LinkedIn might be the crucial piece missing to grow your company, even though it might not seem that significant. You should now have a much better idea of why social media marketing is crucial to your local business's success. There is no reason why your company shouldn't be present there if the majority of your clients and potential clients spend a lot of time there. It's comparable to throwing money on the table. For a free consultation, get in touch with me if you need assistance from a qualified social media specialist to set up and maintain your social media profiles on Facebook, Twitter, G+, and LinkedIn.

6.2.3. Benefits for Businesses Having LinkedIn Social Media Accounts

Users can connect with other professionals, share information about their work, and create a profile. For anyone looking to progress their career, including job seekers and entrepreneurs, LinkedIn can be an invaluable resource.

1. **Increased Brand Awareness:** Since LinkedIn is a professional social media network, it's a fantastic way to connect with prospective clients who are already considering your offerings. You can raise brand awareness and improve website traffic by sharing pertinent content and interacting with your audience.
2. **Enhanced Customer Engagement:** LinkedIn is an excellent resource for establishing connections with both current and prospective clients. It can be used to solicit feedback, offer assistance, and respond to inquiries. In addition to helping you develop client loyalty and trust, this can help you enhance your goods and services.
3. **Targeted Marketing and Advertising:** With the range of targeting options LinkedIn provides, you can make sure the right people see your marketing messages. By industry, job title, company size, location, and other factors, you can target. You can achieve better outcomes and increase the effectiveness of your marketing campaigns by doing this.
4. **Cost-Effective Marketing Channel:** Advertising on LinkedIn may be an affordable method of reaching your intended audience. Although the price of LinkedIn advertising varies based on several factors, it is typically less expensive than traditional advertising channels like print and television.

5. **Increased Website Traffic:** Using LinkedIn to promote your website is a great idea. You can entice your followers to visit your website and discover more about your company by including links to it in your posts and updates.
6. **Market Research and Customer Insights:** LinkedIn is a useful resource for customer insights and market research. It can be used to get client feedback, discover needs and desires, and spot new business opportunities.
7. **Competitive Advantage:** You can learn about the strategies and tactics used by your rivals by keeping an eye on their LinkedIn activity. By using this information, you can maintain your competitive edge and achieve better outcomes.
8. **Recruitment and Talent Acquisition:** LinkedIn is an excellent resource for hiring and locating exceptional personnel. It allows you to post job openings, find candidates, and establish connections with possible employees.
9. **Thought Leadership:** One excellent resource for positioning oneself as a thought leader in your sector is LinkedIn. You can establish yourself as an authority and draw in new business by posting insightful content.
10. **Networking:** A fantastic resource for networking with other professionals in your field is LinkedIn. It can be used to establish connections with possible clients, collaborators, and partners. These are but a few advantages of being active on LinkedIn. The use LinkedIn for business purposes right away if you haven't already. It's an effective tool that can expand your clientele, foster relationships, and boost sales.

6.2.4. LinkedIn and Content Strategy

A strategy is a plan of action or policy that is intended to accomplish a primary or overarching goal, according to the dictionary. In the previously mentioned Content Marketing Institute report, LinkedIn was ranked as the No. One social media platform to assist organizations in achieving particular goals. LinkedIn is crucial to a strategic, goal-based content marketing approach for the following seven reasons:

1. **Targeted Reach:** With over 575 million professionals worldwide, LinkedIn is home to a vibrant professional community. Your B2B clients are most likely on the platform, regardless of who they are. Furthermore, you can fine-tune the reach of your messaging like

never before thanks to the extensive range of filters and targeting parameters available to you for campaign orientation.

2. **Context and Relevance:** Reaching the right people in the right context is just as important to an effective content strategy as reaching the right people in the first place. For business-to-business (B2B) marketers using social media, this can pose a significant obstacle because users are rarely looking for expert content when browsing through their personal feeds. However, many LinkedIn members log in to find helpful professional content. While being helpful is emphasized here, LinkedIn is ultimately almost always a better environment for connecting with buyers and decision-makers in a meaningful way. This clarifies why 80% of B2B social media leads originate from the platform. LinkedIn is a great place to establish authority in your niche when it comes to thought leadership because it has a large number of active influencers, executives, and other people who are serious about improving their skills and expanding their knowledge.
3. **Versatility:** Content marketing strategies of today must incorporate a variety of media, from written posts to infographics to videos and more. Both paid and organic reach ought to have a role. All of these various styles are simple to include into your LinkedIn content mix, especially with the addition of native video functionality. Strategic marketers on LinkedIn have a great opportunity to capitalize on B2B video in particular, as visual content marketing becomes increasingly important in promoting social engagement.
4. **Research:** Acquiring a thorough understanding of clients and potential clients is B2B marketers' top priority. While this is by no means a novel development, the stakes are constantly rising as customers grow accustomed to expecting experiences that are more and more customized and tailored to them. LinkedIn has representation from most businesses and professionals. It can be quite educational to just skim content feeds and ask employees and companies about the insights they share on their profiles. Another excellent way to network and pick up knowledge from people in your industry is to start participating in LinkedIn Groups that are pertinent to your industry.
5. **Inbound Influx:** The main goal of content creation is to raise your brand's profile and draw customers in an organic way. Of course, there are many factors in that equation, but LinkedIn should be one of them. Prospective clients are more likely to find you when you

and your business are active on the platform, particularly if you regularly discuss topics that are relevant. In particular, the LinkedIn Company Page is an important factor. When someone searches for your company on Google, it typically ranks close to the top of the results. It also connects to the network profiles of every employee you have. Avoid the error of not including it in your content strategy.

6. **Relationship-Building:** The long term perspective is crucial to content marketing strategy. While one-off advertisements and campaigns have their place, nothing beats the significance of establishing solid, real-world professional connections outside of your company. LinkedIn serves as a bridge connecting you with global business leaders, influencers, peers, coworkers, and prospects. Follow their activities to keep an eye on them, and stay visible to them by sharing content they might find interesting, leaving sporadic comments on updates, and, when appropriate, sending them an instant message on LinkedIn. The foundation of an account-based marketing strategy is these procedures.
7. **Measurement:** Ongoing measurement and optimization is one of a marketing strategy's most important components—in fact, I could argue its most important component. Whatever strategies you employ, there's almost always room for improvement. You have access to a multitude of analytical tools on LinkedIn that let you monitor who is engaging with your content and how. To keep things moving forward and fine-tune your approach with data, test various headlines, images, copy, and more.
8. **Onward and Upward!:** If you've been debating whether or not to include LinkedIn in your content strategy, hopefully these seven imperatives will help convince you. This year, a lot of new features will be available to support you in pursuing your goals more actively.

6.2.5. The Importance of LinkedIn as a Social Media Platform for Businesses

To maximize your social media strategy in the current era of digital marketing, you must establish your brand across a range of platforms. With an astounding 303 million monthly active users, LinkedIn is one of the most crucial platforms for businesses to use. Although the purportedly largest professional network in the world helps people and businesses connect effectively, it is occasionally disregarded in efforts to raise brand awareness. While creating a winning LinkedIn strategy could seem overwhelming, working with a social media marketing company to increase your brand's visibility on LinkedIn will pay off quickly.

1. **Networking Opportunities:** LinkedIn is a fantastic platform for people to connect with friends, family, and coworkers. Businesses can also use it to connect with prospective employees, and vice versa. Businesses can hire and retain valuable employees through this platform because users can curate their profiles to display their work experience, accomplishments, and other pertinent professional information. LinkedIn additionally facilitates connections between employers and current employees, which, through the employees' connections, increases exposure and engagement for company pages. Additionally, companies can establish connections with their customers on LinkedIn, which can strengthen ties between an organization and the community at large.
2. **Building Credibility:** A company's LinkedIn presence would be greatly enhanced by sharing helpful content related to its industry, as LinkedIn is known as a professional network. Posts of this nature would give the company the opportunity to show off its thought leadership and, in turn, be seen as an extremely knowledgeable and reliable source in its industry. You will ultimately benefit from collaborating with a social media marketing agency to produce imaginative, educational posts for your business page, as it can be challenging to find high-quality content elsewhere. Furthermore, getting recommendations from customers is a great way to build your company's credibility. Since customers are the ones who make the decisions, you should feel free to display any positive reviews you receive on your company page.
3. **Sharing Updates:** Posting updates and accomplishments from your company is a great way to engage with your audience on LinkedIn, in addition to industry-related content. Users will be more interested in and drawn to your company's page if you provide them with an inside look at company highlights and highlight your success to date in your industry. A simple approach to humanize your business and show prospective customers and staff what you have to offer is to share updates and accomplishments.
4. **Improved SEO:** When creating a successful digital marketing strategy, one of the most important components is search engine optimization, or SEO. Building a presence on multiple social media platforms is necessary to optimize your SEO, which makes having a strong LinkedIn presence essential. Since LinkedIn generates 80% of B2B leads, companies would be well advised to spend time marketing on this platform. Increasing the number of online

locations where people can learn more about your business will boost the likelihood that they will visit your page and engage with your content. Having a strong online presence on LinkedIn will help your company attract more leads and reach a wider audience of both potential customers and employees. Your LinkedIn strategy, with the assistance of a social media marketing agency, will enable your business to establish a strong professional network and eventually thrive on the internet.

6.3. THE ROLE OF THE LINKEDIN SOCIAL MEDIA IN BUILDING THE PERSONAL IMAGE

Virtual social networks and social media have emerged as highly intriguing research subjects for the academic and professional community across a variety of fields. The ComScore Company's Lipsman report from May 2011 states that the number of people using social networking websites is increasing quickly. With 157.22 million monthly visitors, Facebook is the most exploited social network. MySpace (34.49 million), LinkedIn (33.4 million), and Twitter (27.0 million) are the next most popular networks. It is especially intriguing that professionals in marketing, public relations, information technology, human resources, and other related fields have distinct perspectives on social networks based on their individual areas of interest. Regardless of how one views the applications and advantages of social media and networks, it is undeniable that professional social networks serve as a platform for service provision, job placement, and the promotion of individuals as authorities in their field. They are also an effective means of connecting with other professionals in the same industry. Prior research has indicated the value of social media for business presentations by individuals and companies, as well as the necessity of tailoring online communication strategies to specific audiences. Businesses use social media and social networks to present brands and people in virtual environments and to obtain information.

More than 2 million businesses, according to Hershberger, have a LinkedIn page since it allows businesses to present themselves online and their employees in their respective fields of expertise. The data presented indicates that online communication is having a growing impact on social networks for individuals and businesses. It is being utilized more and more for the exchange of pictures, videos, and information, as well as for business social network connections. This study's primary goal is to examine how people present themselves online, particularly on Serbia's professional LinkedIn network, in relation to constructing their personal brand. The results provided shed light on how LinkedIn is currently used in Serbia and offer professional and scholarly communities studying this subject an opportunity to comprehend how LinkedIn users view the value of online communication and this specific social network in establishing a personal brand.

6.3.1. Building Personal Image in the Social Media

Experts use LinkedIn, a global social network spanning 170 industries (professions) and 200 countries. In 2003, LinkedIn was formally established. The five website founders invited their 300 most significant contacts to join the network on May 5, which is commonly known as Cinco de LinkedIn, or "The LinkedIn five," according to the staff. After a month, 4500 people were registered users on LinkedIn. The original LinkedIn headquarters were located in Mountain View on Shoreline Road. Around 5,00,000 of LinkedIn's 9 million users in Europe are from German-speaking nations. For comparison's sake, Xing has 65 million users, the majority of whom are from German-speaking nations (Xing does not release country-specific statistics). In terms of German-speaking nations, Xing is the market leader; however, when it comes to other European nations, such as the UK, Italy, and France, LinkedIn has a significant advantage. A LinkedIn profile helps users find and connect with potential customers, suppliers, industry experts, and partners who can provide recommendations. It also helps users explore new business opportunities, look for employment, make connections that can facilitate business dealings, find highly qualified candidates, and connect with other experts through people they already know.

The workplaces and business practices are altered by the constant social and economic changes in our environment as well as by the rapid advancement of technology. As a result, an individual's position and significance are shifting in both personal and professional contexts. Values like lifelong learning, gaining knowledge and skills, enhancing one's own image, and so forth are becoming more and more important. Developing a positive self-image involves constantly influencing behavior to help people blend in with their environment and increase their own influence by highlighting their accomplishments, talents, and positive traits.

Social networks have grown in importance as a source of personal image building material and as a result of the growing number of users and the amount of time they spend on them (Okanović). The aforementioned study indicates that people use the Internet to improve and fortify their online personas. Because an individual's image is a reflection of their physical and behavioral characteristics, an individual's past actions and experiences on social media have an impact on their overall perception. As a result, managing social media presentation, profile creation, communication style, and presented content (videos, images, and comments) is crucial. According to Leder (Leder), social networks like Facebook and LinkedIn can help develop one's personal brand. Managing a personal online image is the most crucial and efficient way to present oneself to target audiences, even though users of social networks have some control over the messages that are launched. Workers at Burger King, Domino's Pizza, and Delta Air Lines have come to realize that their personal social media status updates or messages regarding workplace entertainment may result in termination if they violate the companies' social media policies. It is critical to comprehend the challenges people face when establishing social media profiles. It is noted in the Dalton study that the biggest issue is social network data security. Other barriers include not having the time or expertise to set up or maintain a profile and not having faith in social media as a resource for business. Despite all the negative connotations, it is still advised that people familiarize themselves with all that a particular social network has to offer and, based on their own requirements, create profiles that can enhance their social and professional images.

6.3.2. Activation on LinkedIn Professional Social Network

In the context of constructing a personal brand, research findings illustrate the kinds of information people look for online, including the causes behind and degrees of activity on the professional social network LinkedIn. Additionally, a comparison is offered with a related study that was carried out in the United States in 2009 at the Pew Research Center's initiative in Washington. According to an analysis of the browsing purpose, 90.3% of participants use the Internet to look up personal information about themselves.

It can be concluded that Internet users in Serbia are more interested in the availability of personal information when compared to research done in the USA in 2009, where 57% of participants said they used browsers to look up their own names and personal information. From a demographic perspective, the percentage of men and women who use browsers to verify their digital signatures is nearly equal. Regardless of the participants' occupation, the analysis of the information available on the Internet reveals that birth dates, e-mail addresses, and photos represent the most accessible information. The findings indicate that when it comes to posting information about employers or the organization/group to which an individual belongs, the participants from the human resources and public relations departments are the most lenient.

While the majority of participants use the Internet to look up information about other people, nearly half of them believe that it is incorrect to judge people based solely on what they find online, and 34.7% of them completely agree with this statement. There are differing views on creating a personal online persona.

Around 35% of participants disagree, with nearly 48% of participants believing that it is difficult to establish and maintain a personal image on the Internet.

In Serbia, 33.1% of users use LinkedIn primarily for networking, 18.3% for personal branding as subject matter experts, and 10.6% for locating businesses and individuals for business collaboration. The only real difference in how men and women use LinkedIn is that men use it more frequently to find jobs (16%) than women do, with women typically using it to find people for business cooperation (16.9%). However, when using LinkedIn to find a job, a statistically significant gender difference has been found (X2 = 8.004, p = 0.005), suggesting that there is some evidence to support the hypothesis (H1) regarding the motivations behind using the LinkedIn social network. Analyzing the age differences between groups reveals that there is a statistically significant difference between age groups for most of the stated reasons for using this social network. While participants between the ages of 25 and 35 primarily use LinkedIn for new business endeavors, those over 35 use it for networking and personal branding. Consequently, the hypothesis (H2) regarding the varying motivations for using the LinkedIn business social network among different age groups has been nearly entirely validated (Table 6.1).

Table 6.1. *Differences in the Purpose for Using LinkedIn between Age Groups*

The purpose of use	% of the participants using LinkedIn for the given purposes				
	younger than 25	between 25 and 35	older than 35	X^2	Sig.
Personal branding	13,6%	20,9%	30,8%	5,950	,052
Connections	21,6%	39,0%	65,4%	24,583	,000
Questions and answers	1,2%	3,5%	7,7%		
Finding companies/partners	11,1%	22,7%	23,1%	8,330	,016
Finding a job	8,0%	12,2%	15,4%		
New business endeavours	6,8%	17,4%	15,4%	8,867	,012
n=360					

Source: https://www.researchgate.net/publication/273715566_The_Role_of_the_LinkedIn_Social_Media_in_Building_the_Personal_Image.

Regarding the participants' use of LinkedIn for professional networking (Figure 6.1). According to research, 81.82% of human resources employees, 72.22% of public relations employees, 59.1% of marketing employees, 28.89% of management and organization employees, and 27.4% of ICT and Internet employees use this social network for that purpose. The hypothesis regarding the motivations for using LinkedIn among participants with different professions (H3) is deemed to be proven as the chi square test revealed that there are statistically significant differences among the participants in the majority of cases (Table 6.2).

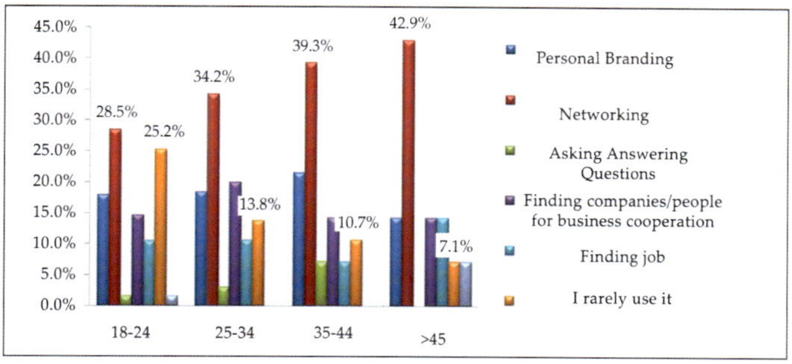

Figure 6.1. *The reasons for activation on LinkedIn according to age groups.*

Source: https://www.researchgate.net/publication/273715566_The_Role_of_the_LinkedIn_Social_Media_in_Building_the_Personal_Image.

Table 6.2. *Differences in the Purpose for Using LinkedIn between the Participants with Different Professions*

The purpose of use	% of the participants using LinkedIn for the given purposes					X²	Sg.
	IT	HR	MARK	MEN ORG	PR/Med Kom		
Personal branding	16,9	45,5	29,5	20,3	38,9	24,483	,000
Connections	27,4	81,8	59,1	29,0	72,2	49,592	,000
Finding companies/partners	16,1	63,6	27,3	17,4	33,3	30,462	,000
Finding a job	10,5	18,2	11,4	15,9	11,1	5,556	,351
New business endeavours	12,1	45,5	20,5	13,0	22,2	22,507	,000
n=360							

Source: https://www.researchgate.net/publication/273715566_The_Role_of_the_LinkedIn_Social_Media_in_Building_the_Personal_Image.

More than half of participants say they network with the same or similar contacts as those on Facebook or other social networks, despite the fact that LinkedIn represents a professional network whose primary goal differs slightly from that of a typical social network. This suggests that, in contrast to participants from the USA, Serbians do not distinguish between their contacts on various social networks based on their purpose (private or business). When it comes to asking questions and responding to specific topics in their field of interest or affiliation, the typical Serbian LinkedIn user is fairly passive. The most engaged participants are the human resources representatives, who use at least one of the aforementioned activities at a rate of 40% and 45% of the representatives between the ages of 35 and 44. Although personal branding ranks second among the reasons people use LinkedIn, 58% of participants have no recommendations, compared to 27% with one to three, 10% with four to seven, and 5% with more than seven recommendations (Figure 6.2).

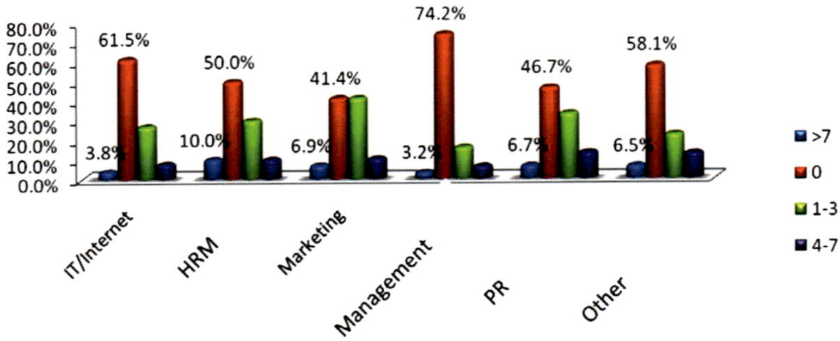

Figure 6.2. *Recommendations on LinkedIn sorted by professions in Serbia.*

Source: https://www.researchgate.net/publication/273715566_The_Role_of_the_LinkedIn_Social_Media_in_Building_the_Personal_Image.

Employees in human resources have at most seven recommendations (10% of them), whereas representatives from management, organizations, and IT have at most no recommendations (74.2% and 61.5%, respectively). Given that a large number of participants have no recommendations on LinkedIn, it is not surprising that 53% of them say they never give recommendations, and 44% say they only give recommendations to people they believe deserve them. Once again, participants in human resources top the list with 77.8% of them making recommendations to deserving parties, compared to 60% of participants in management and organization, IT, and other occupations who make very few recommendations. In addition, men are more likely to write recommendations—47,8% of them—while women are less inclined—40.3% of them feel prepared to write a recommendation for someone they believe deserves it. Regarding employment, only 18% of the participants reported that they had received contact from employers seeking candidates to fill open positions. The IT and Internet sector accounts for one of the three participants who have been contacted about potential employment, with human resources and marketing participants coming in second on the list with 19%. While over half of the participants are unsure but believe it is possible, slightly over one-third of them are optimistic about using LinkedIn to find work. Males are more positive than women; 389 out of them believe that LinkedIn can assist them in their job search, compared to 351% of women.

6.3.3. Key Differences between LinkedIn and Facebook When It Comes to Business

1. **Audience:** Facebook is a general-purpose social media platform, whereas LinkedIn is a professional social network. This indicates that content pertaining to businesses is more likely to pique the interest of LinkedIn users. Facebook users, on the other hand, are more likely to be interested in a greater variety of content, such as news, entertainment, and personal.
2. **Purpose:** LinkedIn's purpose is to facilitate professional connections, job searches, and career growth. Facebook was created to facilitate sharing of ideas and experiences, keeping users informed about current affairs, and fostering relationships with friends and family.
3. **Content:** Sharing professional content, such as job listings, blog posts, and articles, is more common among LinkedIn users. Shares of private content, including images, videos, and status updates, are more common among Facebook users.
4. **Engagement:** Users of LinkedIn are more likely to interact with content that speaks to their interests in their line of work. Funny, intriguing, or thought-provoking content has a higher chance of generating interaction among Facebook users.
5. **Advertising:** LinkedIn provides a range of professional-focused advertising options. Facebook provides a range of advertising options that are intended for a more diverse set of users.
6. **Cost:** Advertising on LinkedIn may cost more than that on Facebook. But because LinkedIn advertising is targeted at a more narrow demographic, it can also be more successful.
7. **ROI:** LinkedIn has been shown to have a higher ROI than Facebook for businesses that are targeting professionals.
8. **User Experience:** LinkedIn has a more professional user interface than Facebook. Facebook has a more casual user interface.
9. **Mobile App:** LinkedIn has a dedicated mobile app that is designed for professionals. Facebook has a mobile app that is designed for everyone.
10. **Overall Value:** LinkedIn is a useful resource for companies looking to market to professionals. Facebook is a useful tool for companies looking to reach a broader demographic. Your unique needs and objectives will determine which platform is best for your company. LinkedIn is a fantastic choice if professionals are your target audience. Facebook is a great choice if you want to reach a wider range of audiences.

6.4. THE SYSTEM OF LINKEDIN ALGORITHM

The posts that appear in each user's feed are chosen by the LinkedIn algorithm, which functions as a recommendation system. What content appears in an individual's feed depends on the subjects, users, and kinds of posts that they are most likely to interact with. There are currently 950 million members on LinkedIn. Every day, the algorithm analyzes billions of posts in order to provide each user with an engaging and educational newsfeed. LinkedIn wants to prioritize high-quality, relevant content and encourage interaction. The algorithm will function more effectively for you the longer you use the platform. Having said that, you shouldn't expect your content to become viral on LinkedIn. LinkedIn states unequivocally that it was not intended to go viral. It's about disseminating updates and knowledge to those who are interested in it and can use it to further their professional lives.

6.4.1. LinkedIn Algorithm Work

1. **LinkedIn Decides if Your Post is Spam or Good Content:** The LinkedIn algorithm starts by categorizing your post to see if it breaks any community policies or spam guidelines on the site. Clear violations are flagged by the AI, and the content is filtered. As per LinkedIn's definition, some blatant instances of spam include:

- Emoji or reaction polls designed to artificially boost engagement;
- Chain letters;
- Requests for likes, reactions, and shares;
- Excessive, irrelevant, or repetitive comments or messages.

The content type is sent for human review if it is not sufficiently clear to filter automatically. Should the content pass the human review process, it stays up on the platform (Figure 6.3).

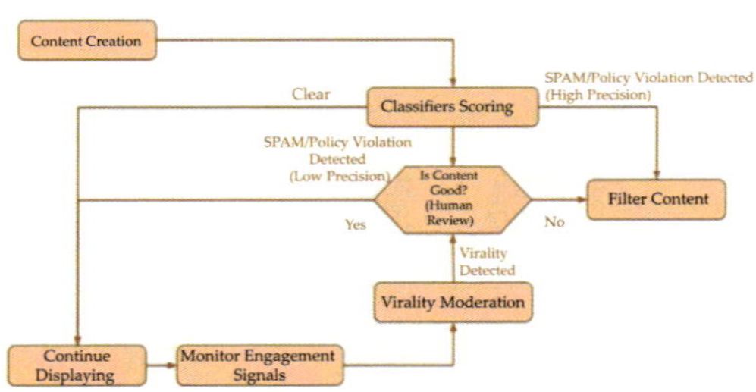

Figure 6.3. *AI classification pipeline for LinkedIn algorithms.*

Source: https://blog.hootsuite.com/wp-content/uploads/2023/10/linkedin-algorithm-1-620x371.png.

2. **LinkedIn Puts Your Post to the Test:** LinkedIn looks for engagement signals to gauge the value of your post to people in your immediate and extended networks, after the algorithm has determined that you haven't posted anything overtly spammy. Although engagement is a positive indicator of the value of your post, not all engagement is equal. Recent adjustments to the LinkedIn algorithm give particular weight to meaningful engagement, as you can see below. That entails intelligent remarks from experts in pertinent domains. (For this reason, unless it's a highly targeted pod of people who are genuinely interested in your content anyway, joining a LinkedIn pod is not likely to result in a significant boost in your distribution).

3. **LinkedIn Delivers Your Most Valuable Content to Relevant Users:** Who gets to see your post from here depends on three ranking signals:

i. **Identity:** The LinkedIn algorithm has recently undergone modifications with the express purpose of making sure more of your content is seen by first-degree connections. Generally speaking, followers are more likely to see your posts if they are closely related to you. This could include members of your extended network who you have previously interacted with. Here, other variables include your profile location and skill set.

ii. **Content:** Here, the LinkedIn algorithm evaluates a piece of content's relevancy to a particular LinkedIn user based on how well it performs among other users on the network. This comprises indications such as.

- How often the content has been viewed and engaged with;
- How relevant the topic is based on the identity signals above;
- Whether the content shares knowledge or professional advice (more on this below!);
- The language of the content;
- How professional and constructive the conversation in the comments section is;
- Which companies, people, and topics are mentioned.

4. **Member Activity:** The groups, hashtags, pages, and users that a user follows are used by the LinkedIn algorithm to determine that user's interests. Additionally, it evaluates a user's interest in a subject matter based on their social media activity, such as posting, liking, or commenting on pertinent posts or articles. Users will see more content from the authors and topics they interact with most

frequently, as well as content that is similar to what they have already engaged with.

6.4.2. Navigating LinkedIn Algorithm Changes

The recent changes to LinkedIn's algorithm have drastically changed how users should approach their content in order to increase visibility and engagement. The platform now places more emphasis on informative posts of a high caliber than on volume, highlighting content that provides insightful analysis and expert guidance catered to particular niches. This change implies that users should concentrate on writing informative and educating posts since they have a higher chance of becoming popular. Posts with genuine value are given priority by the new LinkedIn algorithm. Make sure your content offers expert advice and is packed with insights in order to meet this requirement. To draw in a specific kind of reader, customize your posts to fit into niches. Not only does high-quality content increase your reach, but it also establishes your authority in the industry. Considering the new LinkedIn algorithm, cultivating meaningful engagement is essential. Posts that pose open-ended questions to foster sincere dialogues typically get more attention. The algorithm favors interactive content, which explains this. Expanding the reach of your content can be achieved by actively interacting and responding thoughtfully with your audience. Including rich media in your posts—like videos and images—can significantly increase interaction. Research indicates that posts with images on LinkedIn receive twice as many comments as posts without images, and videos receive up to five times as much interaction as other content types. Therefore, to make your posts stand out, consistently incorporate captivating videos and high-quality images.

Posting at the right time is also crucial. Posting usually occurs at 1:00 p.m. on Mondays works well. To ascertain the optimal times for engagement, it is imperative to take into account the online behaviors of your target audience. Planning your posts for optimal visibility can be aided by analyzing the times of day when your audience is most engaged. LinkedIn's algorithm rewards consistency in posting. Your engagement rates can double if you stick to a regular posting schedule of one post per week at the very least. This keeps your audience interested and shows dedication, which raises the possibility of continued interactions and shares. Enhancing your LinkedIn profile is an additional crucial action. Make sure your profile has a catchy headline, an in-depth synopsis, and pertinent skills. This helps people find and connect with you more easily by enhancing your personal branding and LinkedIn SEO. A profile that is optimized will increase your credibility and draw in more business contacts. Since LinkedIn wants to keep users on the site, outbound links in posts may have a negative effect on performance. Instead, provide external links in follow-up posts or comments. This strategy gives your audience access to useful resources while maintaining your primary content in line with LinkedIn's preferences. You can successfully navigate the new LinkedIn algorithm by concentrating on high-quality content, meaningful engagement, rich media, ideal posting times, consistent posting, and profile optimization. These techniques make sure the appropriate people see and interact with your content, increasing your exposure and influence as a professional on LinkedIn.

6.4.3. Working with the LinkedIn Algorithm

1. **Be Relevant and Informative:** Recall that, in light of members' skills and interests, the LinkedIn algorithm now presents content that seems likely to pique their curiosity. Consequently, you must be aware of the abilities and preferences of the target market you are attempting to reach. For you to be able to speak as a reliable authority on pertinent subjects, those interests and talents should ideally complement you greatly. Your LinkedIn profile tells LinkedIn what areas of expertise you have. Your followers and first-degree connections are not the only people who are likely to see posts on those subjects. Benchmark social media engagement rates for different industries are shared, for instance, in this Hootsuite post on LinkedIn. Many people interacted with and reshared this post because it contains extremely pertinent information that was taken straight from Hootsuite's benchmarking tool. Analytical and intelligence data from your other social media accounts should be examined first. Take a look at your audience's interests to gain more insight into their priorities. Personas can also be created by utilizing the audience of a rival company. Following that, relate those interests to your personal expertise and knowledge domains. As you develop your LinkedIn marketing strategy, start with these findings. Hint: According to LinkedIn members, even if the posts were from people outside of their direct network, 98% of those pertaining to professional knowledge were valuable.

- Relevance can apply to formats, too. LinkedIn members prefer to engage with rich media:
- Posts with images get twice as many comments as text posts;
- LinkedIn videos get five times the engagement.

2. **Schedule Your Posts for the Best Times:** It's crucial to have a strong first hour of engagement. If the people in your audience are sound asleep, you will not be able to start a conversation. Plan your

posts for when most of your followers are most likely to be online and active on the platform to get the most exposure. In general, 1:00 p.m. is the ideal time to post on LinkedIn. Mondays. However, each audience is distinct. To optimize engagement with your own network, the Hootsuite dashboard's "Best Time to Publish" feature provides a tailored recommendation. Make sure to frequently publish new content. According to LinkedIn data, publishing content on a weekly basis increases engagement by twice.

3. **Promote Your Posts (on LinkedIn and Off):** One of the best ways to increase engagement on your posts is to increase the number of people that will see them.

There are several tactics to gain extra traction on LinkedIn:

- Tag people and relevant companies;
- Use keywords strategically;
- Include relevant hashtags.

Here, branded hashtags are also potentially useful. The algorithm will show posts that use a hashtag to its followers if you create one that is worthwhile following. Adobe's *AdobeLife*, Nike's *SwooshLife*, and Lyft's *LifeAtLyft* are a few examples. With the help of Google's *GrowWithGoogle* hashtag, over 21,000 users can interact and exchange experiences on the platform. Share a recent post in Slack or your e-newsletter if you believe it could be useful to staff members or clients. Using your content in this way can be a great way to interact with inactive LinkedIn members. As a result, the interaction will raise your algorithmic ranking. It benefits both parties.

4. **Avoid Outbound Links:** LinkedIn wants you to stay on the network. Therefore, it should come as no surprise that posts with outbound links are not given the same priority by the algorithm as other kinds of content. For the sake of certainty, we conducted an experiment. Our non-outbound link posts consistently perform better than other kinds of posts. Post the link to anything off-platform in the comments if you must share it.

5. **Encourage Meaningful Engagement:** Engagement is rewarded by LinkedIn's algorithm, but only if it is pertinent and significant. You won't reach more people if they make generic remarks. You want comments that demonstrate readers in related fields have read, understood, and considered your post. Consider posing a query that invites comments or insights from the audience. Asking the right questions fosters meaningful conversations and establishes your brand as a thought leader. It also gives you the chance to discover

more about the interests of your audience, which will help you create even more pertinent content. Lastly, remember to participate in the discussion yourself. LinkedIn prefers an active dialogue with you as the main participant over a one-way stream of comments. By making sure you never miss a mention or comment, a tool like Hootsuite Inbox allows you to demonstrate to your followers—as well as the algorithm—that you're knowledgeable, involved, active, and relevant.

6. **Craft Original Content with a Unique Perspective:** Compared to shared posts, original content gets much more attention and is more widely shared. Try to find a way to reframe the content and add your own perspective and insights if you're going to repurpose it or have a user-generated content strategy. Recall that LinkedIn seeks to highlight content that fosters connections and knowledge sharing. It's essential to contribute your own viewpoint to both. For instance, Thinkific added their own viewpoint based on their ThinkinColor event when they shared this post by Keenya Kelly. Remember that asking a thought-provoking question can really help to spark conversation.
7. **Build Your Network Strategically:** Relevance and connections are important signals for the LinkedIn algorithm. This entails developing a robust and dynamic network of industry experts. According to LinkedIn data, the potential for growth increases exponentially once your page reaches 150 followers. Some routes to get there are as follows:

- As much as you can, complete your page and personal profile and keep them updated. (LinkedIn reports that Pages with comprehensive information receive 30% more views every week!) Make sure your Page overview contains pertinent keywords and phrases because LinkedIn members can search by them. To inform your first-degree profile connections about your LinkedIn Page, use the Invite button. Encourage staff members to use your corporate hashtag when demonstrating that they are employed by your company. Permit them to follow your business page and ask their own profile connections to do the same.
- To increase reach and engagement, use employee notifications (located under the three-dot icon when creating content) to notify staff members once a week about your most important posts. Connect with experts in your field and follow other Pages that are relevant to you. Participate in groups on LinkedIn or start your own. To allow

others to find you, add you, and view your posts, make sure your profile is public. Participate in discussions and generally be active on the network. Display links to your LinkedIn profiles on your website and in other relevant areas (e.g., business cards, newsletters, email signatures, staff biographies, etc.). For this, setting up personalized URLs is helpful.

8. **Optimize with Analytics:** If something works well, do the same. Utilize Hootsuite Analytics to determine which posts are most successful and why. This is a crucial method for deciphering the algorithm in light of your individual historical performance. Perhaps it's because you published them all at once? Perhaps every post asked a question? Whatever the reason, figure it out and apply these insights to improve your LinkedIn content strategy.
9. **Post LinkedIn-Appropriate Content:** LinkedIn users want to interact with the professional world. That is something you should take into account when writing your posts. You shouldn't post a video of your dog's birthday celebration here. Instead, remain focused on your business. Don't merely believe what we say. The professional community policies on LinkedIn include this: "Know your niche and make a home in it." You don't have to project an entirely cold, roboto-corporate vibe on LinkedIn. Humor, humanity, and authenticity are encouraged and even rewarded. Adopt an approachable and amiable brand voice. Members of LinkedIn may become less likely to interact with accounts that follow corporate policy or overuse business terminology. If you are genuine and approachable, your audience will be more inclined to reciprocate.

REFERENCES

1. Clark, D. (2011). Reinventing your personal brand: How to change your image and create exciting new opportunities. *Harvard Business Review, 89*(3), 81.
2. Dalton, D. (2011). How women can hone their networking skills. *Financial Management*, 51–52.
3. Damnjanovic, V. (2011). *Marketing in practice – applying the case study method.* FON, Beograd.
4. Diga, M., & Kelleher, T. (2009). Social media use, perceptions of decision-making power, and public relations roles. *Public Relations Review, 35*, 440–442.
5. Dutta, S. (2010). Managing yourself: What's your personal social media strategy? *Harvard Business Review, 88*(11), 127–130.
6. Elmore, B. (2009). Social networking strategies. *Baylor Business Review, 28*(1), 25–27.
7. Eyrich, N., Padman, M. L., & Sweetser, K. (2008). PR practitioners' use of social media tools and communication technology. *Public Relations Review, 34*(4), 412–414.
8. Fatt, J. P. T. (1997). Communicating a winning image. *Industrial and Commercial Training, 29*(5), 158–165.
9. Filipović, V., & Kostić Stanković, M. (2011). *Odnosi s javnošću.* FON, Beograd.
10. Freberg, K. (2012). *Social media & public relations.* University of Tennessee, Knoxville.
11. Hershberger, T. (2012). Using LinkedIn as a marketing tool. *ABA Bank Marketing, 37*, 37.
12. Hood, T. (2010). Your reputation rests on your own personal brand. *British Journal of Administrative Management, 24*, 24.
13. Kazim, A., & Karahan, F. (2011). To be or not to be in social media arena as the most cost-efficient marketing strategy after the global recession. *Procedia Social and Behavioral Sciences, 24*, 260–268.
14. Kostić Stanković, M., & Damnjanović, V. (2011). The social media interaction: Case study in students' perspective. In *1st International Conference Economic System of European Union and Accession of the Bosnia & Herzegovina* (pp. 172–179). Vitez, Bosna i Hercegovina.
15. Leder, G. (2008). Your online brand. *Wall Street Journal, 86*, 86.

16. LinkedIn company information. (2009, March 28). Retrieved from http://www.linkedin.com/static?key=company_info&trk=hb_ft_abtli.
17. LinkedIn opens site in Germany, takes on Xing. (2009, February 4). *AIM Group*. Retrieved from http://aimgroup.com/index.php/article/linkedins-german-portal-to-focus-on-jobs-and-news.
18. Lipsman. (2011, May 6). The network effect: Facebook, LinkedIn, Twitter, and Tumblr reach new heights in May. Retrieved from http://www.baselinemag.com.
19. Madden, S. (2010). Reputation management and social media: How people monitor their identity and search for others online. *Pew Research Center*. Retrieved from http://pewinternet.org/Reports/2010/Reputation-Management.aspx.
20. Matović, V. (2011). *Upravljanje ličnim identitetom, imidžom i reputacijom na društvenim medijima* (Master's thesis). FON, Beograd.
21. McGinley, J. J. (2010, June 17). Well connected. *Money Marketing*, 51.
22. Milićević, V., & Ilić, B. (2011). Konkurentske strategije u uslovima digitalne ekonomije. *Management*, *5*(16), 5–13.
23. Millard, E. (2008). Facebook, LinkedIn: Meet human resources. *Baseline Magazine*, 14–15.
24. Nadkarni, A., & Hofmann, S. G. (2012). Why do people use Facebook? *Personality and Individual Differences*, *52*(3), 243–249.
25. Nguyen, N., & Leblanc, G. (2001). Corporate image and corporate reputation in customers' retention decisions in services. *Journal of Retailing and Consumer Services*, *8*(4), 227–236.
26. Noella, L. (2009). Ten tips to raise your business visibility through social networks. *Financial Executive*, *25*(9), 17.
27. Okanović, M., Milosavljević, M., & Cicvarić, S. (2010). Personal image in social networks context. In *XII Internacionalni Simpozijum SymOrg 2010* (pp. 172–179). Zlatibor, Srbija.

CHAPTER 7

TWITTER ALGORITHM

Contents

Introduction 254
7.1. Overview of Twitter (X) Algorithm 255
7.2. How Does the Twitter Algorithm Work? 257
References 277

INTRODUCTION

With the goal of improving user engagement and satisfaction, Twitter has developed a sophisticated algorithm to curate and prioritize the massive amount of content available on the platform. Fundamentally, the algorithm determines which tweets are most relevant to each individual user by combining machine learning techniques, historical data, and user interactions. It uses a variety of strategies to customize the Twitter experience.

User engagement history is one of the main factors affecting the algorithm. To determine each user's interests and preferences, the algorithm monitors likes, retweets, replies, and the amount of time spent on a particular tweet. This information aids in anticipating the kind of content that a user will probably interact with in the future. For example, the algorithm will give similar content in a user's timeline priority if they regularly interact with tech-related tweets.

The algorithm's consideration of tweets' recentness is another important factor. The algorithm gives more weight to more recent content in order to maintain the feed current and relevant, even though older tweets are not completely removed from the timeline. This harmony makes sure that users can access important or trending conversations that may have begun earlier and still see the most recent updates. The algorithm also considers the user's network of followers and the degree of interaction with the individuals in their network. A user's feed is more likely to display tweets from users who have a high level of engagement or who are well-known within a specific topic. This social component aids in promoting content from people who are regarded as important voices or engaged contributors to particular discussions. Furthermore, contextual relevance is incorporated into Twitter's algorithm, which means that tweet content—including hashtags and keywords—is assessed to make sure it corresponds with users' interests and popular subjects.

The text and media in tweets are analyzed by the algorithm to determine their appropriateness and relevance for each individual user. The algorithm is always changing despite its complexity because of user feedback and behavioral shifts. Twitter modifies its algorithm on a regular basis to address problems such as disinformation, harassment, and the dissemination of dangerous content. The objective is to achieve equilibrium between customizing the user experience and upholding a robust and captivating platform. In general, the Twitter algorithm seeks to produce a dynamic, customized feed that takes into account the interests of each individual user and changes to reflect emerging conversations and trends. Its diverse method of content curation makes it easier for users to navigate the abundance of information on the platform, improving the relevance and engagement of their Twitter experience.

7.1. OVERVIEW OF TWITTER (X) ALGORITHM

The Twitter algorithm is a collection of guidelines that determines the value of each post by ranking content on the network. The algorithm, which determines what we see on Twitter and how we see it, is essentially a central brain. The algorithm, according to the company, selects a small number of tweets to appear on a user's timeline each day after sorting through about 500 million tweets. Numerous factors are taken into consideration when making these decisions, such as the content's location, virality, personal interests, timeliness, and spammy or sensitive nature.

The recommendation engine on Twitter, known as the "X" algorithm, makes recommendations based on machine learning for users' feeds. The posts that you see depend on a number of variables, such as popularity, relevancy, and the kinds of content you interact with. In practice, the combination of factors used to rank posts is far more complex and is continuously being improved, much like any other social media algorithm. In order to guarantee that their Twitter (X) marketing strategy remains effective, marketers must remain up to date on all the most recent developments.

7.1.1. Why Does Twitter Use It?

Twitter shows users the most interesting and relevant content based on an algorithm that enhances user experience. Based on their interests, previous interactions, and other variables, the algorithm makes sure that users see the most significant tweets first. By presenting users with relevant advertisements, the algorithm also aids in Twitter's revenue generation.

The algorithm is able to present ads that have a higher chance of being clicked on and interacted with by examining user behavior and interests. The amount of time spent by Twitter users viewing connect ads—ads related to a particular event, occasion, or trend—is 1.9 times higher. This is a crucial reminder for advertisers who use Twitter to connect with prospective clients and earn a portion of the ad revenue.

7.1.2. Twitter

The most widely used microblogging platform is Twitter. Microblogging is a type of blogging where users post brief text updates—usually no more than 140 characters—that are accessible to the public or members of a particular community. Twitter went live in July of 2006. These 140-character updates, sometimes known as tweets, typically consist of brief ideas or connections to worthwhile articles. With 100 million active users sharing over 500 million tweets per day, Twitter boasts over 328 million monthly active users. Although it was previously believed that Twitter was a site primarily used by older users, the most recent statistics reveal that almost 40% of users are between the ages of 18 and 29, while only 30% of users are between the ages of 30 and 49. With more than 80% of its users accessing the platform via a mobile device, Twitter is undoubtedly a platform that users use on the go (Figure 7.1).

Figure 7.1. *Twitter is the most popular microblogging service.*

Source: https://encrypted-tbn0.gstatic.com/images?q=tbn:ANd9GcTI-h-e2hgz8m-wGfCt4gvj4IgMG_wAUolVM6w&s.

7.1.3. Features

Every Twitter user will have a distinct username, which is indicated by the @ symbol followed by their preferred name; for example, @robstokes for www.twitter.com/robstokes. By beginning a tweet with the user's @username, you can target a specific person with it. They also go by this name on Twitter. Similar to Instagram, Twitter users can categorize their posts using hashtags by adding a word or phrase before the symbol, like "digital marketing." You can click the hashtag to view other tweets that contain this tag. It will turn into a link. The option to follow a hashtag allows users to view all messages posted publicly with that tag, regardless of whether they follow the user who posted it or not. This can be a very helpful method for gathering data at conferences and other events. You can still follow messages from the event if you're not present by following the hashtag. All tagged messages can be broadcast to attendees in a common area.

A hashtag or keyword may become popular and show up to the left of a user's tweet stream if it is used a lot in a short period of time. Globally significant events are typically heavily featured, but occasionally, brands can trend as well (though not always for the right reasons). A tweet may be quote- or retweeted if it is deemed noteworthy. Retweeting is the act of adding another person's tweet and username to your own profile. This is automatically retweeted by Twitter.

You can retweet another post and leave a comment about it by using a quote retweet.

7.1.4. Marketing and Advertising with Twitter

Twitter has grown to be a well-liked and significant marketing tool for a lot of businesses, brands, and people. Many brands, like @jetblue @klm and @ dstvcare, successfully use it for quick customer service. Twitter has developed into an excellent tool for consumer insights and market research. Brands can gain a great deal of insight by tracking indirect conversations and searching for brand keywords on Twitter. Because of its instantaneity, news can be shared with ardent supporters and followers first, as pop sensation Lady Gaga has done with single releases (@ladygaga). Dell maintains a number of Twitter accounts, many of which only share information about their exclusive offers (@delloutlet). Among them are Promoted Accounts, Promoted Trends, and Promoted Tweets (Figure 7.2).

Figure 7.2. *Marketing and advertising with Twitter.*

*Source: https://miro.medium.com/v2/resize:fit:720/format:webp/1*0ZhzN-2EUXmov3HHwOjKCQ.png.*

7.1.4.1. Twitter Analytics

As of right now, anyone who provides analysis using the Twitter API can access Twitter Analytics. Analytics that are integrated into Hootsuite's Twitter management tools can yield useful information. Twitter metrics that are important to track include the number of users who interact with your content by clicking on links, the number of people who reply to you, the number of retweets you get, and the usage of hashtags and trends.

7.2. HOW DOES THE TWITTER ALGORITHM WORK?

Like anything else on social media, the Twitter (X) algorithm is constantly changing and is composed of multiple algorithms. Twitter's algorithm gathers user data by looking at clicks, likes, and replies. It then uses this data and converts it into outputs. In this case, the data aids in the creation of Twitter's primary "For You" feed.

Recently, Twitter (X) added two distinct sections to its home screen. You can see the accounts you have specifically selected to follow in the Following section, and the algorithm-based For You section offers you customized recommendations. You can choose whether or not the For You feed is truly for you, and users can switch between these modes (Figure 7.3).

Figure 7.3. *The Twitter (X) algorithm.*

Source: https://cdn.prod.website-files.com/63ff7c6ecc83f9ec7ffe916b/65fb570b9704dd131a569940_Twitter%20algorithm-p-1080.webp.

Twitter has developed into an essential resource for creators looking to share their work and express their ideas over time. The platform has cemented its standing as a major player in the social media scene with its well-established role as a focal point for networking and discussions.

While the recent transition of the platform from "Twitter" to "X" brought subtle changes to the app's interface, comprehending its algorithm remains crucial for creators striving to navigate and succeed in this dynamic social media environment. Every interaction, including tweets, likes, retweets, and trending topics, affects how the algorithm makes decisions, which in turn shapes content visibility and increases audience engagement. In-depth analysis of the Twitter (X) algorithm's effects on tweet visibility, audience engagement, and the general user experience on one of the most significant social media platforms worldwide is provided in this article.

7.2.1. Twitter Algorithm Works in 2024

Despite being a social media platform, this one consumes content very differently than others. While some users use the app primarily to passively absorb all information available worldwide, others may use it to actively post updates, news, and opinions on a regular basis. But it can be difficult to stay up to date with everything going on the platform because there is so much shared content.

However, users' timelines are largely influenced by Twitter's algorithm.

On Twitter, an algorithm makes sure users see the most intriguing and relevant content first rather than being inundated with updates. Anyone who wants to get the most out of Twitter must comprehend how the algorithm operates.

Understanding how the algorithm functions can help you make the most of your Twitter experience, whether you're a journalist trying to stay up to date on the latest news, a business trying to promote its goods or services, or just an average user trying to follow your favorite accounts (Figure 7.4).

Figure 7.4. *Social media platform.*

Source: https://cdn.prod.website-files.com/64dc619021257128d0687cce/6581721e2ed7aa5f5f227abf_1680692659777.jpeg.

The top tweets that appear on your device's "For You" timeline are chosen by Twitter's recommendation algorithm. Let's take a closer look at how the Twitter algorithm selects tweets from different sources to present you with the best content.

7.2.2. Twitter's Recommendation Algorithm

Twitter wants to provide you with the most up-to-date information on global events. In order to reduce the roughly 500 million Tweets posted every day to a select few top Tweets that eventually appear on your device's For You timeline, a recommendation algorithm is needed. An overview of the algorithm used to choose Tweets for your timeline can be found in this blog. We will go into detail in this post about the various services and tasks that make up our recommendation system. Although the app has numerous sections where Tweets are suggested, such as Search, Explore, and Ads, this article will concentrate on the For You feed on the home timeline.

7.2.3. How Do We Choose Tweets?

A collection of fundamental models and features that draw out latent information from user, engagement, and tweet data form the basis of Twitter's recommendations. These models seek to provide accurate answers to key queries regarding the Twitter network, such as "What is the likelihood that you will interact with another user in the future?" and "What are the Twitter communities and what are the trending Tweets within them?" By providing accurate answers, Twitter is able to provide recommendations that are more pertinent to the user.

The recommendation pipeline is made up of three main stages that consume these features:

1. Fetch the best Tweets from different recommendation sources in a process called candidate sourcing.
2. Rank each Tweet using a machine learning model.
3. Apply heuristics and filters, such as filtering out Tweets from users you've blocked, NSFW content, and Tweets you've already seen.

Home Mixer is the service in charge of creating and delivering the For You timeline. Product Mixer, our proprietary Scala framework for creating content feeds, is the foundation upon which Home Mixer is constructed. This service serves as the backbone of the software that links various candidate sources, heuristics, filters, and scoring functions. This diagram below illustrates the major components used to construct a timeline (Figure 7.5):

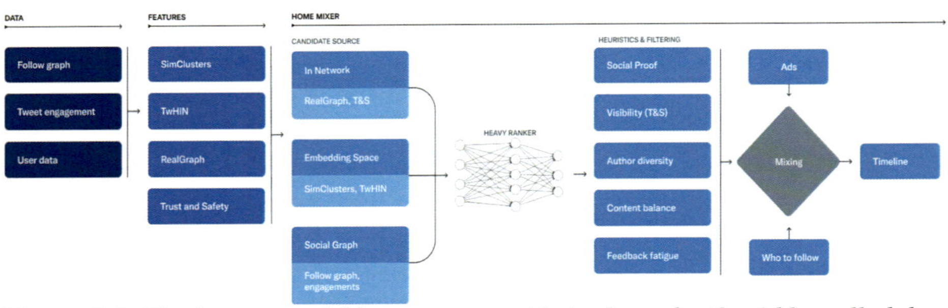

Figure 7.5. *The key parts of this system, roughly in the order they'd be called during a single timeline request, starting with retrieving candidates from candidate sources.*

Source: https://cdn.cms-twdigitalassets.com/content/dam/blog-twitter/engineering/en_us/open-source/2023/twitter-recommendation-algorithm/open-algorithm.png.img.fullhd.medium.png.

Twitter's Recommendation Algorithm combines in-network and out-of-network sources to choose tweets. The algorithm aims to answer important questions such as "What is the most relevant content for this user right now?" and "What is the best way to rank content for this user?"

1. **Candidate Sources:** We use a number of Twitter Candidate Sources to get the most recent and pertinent Tweets for a user. Using these sources, we try to select the top 1500 Tweets for every request out of hundreds of millions. We locate candidates from both your following and unfollowing accounts (In-Network and Out-of-Network). Currently, the For You timeline has an average of 50% In-Network Tweets and 50% Out-of-Network Tweets, though this might differ from user to user. A broad variety of candidate sources are taken into account by the algorithm, such as tweets from accounts you follow, accounts you don't follow, and accounts that are similar to those you follow. In addition, it takes into account trending tweets related to your interests.

i. **In-Network Source:** These are also used by Twitter's recommendation algorithm to select tweets. In other words, it selects tweets from the users you follow and assigns a relevance rating to each one. It records who you follow and how frequently you communicate with them. It takes into account the things you have recently done, like retweet, or reply to tweets. For the In-Network tweets, Twitter employs the Real Graph model, which forecasts the possibility of interaction between two users.

The largest candidate source, the In-Network source, seeks to present the most recent, pertinent Tweets from the users you follow. It employs a logistic regression model to effectively rank the Tweets of users you follow according to their relevance. The best Tweets are then forwarded to the following phase. Real Graph is the most crucial factor in the ranking of In-Network Tweets.

A model called Real Graph forecasts the possibility of interaction between two users. We'll include more of the tweet author's tweets the higher your Real Graph score is with them. At Twitter, recent work has focused on the In-Network source. Fanout Service, a 12-year-old service that was formerly used to deliver In-Network Tweets from a cache of Tweets for every user, was recently discontinued. The logistic regression ranking model, which was last updated and trained several years ago, is also undergoing a redesign!

ii. **Out-of-Network Sources:** The algorithm selects tweets for a user's timeline based on factors including out-of-network sources. It uses signals unrelated to your interactions or activities, such as news events, popular topics, and others, to do this. Twitter uses two methods to address the more difficult problem of finding relevant Tweets outside of a user's network: how can we determine if a particular Tweet will be relevant to you if you don't follow the author?

a **Social Graph:** Our first approach is to estimate what you would find relevant by analyzing the engagements of people you follow or those with similar interests.

We traverse the graph of engagements and follows to answer the following questions:

- What Tweets did the people I follow recently engage with?
- Who likes similar Tweets to me, and what else have they recently liked?

Based on the responses to these queries, we produce candidate Tweets, which we then rank using a logistic regression model. These kinds of graph traversals are crucial to our Out-of-Network recommendations. To carry out these traversals, we created GraphJet, a graph processing engine that keeps track of users' interactions with Tweets in real time. Although heuristics like these for looking up Twitter engagement and follower networks have been helpful (they currently account for 15% of Home Timeline tweets), embedding space approaches are now a more significant source of tweets that are found outside of networks.

b. **Embedding Spaces:** What Tweets and Users are Similar to My Interests? is a more general question about content similarity that embedding space approaches seek to address. Embeddings function by producing numerical representations of users' interests and Tweet content. The similarity between any two users, Tweets, or user-Tweet pairs in this embedding space can then be determined.

As long as we produce precise embeddings, we can substitute this similarity for relevance. SimClusters is one of Twitter's most helpful embedding spaces. SimClusters use a customized matrix factorization algorithm to identify communities that are anchored by a cluster of influential users. Every three weeks, the 145k communities are updated.

Communities represent users and tweets, and they can be a part of more than one community. Communities can have hundreds of millions of members for news or pop culture, or just a few 1000 for personal friend groups.

These are some of the biggest communities (Figure 7.6):

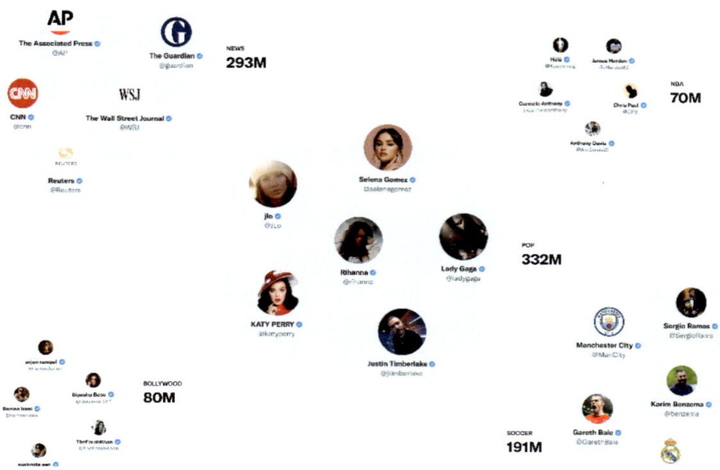

Figure 7.6. *Embedding spaces.*

Source: https://cdn.cms-twdigitalassets.com/content/dam/blog-twitter/engineering/en_us/open-source/2023/twitter-recommendation-algorithm/simclusters.png.img.fullhd.medium.png.

We can embed Tweets into these communities by looking at the current popularity of a Tweet in each community. The more that users from a community like a Tweet, the more that Tweet will be associated with that community.

2 **Ranking:** The main goal of Twitter's ranking algorithm is to make user content more relevant to them based on their interactions, likes, shares, and replies. These consist of the user's interaction (likes, retweets, replies), the tweet's recentness, the user and tweet author relationship (like mutual follows), and the user's previous interactions with related content. For example, tweets from sports-related accounts may have a higher ranking if the user engages with sports content on a regular basis. Providing you with pertinent Tweets is the aim of the For You timeline.

We currently have about 1500 candidates in the pipeline that could be relevant. The main factor used to rank Tweets on your timeline is scoring, which accurately forecasts each candidate Tweet's level of relevance. All candidates are given the same treatment at this point, regardless of the source of the candidate information.

A neural network with approximately 48 million parameters is utilized to rank content. It is trained on Tweet interactions in real time to maximize positive engagement (e.g., Likes, RTs, and Commenting).

To assign a score to each Tweet, this ranking algorithm considers thousands of features and produces 10 labels, each of which denotes the likelihood of an engagement. The Tweets are ranked based on these scores.

3. **Heuristics, Filters, and Product Features:** Heuristics are rules that are applied to content filtering. Heuristics, for instance, might be used by Twitter to hide spam and repetitive content. Twitter uses filters to control the quality of its content. For example, it removes hate speech and false information. Additionally, it excludes tweets from users that you have muted or blocked.

   These filters are updated frequently to take into account the changing discourse on the internet. Product features include things like "Topics," which allow users to track particular topics. These features align content with user-selected interests, which has an impact on the recommendation algorithm.

   After the Ranking stage, we apply heuristics and filters to implement various product features. These features work together to create a balanced and diverse feed. Some examples include:

- **Visibility Filtering:** Filter out Tweets based on their content and your preferences. For instance, remove Tweets from accounts you block or mute.
- **Author Diversity:** Avoid too many consecutive Tweets from a single author.
- **Content Balance:** Ensure we are delivering a fair balance of In-Network and Out-of-Network Tweets.
- **Feedback-based Fatigue:** Lower the score of certain Tweets if the viewer has provided negative feedback around it.
- **Social Proof:** Exclude out-of-network tweets without a second degree connection to the Tweet as a quality safeguard. In other words, ensure someone you follow engaged with the Tweet or follows the Tweet's author.
- **Conversations:** Provide more context to a Reply by threading it together with the original Tweet.
- **Edited Tweets:** Determine if the Tweets currently on a device are stale, and send instructions to replace them with the edited versions.

4. **Mixing and Serving:** In the process of displaying tweets on a user's feed, this is the final stage. This describes the way that news, advertisements, and tweets are mixed together in a user's feed. The

objective is to produce a stream of interesting and varied content. It takes into account content delivery networks, server load, and real-time modifications made in response to user interaction.

A thorough explanation of Twitter's recommendation algorithm's operation and effects on user experience can be obtained by combining all of the aforementioned components with pertinent data and real-world examples. Home Mixer is now prepared to send a selection of Tweets to your device.

Finally, the system combines non-Tweet content (Ads, Follow Recommendations, and Onboarding prompts) with Tweets, which are then sent back to your device for display. The aforementioned pipeline runs about 5 billion times a day on average, taking less than 1.5 seconds to complete. Around 220 seconds of CPU time are needed for a single pipeline execution, which is almost 150 times more latency than what you see in the app.

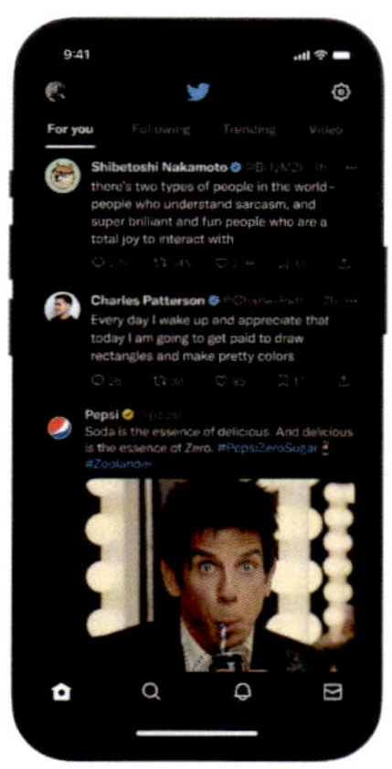

Source: https://cdn.cms-twdigitalassets.com/content/dam/blog-twitter/engineering/en_us/open-source/2023/twitter-recommendation-algorithm/phone-frame-padded.png.img.fullhd.medium.png.

Our open source project aims to fully disclose to you, our users, the inner workings of our systems. To help you better understand our algorithm, we've made the code underlying our recommendations available for viewing here (and here). We're also working on a few features to give you more transparency within our app.

Some of the new developments we have planned include:

- A better Twitter analytics platform for creators with more information on reach and engagement

- Greater transparency into any safety labels applied to your Tweets or accounts
- Greater visibility into why Tweets appear on your timeline

7.2.3.1. What's Next?

Worldwide conversations revolve around Twitter. We deliver more than 150 billion Tweets to users' devices every day. Making sure that our users are receiving the greatest content available is a difficult but fascinating task. With one of the most intriguing datasets and user bases in the world, we're working on new opportunities to expand our recommendation systems—new real-time features, embeddings, and user representations. The town square of the future is what we are creating.

7.2.4. Twitter Algorithm Ranking Signals

You must respect the algorithm if you want to make big moves on Twitter. The Twitter algorithm uses various signals to decide which tweets to show in users' timelines. Understanding these signals can help you optimize your tweets for maximum visibility:

1. **Recency:** It is one of the most significant signals. Recent and pertinent tweets are given priority on Twitter. Thus, be sure to tweet at the appropriate time if you want it to be seen by as many people as possible.

   Twitter (X)'s "For You" timeline no longer has a reverse chronological order, but the algorithm still considers the time since a tweet was posted when determining its ranking.

   The algorithm is aware that users frequently want to view the most recent and updated content. Thus, when tweeting about popular subjects (e.g., AI) and current affairs, your posts are more likely to stimulate interaction, which increases your visibility.

2. **Relevance:** In order to display the tweets on your timeline, Twitter takes into account a user's previous actions and engagements. You will only see content that is pertinent to your interests thanks to the relevance factor. Prioritizing tweets that are more likely to be interesting and helpful to the user is done by looking at the user's previous interactions, including likes, retweets, and follows. People should see content on the platform that aligns with their interests, preferences, and behavior, according to the algorithm.

   Twitter's (X) algorithm analyzes a variety of signals, such as the people you follow and the subjects you enjoy engaging with, to determine what content is relevant. When assessing a Tweet, the algorithm also considers the trending topics, keywords, and hashtags that are relevant. In other words, content that is relevant, educational, and helpful to the user will appear higher on their customized For You feed.

3. **Diversity:** This is another crucial ranking signal which provides users with a wide variety of content. It includes a bit of news, personal opinions, entertainment – all in all to present different perspectives. This allows users to be open to new ideas and diversify visibility.
4. **Media Files:** Last but not least, the algorithm prefers tweets with media components so that your timeline isn't overrun with text. People with polls, GIFs, photos, and videos are displayed further down the timeline. Make sure your photos are sized correctly and optimized to avoid cropping for the best viewing experience. Another method of promoting tweets with media files is the addition of a section called "Popular Videos" to the platform, which you may have noticed recently.

7.2.5. What the Twitter (X) Algorithm Doesn't Show

Certain content that could have a negative effect on how you use the platform is filtered out of your feed by the Twitter (X) algorithm. This covers content that is spam or potentially dangerous, posts that you have already seen, posts from accounts that have been blocked or muted, and excessively frequent posts from the same author.

7.2.5.1. Tips for Working with the Twitter Algorithm to Maximize Engagement

Understanding how the Twitter (X) algorithm works is just the start. To get more visibility on your posts, you're going to need to do the work.

The tips below will set you up with some of the essential ways to adapt to the Twitter algorithm and stay flexible when it appears to affect your social media metrics.

1. **Post Consistently:** Many of them spend a few minutes a day sending all of their Tweets at once and commenting on the first few posts they come across on Twitter (X). It's crucial for brands to stay active on Twitter (X) all day long to increase the likelihood that your audience will see your posts.

Organizing your content ahead of time is one method to maintain consistency on social media. A social media publishing tool like Sprout Social, which allows you to easily draft and schedule posts and see an overview of your upcoming publishing calendar, can help you achieve that.

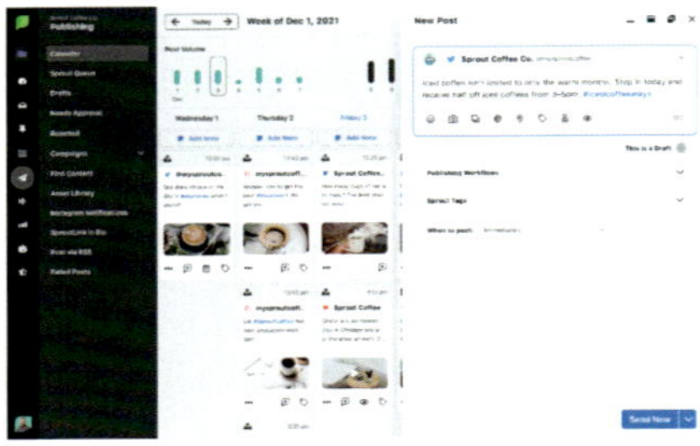

Source: https://media.sproutsocial.com/uploads/PI_Publishing_Calendar_Week_Compose_Twitter.png.

There are varying opinions on when and how many Tweets you should post a day in order to get the most Twitter engagement from your efforts. Which leads into our next tip… (Figure 7.7).

2. **Post at the Best Times:**

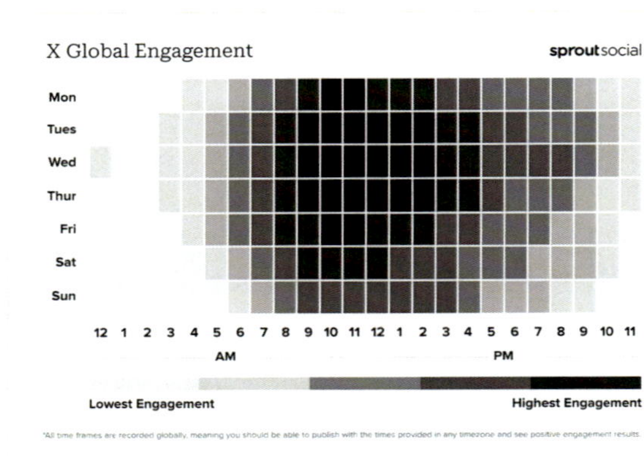

Figure 7.7. *The Twitter algorithm to maximize engagement.*

Source: https://media.sproutsocial.com/uploads/2024/04/Best-times-to-post_2024_X_heatmap-global.png.

With Sprout's patented ViralPost technology, you can take your strategy one step further. Our Optimal Send Times feature analyzes the behavior of your specific audience and zeroes in on the top times to post that are specific to your account.

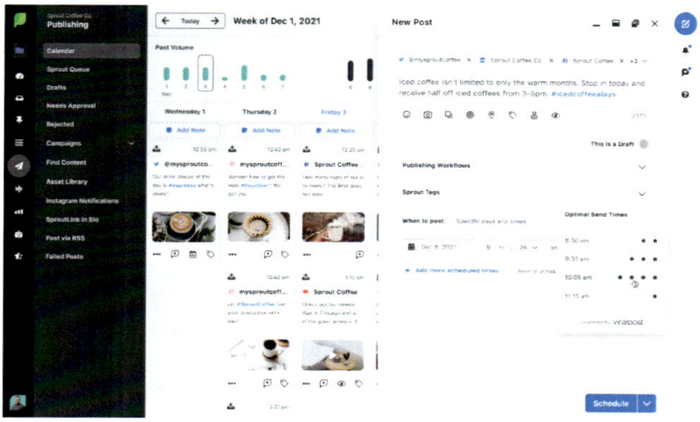

Source: https://media.sproutsocial.com/uploads/PI_Publishing_Calendar_Week_Compose_Optimal_Send_Times.png.

This frees up time to focus on amplifying your strategy, such as by measuring success using Sprout's Twitter analytics and building on what works for your next campaign.

3. **Choose the Right Content Types and Formats:** It is imperative for brands to consistently publish high-quality, relevant, engaging, and helpful content on all social media platforms, including Twitter (X). Posting the appropriate kind of content is another aspect to take into account.

   Because rich media encourages user engagement, the Twitter (X) algorithm takes this into account when ranking content. This covers GIFs, photos, carousels, videos, and even polls.

Source: https://media.sproutsocial.com/uploads/2024/05/sprout-social-tweet-example-poll.png.

However, videos seem to be the way to go if you want to drive engagement. According to Twitter (X) data, four out of five user sessions on the platform now include watching video. Interestingly, Sprout Social's research points out the same.

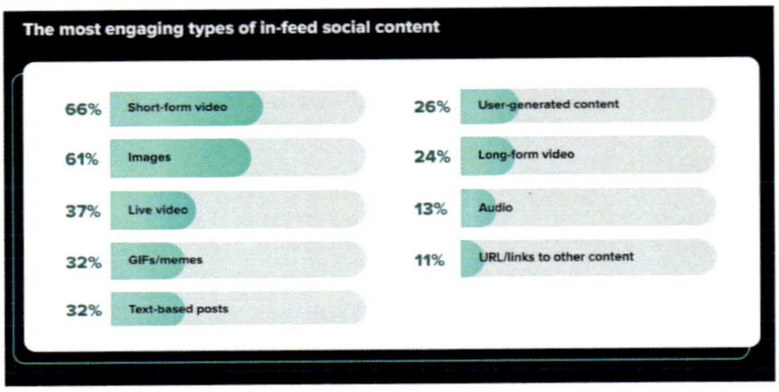

Source: https://media.sproutsocial.com/uploads/2023/03/list-of-most-valuable-types-of-social-media-content-2023.png.

4. **Optimize for Engagement:** It's crucial to create content that motivates people to like, comment on, and retweet your posts because of how much engagement affects the algorithm. There are various ways to encourage interaction on your Tweets, but rich media is one of them.

You can:

- Ask thought-provoking questions;
- Use relevant trending hashtags and piggyback on viral memes and trends (just be sure they fit your brand!);
- Participate in popular Twitter (X) campaigns;
- Tag other users;
- Respond.

Source: https://media.sproutsocial.com/uploads/2024/05/twitter-x-semrush-example-meme.png.

5. **Respond Quickly to Replies:** The Twitter (X) algorithm prioritizes recent content, and engaged users. It's important to respond to any

engagement your post, and even your brand, receives as soon as possible, preferably in the first 2–3 hours (Figure 7.8).

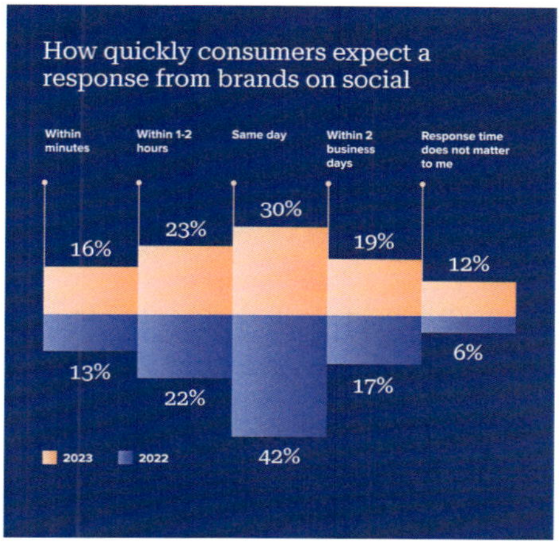

Figure 7.8. *Respond quickly to replies.*

Source: https://media.sproutsocial.com/uploads/2023/12/1_1-Index-2023-Customer-Care-Chart-1-1-1.png.

For example, you should:

- Respond when someone tags or mentions you;
- Respond to any replies your post gets;
- Respond to reposts by replying, even if it's just to say thank you.

Source: https://media.sproutsocial.com/uploads/2024/05/procreate-twitter-x-example-respond-to-replies.png.

Even if you're not tagged, using a social media monitoring tool like Sprout Social is a great way to be informed when your brand is mentioned on Twitter (X). You have the ability to designate particular brand terms that you wish to track in order to keep track of every post that mentions your goods, promotions, or other significant brand terms.

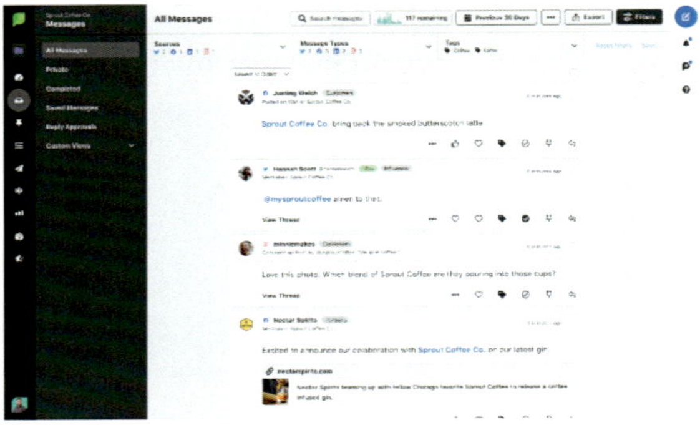

Source: https://media.sproutsocial.com/uploads/PI_Engagement_Smart_Inbox_Tag_Filter.png.

6. **Consider Running Twitter Ads:** If you're finding it challenging to attain organic reach, Twitter's advertising could prove to be an excellent solution, providing your content with the additional boost it requires. This is particularly beneficial for new businesses on Twitter, as it offers them an opportunity to gain extra visibility as they embark on their journey.

Source: https://media.sproutsocial.com/uploads/2024/05/twitter-x-ad-example.jpg.

Don't have the budget for ads? Try your hand at some of the non-paid tactics on this list first. If you're interested, you can learn more about how to run successful Twitter (X) ads here.

7.2.6. Tips to Beat the Twitter Algorithm

1. **Get Verified:** Twitter conducts account verifications to guarantee that users can rely on the legitimacy of the content. If you meet the requirements, it's worthwhile to apply for verification because verified accounts are more visible. Elon Musk declared that verified accounts would be given priority after seizing control.
2. **Tweet at The Right Time:** On Twitter, timing is everything. Tweeting at the peak of your followers' activity can boost visibility and interaction. Start keeping an eye on Twitter to see when your followers are most likely to interact, then plan your tweets around that time. According to a Buffer study, tweets posted in the US at nine o'clock at night typically receive the most favorites and retweets.
3. **Be Consistent:** Increasing your presence on Twitter can also be largely attributed to your consistency there. Users can increase their visibility and reach by regularly sharing valuable tweets, engaging with followers, and posting high-quality and engaging content.

   This is because the algorithm rewards these accounts. An account that consistently posts content is seen by the algorithm as active and dedicated to meaningful interactions, and this can result in a higher ranking in users' feeds.
4. **Use Tags Purposefully:** Making use of pertinent hashtags can help you build relationships and make your tweets more visible. But don't go overboard. Adding too many tags can make your tweets appear spammy and reduce interaction. The marketing process is improved by the use of hashtags, which raises brand awareness and message association.
5. **Use Visual Elements:** Tweets with images typically receive higher engagement rates than those with just text. To improve the engagement and visibility of your tweets, include images, videos, and GIFs. According to a very early analysis by Twitter, tweets containing photos received an average of 35% more Retweets than tweets containing videos, which received 28% more. If you want to use GIFs from Twitter as a humorous tool to connect with your audience, there are a few different ways to save them.
6. **Encourage Followers to Engage:** Increasing the number of people who see your tweets depends on engagement. To boost interaction and visibility, ask your followers to like, retweet, and reply to your tweets. Remember that engaging goes beyond simply getting likes and retweets. Engaging with the replies and bookmarks you receive

on your tweets is one of the few other factors that determines whether or not they show up on other people's feeds. Earlier this year, Twitter included an action button for bookmarks. Thus, the quantity of bookmarks your tweet receives will also raise the likelihood that it will be seen.

7. **Try Twitter Polls:** Twitter polls are a fantastic method to raise visibility and interaction. You can use polls to collect feedback from your followers and they are very simple to create. With just one click, you can find out about a user's preferences and viewpoints. Before launching a new product, brands can creatively use surveys and market research.
8. **Join Relevant Trends and Topics:** Participating in pertinent trends and discussions can boost exposure and interaction. Everyone who is following or debating a particular subject will also be able to interact and follow your opinions. Joining discussions that are pertinent to your brand or message is important, though. By being able to mute words on Twitter, you can block content that is offensive, irrelevant, or bothersome.
9. **Repackage Top Content:** If you have a tweet that performed well in the past, consider repackaging it and tweeting it again. This can increase visibility and engagement.
10. **Apply Insights from Analytics:** Utilize Twitter analytics to monitor the effectiveness of your tweets and modify your approach as necessary. To increase visibility, look for trends in engagement and modify the timing and content you offer. You can maximize the visibility and engagement of your tweets on Twitter by comprehending these ranking signals.

7.2.7. Algorithmic Choices

What users see on their feeds is greatly influenced by Twitter's algorithmic decisions. These selections have come under fire for spreading harmful content such as conspiracy theories and fake news. Twitter has responded to these worries, though, by making its algorithmic processes more transparent. For instance, Twitter has made a large portion of its source code available to the whole world on GitHub, enabling academics and developers to gain a deeper understanding of the platform's operation.

Additionally, it has experimented with different approaches to enable custom algorithm controls, letting users select an algorithm other than Twitter's Home Timeline algorithm of their choice. It aims to provide more control over what users see on their feeds so that everyone has a more interesting and personalized experience.

7.2.8. Impact of the Twitter Algorithm

1. **On Users:** The way users interact with Twitter is greatly impacted by the algorithm. The algorithm creates a customized timeline for every user by utilizing machine learning to identify the tweets that they are most likely to interact with. Users will therefore be more likely to see tweets that are interesting to them, which will improve their overall experience on the platform. Some users, however, find the algorithm to be frustrating and unpredictable at times.

   They might not see tweets from accounts they follow in their timeline, but they might see more tweets from accounts they don't follow. Furthermore, because the algorithm presents them with tweets that are similar to those they have already interacted with, some users might feel that it confirms their preexisting opinions and biases.

2. **On Advertisers:** Similar to other social media platforms, Twitter primarily depends on advertising for revenue generation. Just like users, advertisers who use Twitter to reach their target audience are greatly impacted by the platform's algorithm. Twitter can increase the effectiveness of advertising campaigns by showing ads to users who are most likely to interact with them through the use of the algorithm. Every time they launch a new campaign, ad publishers charge them based on various metrics like impressions, website visits, app installs, and so forth. But the algorithm also means that marketers need to target and create content more strategically.

   They must comprehend who their target audience is in order to produce content that appeals to and engages them. Additionally, since consumers might grow weary of seeing the same advertisements over and over again, advertisers must consider the possibility of ad fatigue. According to a Deloitte survey, 6 out of 10 consumers said they would be happier with advertisements if they were more relevant and targeted to them.

   Overall, users and advertisers are impacted by the Twitter algorithm in both positive and negative ways. It can boost the efficacy of advertising campaigns and enhance user experience, but it can also be unpredictable and reinforce preexisting biases. To maximize the algorithm, advertisers must target and create content strategically, and users may need to modify their expectations and engagement patterns to fully utilize the platform.

7.2.9. Twitter Algorithm: Final Reflections

In conclusion, anyone hoping to build a significant online presence on Twitter must comprehend the workings of the algorithm. The algorithm is a sophisticated system made up of phases for sourcing, ranking, and filtering candidates. Its goal is to show users the most relevant content based on their engagement history and interests. You need to produce excellent content that appeals to your target audience if you want to outshine the algorithm. This entails keeping up with the most recent fashions, utilizing pertinent hashtags, and consistently interacting with your followers. This can be tiresome, so why not use software to make it easier? Check out our High-performr social media management tool for a smooth and enjoyable experience. With the aid of cutting-edge AI technology, you can create captivating headlines, include multimedia content like photos and videos, and make effective use of advertising tools to reach a larger audience. With the software's numerous free tools, you can create an engaging bio or even automate tweets.

Finally, it's critical to routinely assess your performance and modify your plan of action. Utilize the analytics tools provided by High-performr to monitor your engagement metrics and pinpoint areas on Twitter that require work. Keep in mind that giving your audience something of value and being persistent in your efforts are the keys to success on Twitter. Having a thorough understanding of Twitter's algorithm can help you manage your presence there more effectively. Let High-performr help.

REFERENCES

1. Anderson, J. (2022, February 4). Introducing a new Swift package for Apache Thrift.
2. Ashworth, L. (2023, July 24). The logo of X, formerly Twitter, wasn't actually stolen. *Financial Times*. Archived from the original on July 24, 2023. Retrieved July 25, 2023.
3. Carlson, N. (2009, June 2). Stunning new numbers on who uses Twitter. *Business Insider*. Archived from the original on February 5, 2021. Retrieved January 9, 2021.
4. Del Nano, D. (2021, August 11). Applying flame graphs outside of performance analysis.
5. Fitton, L., Gruen, M. E., & Poston, L. (2009). *Twitter for dummies* (Foreword by Jack Dorsey). Hoboken, NJ: Wiley Publishing.
6. Halliday, J. (2012, June 7). No flipping the bird! Twitter unveils strict usage guidelines for new logo. *The Guardian*. Archived from the original on April 27, 2019. Retrieved October 11, 2014.
7. Houston, T. (2011, December 8). Twitter app and website redesign: Hands-on pictures and video. *The Verge*. Retrieved July 17, 2019.
8. Kelly, R. (Ed.). (2009, August 12). Twitter study – August 2009. *Twitter study reveals interesting results about usage* (PDF). San Antonio, TX: Pear Analytics. Archived from the original (PDF) on July 15, 2011.
9. Laurent, O. (2011, May 11). Photo agency's CEO addresses TwitPic controversy. *British Journal of Photography*. Archived from the original on August 3, 2011. Retrieved August 17, 2011.
10. Lee, D. (2019, July 15). Twitter desktop redesign adopts some of its mobile app's best features. *The Verge*. Retrieved July 17, 2019.
11. Niwa, Y. (2021, January 25). Introducing Twitter text editor.
12. O'Carroll, L. (2012, September 18). Twitter redesign makes more of photos. *The Guardian*. Retrieved July 17, 2019.
13. Rodríguez-Ruiz, J., Mata-Sánchez, J. I., Monroy, R., Loyola-González, O., & López-Cuevas, A. (2020). A one-class classification approach for bot detection on Twitter. *Computers & Security*, *91*, 101715.
14. Streams, K. (2012, November 11). Tweetro says it's 'completely crippled' by Twitter's strict 100,000 user token limit. *The Verge*. Archived from the original on February 2, 2021. Retrieved December 18, 2016.
15. Su, P. (2018, November 28). Twitter's Kafka adoption story.

16. Tufekci, Z. (2017). *Twitter and tear gas: The power and fragility of networked protest*. Yale University Press.
17. Vaughan-Nichols, S. (2012, August 30). How Twitter tweets your tweets with open source. *ZDNet*. Archived from the original on October 5, 2014. Retrieved September 10, 2012.
18. Venners, B. (2009, April 3). Twitter on Scala. *Artima Developer*. Archived from the original on June 19, 2009. Retrieved June 17, 2009.

CHAPTER 8

PINTEREST ALGORITHM

Contents

Introduction 280
8.1. What Is the Pinterest Algorithm? 280
8.2. How Does the Pinterest Algorithm Work? 284
8.3. Pinterest Algorithm Changes – A Timeline of Important Updates 297
8.4. How to Beat the Pinterest Algorithm 298
References 307

INTRODUCTION

The complex algorithm used by Pinterest is intended to provide users with content that is tailored to their interests, preferences, and actions. It uses a lot of data to provide a highly customized experience and works on the principles of machine learning. The information is gathered by the algorithm when a user engages with Pinterest—by saving, sharing, or clicking on pins—in order to better understand their preferences. The most likely-to-be-interesting pins are displayed in a personalized feed that is created using this information. When determining what content to display, the Pinterest algorithm takes into account a number of factors. The user's past activity, which includes the kinds of pins they've interacted with, the boards they've made, and the searches they've done, is a crucial component. In addition, the algorithm considers how popular a pin is, favoring those with higher engagement metrics—such as more clicks or saves. Furthermore, it prioritizes pins that are relevant to the user's previous behavior by taking into account the content's relevance based on keywords.

The utilization of "related pins," which are recommendations made in response to content a user has previously expressed interest in, is another crucial component of the Pinterest algorithm. By presenting users with engaging, up-to-date content that suits their interests, these recommendations help maintain user engagement. To further improve the user experience, the algorithm takes into account the time of day and the demographics of the user when determining what to display. The goal of the Pinterest algorithm is to give users access to a dynamic, personalized space where they can find fresh inspiration and ideas. The system keeps Pinterest a very interesting platform by continuously gaining insight from user interactions and adapting to trends.

8.1. WHAT IS THE PINTEREST ALGORITHM?

Pinterest is a visual search engine that is often misinterpreted as a social media platform. Because search engines base their content rankings on specific information, it is essential to comprehend the fundamental SEO techniques in order to learn the Pinterest algorithm. What matters more for your traffic strategy is how Pinterest's search engine algorithm selects which pins to show users when they enter search terms (Figure 8.1).

Like most people, you typically use Pinterest to find inspiration for home décor, new recipes, and fashion. As is common with well-known social media networks, Pinterest uses its social media algorithm to select the content that users see. Comparing Pinterest to some other websites, the internal workings of the algorithm are more transparent.This helps marketers in terms of drawing viewers to content. You may be surprised to learn that the platform is heavily reliant on science. This social media platform updates its algorithm frequently to deliver the best content to users. Becoming proficient in the algorithm is necessary to succeed on Pinterest. What pins show up in a user's stream depends on the search algorithm. As a result, it's critical to stay current with the latest developments in content marketing, as these are always evolving.

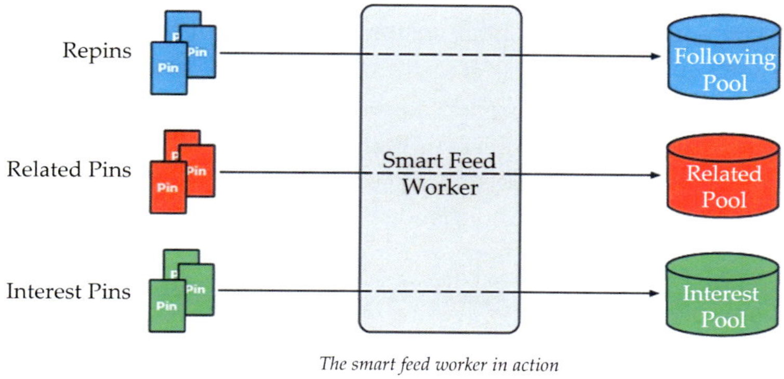

Figure 8.1. *The smart feed worker in action.*

Source: https://blog.contentstudio.io/wp-content/uploads/2022/09/image15.jpg.

A higher level of engagement increases your chances of showing up in someone's feed. The most recent algorithm change on Pinterest has made it so that users are seeing much more relevant pins. The system examines a user's previous pins and finds pins that are similar to them.

8.1.1. Advantage and Disadvantage of Pinterest Algorithm

8.1.1.1. Advantages of Pinterest Algorithm

1. **Personalized Content Recommendations:**

- **User Experience:** One of the most significant advantages of Pinterest's algorithm is its ability to provide personalized content recommendations. By analyzing user behavior, such as pins they've saved or boards they follow, the algorithm suggests content tailored to individual tastes. This increases user engagement and satisfaction as users are more likely to find pins that interest them.
- **Content Discoverability:** For content creators, the algorithm increases the chances of their pins being discovered by users who are genuinely interested in that type of content. This targeted approach can lead to higher engagement rates for pins.

2. **Improved Content Visibility:**

- **Increased Reach for Creators:** The algorithm allows creators to reach a broader audience beyond their followers. If a pin is well-received by a small group, the algorithm may promote it to a larger audience. This can be particularly beneficial for small businesses and individual creators who may not have large followings but can still reach potential customers or fans through the algorithm's recommendations.
- **Long Tail Content:** Unlike social platforms where content may have a very short lifespan, Pinterest's algorithm enables older pins to resurface if they match current user interests. This gives content a longer shelf life and continuous visibility, which can be advantageous for creators.

3. **Efficient User Engagement:**

- **Active Engagement:** The algorithm promotes pins that users interact with the most, whether through saves, clicks, or comments. This encourages users to engage more actively with the content they like, further refining the algorithm's recommendations.
- **Encourages Diversity in Engagement:** Pinterest's algorithm doesn't just focus on popular pins but also surfaces niche content. This encourages users to explore a wider range of topics and engage with different types of content, leading to a more diverse user experience.

4. **Enhanced User Retention:**

- **Continuous Learning:** The Pinterest algorithm continuously learns from user interactions. As users spend more time on the platform, the algorithm refines its recommendations, which can lead to increased user retention as people find more relevant and interesting content over time.
- **Habit Formation:** The algorithm's ability to consistently provide users with content they enjoy can contribute to the formation of a habitual use of the platform. Users may find themselves returning regularly to Pinterest because they know they'll discover something new and engaging each time.

5. **E-Commerce Integration**

- **Product Discovery:** Pinterest has increasingly integrated e-commerce features, and its algorithm plays a crucial role in product discovery. By recommending products based on user interests and previous interactions, the platform becomes a powerful tool for online shopping.

- **Conversion Optimization:** For businesses, the algorithm can optimize conversions by showing products to users who are most likely to purchase them, based on their browsing and pinning behavior. This targeted approach can lead to higher sales and more efficient advertising spending.

8.1.1.2. Disadvantages of Pinterest Algorithm

1. **Algorithmic Bias:**

- **Limited Exposure for New Content:** One of the primary disadvantages of the Pinterest algorithm is that it may favor well-established content over new content. This can make it difficult for new creators to gain visibility, as their pins may not be promoted as much as those from more established accounts.
- **Reinforcement of Trends:** The algorithm tends to reinforce popular trends, which can lead to a homogenization of content on the platform. Users may see the same types of pins repeatedly, limiting exposure to diverse ideas and content.

2. **Over-Personalization:**

- **Echo Chambers:** While personalized content can enhance user experience, it can also create echo chambers where users are only exposed to content that aligns with their existing interests and beliefs. This can limit the discovery of new ideas and perspectives, reducing the platform's potential for broadening user horizons.
- **Reduced Discovery of Serendipitous Content:** The focus on personalization can reduce the likelihood of users stumbling upon content that is outside their usual interests. This can limit the sense of discovery that many users enjoy when using Pinterest.

3. **Impact on Content Creators:**

- **Unpredictable Reach:** The algorithm's decisions on what content to promote can be unpredictable, making it difficult for creators to consistently reach their audience. A change in the algorithm or a shift in user behavior can lead to a significant decrease in visibility for certain pins, affecting the creator's overall reach.
- **Dependence on Algorithm:** Content creators may become overly reliant on the algorithm to drive traffic to their pins. If the algorithm changes, it could significantly impact their ability to attract views and engagement, making them vulnerable to fluctuations in platform policies.

4. **Privacy Concerns:**

- **Data Usage:** The algorithm relies on collecting and analyzing vast amounts of user data to make personalized recommendations. This can raise privacy concerns among users who may be uncomfortable with the extent of data being collected and how it is used.
- **Potential for Data Misuse:** There is always a risk that user data could be misused or improperly secured. If data were to be leaked or used in ways that users did not consent to, it could lead to a loss of trust in the platform.

5. **Commercialization and Ads:**

- **Commercial Bias:** As Pinterest has integrated more e-commerce features, the algorithm may prioritize sponsored content or pins from advertisers over organic content. This can lead to a commercial bias where users see more ads and fewer organic pins, which could detract from the user experience.
- **User Experience:** An increase in ads and promoted pins can clutter the feed, making it harder for users to find the content they are genuinely interested in. This could lead to frustration and a decline in user engagement over time.

8.2. HOW DOES THE PINTEREST ALGORITHM WORK?

Users can find pins that are relevant to their interests by using the Pinterest search algorithm. Determining the exact ranking components that make up the Pinterest algorithm is challenging. But some of the factors the algorithm takes into account when judging how relevant a pin is are the user's search query, the user's Pinterest activity, and the content of the pin (Figure 8.2).

Figure 8.2. *Steps of Pinterest algorithm work.*

Source: https://www.socialchamp.io/wp-content/uploads/2022/04/Pinterest-Algorithm_v1_01-scaled.jpg.webp.

The algorithm emphasizes the four key elements:

- Domain quality;
- Pin quality;
- Pinner quality;
- Topic relevance.

8.2.1. Pinterest Algorithm Factor 1: Domain Quality

Pinterest rates the overall quality of your domain, just like Google does. It's their opinion of your website's overall quality. You will need to have patience and a well-thought-out plan for this, as Pinterest will take some time to begin trusting your domain.

Broadly speaking, Pinterest looks at how popular pins from your website are. As a result, you want to maximize the amount of interaction with your pins. You want users to click, save, and engage with them. This will inform Pinterest that your website is a reliable source of excellent content.

So how can you improve your domain quality for the Pinterest algorithm? Let's look at five key steps you can take:

- **Step 1: Create a Business Account:** Making a business account is the simplest and most basic method to ensure that Pinterest accepts your domain.

If you have a private account already, convert it to a business account now.

- **Step 2: Claim Your Website:** Secondly, ensure that you link your business account to your website. This is merely a means of confirming that the website listed on your profile is owned by you.

  Navigate to your account settings to claim your website. On Pinterest, they are located in the top-right menu:

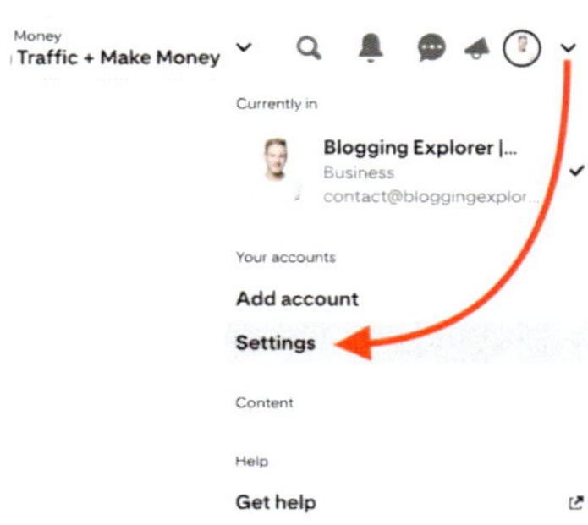

Source: https://bloggingexplorer.com/pinterest-algorithm/.

Next, navigate to Claimed accounts > Websites > Claim and enter your website URL in the field:

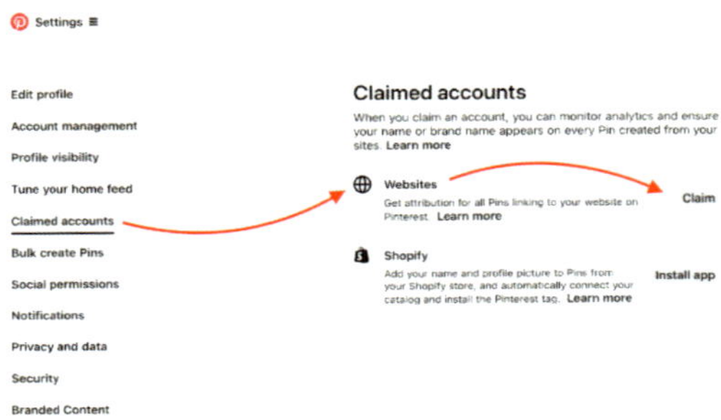

Source: https://bloggingexplorer.com/pinterest-algorithm/.

Finally, you need to either add a meta tag to your website or upload an HTML file to your website's root folder.

- **Step 3: Enable Rich Pins on Your Blog:** Rich pins are simply pins that have been enhanced with additional details and useful information. Despite being simple to set up, they are a potent tool for raising your Pinterest ranking.

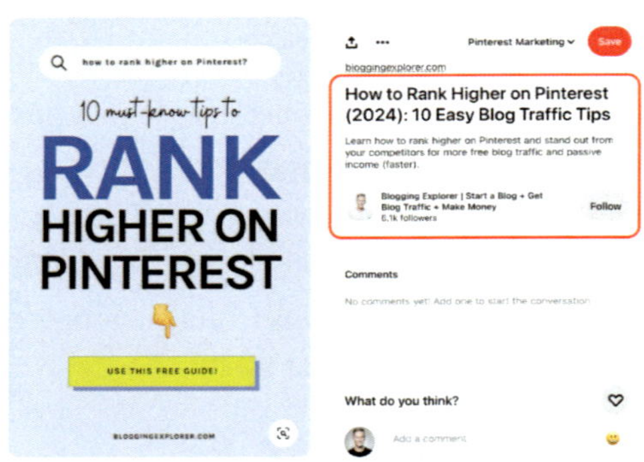

Source: https://bloggingexplorer.com/pinterest-algorithm/.

- **Step 4: Publish Pins that Encourage Interaction and Engagement:** Every interaction your pins get from users counts towards your domain quality. Saves, clicks, comments — you want it all!

  The more users engage with your pins, the better. We'll cover some helpful tips for this in a minute.

- **Step 5: Pin Consistently:** The most crucial thing to think about when developing a Pinterest marketing strategy is consistency, especially if you want to see actual results.

Hence, the only way to generate consistent traffic is by being a consistent pinner. To do this, create a pinning schedule you can follow every day.

- Instead of popping by once a week and pinning 100 pins, spend a few minutes on Pinterest every day and pin a few helpful pieces to your boards.
- The easiest way to pin consistently is to use a Pinterest scheduling tool. There are a few good ones out there you can choose from.

8.2.2. Pinterest Algorithm Factor 2: Pin Quality

Pin quality is a measure of how popular and current a specific pin is.

If tons of users interact with your pin — save, comment, click through, or closeup — Pinterest knows it's high quality.

And the idea here is simple – users who engage with pins are content ones. Furthermore, users are more likely to stick with Pinterest if they are happier. With this scoring system, Pinterest is caving in to its own itch. In order to encourage users to stay on the platform longer, they want their users to be satisfied. After all, Pinterest can operate profitably on the basis of having as many active users as possible.

Furthermore, it's crucial to pay close attention to how your own followers interact and engage with your pins. Pinterest distributes your newly published pins to your followers first. When a pin gains traction with them, the algorithm begins displaying it to more people.

The correlation between "freshness" and popularity is another fascinating feature of pin quality. Over time, even the most well-liked pins begin to wane in popularity. As a result, while a viral pin might be a true traffic generator for a while, its effects wear off.

- **Step 1: Create Click-Worthy Pin Images:** Having excellent blog posts won't be enough to get people to click on your pins and read your blog. Actually, it's more the other way around: a great pin image that leads to a mediocre article can drive a ton of clicks.

  Naturally, you want to ensure that your target audience will find value and utility in both your article and your pin.

Here are six best practices for creating click-worthy, viral pin images:

1. **Use a High-Quality, High-Resolution Image**: Take your own photos or use free high-res stock photos from Unsplash or Pexels, for instance.

2. **Make Sure Your Pin Graphic is Tall:** Pinterest recommends a 2:3 ratio, width to height. Think vertical!
3. **Use the Right Image Size:** For example 1,000 x 1,500 pixels.
4. **Use Text Overlays:** Add a benefit-driven title or a teaser on top of your image. Keep it short, use a clear font, and make sure it's readable on smaller screens.
5. **Include Your Logo:** Place your logo or your website URL on of every pin you publish.
6. **Include a Giveaway Preview:** If your article includes a free downloadable giveaway, use a small cover image on your pin. This gives users a quick preview of what's inside, making your pin more clickable.
7. **Add a Link to Your Website:** Finally, make sure you add a link to your blog. Also, double-check that it's working and the page loads quickly.

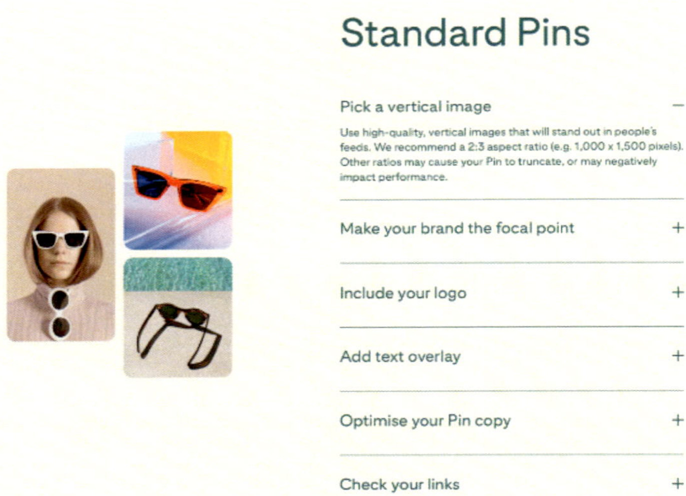

Source: https://bloggingexplorer.com/pinterest-algorithm/.

Here's an awesome click-worthy pin from Elna at TwinsMommy.com, for example:

Source: https://bloggingexplorer.com/pinterest-algorithm/.

- **Step 2: Write Irresistible Blog Post Titles:** Your blog post titles need to grab readers' attention if you want them to click through to your blog. Your post titles will appear beneath your pins in the feed if you followed the previous section's instructions and enabled rich pins.

Source: https://bloggingexplorer.com/pinterest-algorithm/.

Also, when people closeup your pin, they'll see the title on the right:

Source: https://bloggingexplorer.com/pinterest-algorithm/.

It goes without saying that creating a blog post title that is motivated by benefits will raise the likelihood that each pin will prompt a click.

- **Step 3: Track Your Best-Performing Pins:** Let's look at how to determine which pin kinds work best for improving your pin quality next. After some time spent pinning, you want to know which kind of pin designs are getting more interaction than others. This will assist you in the future in producing pins that are better and more effective.

Start by navigating to Pinterest > Analytics > Overview:

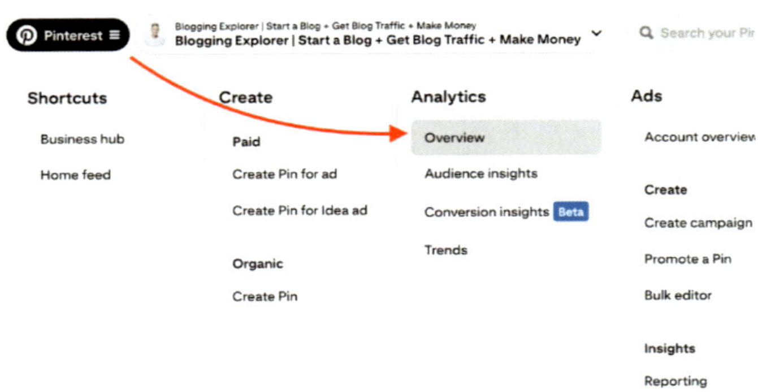

Source: https://bloggingexplorer.com/pinterest-algorithm/.

Next, choose a Date range:

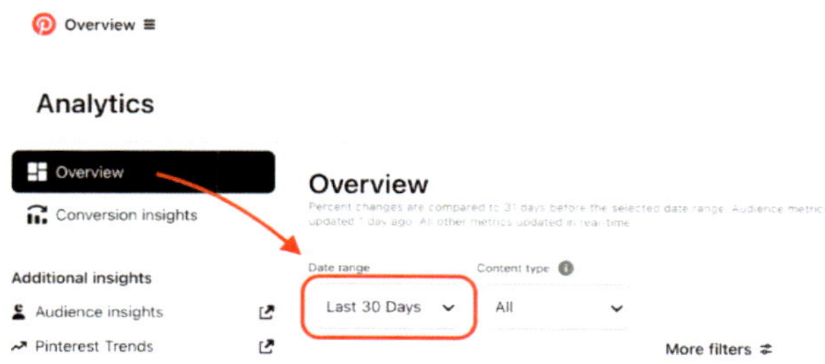

Source: https://bloggingexplorer.com/pinterest-algorithm/.

Now scroll down to your Top Pins further down the page. Use the dropdown menu on the left to find your pins with the most clicks:

Source: https://bloggingexplorer.com/pinterest-algorithm/.

These are your top-performing pins in the date range you selected.

8.2.3. Pinterest Algorithm Factor 3: Pinner Quality

Pinner quality is a rating that Pinterest uses to assess your abilities as a content producer, blogger, and pinner. The content you repin from other users is included in the pinner quality score in addition to your own pins. As a result, Pinterest considers how high-quality the pins you share from other people are.

The more people interact with your pins and your profile, the higher your pinner quality score will be. Here are a few helpful questions to get started:

1. How often do you pin?
2. Do you pin actively and consistently?
3. How many saves and comments do you receive?
4. Do you save content that Pinterest views as high quality?

All in all, pinner quality is a score you can boost with these four key steps:

- **Step 1: Pin Actively Throughout the Day:** Maintaining an active and consistent pinnership is essential to maintaining a high pinner quality score.

  If you are unable to visit Pinterest multiple times a day, you can purchase a Pinterest scheduler tool. By setting up automated pins, you can maintain account activity all day long, even at night.

  Additionally, Tailwind and other Pinterest scheduling tools assist you in determining the ideal time to publish your pins. They can pinpoint precisely when your followers are online and actively pinning thanks to their extensive database.

  Also, Tailwind comes with powerful analytics tools to help you find your top-performing pins and boards. You can use these insights to further improve your pins and optimize your boards.
- Step 2: Create Fresh Pins Weekly:

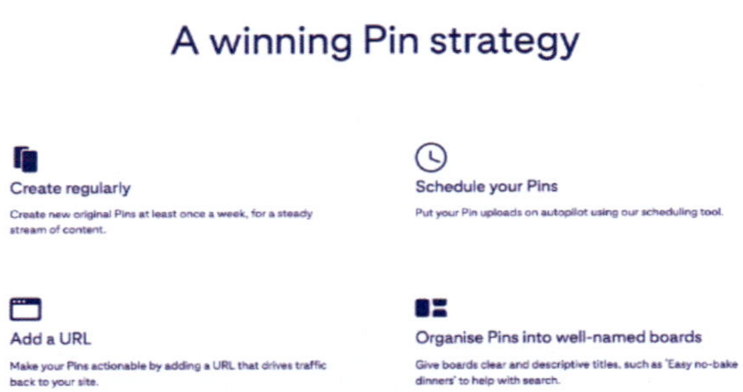

Source: https://bloggingexplorer.com/pinterest-algorithm/.

For a few years now, Pinterest has sent a clear message to all bloggers and creatives: the Pinterest algorithm favors new, fresh pins, and we should publish them as often as we can. We know there has been a lot of confusion about fresh pins.

What's a new, fresh pin exactly?

Fresh pins are images that Pinterest hasn't seen before:

1. When you create a new pin for an old blog post, that's going to be a fresh pin.
2. When you create a new pin for a new blog post, that's a fresh pin, too.

So it doesn't matter whether your content is brand new. Any new pin image you create counts as a fresh pin.

The easiest way to keep the Pinterest algorithm happy is to create and publish new pin images weekly. If you can, create fresh pins every day.

- **Step 3: Increase Your Saves and Comments:** Improving your pin quality is the key to increasing the amount of saves. Thus, adhere to the instructions mentioned in the section above on "pin quality."
- **Step 4: Boost your Overall Engagement Rate:** Again, head over to your Pinterest Analytics to find the pins with the highest engagement:

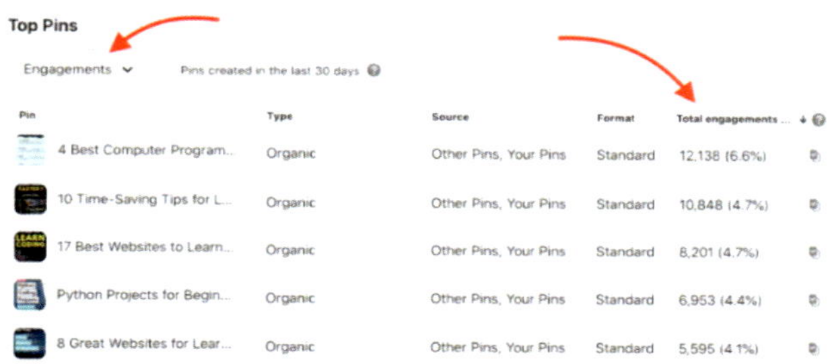

Top Pins

Engagements ⌄ Pins created in the last 30 days

Pin	Type	Source	Format	Total engagements ...
4 Best Computer Program...	Organic	Other Pins, Your Pins	Standard	12,138 (6.6%)
10 Time-Saving Tips for L...	Organic	Other Pins, Your Pins	Standard	10,848 (4.7%)
17 Best Websites to Learn...	Organic	Other Pins, Your Pins	Standard	8,201 (4.7%)
Python Projects for Begin...	Organic	Other Pins, Your Pins	Standard	6,953 (4.4%)
8 Great Websites for Lear...	Organic	Other Pins, Your Pins	Standard	5,595 (4.1%)

Source: https://bloggingexplorer.com/pinterest-algorithm/.

Can you find a pattern in your top pins?

- What colors are you using?
- What fonts resonate most with your audience?
- Are there people in your pin images or not?
- Is your background dark or light?
- How is your text overlay formatted?

Use your findings to find content that your audience responds well to. Also, could you create additional, related posts on these topics?

- **Step 5: Pin Popular Content to Your Boards:** The content you pin from other people also matters when it comes to pinner quality. Pinterest pins that are already well-liked are the ones you should bookmark and share.

  Regretfully, Pinterest has taken down the specific save numbers for individual pins. Your best option is to search for your topic quickly and peruse the top results. With hundreds of thousands of saves and repins, these are typically the most popular pins.

8.2.4. Pinterest Algorithm Factor 4: Topic Relevance (Pinterest Keywords)

So far, we've looked at how you can make sure your domain, pin, and pinner quality scores are optimized. These three measures aim at improving your *overall score and authority* on Pinterest.

Now, *topic relevance* is perhaps the most abstract – yet also the most important – factor for the Pinterest search algorithm.

Earlier in this article, we learned that Pinterest wants to show the best possible, most relevant results for each individual search.

To distribute your pins to the right users, Pinterest needs to determine what topic they're related to and how relevant they are to users interested in that topic.

When you publish a new pin, Pinterest assigns it to a specific topic using keywords.

Just like on any other search engine, Pinterest SEO is heavily focused on knowing why, where, and how to use the right keywords.

You can think of topic relevance as telling Pinterest what your pins are about. So, how do you find and use keywords on Pinterest to show them that your content is relevant for a given search query? Let's have a look:

- **Step 1: Find the Right Pinterest Keywords:** You should first conduct some keyword research before you begin pinning your blog entries to Pinterest. With less effort, you can increase traffic once you know where to look and how to use the appropriate keywords on the platform.

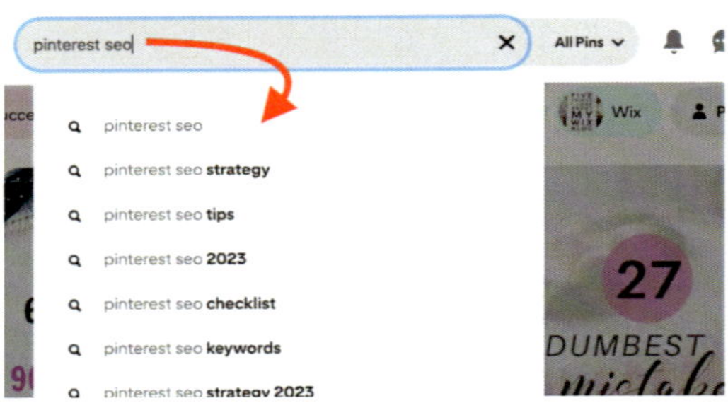

Source: https://bloggingexplorer.com/pinterest-algorithm/.Source: https://bloggingexplorer.com/pinterest-algorithm/.

Prioritizing topic relevance over anything else on the platform should always be your first goal, as it is crucial to your success there.

The quickest way to find keywords on Pinterest is to use the built-in search bar. Say your blog or website is about *travel tips*. Thus, you want to find related keywords to help Pinterest show your pins to the people searching for that specific topic.

Let's type "Pinterest SEO" in the search bar and see what the autofill feature suggests:

See how Pinterest automatically suggests more specific keywords for your search:

- Pinterest SEO strategy;
- Pinterest SEO tips;
- Pinterest SEO 2023;
- Pinterest SEO checklist;
- Pinterest SEO keywords, and so forth.

These are related, popular keywords you should use in your Pinterest SEO strategy.

- **Step 2: Use your Keywords in the Right Places:** Once you've found the keywords you want to use, it's time to put them to work.

  So, where should you place your keywords, then? Let's look at a few key spots to get started:

1. **Optimize Your Profile:** First, you want to add keywords to your Pinterest profile. Start by updating the following details:

- **Your Username:** This is the URL of your Pinterest profile.
- **Business Name:** This is the title of your Pinterest profile page. You have 60 characters, so add the most important keywords to your business name.
- **Profile Bio:** Write a short and snappy, benefit-focused profile description. You have 160 characters, so use them wisely!

2. **Optimize Your Pinterest Boards:** It's now time to check that your Pinterest boards have the most relevant keywords optimized. Boards function on Pinterest in the same way as individual pins and other content. If someone isn't interested in all of your content, they can search for them and follow specific boards.

   You want to add keywords to your board titles and descriptions. Make sure your board descriptions sound natural – don't just stuff them with keywords.

For example, I have a board titled "How to Start a Blog." That's my collection of the best content I've found on the platform related to starting a blog from scratch.

Hence, both the board title and the board description below include relevant, popular keywords for this specific topic:

Source: https://bloggingexplorer.com/pinterest-algorithm/.

3. **Optimize Your Pins:** It's time to make and publish your first pins now that your boards and profile are setup. Using keywords in your pin title and description is the most crucial aspect of pin optimization.

   The primary keyword you want to target should come first in your pin title. This data will be used by Pinterest's search algorithm to identify the topic of your pin.

Source: https://bloggingexplorer.com/pinterest-algorithm/.

As for pin descriptions, make sure you include relevant keywords and highlight the value for your target audience.

- Why should they head over to your website?

- What will they get from your article?

  Bear in mind that using the right keywords helps the Pinterest search algorithm match your pins with the users who are most likely to click through to your blog.

8.3. PINTEREST ALGORITHM CHANGES – A TIME-LINE OF IMPORTANT UPDATES

Like all other platform policies, Pinterest's algorithm is subject to periodic changes. As a result, the timeline of updates from the start to the present provides you with a summary of the modifications made to the Pinterest algorithm over the years.

- **2015 – Pinterest Shows Local Search:** The platform began displaying local searches according to the language and nation. For example, Pinterest will display results from Brazilian websites and descriptions if a user from Brazil searches for gift ideas.
- **Streamlined Suggestions**: In order to connect with users worldwide, Pinterest redesigned the "Pin" button to the "Save" button.
- **2016 – Save Button Went Global:** Pinterest changed the 'Pin button' to the 'Save' button so that it can equally resonate with other users in the World.
- **Pins Ratio:** Anything larger than this ratio would be cropped on Pinterest, which introduced the shorter aspect ratio of 1:3:5 to 1:2:8.
- **Removal of Rich Pin Descriptions from Feeds:** Pinterest made the decision to only display rich pin descriptions in closeups and remove them from the feed in an effort to declutter the platform.
- **2017 – Invitations to Hashtags:** Hashtags were initially frowned upon on Pinterest; however, later in 2017, hashtags were allowed.
- **Introduced Board Sections:** In order to assist pinners in creating more general boards and organizing them according to various themes, the platform introduced board sections.
- **Lens (Beta) Launched:** Pinterest introduced lens technology that enables users to take advantage of fresh concepts derived from actual objects with their cameras.
- **2018 – Introduction to Following Tabs**: "Following tabs" is a new feature that Pinterest launched that primarily highlights all of the users and boards you follow on the platform. Furthermore, the order of these pins is chronological.

- **Profile Covers:** Introduced a profile cover featuring a selection of the newest pins. You have the option to select the most recent pins or personalize the ones that show up.
- **Monthly Reach Made Public:** Everybody can view the analytics on your profile because the platform made the monthly reach publicly available.
- **The Launch of Activity Tab**: The activity tab was introduced by Pinterest and displays every pin that has been saved from your website.
- **2019 – Released New Analytics Dashboard:** Pinterest changed the analytics dashboard to a newer and cleaner version than the old one.
- **2020 – Today Tab on Mobile Apps:** Pinterest introduced the 'Today tab' on the mobile app, which is a source of inspiration with curated topics and trending pins.
- **Fresh Pins:** During a live webinar hosted by Tailwind and Pinterest, the latter highlighted the value of recent pins by stating, "Fresh pins can generate more leads." After that, the website introduced a new algorithm that rewards recently added pins.
- **Controllable Distribution:** Diversifying the types of content on the home feed was the primary objective of the new algorithm, as the tool explicitly stated in an article it published.
- **2022 – Idea Pins Taking Up the Space:** Regular pins are receiving less views as a result of idea pins, formerly known as story pins, which require a lot of spacing.

8.4. HOW TO BEAT THE PINTEREST ALGORITHM

Like traditional website SEO, you should make sure that your content contains keywords. Pinterest, though, goes one step further. As a visual platform, Pinterest requires proper image formatting, audience engagement, and activation of its special features, such as the "Save" button and "Rich Pins." ."

To help you use Pinterest as an effective marketing tool, the following Pinterest tips will be helpful. Let's start now!

1. **Switch to Business Account:** If you use Pinterest for business, you have to upgrade to a business profile. This is important because using a private account for business purposes is prohibited by Pinterest's terms of service. With a business account, which is completely free, you can access Pinterest statistics and discover important details about user behavior. You can use Rich Pins and other Pinterest

features because of it. Your company account can be quickly, and cost-free setup. It also offers advantages like:

- Place a link to your website in your profile's bio to increase traffic.
- Utilize analytics to evaluate the effectiveness of your material
- Build the authority of your brand.
- Run adverts to raise awareness and interaction

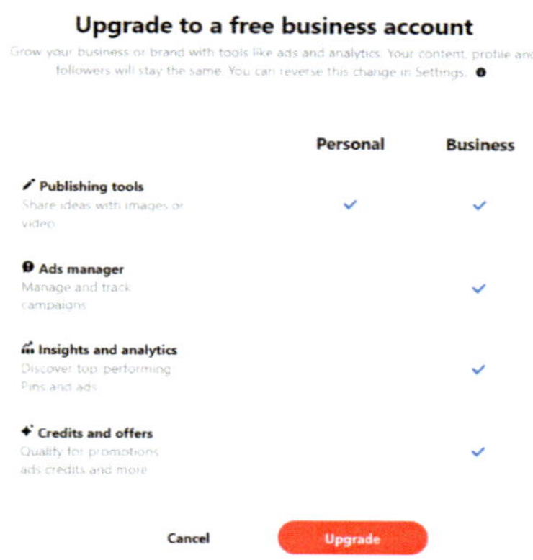

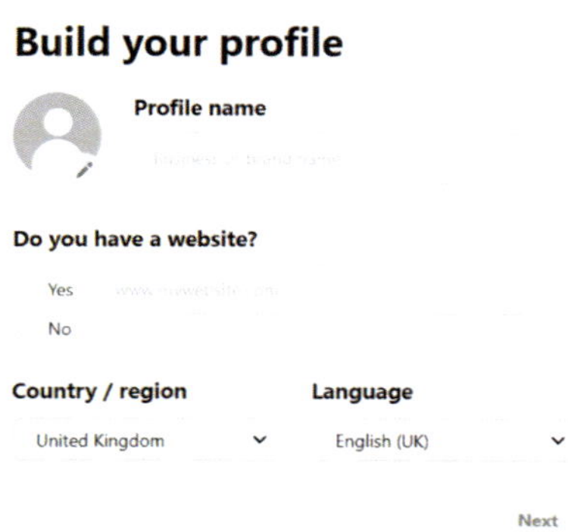

2. **Verified Pinterest Account:** A red or blue checkmark appears on your Pinterest account next to your name if it has been validated. A verified merchant is indicated by a blue checkmark, and a well-known individual or brand is indicated by a red checkmark. Regretfully, it doesn't appear that you can enable or request this on your own. All you can do is increase your audience and take charge of your website. Even though Pinterest chooses which accounts to validate, adding it will at the very least make you appear more credible.
3. **Claim Your Website:** The next step is to make your business a Pinterest claim. By doing this, you formally inform Pinterest that

the business you represent is who you claim it is. This step requires adding a code link to your website and verifies that you are the owner of the specified domain. Once more, everything is very easy to understand.

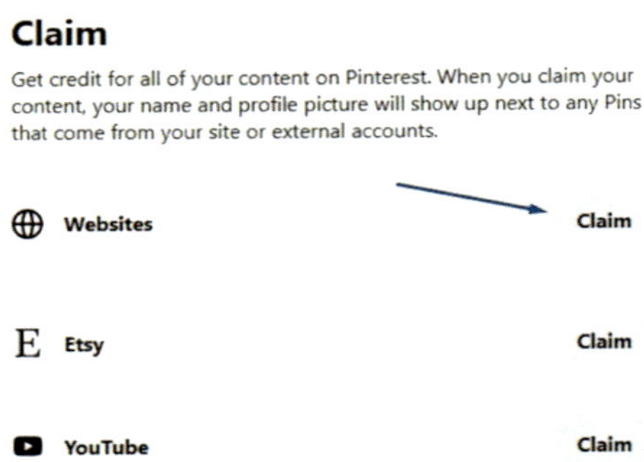

Verify

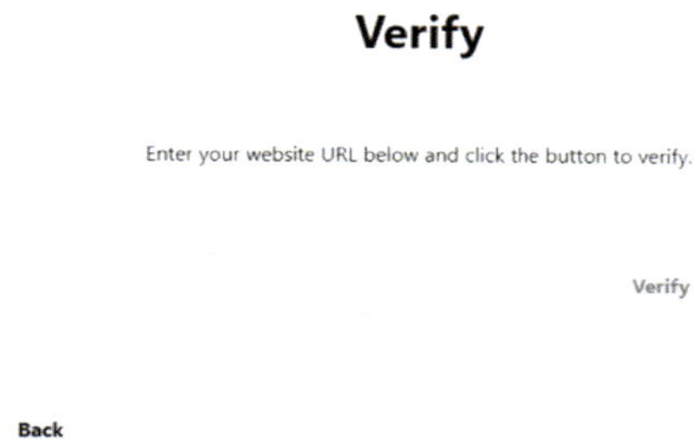

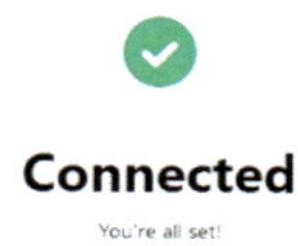

4. **Pin Engaging and Valuable Content:** In any SEO conversation on Pinterest, your website, or any other platform, quality content must come first. There's simply no avoiding it.

   These days, search engine algorithms are very good at figuring out what people want to see. As a result, simply stuffing a website with a ton of useless, badly written content and adding as many keywords as you can is no longer enough to get it to rank. That might work if you build a time machine and go back to 1995, but right now you have to make something valuable. It's the same with Pinterest. If you don't start with high-quality content, people won't interact with your pins. You won't succeed very far as a result.

   Put another way, they won't save it, share it, or comment on it. Not only will they not be inspired to follow you, but more importantly, Pinterest's algorithm will detect that you are producing boring content, which will make it harder or impossible for you to draw in the intended audience organically.

5. **Guide Content Creation by People's Requirements:** Before engaging in formal keyword research, you can obtain an idea of what Pinterest users are searching for by simply visiting your Pinterest account and entering search terms related to your business into the search field.

   Assume for the moment that you sell specialty bedding on your website. You want to know what kind of products Pinterest users are looking for that are similar to your lovely little niche in that industry. One can start a Pinterest search by typing "bed sheets," and similar to Google, results will start to show up based on what other users are also entering.

The next step is about quantitative data on Pinterest search volume, which the search terms that come up won't give you. Instead, think of this phase as the concept generation stage. It's an opportunity to look into every possibility. It's unlikely that you would have looked up the term "bed sheet aesthetic" on your own, but since a lot of people are searching for it on Pinterest, you can now explore further and find related terms.

One of Pinterest's many beautiful features is the way users group their work into "boards" with a shared subject. Take a close look at those searches and browse the forums of competitors' businesses to see what ideas spring to you. Look for novel ideas and investigate them. You can then produce content around them and target visitors who are ready to buy if they appear to be trending topics.

6. **Research Keywords:** After learning more about guided search, it's time to apply what you've learned and see what Google has to say. Make use of Google's complimentary keyword research tool to find terms and phrases related to your subject. You'll also be able to find out which keywords are more popular and have less competition.

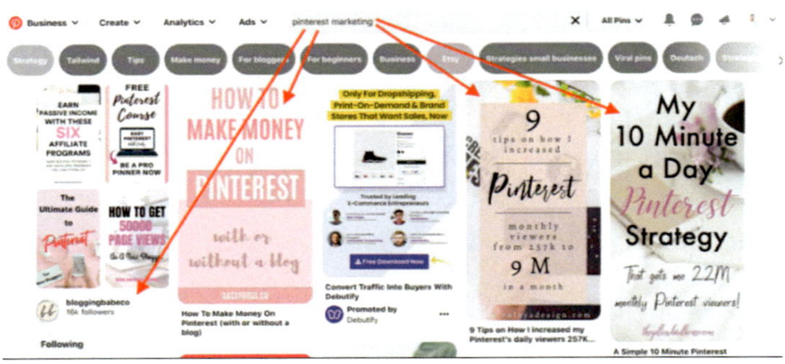

Source: https://blog.contentstudio.io/wp-content/uploads/2022/08/image10.png.

Google Trends is a useful tool for keyword planning, and if you're willing to pay for it, you can get even more data by using paid services like Ahrefs or Mangools. Therefore, even though the focus of this analysis is on Google searches generally rather than Pinterest searches specifically, it is nevertheless significant information for a number of reasons.

First off, a tonne of search data from Google will still give you a decent idea of what the market wants to see, even if it doesn't exactly match Pinterest users' interests. Secondly, quality content may draw some outside traffic to Pinterest, as the platform gets traffic from Google searches.

7. **Use Keyword-Rich Description:** Now that you have a general idea of what your target audience wants to see and is searching for, it's time to create content that engages them. Furthermore, make sure each piece of content that makes use of the lucrative long tail keywords you discovered has a thorough description. In the same way, arrange your belongings on the boards you create.

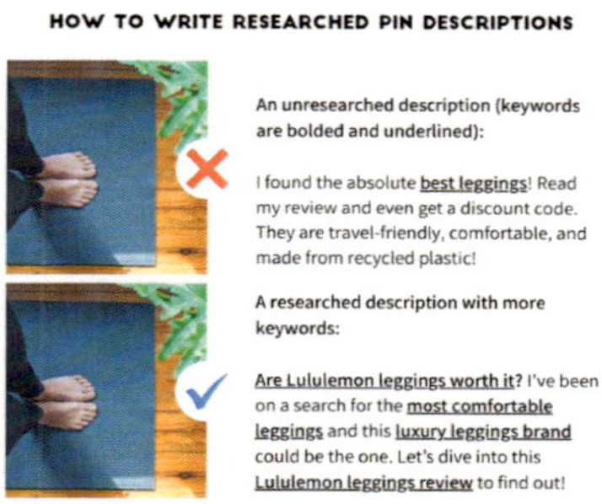

Source: https://blog.contentstudio.io/wp-content/uploads/2022/08/image11.png.

8. **Choose Hashtags Wisely and Freely:** Hashtags are widely used to tag content on all major social media platforms, including Pinterest, since they first appeared on Twitter. Theoretically, by including up to 20 different hashtags in each pin description, you can concentrate on keywords or related topics. However, you should never use more than four in a single post. Overusing hashtags can come across as spammy and invasive.

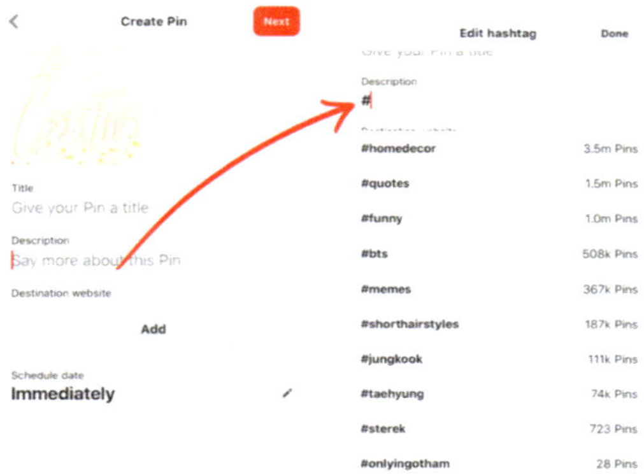

Source: https://blog.contentstudio.io/wp-content/uploads/2022/08/image12.png.

It's important to make sure your hashtags relate to the content you are pinning. Of course, if you do that, your exposure won't suffer. Conversely, some Pinterest users believe that pinning something increases views in the initial minutes.

9. **Tag Pinterest to Your Website:** The Pinterest tag is a piece of code that you can add to your website's source code to track traffic from Pinterest and find out what users are doing there. You can track any activity, such as purchases or newsletter enrollments, using the Pinterest tag, regardless of whether your ads are sponsored or organic. The information you gather from tracking conversions will help your SEO efforts going forward, even though adding the Pinterest tag won't have a direct effect on your SEO. You can ascertain which keywords drive revenue to your website, for instance, by tracking conversions using the Pinterest tag.

10. **Employ Pinterest Save Button on the Website:** One can configure the "Save" button to show up automatically or only when the user's mouse is hovering over the image's upper-left corner. If Pinterest is a major source of traffic for your website, it might be advantageous to have the "Save" button displayed prominently.

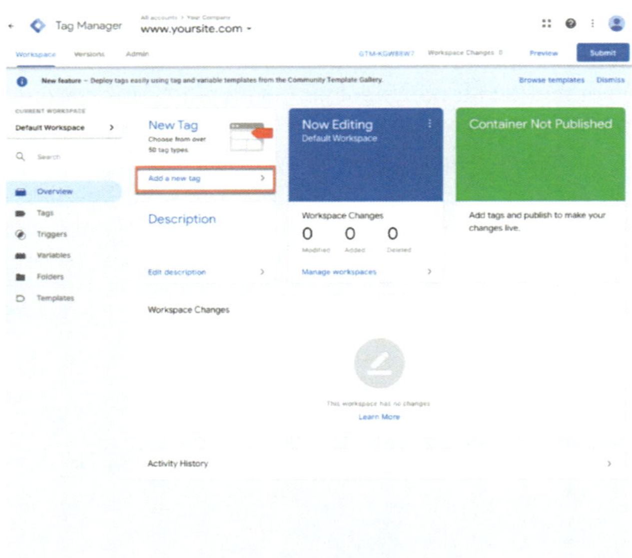

Source: https://blog.contentstudio.io/wp-content/uploads/2022/08/image13.png.

You can improve visibility, drive more traffic to your Pinterest page, and gain more followers by adding the Pinterest "Save" button to photos on your website. If you sell jewelry or clothing, for example, your website probably has a ton of pin-worthy content. With the addition of a "Save" option, pinners can now instantly add these images to their boards and pins.

11. **Rich Pins:** These are vital for e-commerce companies that use Pinterest to showcase their products because they update product descriptions, prices, and other information on the site. Stated differently, in the event that you modify a product's price on your website, the system will promptly update your Product Rich Pin. By taking this action, Pinterest users will not click on a link to your store only to find that the price is different from what they were originally shown on the platform.

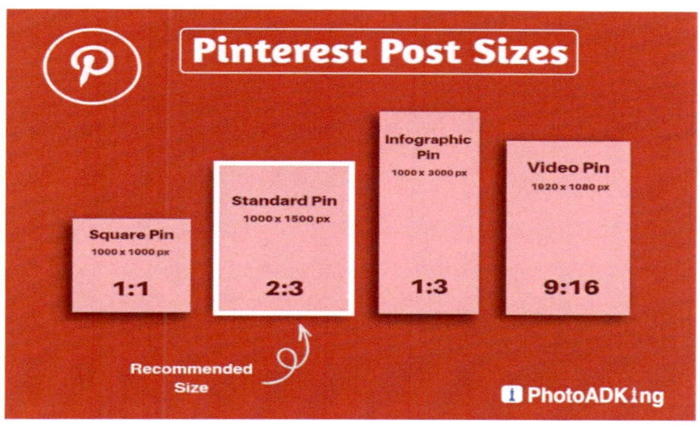

Source: https://blog.photoadking.com/wp-content/uploads/2023/02/pinterest-post-sizes.jpg.

In addition to Product Rich Pins, you can also activate Article Rich Pins to have blog entries updated automatically. You can create coordinated ads that highlight the most recent information from your website by utilizing both. You do this by adding a small bit of HTML code to your website.

12. **Format Images Meticulously:** The ideal picture format is significantly affected by the fact that, according to the most recent data, mobile devices account for 85% of Pinterest traffic. In other words, longer is better; the ideal pin size is 1,000 by 1,500 pixels, and the ideal aspect ratio is 2:3. In order to prevent your incredible content from getting lost in a sea of other images, you should also use bold colors that stand out on the website.

13. **Use Analytics:** One of the many benefits of having a Pinterest business profile is the abundance of information available to you. Additionally, by utilizing Pinterest statistics, you may discover terms

that promote engagement, generate traffic, and lead to conversions. And that's just the start even then.

14. **Try Pinterest Ads:** To improve engagement and drive traffic to your page, you might want to try your hand at paid Pinterest ad campaigns. They share Google Adsense's Pay-Per-Click (PPC) business model, so you can set a budget and experiment with paid ads without taking a big chance. Prior to making a Pinterest advertisement, choose your goals. For instance, do you want to increase blog click-through rates, get more views for your video, or increase conversions? Different Pinterest ad types are made for different purposes.

Source: https://encrypted-tbn0.gstatic.com/images?q=tbn:ANd9GcT1-e3kCkA-cYFSCgsvpyx_aV6-y5RelJoN9tA&s.

REFERENCES

1. Bigger than ever, Pinterest opens up to all. (2012, August 12). *The Sydney Morning Herald*. Archived from the original on November 13, 2012. Retrieved August 15, 2012.
2. CMS Social. How Pinterest is different from other social media platforms – CMS Social Media Company Miami FL. Archived from the original on August 6, 2020. Retrieved May 7, 2020.
3. Constine, J. (2012, January 31). Congratulations Crunchies winners! Dropbox is the best overall startup. *TechCrunch*. Archived from the original on November 24, 2020. Retrieved February 7, 2012.
4. Coyle, J. (2012, May 1). Louis C.K., Instagram, Pinterest, and Facebook win Webby Awards. *Mercury News*. Archived from the original on May 11, 2012. Retrieved May 3, 2012.
5. Farrell, M. (2019, February 22). Pinterest files confidentially for IPO. *The Wall Street Journal*. Archived from the original on February 22, 2019. Retrieved February 22, 2019.
6. Gershgorn, D. (2019, March 23). Pinterest is distancing itself from social networks as it goes public. *Quartz*. Archived from the original on April 4, 2020. Retrieved May 7, 2020.
7. Pinterest is getting rid of its like button, moving away from 'social network' label. (2017, April 22). *Social Media Today*. Archived from the original on September 24, 2021. Retrieved September 24, 2021.
8. Price, E. (2013, February 5). Pinterest updates iOS app to make editing pins easier. *Mashable*. Archived from the original on February 8, 2013. Retrieved February 8, 2013.
9. Trentmann, N. (2021, April 28). Pinterest CFO looks to ramp up spending on marketing, product investments. *The Wall Street Journal*. Archived from the original on April 29, 2021. Retrieved April 29, 2021.
10. Vanian, J. (2023, February 6). Pinterest shares slip on fourth-quarter revenue miss and weak forecast. *CNBC*. Archived from the original on February 7, 2023. Retrieved February 7, 2023.

CHAPTER 9

THREADS ALGORITHM

Contents

Introduction 310

9.1. Define Thread 310

9.2. Working Threads Algorithm 312

9.3. Tips for Working with the Threads Algorithm 314

9.4. Understanding the Threads Algorithm and User Control 318

9.5. Things the Threads Algorithm 320

9.6. Create a Threads Account 328

References 339

INTRODUCTION

Social media platforms rely on complex algorithms to determine the content users see in their feeds, and Threads—a text-based social platform launched by Meta—is no exception. These algorithms are central to user experience, as they personalize content, prioritize interactions, and help users discover relevant posts and conversations.

The core of Threads' algorithm likely revolves around a combination of machine learning models, including collaborative filtering, natural language processing (NLP), and deep learning techniques. These models analyze user behavior, such as likes, follows, and the types of content engaged with, to predict and recommend new content. Additionally, the algorithm likely considers recency and relevance, ensuring that users see timely and pertinent posts.

Social media algorithms, including those in Threads, are designed to increase engagement by keeping users active on the platform. This is achieved by surfacing content that aligns with user interests while also introducing diversity to encourage exploration. The algorithm continuously learns from user interactions, refining its predictions and recommendations over time.

However, these algorithms are not without controversy. They have been criticized for creating "filter bubbles" by showing users content that reinforces their existing beliefs, potentially limiting exposure to diverse perspectives. Furthermore, the opacity of these algorithms often raises concerns about bias, privacy, and the potential for manipulation.

In conclusion, the algorithm behind Threads plays a crucial role in shaping user experience by curating content that aligns with individual preferences. While it enhances personalization and engagement, it also brings challenges related to transparency and the broader impact on social discourse. Understanding how these algorithms work is essential for both developers and users in navigating the digital landscape.

9.1. DEFINE THREAD

0A thread is an organized conversation created by a sequence of responses or comments on a social media post, usually centered around a specific idea or topic. On some social media sites, a thread can also refer to a collection of posts that are published one after the other on the same topic.

A sequence of emails or replies to emails can also be referred to as threads. Digital communications are made possible by threads, which are widely used in social media. A thread is an arrangement of connected posts or messages about a particular topic or concept. Social media sites such as Facebook Groups,

Reddit, Twitter, and online forums are popular places to find threads.Social media threads give users and brands an organized way to post, allowing them to elaborate on their initial message and add more context. This allows users of social media to interact with a particular concept, subject, or piece of content.

Additionally, it makes it possible for users to take part in online chats and discussions in a more structured manner by answering previous responses or remarks made by other users.

As more people respond to or comment on posts on social media, the content or posts themselves eventually gain more reach and visibility. Threads can be used for a number of things, such as talking about an event, sharing a collection of related photos or videos, or publishing a story in several parts that are published in order.

Users of Meta's text-based social media platform Threads can post updates and share viewpoints in a manner akin to the well-known X (formerly Twitter) network. By employing data from Instagram to recommend accounts for users to follow and interact with, Threads makes use of the platform's user base to increase its reach. It has become a rival to Twitter, which has long dominated text-based social media.

There were threads in the Instagram universe before 2023, when it saw a comeback. The first version of Instagram Threads, a video messaging service akin to Snapchat, was released in 2019. This first Threads faded into obscurity in spite of its potential.

Once the clear leader in real-time updates and conversation, X had experienced substantial changes under Elon Musk's ownership by 2023, leaving many users disenchanted and searching for alternatives. Musk made a number of platform modifications, one of which was charging users for the blue verification check mark—which had hitherto verified the legitimacy of accounts—on the platform. But soon, X's algorithm was favoring content from blue-checked accounts—a large portion of which was offensive or untrue. Following his acquisition of Twitter, Musk also let go of thousands of workers. His far-right politics increased the mistrust among users.

In July 2023, Threads returned to the digital scene with a whole new set of features. Its design concept revolves around allowing users to share images and videos and setting a character limit of 500 per post. Combining writing features with Instagram's community-building potential is Meta's vision for Threads.

In just the first week of its launch, the platform saw a spike in activity that attracted over 100 million users and clearly challenged X's dominance.

Instagram users can begin "threading" without creating a new account thanks to Threads' sign-up process. Users can follow accounts automatically thanks to the integration between Threads and Instagram, which guarantees that users' networks on Instagram are immediately available on Threads. Users could share content between Threads and Instagram, interact with posts using well-known icons, and even transfer their Instagram verification status over to Threads.

When Threads first launched, it was unique in that it offered an uninterrupted, ad-free scrolling experience. Users found this feature of the platform especially appealing because it offered a clutter-free setting for interaction and communication.

Social media sites incorporate threads in particular ways to enable organized posting, discussion, and idea sharing by users. Additionally, they usually adhere to specific formatting guidelines to distinguish between different reply levels and improve thread readability:

- **Twitter:** Here, a thread starts with a comment on a tweet. A threaded conversation is created when individuals post comments below the original tweet. Users can keep commenting on subsequent tweets in the thread, and the conversation can stay focused and well-organized. On Twitter, users generally number tweets within a thread (e.g., 1/5, 2/5, etc.) or employ indentation to mark the hierarchy of replies.
- **Online Forums:** These or social groups are built around threaded discussions. Users can add new posts on specific subjects, building upon the comments or responses from other users to expand the discussion. Like Twitter, forum threads also have a hierarchical format. It starts with the initial post at the top and continues with subsequent replies chronologically.
- **Reddit:** This revolves around the notion of threads, referred to as 'posts' or 'threads.' Users can add comments on posts to join a discussion. Other users can upvote or downvote comments for visibility on the discussion. Reddit threads are arranged by subreddit (topic-specific forums), covering an extensive range of topics.
- **Facebook Groups:** Thes integrate threads to start and coordinate discussions. Group members can publish content, and others may leave comments on those posts to continue the conversation.

9.2. WORKING THREADS ALGORITHM

Posts that are prioritized in each user's "For You" feed are chosen by the Threads app algorithm, a secret formula. (Also, Facebook and Instagram are not the only social media sites with algorithms. Users are presented with content on Threads through two distinct tabs: the Following tab and the For You tab.

The Following tab presents content from accounts you follow in a chronological order, which is pretty simple to understand. However, the For You tab provides a combination of user recommendations and content from your friends.

Posts on your For You feed ought to be relevant to your particular interests if the algorithm is functioning properly. Its forecasts are dependent on several variables, such as the type of content you have previously interacted with or the creators you are currently following. For instance, content with a magic theme is likely to appear if you follow magicians.

9.2.1. Threads Generator [Free Tool]

It takes a lot of pressure to produce content that will impress the Threads algorithm as well as your followers. It's okay to ask for assistance if you're having a Threads block—a shorter version of writer's block.

Your content calendar will be filled and your creative juices will quickly flow again with our Threads generator. The AI system at Threads makes predictions about the kind of content you will find most valuable based on your usage patterns throughout the platform.

It first compiles content from the accounts you follow and publicly accessible content from Threads. Subsequently, the Threads algorithm examines a set of input signals derived from that content, such as your interaction with related content or the subjects that pique your interest.

The content is then ranked by the algorithm, which also predicts which posts will pique your interest the most. The ones that are most likely to be useful to you appear higher in your personalized feed. It's a rather complicated three-step process that goes on continuously in the background while you're carelessly using your Threads. It's up to you whether you find it comforting or a little creepy.

9.2.2. Threads Algorithm Ranking Factors

Each time you use Threads, you are providing the Meta robot with additional data about your preferences. It sees the number of posts you've liked, the writers you've followed lately, the number of replies you've seen, and other information.

The Threads algorithm looks at each post and considers the following:

- **Whether or not you'll like the post?:** Meta claims that the number of posts you've liked, the number of posts by a specific author you've liked, and the number of posts you've seen in your feed are among the signals that affect this prediction.

- **How likely you are to click to view replies on a Threads post?:** Based on how often you interact with an author's content, how many times others have done the same thing, and how long it has been since you were active on Threads, Meta can forecast a user's propensity to view replies on a post.
- **How likely you are to give the post author a follow?:** The Threads algorithm is tracking all of this behavior to figure out just how likely you are to follow the author of a given post. Are you active on Threads? How many posts have you seen in your feed? Who have you followed recently? Have you been stalking the author on Instagram?
- **How likely you are to click on the author profile of a post?:** The frequency with which other users have clicked on a Threads author's profile and the frequency with which you have viewed the author's Instagram post are two factors that affect your likelihood of clicking on their profile.
- **How likely you are to scroll past something instead of engaging with it?:** The likelihood that you will interact with something increases if you have liked or viewed a post several times. They also increase if a significant number of people have viewed the post. And those are the only variables under your control. The Threads algorithm also considers how many other users are enjoying a given post in addition to you.

Meta will take note of posts that have received a lot of views from users who share your interests and may add them to your feed. "It's an alligator escape video that this guy is going to love!."

9.3. TIPS FOR WORKING WITH THE THREADS ALGORITHM

All of the information above explains how Meta chooses the ideal Threads feed for you, but what more can we learn about how to make the Threads algorithm work in your favor and increase the reach of the content you produce?

In the end, the Threads algorithm is made to present users with content that they are likely to enjoy, including content that is relevant to their interests and that other users have liked. Hence, producing excellent content that users enjoy is the true key to becoming popular on the app. Now, we realize that might not seem like much of a hack ("What if you were just… good?"), so continue reading for some more helpful tips on how to write interesting, widely shared Threads posts that will wow that mighty, powerful Threads algorithm.

9.3.1. Understand Your Audience

If you've read any other social media engagement guides, you already know that Rule 1 is always this. While analytics for Threads are currently nonexistent, use your brand's other social media platforms as a baseline: who follows you on Instagram or Twitter/X? How can you ever capture the interest of your audience if you don't know who they are?

The demographics of your followers can be found in these apps' own internal analytics systems, but allow us to be slightly biased here: Hootsuite analytics also offer a wealth of insightful information. (Plus, it has a sleek reporting feature. After gathering these specifics and reviewing our guide on identifying your target market, you'll be prepared to Thread. (Are we still using the verb "thread"? That's disappointing, to be honest.).

9.3.2. Offer Content with Value

Each Threads user who engages with your account is providing the app with precise feedback about the value they place on your content. It goes without saying that likes and follows are signs that you're contributing quality content to the Thread-iverse. However, if people are hiding, unfollowing, or blocking you, that will suggest a completely different situation.

Thus, maintain their happiness. This entails producing valuable Threads content, such as amusing, educational, or inspirational content. A follower's day will be brightened by watching a behind-the-scenes video of you creating that insane soda can display, but advertising your grocery store's daily big BOGO sale isn't really worth much.

9.3.3. Schedule Your Threads

To delight and engage a large number of people, you must first reach a large number of people. If you post your content when your audience is most engaged, you'll have the best chance of accomplishing that.

9.3.4. Engage with Other Accounts

Users are recommended threads posts according to the popularity of the author. That implies that it's time to start a friendship. Recall that social media is meant to be conversational, not broadcast. Thus, venture forth and interact with other accounts. Seeking to attract other app users' attention? A clever or encouraging remark on someone's Threads post, or a response to someone's query or survey, can make a big difference. Engage in regular, active participation to gain attention from both the algorithm and other Threadsters.

9.3.5. Post Consistently

The Threads algorithm considers your level of activity on the app when deciding which of your content to recommend to someone. While viral content garners a lot of attention, the most successful social media creators have typically developed their audiences over years, gaining followers one post at a time.

By using a scheduling tool, you can demonstrate your reliability as a contributor to the Threadscape and maintain a regular schedule.

9.3.6. Join Trending Topics

Users of Threads in the U.S. now, when they click on the search tool or open their For You tab, they can see Trending Topics.

As per Meta, "Our AI systems use various signals, such as the quantity of posts made on a particular topic and the number of people who have interacted with those posts, to determine what the Threads community is talking about. The AI systems choose topics from among all the posts that users discuss on Threads; they are not just limited to the news articles that users share. ."

Take advantage of this feature if you have access to it by joining the discussion and attempting to add something useful. It's time to contribute some amusing puns about this year's Best Picture titles if the Trending Topics show that everyone is chatting endlessly about the Oscars. Take that wave!

9.3.7. Don't Neglect Your Instagram Account

Your Threads account is closely linked to your Instagram account. As you may recall, in order to create your Threads profile in the first place, you required an Instagram account. Threads is a good funnel for expanding your audience because it asks your Instagram followers to join you there. However, what users see in their Threads feed on Instagram can also be influenced by their actions.

For example, the Threads algorithm interprets a user viewing your Instagram profile as indicating that the user is likely interested in your Threads content as well. All of which is to say that it's crucial to maintain the excitement and engagement of your Instagram content at least as high as it is on Threads. Refresh your knowledge of Instagram marketing to ensure you don't pass up any opportunities.

9.3.8. Get Interactive

Post on Threads to start a discussion, pose a question, or conduct a poll. These kinds of posts are a great way to get engagement because they essentially instruct readers on how to communicate with you. Using this format to your advantage is a timeless and low-risk strategy that works on any social media platform.

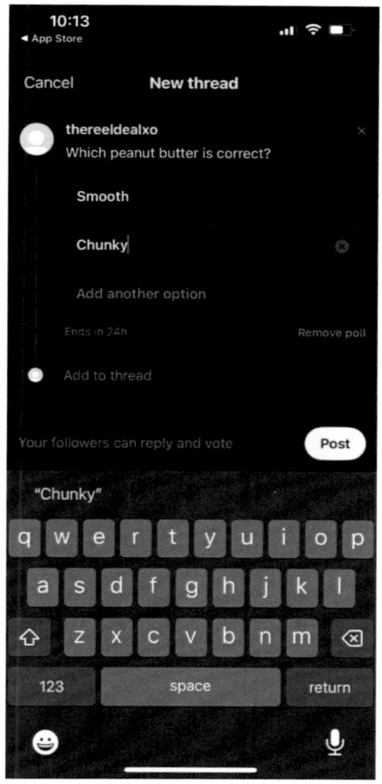

9.3.9. Issue a Challenge

The social media superstar Meta urged brands and content producers to launch competitions and challenges for their followers in an email that was leaked.

Similar to surveys and inquiries, challenges have the power to engage your audience and encourage them to create original posts on Threads. If the algorithm is fond of anything, it is content that generates more content. That might be as intricate as creating a multi-stage, bracketed competition with unique dance moves and video submissions, or it could be as straightforward as offering a prize for reaching a particular follower milestone ("If I get 10,000 likes, I'll shave our office manager's head!").

9.3.10. Use Threads' Tools and Features

The head honchos would really love for creators to start utilizing Threads features, according to that same leaked Meta email. Yes, the text posts that resemble tweets take center stage, but users can also share up to 10 photos and five-minute videos. Try experimenting with the current and upcoming tools; you might just receive a small boost from the algorithm. (Threads, I'm a little thirsty.).

9.3.11. Play by the Rules

Be ready to face consequences if you break the community guidelines on Threads, which are identical to those on Instagram. If you're not following the rules, there's no way you'll get an algorithmic boost. You know the drill: don't post explicit photos of yourself online, don't spam others, don't glorify violence or self-harm. You should not experience any issues if you post in a typical manner. Alright, so you're prepared to use the Threads algorithm to its full potential and can now begin writing those drafts. Have some fantastic ideas for your next Threads post right here on the house.

9.4. UNDERSTANDING THE THREADS ALGORITHM AND USER CONTROL

We understand; sometimes it can feel as though you're trapped in a time loop where new content is as scarce as a two-dollar bill. Have you ever felt like you're just scrolling through your social media feed, seeing the same old stuff, from the same people, over and over? It's time to make some changes, then. Because using Threads is about exploring and discovering in a way you've never done before, rather than just connecting with people you know. An algorithm created to escape the echo chamber and provide a novel, interesting social experience.

9.4.1. Dissecting the Algorithm Behind Threads

Now, let's get right to the point. When we discuss algorithms, we're referring to the internal mechanisms that determine what appears on your feed. With Threads, they've taken the traditional formula and added their own twist, resulting in a special hybrid system that offers you a wide variety of new and interesting content.

1. **Breaking Down the Threads Feed:** Consider Threads to be a party DJ. It creates a special mix that keeps the party going by taking the beats you're feeling (from the accounts you follow) and adding some unexpected tracks (posts from undiscovered creators).

   So how does Threads choose these unexpected songs—it's not like they do it at random. Rather, it scans and learns from your likes, shares, and engagement patterns using an algorithm. It then employs this intelligence to identify more content that it believes you'll enjoy.

This implies that the content in your Threads feed is carefully chosen (by means of an algorithm) to provide you with entertainment. Some of it is old, some is new. The really amazing thing is that Threads does more than just mix the songs. It also attempts to find a middle ground between encouraging you to venture outside of your comfort zone and keeping you there.

2. **Post Ranking versus Content Discovery:** Imagine that you are at a buffet. You always go for your favorite dishes, but every now and then you see something new. The way that Threads balances between displaying posts from accounts you follow (your favorites) and posts from new creators (the new dishes) is exactly what this algorithm does. Have you tried it?

   In contrast to other platforms where your favorites always hold the top spots, Threads gives new dishes an equal opportunity to shine. The algorithm employs a content discovery strategy, aggressively pushing content from unknown creators and encouraging you to try these new dishes, rather than favoring the accounts you follow.

   But why does Threads do this? It's easy to understand: it diversifies the way you consume content. Threads encourages you to venture out, meet new creators, and extend your horizons rather than staying with what you already know.

   Please understand that your favorites are not ignored by the algorithm. It simply does not elevate them. You will therefore receive a substantial portion of content from creators you may not be familiar with, in addition to posts from accounts you already follow.

9.4.2. Threads Algorithm and User Control

Although Threads' algorithm undoubtedly has its own style, it is not a totalitarian one. It all comes down to giving you, the user, the freedom to make decisions. It maintains a high standard of user experience while integrating a variety of user actions, such as reporting, blocking, and restricting…

1. **Algorithm's Role in Synchronized Blocking:** Threads is on the same page as how you can block those annoying Instagram profiles that keep showing up. Instagram gets a hint when you press the block button on Threads. Since Instagram's algorithm is intelligent enough to recognize the message and block the account there as well, there's no need to repeat the process there.

   The Instagram and Threads synchronization is a feature of the algorithm's architecture. Its goal is to maintain your sense of security, safety, and comfort on both platforms. Unwanted content is not allowed here. You can still interact freely in your Threads feed without being interrupted by profiles you'd prefer not to see.

2. **How 'Hidden Words' Influence Content Delivery?** With its "hidden words" feature, a clever tool that lets you designate specific words or phrases that you'd prefer not see in your feed, Threads goes one step further. The algorithm filters out any content that contains your list of "hidden words" by screening each and every post, acting as a bouncer at the entrance to your feed. It serves as your own personal filter, removing anything that doesn't appeal to you from your feed.

However, it doesn't end there. In addition to blocking posts that contain your "hidden words," the Threads algorithm is perceptive and learns from them. It makes use of this data to better understand your preferences and present you with material that appeals to you. This indicates that the "hidden words" are a tool for customizing your feed rather than just a filter. Since the Threads algorithm is ultimately created to serve you, it uses these terms to curate a feed specifically for you…

9.5. THINGS THE THREADS ALGORITHM

Finally, the Threads algorithm's inner workings are revealed to us. And while many of the things on the list shouldn't come as a surprise (particularly if you know how the Instagram algorithm operates), Meta is coming up with some fresh and creative ways to give users a special experience…

On the Meta transparency site, the Threads team quietly released this guide on the Threads Feed AI system. It contains some insightful tips on how to increase your following on Threads immediately…

That being said, the social network is still in its infancy, despite the new app's historic launch in July 2023 and its quick ascent to over 130 million monthly active users. Additionally, the team is developing new Threads features at a rapid rate, so as the social media platform changes and expands, expect the algorithm to change as well. Here is a summary of all the information currently available about the functioning of the Threads algorithm, along with some future projections…

9.5.1. Threads' Feed is Ranked by an AI System

The most intriguing thing about Thread's most recent revision to their ranking system is that the word "algorithm" is not used once. Alternatively, it is referred to as an artificial intelligence (AI) system. According to the company, "an artificial intelligence (AI) system selects, ranks, and delivers the content that you see on your Threads feed." Several machine learning models collaborate within a single AI system to provide your experience. ."

Although it may seem unfamiliar and a little scary at first, this isn't really the case. This type of reactive machine learning AI is used by most social networks to customize their feeds (though Threads is the first to drop the word algorithm in favor of AI, probably because most users will understand the term better following the AI boom in 2023).

9.5.2. Threads' AI System Only Impacts the For You Feed

Early adopters clamoured for a "Following" feed, where they would only see content from accounts they already followed, following the launch of a basic "For You" feed, which is a curated feed of the content the algorithm predicts a user will enjoy. Threads was pleased to comply.

Source: https://lh7-us.googleusercontent.com/NC5vrWoHUBTx7QRpHnaDLF-h86zFm12ZpHTm-Tf19J8soXjNade8IsM2T6ARV8ZBEYksGDqLOW0J-TryLp4701VlXEJYL_D9m01DIBz0GMUlZKBamk0O-gZ9XkIF-JxGLZoFdjQX-v4Grw0H9KZBn8ux6g.

The experience currently feels like the For You Page (FYP) and Following feeds on TikTok, which you can quickly switch between at the top of the app…

By tapping the Threads logo at the top or the home button at the bottom of the app, users can navigate between the two feeds. The For You or Following tabs will then appear directly beneath the Threads logo. There is a For You/ Following toggle button on the bottom right of the Threads web page… It's interesting to note that the Following feed appears to be back to the company's traditional chronological feed, with no influence from the algorithm. According to the company, "you can see content only from accounts that you follow, in reverse chronological order, by clicking the Threads logo on your home screen and then clicking Following." You will not be presented with suggested content if you choose this option."

9.5.3. Ranking Is a Three-Step Process

Before any content appears in users' feeds at all, three things happen extremely quickly. Here's how Threads breaks that process down:

1. **Gather Inventory (Content):** "The system gathers a portion of the public content available on Threads and all the content posted by accounts that you follow, which may include text posts, photos, and videos that follow our quality and integrity rules."
2. **Leverage Signals (Engagement):** "Next, the AI system considers a variety of input signals about the content. These signals might include how you've engaged with similar accounts, content, or your interests."
3. **Rank Content: "**Finally, the system ranks content from the previous step. Content that the system predicts will provide more value for you is shown higher in your feed. This helps the system make content recommendations that more closely match your preferences."

It may appear that as a brand or content creator on Threads, you have no control over this behind-the-scenes operation. However, contend that this system contains some crucial hints for optimizing the chances of success for your content…

Making sure your posts are part of "the portion" of content that the Threads algorithm gathers in step one is essential first. The weighting of engagement in ranking is the second (and comparatively standard practice for social media platforms). The third, and possibly most crucial, is the last step's mention of value.

9.5.4. Instagram's Community Guidelines Apply

Breaking the rules is the best way to stay inactive on Threads and could potentially result in bans. Only "text posts, photos, and videos that follow our quality and integrity rules" are examined in accordance with the different ranking signals (below), as you can see in the procedure above.

The Instagram Community Guidelines, which can be summed up as follows: "We want Instagram to continue to be an authentic and safe place for inspiration and expression," are stipulated in Threads' Terms of Use. Assist us in building this community. Share only your personal images and videos, and always abide by the law. Respect everyone on Instagram by avoiding posting nude content or spamming users. ."

Additionally, you should make sure that your content complies with Instagram's recommendation guidelines. Although content that violates these rules is not removed from Instagram-recommended feeds like the Explore Page or the Instagram Reels Feed, it is still technically permitted on the platform. This probably affects the Threads' For You Feed as well.

That means avoiding anything that:

- Depicts/discusses self-harm, suicide, eating disorders, or violence;
- Is sexually explicit or suggestive;
- Promotes the use of certain regulated products, like tobacco.

9.5.5. The Signals That Shape Users' Feeds

Similar to other social networks, Threads users' feeds display content based on a variety of signals that determine what gets displayed first and in what sequence…

The social network deconstructs a number of the algorithm's predictions and the signals that affect them in their explainer. Their framing of this is fantastic because it emphasizes how even the smallest actions on your content—beyond likes, comments, and reposts—can have a significant impact…

- **Whether or not a user will like a post?:** This prediction is influenced by:
  - How many posts they've seen on their feeds
  - How many posts they've clicked to like
  - How many times they've clicked to like the author's posts in their feed
  - How many posts they've clicked to like from this author, of those that they've seen
- **How likely a user is to click to view replies on a post?:** This prediction is influenced by:
  - How many times others have clicked to reply to the post
  - How many replies they've seen
  - How many times they've clicked to like the author's posts in their feed
  - How long it's been since they were active on Threads
- **How likely they are to follow the author of a post?:** This prediction is influenced by:
  - How many posts they've seen in their feed
  - How long it's been since they were active on Threads
  - Which authors they've followed recently

  - Whether or not the post was predicted to contain language that goes against the Instagram Community Guidelines
  - How many times they've viewed the author's profile on Instagram
- **How likely a user is to click on the profile of a post's author?:** This prediction is influenced by:
  - How many times the author's profile has been clicked
  - The profile click rate on the author of the post
  - Whether or not the post was predicted to contain language that goes against our Community Guidelines
  - How many times they've viewed the author's profile on Instagram
  - The number of times that people have clicked on the author's profile
- **How likely a user is to scroll past a post rather than engage with it?:** This prediction is influenced by:
- The number of times that they've viewed a post
- How many times they've clicked to like the author's posts
- How many times others have viewed the post

Although Threads hasn't stated clearly how much weight each of these actions carries, it's likely that the more work an action takes, the more it affects the predictions and, consequently, the ranking of your content…

9.5.6. Actions on Instagram Affect Threads' Feeds

Although Threads is owned by Meta, the company that also owns Facebook, Instagram, and WhatsApp, it is frequently promoted as an Instagram companion app. Creating an account on Threads requires an Instagram profile, but sharing content and navigating between the two platforms is simple. Your Instagram followers will also be encouraged to follow you on Threads once you sign up for the platform…

Therefore, it should come as no surprise that actions on Instagram have a significant influence on the Threads algorithm. Looking at an author's Instagram profile influences not one, but two predictions, as you can see above. To switch between apps, navigate to the author's Threads profile and tap the Instagram logo on their page. This is a relatively high-friction action…

After all that work, viewing someone's Instagram profile is a strong sign that the author is interested in their work and will probably have a big influence on ranking. This is a clear indication that, at least for the time being, Threads' growth will be closely linked to success on one platform.

9.5.7. Users Can Customize Their Experience

Users of Threads have more explicit control over what they see and don't see, even though their feeds are all shaped by how they interact with and consume content on the platform.

Some of these options include:

- **Unfollow:** This one is pretty self-explanatory (though Threads doesn't say whether an unfollow on Threads might impact Instagram feeds and vice versa).
- **Share:** This includes sending a post to a chat and sharing it on another platform or site.
- **Mute:** Via the three dots to the right of every post, users can mute Threads creators so their content no longer appears in the users' feeds without unfollowing.
- **Hide:** Also via the three-dot menu, users can hide a specific post so that they won't see that post again. "This action also helps to limit similar content from appearing in your feed," Threads says.
- **Report:** Users can report content they think goes against Threads' (read: Instagram's) Community Guidelines and posts they believe are spam or false information. The system will try to show the user less content like the post they reported, whether Threads rules that the content violates their guidelines or not.

Again, Threads is silent on the relative importance of each of these actions, but I would guess that the more difficult or one-click actions—like clicking on a picture—have a greater impact. ."

9.5.8. Threads Is Exploring Trending Topics

Though not directly related to the algorithm, the recent release of a feature on Threads may portend future developments. Adam Mosseri, the CEO of Instagram, recently revealed that Threads is testing trending topics, a much-needed feature. He posted on Threads in February, saying, "For those of you who have been calling for a trending feature, we're rolling out a small test to help you find timely topics people are talking about."…

The Threads topics for today can be found in the For You feed and on the search page. Our AI systems choose the topics based on what users are currently talking about on Threads. Currently, only a small percentage of English users can access trending topics in the U.S. market. However, Mark Zuckerberg, the CEO of Facebook, stated that after it is optimized, they plan to "roll it out in more countries and languages." ."

Source: https://lh7-us.googleusercontent.com/_a6Tw_p43dAJLdPh5sz_JdOPApr-j_JFjLZRStXGQZURsUTXV0scQESyxYM1hFqmGWQ-vkkoWx9raSI_kSKIH4OF-GTZ1zfO-xQMQmrBd_QFcuObXDxwG7eiAGE6jWnyw-DvCP91-7MHPDtaXk-2ounvA.

When it makes sense to weigh in on a hot topic associated with your niche, this could be a potent method of content discovery and a way to connect with a new audience. This addition is definitely worth watching because it closely resembles the strategies that many influencers and content producers used to gain popularity on X (formerly Twitter)…

Despite the inevitable parallels to X, Threads hasn't avoided them in an attempt to appease a large number of disappointed X users. For instance, Threads swiftly added an edit function after its launch, probably in response to the popular request from users on Twitter to modify tweets, a feature that is currently exclusive to X Premium subscribers. These and other new features raise the possibility that Twitter growth strategies could also work on Threads…

9.5.9. Fediverse Features Are Worth Watching Out for

The fediverse's arrival, which Threads has been promising since its launch, should bring intriguing new aspects to the platform's ability to attract users…

One thing to note is that soon, people who follow you on Threads won't even need to have accounts there. For those who are unaware, Threads will work with other social media sites like Mastodon and Bluesky that are based on the ActivityPub protocol, so the people you are targeting will be much larger than the 130 million users of Threads alone. That is a big deal, if you can say that at all. The social media landscape could be altered by the fediverse… While the Threads team works on these features, you can already follow prominent writers from other platforms on Threads, including Adam Mosseri. Although it's unclear currently how this might affect the Threads algorithm and the algorithms of other platforms based on the ActivityPub protocol, it's definitely something to consider as your following grows…

9.5.10. Providing Value Is the Key to Threads' Success

Though their ranking explainer has a small detail that caught my attention, it is helpful to understand the inner workings of the Threads algorithm: "Content that the system predicts will provide more value for you is shown higher in your feed." ."

That framing is fantastic because it highlights the ultimate objective that Threads seeks to accomplish with its potent AI ranking system: posts that are valuable to Threads users. Therefore, concentrate on the caliber of your content rather than on Threads engagement tricks or the appropriate tags to use. When reading or viewing your posts, what do you want your readers to take away?

There are so many ways to do that. It might involve:

- Teaching them something new from your unique areas of expertise
- Helping solve a particular problem your target audience often faces
- Kickstarting a conversation in an area they have knowledge of or want to learn more about
- Just making them laugh!

Of course, that is easier said than done, but fortunately, we have a ton of resources available to help you as you expand your Threads following…

It's also important to note that Threads offers a number of features that facilitate finding, interacting with, and finding value in your content. Although Threads' algorithm update makes no mention of any of these features, it's always a good idea to take advantage of all the options a social network has to offer in order to make sure you're providing as much value as possible. That means:

- Using tags (Threads' version of hashtags) to start or join conversations in your niche
- Leaning into polls, GIFs, memes, photos, and videos to stop the scroll
- Joining ongoing conversations in Threads rather than just trying to start your own

9.6. CREATE A THREADS ACCOUNT

Here's how easy it is to get up and running on the platform:

1. **Download and Install the Threads App:** Download Threads from the Apple App Store (iOS) or Google Play Store (Android).
2. **Log in with Instagram:** Use your Instagram account to log in. If you don't have an Instagram account, you'll need to create one on Instagram.com or the app. There's no need actually to use this Instagram profile if you don't want to. You can opt for a private profile and don't need to post on the Instagram account in order to use Threads. Your Threads and Instagram accounts are effectively the same accounts — you cannot create a Threads account separately. If you have multiple Instagram accounts, you can create a separate (but connected) Threads account for each one.
3. **Set Up Your Threads Profile:** Customize your Threads account by adding a profile picture, a bio, and a link (Buffer's Start Page is a great link-in-bio option) so followers can find you and your other accounts. You can sync your profile picture and bio from Instagram, which is handy. You can also choose to make your profile private here if you wish (if you change your mind and want to adjust this later, it's easy enough to change in account settings.)
4. **Follow Accounts in Your Niche:** Threads will prompt you to follow users you already follow on Instagram who are active on Threads. It's worthwhile spending some time exploring how others in your industry or niche are posting on the platform, too.

9.6.1. Post on Threads

Posting on Threads is very straightforward on both the app and web version. Here's how to share your first thread, plus tap into all the neat features Threads has to offer:

9.6.1.1. How to Post on the Threads App?

To start a new thread on the app:

- Open the app and tap on the + icon at the bottom of your screen, or tap in the composer right at the top (where it says 'What's new?') to start your Threads post.
- Add your text in the composer window. To create a multi-post thread, tap the 'Add to thread' button underneath the text box.

- The buttons underneath allow you to upload multimedia and use other features:

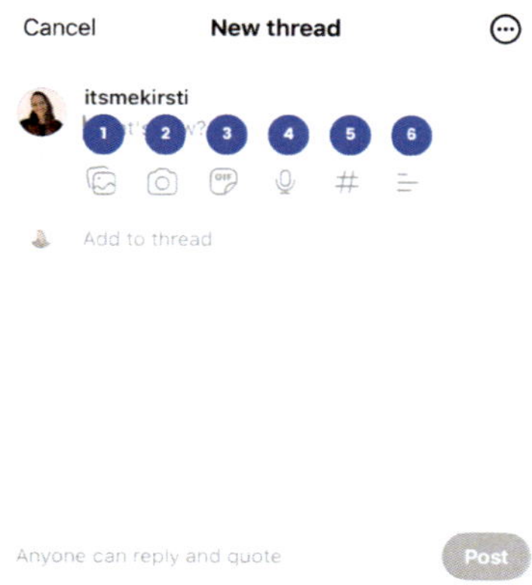

Source: https://buffer.com/resources/content/images/2024/06/how-to-use-Threads-1.png.

  - **Image Icon:** Upload from camera roll.
  - **Camera Icon:** Take a photo or video.
  - **GIF Sticky Icon:** Add a GIF to your post.
  - **Microphone:** Record a voice note.
  - **Hash Symbol Icon:** Add a tag to your post.
  - **Horizontal Line Icon:** Add a poll.
- Choose who can view your post by tapping 'Anyone can reply and quote' (the default setting). Your other options are: 'Anyone,' 'Profiles you follow,' or 'Mentioned only.' If you want others to be able to comment on, repost, or quote your thread, keep the default setting.
- When you're ready, hit the Post button. Congratulations — you just shared your first thread!

9.6.1.2. How to Post on Threads Web

To start a new thread on threads.net:

- Log in to threads.net and click the + button on the bottom right of your screen, or click on the composer at the top of your For You feed.
- Add your text in the composer window. To create a multi-post thread, tap the 'Add to thread' button underneath the text box.

- The buttons underneath allow you to upload multimedia and use other features (note that your options are more limited in the web version of Threads):

Source: https://buffer.com/resources/content/images/2024/06/how-to-use-threads--3-.png.

  – **Image Icon:** Upload image from device folders.
  – **GIF Sticky Icon:** Add a GIF to your post.
  – **Symbol Icon:** Add a tag to your post.
  – **Horizontal Line Icon:** Add a poll.
- Choose who can view your post by clicking 'Anyone can reply and quote' (the default setting). Your options are the same as those above.
- When you're ready, hit the Post button.

9.6.1.3. How to Customize Your Threads Home Page on Web

The web experience on Threads is fantastic (and a game-changer if you prefer to type your posts out on a laptop keyboard instead of tapping away on your phone)…

It's also fantastic because of a June 2024 feature update that lets you pin various Threads feeds to your home page. To see everything at a glance, you can choose to pin your activity, search page, Following, For You, Threads profile, and more to a single page…

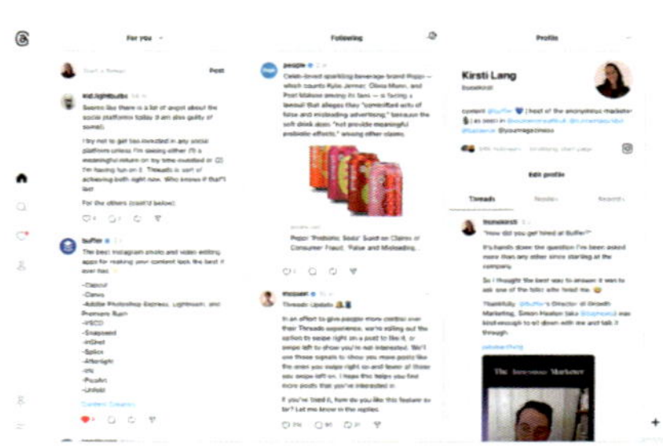

Source: https://buffer.com/resources/content/images/2024/06/how-to-use-threads--1-.png.

To do so:

1. Log into the Threads website via threads.net.
2. Click the pin icon on the bottom left of your screen.
3. Choose the feeds you'd like on your Threads home page, or use the search bar to pin a specific Threads profile.

9.6.2. Threads Best Practices for Growth

Check out our tips and tricks for Threads growth for a detailed look at how the Buffer team is expanding their followings on the platform. This is an overview of some of the lessons we've learned so far as we investigate the developing platform…

9.6.2.1. Post Regularly

Growing on any platform requires consistent posting, and if the new app's behavior is similar to that of Twitter, it might be wiser to post more frequently on Threads than on other platforms…

Although there isn't a set amount of posts you should share daily to get the best results, we should suggest starting with at least one thread each day and experimenting with posting more and less frequently to see what works best for you…

9.6.2.2. Start Conversations

The purpose of Threads is to facilitate conversations. A great way to start interacting on the platform and, hopefully, generate the kind of interactions that will increase the reach of your posts is by using conversation starters. Utilize polls, pose inquiries, and solicit feedback from your followers…

9.6.2.3. Engage Consistently

At the very least, you should reply to comments on your own Threads. Several of my Buffer colleagues have found that thoughtful responses to other creators in their niches on Threads have yielded greater growth than simply sharing their own content…

9.6.2.4. Tap into Tags

To organize your content and make it searchable, use pertinent tags. By doing this, you may appear in Threads users' For You feeds who have interacted with related content. Since you can only use one tag per thread, it's a good idea to investigate what tags other people in your niche or industry are using to congregate…

9.6.2.5. Experiment with All the Features

As was previously mentioned, Meta enjoys seeing users take advantage of their new features. Trying out different content types on the platform, such as GIFs, polls, videos, images, and more, is a great way to keep your followers interested and learn more about what appeals to them…

9.6.2.6. Try Out New Trends

Reels and TikToks are much harder to personalize than Threads trends, which are much more entertaining. This fantastic example from @ instagramforbusiness—a fantastic brand account that social media managers should follow for inspiration—makes fun of the popular TikTok and Instagram song, "Looking for a man in finance." ."

Source: https://buffer.com/resources/content/images/2024/06/image.png.

Source: https://lh7-us.googleusercontent.com/docsz/AD_4nXfB4MuuquSiyyS0q7-4WxxxUQ2ILeJTrjaUq5JrOzLthsuy4CBKJKrm_3Nda0k6zdvIoLPRRF9QocEFA0d5fSKNPmkNVKaL1fzFcrmDv1lDKmPQLx1oR4yrz5mo3xtT10dYjM4Zc2uujGn9IXgOc3zJ9F7s?key=riEbQTef3D7ff1TZF6B9Ww.

9.6.2.7. Cross-Post on Other Platforms

To let your audiences know you're on Threads, share your threads on other apps. Naturally, Instagram is a great place to do this because the app automatically converts text-only threads into visually appealing Instagram posts, such as the one below…

To share a thread to your Instagram Stories or directly to your feed, tap the paper airplane icon located beneath the thread…

Should you choose to post, your thread will show up over a background of Threads similar to the one below. Should you select an Instagram Story, it will be displayed on top of a simple colored backdrop. Please be aware that no media you upload to Threads will be shared automatically like an Instagram post.

It's interesting that cross-posting in the opposite direction isn't as seamless. Sharing your Instagram photos on Threads is as simple as tapping the paper airplane icon beneath the images. However, instead of sharing these Instagram posts directly, they appear as links.

Here's an example of how Instagram posts look when shared on Threads:

Source: https://buffer.com/resources/content/images/2024/06/how-to-use-threads--2-.png.

You'll soon be able to cross-post Instagram posts on Threads (as well as your other connected channels, like LinkedIn, Twitter, TikTok, and more) with just a few clicks when you schedule them in Buffer…

9.7. Threads Strategy for Business

With multimedia options and a character limit of 500, Threads is a content creation tool that emphasizes conversational content. In July 2023, its popularity skyrocketed, with over 100 million users in just one week. Making posts that are interesting and meaningful requires utilizing the Threads algorithm.

In contrast to Twitter's platform, Threads is exclusive to mobile devices, integrates with Instagram, and shows content in an algorithmic manner, including accounts that are not followed. Instead of using hashtags or trending content like Twitter does, it uses content selected by an algorithm.

Because Threads' content lifecycle is limited to a few hours, businesses looking to leverage the platform must produce original content on a regular basis. It's also advised to use techniques like resharing and repurposing content to increase its lifespan.

9.7.1. Differences Between Threads and Twitter

One quickly developing app that has made its way onto social media is called Threads. Thoughts can be shared textually in up to 500 characters using Threads, which is primarily a platform for content creation. Users can also attach multimedia files, such as images and videos. As stated on Meta's official blog, it is mobile-friendly and easy to use, and it can be downloaded in more than 100 countries. It seamlessly links with Instagram, extending an invitation to your followers on Instagram to follow along on your Threads journey.

Category	**Threads**	**Twitter**
Purpose	Content creation	Microblogging, news sharing
Content length	Up to 500 characters	Up to 280 characters
Multimedia	Supports photos and videos	Supports photos, videos, and GIFs
Platform Integration	Integrates with Instagram	Standalone platform
User base	Over 100 million (as of July 2023)	Over 330 million (as of 2021)
Content display	Algorithm-driven, includes non-followed accounts	Reverse chronological timeline/'For You' feature
Accessibility	Mobile-only	Mobile and desktop
Content discovery	Algorithm-driven, no trending section or hashtags	Hashtags, trending section, search functionality

Source: https://www.talktomira.com/post/threads-strategy-for-business-how-go-to-viral.

A side-by-side comparison with Twitter, the largest social media platform, highlights some significant distinctions between the two. In contrast to Twitter, where posts are limited to 280 characters, Threads gives users more freedom to express themselves with much longer posts. More importantly, unlike Twitter's reverse chronological timeline or its 'For You' feature, Threads' content display is powered by an algorithm that even displays posts from accounts that are not followed…

The platform's accessibility is another important difference: although Twitter offers features on its website as well, Threads currently limits its experience to mobile users only. In contrast, Twitter maintains a more flexible approach…

The "trending section" or hashtag usage feature that would enable users to look for particular content or trending topics on Twitter is absent from Threads; instead, viewers must rely solely on what Meta's algorithm presents to them in order to stay interested in the content.

9.7.2. Threads Prioritize Conversation-Driven Content

It is the purpose of the Threads algorithm to present a variety of content from different users so you can find new posts and participate in new discussions. The algorithm gives priority to threads that have received a lot of reports, likes, and comments, as the name would imply. This implies that posts that receive more interactions stand a greater chance of being seen by a larger number of users. Users are encouraged to engage in conversation and active participation by this type of algorithm.

Source: https://d3qug4wxaelkyn.cloudfront.net/IMG_0180_fdf0896ced.jpg.

9.7.2.1. How Is the Threads Algorithm Different from Twitter and Instagram

The algorithms used by Threads and Instagram are essentially distinct from one another. In contrast to Instagram, which places a premium on image relevance, Threads is heavily conversation- and contextual-driven. It pays more attention to the quality of conversations within a thread than it does to the original post…

In terms of being conversation-centric, Twitter and Threads are similar, but Threads goes one step further by surfacing posts from different users at random, resulting in a more dynamic and varied content discovery experience.

9.7.2.2. What Do You Have to Do Differently to Go Viral on Threads?

It takes more than just posting content to become viral on Threads; it also takes meaningful conversations to start. This entails creating posts that provoke discussion and inspire other users to join in. Social media strategists claim that sharing original ideas or posing open-ended questions can spark conversations, which raises the likelihood of your content becoming viral on the network.

	Threads	**Twitter**	**Instagram**
Working Principle	The Threads algorithm prioritizes conversation-driven content and threads with high engagement.	Twitter's algorithm is also conversation-centric.	Instagram's algorithm prioritizes image relevancy.
Content Discovery	The algorithm surfaces diverse content from various users to enable discovery of new posts.	Shares some similarities with Threads but does not randomly surface posts from different users.	Discovery depends on the relevancy of the images and their interactions.
Impact of Engagement	High engagement (reports, likes, comments) increases the chance of the posts being surfaced to more users.	Engagement impacts visibility, but not to the extent as in Threads.	High engagement does help in surfacing the content, but it is not the primary factor.
How to Go Viral	To go viral, meaningful conversations are needed, not just the posting of content. Ask open-ended questions or share unique insights to spark dialogue.	Virality often comes from high sharing or retweets, not just conversation.	High-quality, relevant images with engaging captions can drive virality.

Source: https://d3qug4wxaelkyn.cloudfront.net/IMG_0180_fdf0896ced.jpg.

9.7.3. Content Strategies for Threads

9.7.3.1. Unique and High-Frequency Posts

Because Threads drastically shortens the content lifecycle, it has just made things much more difficult for content creators. Content lifecycle: the amount of time that information is relevant…

- **Google Article** – 1–2 years;
- **YouTube Video** – a few months;
- **TikTok Video** – a few weeks;
- **Instagram Post** – a week;
- **Tweet** – a day;
- **Threads** – a few hours.

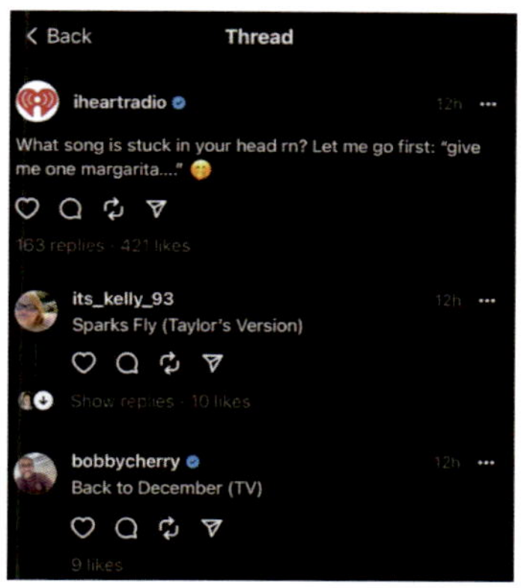

Source: https://mira-strapi-blog.s3.amazonaws.com/IMG_0179_c659a8be56.jpg.

It's critical for companies using Threads to comprehend the value of original and consistent posts. The new platform has significantly shortened the content lifecycle to a few hours, according to Threads App Guide. This indicates that the content on Threads is less relevant for a longer period of time than that of Google articles, YouTube videos, or even Tweets. For this reason, in this high-frequency post environment, it's critical to continuously produce original and captivating content in order to remain visible and relevant.

9.7.3.2. Prolonging Content Life Cycle

Extending the lifespan of your content on Threads can be a calculated approach to optimize its influence and audience. As per multiple marketing research studies, companies can implement tactics like rotating content, repurposing it on different channels, and generating a sequence of connected articles to sustain the dialogue. This strategy guarantees that your content reaches a larger audience in addition to prolonging its life.

9.7.3.3. Utilizing the Extended Character Limit

The extended character limit of 500 on Threads is one of the characteristics that distinguish it from Twitter. Businesses now have the chance to provide more complex and interesting content. Several content marketing blogs claim that you can take advantage of this by providing more thorough insights into your company, storytelling, or sharing more in-depth updates. With the longer character limit, you can better engage your audience by giving them more detailed and educational content.

9.7.3.4. Leverage Images and Videos

Users can share links, images, and videos up to five minutes long on Threads in addition to text. This implies that companies can use richer content formats to better draw in and interact with their audience. An eye-catching infographic or an engaging video, for example, can make your Threads post stand out. To increase your reach even more, the platform lets you share your Threads post as a link to your Instagram story or any other platform of your choosing.

REFERENCES

1. Aggarwal, C. C. (2016). *Recommender systems: The textbook*. Springer.
2. Bakshy, E., Messing, S., & Adamic, L. A. (2015). Exposure to ideologically diverse news and opinion on Facebook. *Science*, *348*(6239), 1130–1132.
3. Bessi, A., & Ferrara, E. (2016). Social bots distort the 2016 U.S. presidential election online discussion. *First Monday*, *21*(11).
4. Cheng, J., Adamic, L., Dow, P. A., Kleinberg, J. M., & Leskovec, J. (2014). Can cascades be predicted? In *Proceedings of the 23rd International Conference on World Wide Web (WWW '14)* (pp. 925–936).
5. Covington, P., Adams, J., & Sargin, E. (2016). Deep neural networks for YouTube recommendations. In *Proceedings of the 10th ACM Conference on Recommender Systems (RecSys '16)* (pp. 191–198).
6. Domingos, P. (2015). *The master algorithm: How the quest for the ultimate learning machine will remake our world*. Basic Books.
7. Easley, D., & Kleinberg, J. (2010). *Networks, crowds, and markets: Reasoning about a highly connected world*. Cambridge University Press.
8. Facebook Research. (2021). How does Facebook's news feed ranking work? Available at: https://research.fb.com.
9. Instagram Engineering. (2016). Improving content ranking on Instagram with machine learning. Available at: https://instagram-engineering.com/improving-content-ranking-on-instagram-with-machine-learning.
10. Lü, L., Medo, M., Yeung, C. H., Zhang, Y.-C., Zhang, Z.-K., & Zhou, T. (2012). Recommender systems. *Physics Reports*, *519*(1), 1–49.
11. Meta AI Research. (2022). Responsible AI for social media algorithms. Available at: https://ai.facebook.com/blog.
12. O'Neil, C. (2016). *Weapons of math destruction: How big data increases inequality and threatens democracy*. Crown Publishing Group.
13. Russell, S., & Norvig, P. (2020). *Artificial intelligence: A modern approach* (4th ed.). Pearson.
14. Twitter Engineering. (2020). Using machine learning to improve relevance in Twitter's timeline. Available at: https://blog.twitter.com/engineering.w

INDEX

A

Aartificial intelligence (AI) system 320, 321
Advertising campaigns 167, 275
Advertising industry 148
Advertising objectives 170
Affiliate marketing 147
AI-driven algorithms 27, 28
Algorithm controls 274
Algorithmic content moderation 31
Algorithm modifications 26
Algorithms control 147
Artificial intelligence (AI) 27
Audience comments 188
Audience engagement 258
Audience response 114
Audience segment 168
Autofill feature 295

B

Background information 159
Block button 319
Brainstorming 31
Brand ambassadors 226
Brand awareness 143
Brand-controlled content 126
Brand-customer relationship 208
Brand recognition 77
Brand-related initiatives 227
Brand statement 196
Brazilian websites 297
Buffer team 331
Business connections 219
Business-focused social media platform 218
Business page 236
Business-to-business connections 230

C

Calls to action (CTAs) 195
Channel style 184
Child sexual abuse material (CSAM) 39
Cold emailing 141
Comment sections 72
Commercial framework 7
Commodity audience 3
Community control 61
Community guidelines 117
Community standards 144
Company pages 236
Competitive environment 194
Complex algorithm 280
Complex system 108

Computer programming 13
Computer programs 36
Conditional formatting 189
Consumer-brand communication 130
Consumer collective intelligence 48
Consumer-generated stories 123
Content marketing 17
Content recommendations 108, 281
Content strategy 233, 234, 235, 249, 250
Co-watching 52
Cultural industry 6
Customer service 257
Customer-to-business (C2B) 124
Customer to customer (C2C) 124

D

Data analysis 158
Datafication 9
Data portability 51
Deep neural networks 179
Demographic information 168
Digital businesses 39
Digital communications 310
Digital landscape 310
Digital marketing strategy 236
Digital Services Act (DSA) 115
Disinformation 254
Domain quality 286
Dropdown menu 168
Dynamic process 197
Dynamic system 113

E

Economic subsystems 8
Effective marketing tool 298
Embedded feature 47
Embeddings function 262
Embedding space approaches 262
Emotional response 110
Empirical data 132
Employee advocacy 224
Employment placement 230
Engagement metrics 280
Explore tab 50, 55, 68, 69, 71, 72
Extensive database 292
Eye-catching images 71

F

Facebook algorithm 138, 139, 140, 142, 143, 145, 146, 147, 149, 166, 169, 170
Facebook engagement 146
Fact-checkers 144
Fact-checking organizations 61
Fact-checking systems 149
False information 179
Financial markets 5
Financial speculation 4
For you page (FYP) 108

G

Gaming channels 181
Geographic identification metadata 47
Geolocated data 47
German-speaking nations 238
Google searches 302, 303
Graphic content 117
Greedy algorithms 151

H

Hash-matching technologies 39
Hashtags 47
Heuristics 264
Hootsuite's benchmarking tool 247
Hootsuite's Twitter management tools 257
Horizontal scroll 62
Human behavior 33

I

Image editing tool 142
Image matching technology 62
In-depth analysis 118
Infographics 167
Information and communication technologies (ICTs) 3
Informative hashtags 89
Initial public offering (IPO) 219
In-network tweets 261
Instagram algorithm 46, 63, 66, 67, 68, 70, 76, 87, 97
Instagram post 314, 333
Instagram profile 316, 324, 328
Instagram shopping tools 71
Instagram stories 58, 333
Internal analytics systems 315
Internal search 119
Internet economy 7, 8
Internet monitoring 2
Interpersonal communication 2

J

Job placement 237
Journalistic credibility 154

K

Keywords 69
K-Nearest-Neighbors (KNN)-based clustering algorithms 161

L

Language preferences 112
LinkedIn 217, 218, 219, 220, 221, 222, 223, 224, 225, 226, 227, 228, 229, 230, 231, 232, 233, 234, 235, 236, 237, 238, 239, 240, 241, 242, 243, 244, 245, 246, 247, 248, 249, 250, 251, 252
LinkedIn's algorithm 16, 23
LinkedIn's operations 223
LinkedIn strategy 235, 236
Logistic regression model 262
Logistic regression ranking model 261
Long-term user satisfaction 156
Low-quality publishing 144
Low-risk strategy 317

M

Machine learning algorithm 37
Machine learning models 23
Marketing tool 60, 231
Merchandising 200, 213, 214
Meta email 317
Meta platforms 46
Meta robot 313
Meta's text-based social media platform 311
Meta transparency site 320
Microblogging 255
Microblogging platform 255
Misleading content 200
Mobile device 256
Monetization journey 197
MTV television network 48
Multimedia files 334
Multinational corporations 39
Multiple channels 189
Multi-post thread 329

N

Natural language processing (NLP) 36
Networking tool 223
News ecosystem 153
News feed 149
News feed algorithm 150
Niche content 26

Non-fungible tokens (NFTs) 53

O

Offline consequences 31
of Instagram marketing 316
One-on-one live chats 201
Online business networking 230
Online chats 311
Online communication strategies 237
Online experience 67
Online market 3
Online news 158
Online shopping 282
Open-ended questions 336
Open-source crawlers 160
Original publication 158

P

PageRank calculation 161
Pairwise-labeled data 153
Peer recognition 157
Performance metrics 166
Personal image building material 238
Personalization 109
Photographic filters 55
Pin description 303
Pinner quality 285, 291
Pinterest advertisement 306
Pinterest algorithm 280, 282, 283, 284, 285, 292, 293, 297
Pinterest analytics 293
Pinterest's algorithm 281, 282, 297, 301
Pinterest scheduling tool 287
Pinterest scheduling tools 292
Pinterest's search algorithm 296
Pinterest statistics 298, 305
Platform modifications 311
Platform policies 283
Potential customers 238
Private messages 57
Professional appearance 187
Professional contexts 238
Professional information 236
Professional networks 218
Professional network system 222
Professional relationships 218
Professional services 219
Progressive web application (PWA) 51
Promoted tweets 257
Propaganda function 2
Publisher authority data 156

R

Ranking signals 18
Ranking systems 153
Real-time data collection 4
Recommendation system 114, 143
Reels 46, 52, 54, 56, 62, 63, 64, 65, 67, 68, 69, 71, 72, 73, 76, 77, 78, 80, 86, 87, 88, 89, 90, 91, 93, 94, 95, 96, 97, 98, 99, 100, 101, 103, 105
Regular pins 298
Regular posting schedule 140
Regular programming 4
Regulatory mechanisms 151

S

Scala framework 260
Scoring functions 260
Scripted miniseries 114
Search engine algorithms 139
Self-linking edges 161
Semistructured data 219
SEO techniques 280
Service provision 237
Sexually suggestive content 62
Social experience 318
Social graph 190
Social groups 312

Social media 1, 2, 3, 4, 5, 9, 12, 13, 14, 17, 21, 27, 28, 32, 33, 35, 42
Social media apps 52
Social media landscape 327
Social media managers 78
Social media network 18
Social media platforms 5
Social media posts 123
Social media scene 258
Social media sites 47
Social media space 204
Social movements 6
Social network connections 237
Social network website 47
Source code 274
Spam content 117
Spreadsheet 189
Stereotype-promoting content 35
Sub-company profiles 228
SWOT analysis 195

T

Target audience 71
Target market 192, 315
Technological innovation 225
Technological systems 10
Text-based social media 311
Text-based social platform 310
Third-party scheduling tool 94
Threads 309, 310, 311, 312, 313, 314, 315, 316, 317, 318, 319, 320, 321, 322, 323, 324, 325, 326, 327, 328, 329, 330, 331, 332, 333, 334, 335, 336, 337, 338
Threads algorithm 313, 314, 316, 318, 320, 322, 324, 327, 334, 335, 336
Threadsters 315
Thumbnail image 200
TikTok algorithm 108, 109, 110, 111, 113, 115, 116, 117, 121
TikTok's algorithm 22
Traditional marketing 123
Twitter algorithm 254, 255, 259, 266, 267, 268, 275
Twitter experience 254, 259
Twitter metrics 257
Twitter's algorithmic decisions 274
Twitter (X) campaigns 270
Twitter (X) marketing strategy 255

U

Unidirectional communication 11
Up-to-date information 259
User engagement 14
User experiences 14
User-generated content 122
User interaction 128

V

Vector-based clustering algorithms 161
Verification feature 59
Vertical scroll 62
Video editing app 94
Video marketing 140
Viewer engagement 115
Viewer satisfaction 179
Vlogging channels 181

W

Watermarks 88
Web experience 330

Y

Young photographers program 198
YouTube algorithm 178, 180, 191
YouTube marketing 186, 192, 193, 194, 205, 208
YouTube partner program (YPP) 197